Music and Exile

Yearbook of the Research Centre for German and Austrian Exile Studies

Editorial Board

Charmian Brinson, *Imperial College London*
Jana Barbora Buresova, *IMLR, University of London*
Rachel Dickson, *Ben Uri Gallery and Museum*
Richard Dove†
Anthony Grenville, *Association of Jewish Refugees*
Andrea Hammel, *Aberystwyth University*
Stephanie Homer, *IMLR, University of London*
Bea Lewkowicz, *IMLR, University of London*
Sarah MacDougall, *Ben Uri Gallery and Museum*
Marian Malet, *IMLR, University of London*
Angharad Mountford, *IMLR, University of London*
Anna Nyburg, *Imperial College London*
Rachel Pistol, *King's College London*
Andrea Reiter, *University of Southampton*
J.M. Ritchie†
Jennifer Taylor, *IMLR, University of London*
Ian Wallace†

VOLUME 22

The titles published in this series are listed at *brill.com/ygae*

Music and Exile

From 1933 to the Present Day

Edited by

Malcolm Miller
Jutta Raab Hansen

BRILL

LEIDEN | BOSTON

Cover illustration foreground: Norbert Brainin and Peter Schidlof, Austrian-born members of the Amadeus Quartet. 1960s pen and ink drawing by Milein Cosman (1921–2017), part of The Milein Cosman Collection of The Wigmore Hall Trust. Reproduced by kind permission of The Wigmore Hall Trust; © The Cosman Keller Art & Music Trust.

Cover illustration background: Manuscript Score of the final bars of *The Cats*, a movement for string quartet, by Peter Gellhorn (1912-2004), composed in 1940 whilst interned at Mooragh Camp on the Isle of Man. Reproduced by kind permission of the Gellhorn Family Archive.

The Library of Congress Cataloging-in-Publication Data is available online at https://catalog.loc.gov
LC record available at https://lccn.loc.gov/2022061992

Typeface for the Latin, Greek, and Cyrillic scripts: "Brill". See and download: brill.com/brill-typeface.

ISSN 1388-3720
ISBN 978-90-04-54065-1 (paperback)
ISBN 978-90-04-54410-9 (e-book)

Copyright 2023 by Malcolm Miller and Jutta Raab Hansen. Published by Koninklijke Brill NV, Leiden, The Netherlands.
Koninklijke Brill NV incorporates the imprints Brill, Brill Nijhoff, Brill Hotei, Brill Schöningh, Brill Fink, Brill mentis, Vandenhoeck & Ruprecht, Böhlau, V&R unipress and Wageningen Academic.
Koninklijke Brill NV reserves the right to protect this publication against unauthorized use. Requests for re-use and/or translations must be addressed to Koninklijke Brill NV via brill.com or copyright.com.

This book is printed on acid-free paper and produced in a sustainable manner.

Printed by Printforce, the Netherlands

In memory of Professor Richard Dove

Contents

List of Figures IX
Notes on Contributors X

Introduction. Music and Exile: From 1933 to the Present Day 1
Malcolm Miller and Jutta Raab Hansen

1 The Musical Identity of the Austrian Exile 10
 Michael Haas

2 An Ambiguous Story – Austrian Music Exile in the Netherlands 29
 Primavera Driessen Gruber

3 Vom Kitchener Camp in australische Wüstenlager: Der Weg jüdischer Exil-Musiker über Großbritannien nach Down Under 53
 Albrecht Dümling

4 Creation of Jobs, Union Work and Cooperation: The Institutionalisation of Musical Life by the European Jewish Artist Society, the Shanghai Musicians Association, and the Association of Jewish Precentors in the Shanghai Exile, 1938–49 75
 Sophie Fetthauer

5 'A State of Crass Ideological Confusion': Avant-Garde Music and Antisemitism in the Free German League of Culture 94
 Florian Scheding

6 'Almost as Impressive as Its Legacy in the Visual Arts': Ben Uri Art Society and Music in Exile, 1931–60 113
 Rachel Dickson

7 Goldschmidt and Hamburg 134
 Peter Petersen

8 Preisgekrönt und doch kein Glück? Anmerkungen zu Berthold Goldschmidts Belcanto-Oper *Beatrice Cenci* 155
 Barbara Busch

9   'A Place of Refuge in Your Arms': Reizenstein's *Anna Kraus* as Holocaust Opera   168
    Malcolm Miller

10 Von großen Erfolgen in der Zwischenkriegszeit zu relativer Vergessenheit: Die Komponisten Bruno Granichstaedten und Robert Katscher im Exil   192
    Hanja Dämon

11 Encounters with the Émigré Experience: Discovering the Chamber Music and Songs of Peter Gellhorn   217
    Norbert Meyn

12 Visits in Four Cities: Stations in the Musical and Familial Life of the Song Composer Max Kowalski (1882–1956)   237
    Nils Neubert

13 Der österreichische Musiker Ferdinand Rauter als Musiktherapeut in Camphill bei Aberdeen in Schottland (1945 bis 1947)   259
    Jutta Raab Hansen

14 Mischa Spoliansky's Music for the Movie *Mr. Emmanuel* (1944)   284
    Jörg Thunecke

Index   303

Figures

1.1 Map taken from the https://www.xn--sterreich-ungarn-lwb.de/demografie.html page which goes on to breakdown the linguistic make-up of Austria-Hungary, with German being the first language of only 23.36%, and *c.*45% speaking one of several Slavic languages   16
3.1 Plakat zum Konzert des Kitchener Camp Orchestra am 2. November 1939 in der St. Clement's Church, Sandwich   67
3.2 Einladung zur Show ‚Hay-Fever' aus dem australischen Internierungslager Hay vom November 1940   69
3.3 Handgeschriebener Programmzettel für ein Konzert mit unterhaltsamer Klassik aus Hay   71
6.1 'Lectures and Recitals, Nov.–Dec. 1951' printed leaflet, Ben Uri Art Gallery   124
7.1 The Goldschmidts' headstone in the Jewish cemetery in Ohlsdorf   135
7.2 Berthold Goldschmidt's birth certificate   136
7.3 The house – Steinstrasse 12 – in which Berthold Goldschmidt was born   137
7.4 Cover of the book *Zündende Lieder, verbrannte Musik*   142
7.5a The title page of Goldschmidt's *Third String Quartet*   146
7.5b Transcription of the title page of Goldschmidt's *Third String Quartet* (by Peter Petersen)   147
7.6 Poster advertising the first showing of *Draußen vor der Tür*   150
9.1 Newspaper photo cutting of a 1954 recital in Bath by Franz Reizenstein and Christopher Hassall, highlighting their lifelong professional relationship and friendship subsequent to *Voices of Night* (1951) and *Anna Kraus* (1952)   175
11.1 Gellhorn's Gold Medal from the Prussian Academy of the Arts for outstanding achievements as a student   221
11.2 Portrait of the young Peter Gellhorn (year unknown)   224
11.3 Peter and Olive Gellhorn on their wedding day in 1943   229
11.4 Peter Gellhorn on a London street in 1951   230
11.5 Peter Gellhorn at St. James's Palace, 1984   233
13.1 Engel Lund and Ferdinand Rauter   263
13.2 Rehearsal in Rauter's home, 74 Carlton Hill, London NW8: Norbert Brainin, violin; Ferdinand Rauter, piano; photomontage on the back wall portrait of Hans (Peter) Schidlof, violist   283

Notes on Contributors

Barbara Busch
is Professor of Music Education at the Manheim State University for Music and Performing Arts. She studied flute, school music, educational science and historical musicology and is co-editor of the journal *üben & musizieren* as well as a member of the board of directors of the Federal Academy for Musical Youth Education in Trossingen. For her monograph *Berthold Goldschmidts Opern im Kontext von Musik- und Zeitgeschichte*, Dr Busch was awarded Hamburg's Kurt-Hartwig-Siemers Science Prize.

Hanja Dämon
studied history at the University of Vienna and obtained her PhD at King's College London's German department where she was part of the European Research Council (ECR)-funded project 'Beyond Enemy Lines: Literature and Film in the British and American Zones of Occupied Germany, 1945–1949'. Her research interests include the topics of exile, and her article on Granichstaedten and Katscher in this volume was stimulated by work undertaken in the context of a Science Scholarship offered by the City of Vienna ('Wissenschaftsstipendium der Stadt Wien').

Rachel Dickson
former Head of Curatorial Services, Ben Uri Gallery and Museum, has a research specialism in the artists and designers who fled Nazi-occupied Europe for the UK and has published widely on the topic. A committee member of the Research Centre for German and Austrian Exile Studies, she continues to act as Consultant Editor for the Ben Uri Research Unit.

Albrecht Dümling
is a musicologist based in Berlin. After receiving his doctorate in 1978, he was a music critic for the *Tagesspiegel* until 1998. From 1988 he was in charge of the exhibition 'Entartete Musik. Eine kommentierte Rekonstruktion' ('Degenerate Music. An Annotated Reconstruction'). Since 1990 he has been heading the 'musica reanimata' association. In 1994 he was a co-founder of the International Hanns Eisler Society. He has published books and articles including on his research subject of musicians' exile in Australia.

Sophie Fetthauer

studied musicology, gaining her PhD in 2002. Since then, she holds a Research Associateship at the University of Hamburg and the Hochschule für Musik und Theater, Hamburg. Her research on music and musical life in the Third Reich and in exile, focuses on biographies, company and institutional history, Displaced Person camps, remigration, and exile in Shanghai. She is co-editor of the online *Lexikon verfolgter Musiker und Musikerinnen der NS-Zeit* (www.lexm.uni-hamburg.de).

Primavera Driessen Gruber

is a cultural manager and scholar in exile studies. She studied Dutch language and literature at the university of Leiden and received her doctorate in law at Vienna university. In 1996 she established the *Orpheus Trust – Verein zur Erforschung und Veröffentlichung vertriebener und vergessener Kunst* and was its artistic and scientific director until 2006. In 2002 she initiated and until 2005 collaborated in the Austrian Science Fund (FWF) research project 'Persecuted Music'. She has published widely on music in exile and is currently working on an *Austrian Biographical Dictionary of Music Professionals persecuted during Nazism*.

Michael Haas

was a recording producer from 1977 until 2017, working for most major labels and initiating Decca's recording series 'Entartete Musik'. From 2002 to 2010, he was Music curator at Vienna's Jewish Museum. In 2013 his book *Forbidden Music – the Jewish Composers Banned by the Nazis* was published by Yale University Press. In 2016 he co-founded the Exilarte Research Center at Vienna's University of Music and Performing Arts.

Norbert Meyn

is a German-born singer, language coach and researcher based in London. He has been teaching German diction and Lieder at the Royal College of Music since 2005. He has a particular interest in practice-based research and is Principal Investigator of the Arts and Humanities Research Centre-funded project 'Music, Migration and Mobility' (2019–23).

Malcolm Miller

is Honorary Associate and Associate Lecturer in Music at the Open University, UK. He received his doctorate from King's College London and has published widely on Beethoven, Wagner and contemporary music, including articles and chapters on topics related to music in exile, and entries in *Grove Music Online* and MGG. His essay 'Music as Memory: British Émigré Composers and their Wartime Experience' appeared in *The Impact of Nazism on Twentieth-Century Music* (ed. Erik Levi, Böhlau Verlag, 2014).

Nils Neubert
born and raised in Hamburg, Germany, tenor, DMA, is active as a performer, educator, coach, and scholar in the United States and abroad. He teaches at the Juilliard School and the Manhattan School of Music in New York City and also serves on the music staff at the Metropolitan Opera.

Peter Petersen
born in 1940, taught musicology at the University of Hamburg until his retirement in 2005. He is co-editor of the online encyclopaedia of persecuted musicians of the Nazi era (www.lexm.uni-hamburg.de) and editor of the series *Musik im 'Dritten Reich' und im Exil*. Recent books include *Music and Rhythm. Fundamentals – History – Analysis* (2013); *'Friedenstag' von Stefan Zweig, Richard Strauss und Joseph Gregor. Ein pazifistisches Opernprojekt im 'Dritten Reich'* (2018); and *Isolde und Tristan: Zur musikalischen Identität der Hauptfiguren in Richard Wagners 'Handlung' Tristan und Isolde* (2019).

Jutta Raab Hansen
studied musicology at Berlin Humboldt University and, in 1988, joined Peter Petersen's exile music research group at Hamburg University, resulting in her PhD thesis *NS-verfolgte Musiker in England: Spuren deutscher und österreichischer Flüchtlinge in der britischen Musikkultur* (Hamburg, 1996). Research in the UK, Australia and Jerusalem (2003–11) included a contribution to ORT's 'Music and the Holocaust' project, followed by her translation and edition of émigré singer Elena Gerhardt's 1953 memoirs (Altenburg, 2012). She worked as a music therapist, between 2012–18 in Thuringia, Germany.

Florian Scheding
is Senior Lecturer in Music at the University of Bristol. His main research area is music and migration, with a focus on the displacements caused by the catastrophes of the 20th century. He has published widely on migratory musics including functional, popular, and art musics. His first book, *Music and Displacement: Diasporas, Mobilities and Dislocations in Europe and Beyond*, was named 'Outstanding Publication of the Year' by *Choice Magazine*. His second book, *Musical Journeys: Performing Migration in 20th-century*

Music, received the Royal Musical Association/Cambridge University Press Monograph Prize 2020.

Jörg Thunecke was Senior Lecturer in German at Nottingham Trent University (1970–97) and Wissenschaftlicher Mitarbeiter at the Westdeutsche Akademie für Kommunikation in Cologne (1998–2006) until his retirement. He has published extensively on music and exile in relation to the Nazi era, including editions and translations of novels such as *Robert Neumann: Blindekuh – Roman* (trans. & amp; ed.; 2022) which received the 2021 translation prize of the Federal Republic of Germany (BRD). From 2013–18 he was editor of the *Newsletter of the International Feuchtwanger Society*.

Introduction. Music and Exile: From 1933 to the Present Day

Malcolm Miller and Jutta Raab Hansen

The present bilingual Yearbook 22 is devoted to the topic 'Music and Exile' and offers new insights to deepen knowledge and understanding of this increasingly significant field of research, which is of particular relevance to musicologists and scholars of performance practice as well as historians. Responding freely to the broad call for contributions, the authors' choice of topics fortuitously created a remarkably coherent and cogent pattern, arranged into three main sections that reflect a multi-perspectival approach to the refugee experience. Firstly, a focus on geographical regions, secondly on institutions and organisations, and finally, on individual composers and compositions. One also senses, within that division, the larger three-part pattern of the refugee experience itself: persecution in one's homeland; dislocation, escape and immigration; and acculturation and a sense of belonging to an adopted home.

The essays presented here flesh out that tripartite pattern in their social-historical and musical contexts. Firstly, the process of being driven out of Germany and Austria after 1933, and the attempts to work and settle in a foreign host country, where the musicians travelled to, including the Netherlands, Britain, the USA, Shanghai, and Australia (including those transferred there from Britain). Secondly, that process is explored in both directions, looking at how, for instance, cultural and political organisations in Britain and Shanghai welcomed musicians from the continent in different periods. Finally, the essays on individual émigré musicians and composers in Britain and the USA explore in detail the mutual give and take with their adopted home. Often involving rejection, overcoming hurdles, and disappointments, their experiences led to both success and failure in their careers, yet also to the fulfilment of finding safe haven for themselves and family members, whilst preserving the memory of those who perished.

In that the issue of 'exile' within recent musicology has received much discussion in the context of such fields as migration and mobility studies, our present volume seeks to use a wide-ranging terminology to provide a more nuanced understanding of phenomena within a single, if broad and pluralistic, over-arching concept of music and musicians affected by the Holocaust. Thus, as well as 'exile' and 'music and exile', we include terms such as émigré, refugee, displacement and forced displacement, migration and forced migration, emigration, immigration, acculturation. All of these terms appear relevant to the task of shedding light on the contexts surrounding individuals who suffered from Nazi persecution and its impact before, during and after the Second World War and the Holocaust.

1 'Music and Exile' in Previous Yearbooks

Even before the publication of the current Yearbook, previous Yearbooks from the last two decades have made significant contributions to the burgeoning field of music and exile. Indeed, closely related to the current volume is the Yearbook *Arts in Exile in Britain 1933–1945: Politics and Cultural Identity* (Vol. 6, 2004). Similarly, the Yearbook *'I Didn't Want to Float; I Wanted to Belong to Something.': Refugee Organizations in Britain 1933–1945* (Vol. 10, 2008) features an essay about the Free German League of Culture, which played an important role, socially and musically, by presenting 'chamber music from home', makeshift opera performances, satirical sketches and plays for refugee members. The counterpart for Austrian refugees was the The Austrian Centre in London's Paddington district, which provided a more comprehensive cultural and musical program. Its political agenda focused on 'democratic post-war Austria' and was discussed in Richard Dove's essay in *German Speaking Exiles in Great Britain* (Vol. 2, 2000).

Whilst the German language was strictly forbidden for broadcast on the BBC Home Service during the Second World War, within the European Service refugee musicians, composers and writers could make use of their mother-tongue and cultural and musical background for radio listeners in Germany and Austria. Musicians like Berthold Goldschmidt, Georg and Paul Knepler, Ferdinand Rauter and Mischa Spoliansky all appeared on the BBC payroll to fight against the Nazis via short-wave-transmitter, a topic covered in the Yearbook *'Stimme der Wahrheit': German-Language Broadcasting by the BBC* (Vol. 5, 2003). The significant role music played for Austrian, German, Turkish and Italian 'enemy aliens', including Jewish refugees, in internment on the Isle of Man during two world wars is discussed in two essays by Jutta Raab Hansen and Richard Dove in the Yearbook *'Totally un-English'? Britain's Internment of 'enemy aliens' in two World Wars* (Vol. 7, 2005).

Richard Tauber was known to be the best 'Viennese export-hit' during his exile in Britain, both in concert and in three Viennese operetta-style British films, including *Blossom Time* (1934), a story about Franz Schubert. Christian Cargnelli's essay on the topic appears in *'Immortal Austria'? Austrians in Exile in Britain* (Vol. 8, 2007).

In connection with a compilation on *Refugee Archives: Theory and Practice* (Vol. 9, 2007), the essay by Charmian Brinson '"Between our two peoples": The archives on the Anglo-Austrian Society and Anglo-Austrian Music Society' tells the unique story of both societies, founded in 1944, and how music-making brought audiences together, offering a significant social bond.

In the Yearbook *Exile in and from Czechoslovakia during the 30s and 40s* (Vol. 11, 2009), Jutta Raab Hansen discusses musicians who fled to Britain in 1938, and who, in contrast to German and Austrian refugees, were deemed 'friendly aliens'. The Czechoslovakian government-in-exile in London gave financial support for performances by musicians, many of whom remained in Britain after 1945. In the Yearbook focused on British Overseas Territories, Albrecht Dümling discusses the career of émigré Berlin –born organist Werner Baer who found refuge in 1939-40 in Singapore, before being interned in Australia (Vol. 20, 2019).

The most recent Yearbook, *Émigré Voices: Conversations with Jewish Refugees from Germany and Austria* (Vol. 21, 2021), edited by Bea Lewkowicz and Anthony Grenville, features an interview with violinist Norbert Brainin (1923–2005) from Vienna. As a fifteen-year-old teenager Brainin arrived in London with his violin in 1938, studied with Professor Max Rostal from Berlin, and became the first violinist of the successful and world-renowned Amadeus Quartet, performing and recording mainly Viennese classics for nearly forty years all over the world.

As a whole, this brief survey underlines the contribution the Yearbooks have made over the years to the study of 'music and exile', the topic with which the current volume engages in depth.

2   Contents of the Current Yearbook

The varied selections of essays are arranged in three main parts: firstly, geographical identities and communities; secondly, refugee institutions and organisations; and finally, individual musicians and works. The volume opens with MICHAEL HAAS's study of 'Austrian Musical Identity in Exile'. Haas has worked extensively in the field of exiled musicians, as a music producer, historian, and museum curator. Enriched by his deep historical understanding of the shifting geo-political borders and identities of the early 20th century, Haas tracks the biographies of refugee composers, and their subtly different Austrian and German cultural or linguistic identities. He focuses on those shaped by three distinct states of Austria and its traditions, culture and politics: pre-1918 (Austrian Empire), that from 1918 to 1933 after Austria's humiliating loss of all but the German nations, and from 1934 to 1938 (the Christian-German Corporate State) – and who found refuge in Europe and USA. Haas also considers the identities of Austrian composers who suffered political and racial hostility, followed by personal uprooting in exile and its new reality, with different and contradictory responses. Some of those composers had recourse, for example, to the traditional four-movement symphony (Wellesz, Toch, Rathaus, Krenek, Rankl, Eisler) as though a genre of the Austrian past. In addition, Haas discusses works composed in exile never intended to be performed, bringing to light unfamiliar composers (Winterberg, Fürstenthal and Arlen), comparing those to the works of 'inner exile' by composers in Nazi-Germany at the same time. Haas stresses that their common idealisation of an Austrian and/or German culture was distinct from the Nazi reality.

Extending the notion of Austrian identity, the second essay by PRIMAVERA DRIESSEN GRUBER, focuses on Austrian musicians in the Netherlands. The number of Jews deported and murdered by the SS in the Netherlands was proportionally the highest compared to the Jewish population of Europe. Gruber's essay represents the first-ever overview of the exile of about three hundred Austrian Jewish professional musicians. Her account offers detailed insights into those who already lived there professionally before the *Anschluss* in 1938, and those who arrived there later and were waiting in transition or became trapped after the German *Wehrmacht* overran its neighbour country in May 1940. Their fate became intertwined with the threatened Jewry of the Netherlands. The author's focus on these Austrian musicians draws on her own extensive database, several archives in the Netherlands and Vienna, and a wide range of published sources and private letters, all illuminating the whereabouts of lost or saved musicians in the Netherlands. This article is remarkable, as it represents only a fraction of a far larger research project.

ALBRECHT DÜMLING's essay traces the trajectories of four musicians who escaped to Britain, following their progress after their arrival from Europe at Kitchener Camp, which was temporarily set up for refugees from the German Reich. There they were allowed to participate in making music, even together with British colleagues before a British public. After 'the darkest hour' in 1940, some of them were shipped to Australia on the *Dunera* and interned. Dümling here brings fresh sources to shed new light on the contexts of their professional lives in Australia. His essay represents new research into a topic pioneered in his seminal book *Die verschwundenen Musiker* (Böhlau, 2011), translated as *The Vanished Musicians* (Peter Lang, 2016), which deals with musicians in exile in Australia. Indeed, Dümling has been involved for several decades in research into the Nazi period and its effect on Jewish musicians and German musical life. He authored, together with Peter Girth, the catalogue for the 1988 reconstruction of the 1938 NS-Exhibition in Düsseldorf 'Entartete Musik' ('Degenerate Music'). As chairman of Musica reaninmata e.V., founded in Berlin in 1990 and devoted to the rediscovery of composers persecuted under

Nazism, he regularly invited musicians and composers to his lecture-concerts in connection with the Berlin Konzerthaus, which was frequently broadcast on German Radio.

The next three essays focus on the role of organisations and institutions in the shaping and promotion of musical life in refugee communities. Firstly, SOPHIE FETTHAUER visited Shanghai, New York, and various other locations, publishing her research in a recent book *Musiker und Musikerinnen im Shanghaier Exil 1938–1949* (Neumünster, von Bockel Verlag, 2021). In her essay, Fetthauer explores the case of Shanghai, where there were some 18,000 Jewish refugees after 1938. Although no restrictions to work had been set up by the Chinese authorities for the refugees, it was nonetheless hard for the 450 musicians to survive in an Asian city with its unfamiliar culture and difficult living conditions. After Pearl Harbor in December 1941, the Japanese occupied Shanghai and set up a 'designated area' for the refugees from 1943 until 1945. Fetthauer considers the initiatives of European refugee-musicians who established their own associations, hitherto unknown to Chinese musicians, in order to represent their social, cultural, and economic interests in the Asian wartime conditions.

Turning to refugee organisations in Britain, FLORIAN SCHEDING's discussion of the Free German League of Culture, founded by communists from Germany in 1939 (as mentioned above, a topic treated in Yearbook Vol. 10) focuses on the so-called 'ideological battles' within this German refugee-community. In particular, he explores the attitudes to modernist composers, as shown in the concert programmes, and the role of the Berlin-born émigré musicologist, composer, and choir conductor Ernst Hermann Meyer, who came to Britain in 1933. Scheding discusses the interesting interaction of communist ideologies and pre-echoes of antisemitism within the League, and how the League anticipated some of the ideas later espoused by the Association of Composers and Musicologists founded in 1949 in the GDR, where Meyer settled from 1948.

Concluding our discussion of organisations which provided platforms for refugee musicians in Britain is a first-ever study of the musical holdings of the archive of the Ben Uri Art Society in London. As a former curator at Ben Uri Museum, RACHEL DICKSON is an experienced researcher at the Ben Uri archives. Here she draws upon its rich resources to produce a fascinating survey of the history of the society before, during, and after the war, highlighting the complementation of art exhibitions and musical performances in those challenging times. Her essay brings to light both familiar musicians at early stages in their careers and introduces less well-known musical personalities, highlighting the rich interaction of the different arts, and affirming the continued value of such archives for the treasures they contain.

The final part features studies of individual musicians from Germany and Austria who found refuge in Britain and the USA, all of whom were involved during their careers in the world of concerts, opera, operetta, film and radio music, as composers and interpreters. Two essays are devoted to the Hamburg-born composer Berthold Goldschmidt. His presence in interviews during a renaissance of interest in his music in Germany after 1987 brought the story of his exile, and that of fellow émigrés to Britain, to wide public awareness, especially in Germany.

Goldschmidt was born in Hamburg in 1903 and died in London in 1996. Both the city of Hamburg, the Hanseatic port-town on the Elbe, and his family who lived there, played an important part in Goldschmidt's life. PETER PETERSEN, who was also born there, invited Goldschmidt for his first revisit to Hamburg in 1989, with concerts of his music. In his essay, he examines Goldschmidt's ties to Hamburg before and after he fled to London and during his visits to his native city until shortly before his death. Inspired by the revival of his long-neglected compositions for concert and stage, Goldschmidt started composing again in the 1980s and 1990s, at last experiencing at first-hand their performances in Europe. Significantly, two of his late compositions based on notated word-abbreviations for Hamburg (Hbg) and Schleswig-Holstein (SCH-H), the area in the North attached to Hamburg, are used in late works within which Goldschmidt recalls his childhood years. Peter Petersen, emeritus professor of music history at Hamburg University, initiated there a research group in the mid-80s to collect and study exiled musicians connected with Hamburg. The group even invited some of them and performed their 'forgotten' compositions, eventually widening the scope to include all exiled musicians.

BARBARA BUSCH considers the background, plot and reception history of the Belcanto-Opera *Beatrice Cenci*, which was the winner of an opera competition as part of the Festival of Britain in 1951. Busch, who has published a monograph about Goldschmidt's operas, explores the reasons it was never produced at the time and had to wait some forty years to be performed, firstly in 1988 in concert and then staged in Magdeburg in September 1994, in the presence of the composer. Busch also curated the travelling exhibition on Berthold Goldschmidt on the occasion of the first modern revival of his first opera, *Der gewaltige Hahnrei* (1932), at the Berlin Komische Oper 1994. The exhibition then was revised and shown in Oldenburg, Bremen, Erfurt, and Munich.

Also an émigré to Britain in the mid-1930s, the notable composer and pianist Franz Reizenstein, born in Nuremberg, forms the subject of the essay by MALCOLM MILLER. The essay traces Reizenstein's life and career, focusing on the 1952 radio opera *Anna Kraus*, one of three settings of English texts in collaboration with the British poet and librettist Christopher Hassall. Bringing to light for the first time primary sources including the BBC Written Archives, Miller discusses in detail the context and content of Reizenstein's little-known radio opera, claiming it as one of the earliest operas to deal with Second World War refugees and a reflection on the composer's own experience.

HANJA DÄMON's essay compares the biographies of two well-known Viennese operetta and film composers, and textbook writers, Bruno Granichstaedten and Robert Katscher, who were active before the Nazis came to power. They both fled to the USA, aiming to start new careers in New York and Hollywood. Although they had achieved personal and professional success in the USA earlier, their much hoped for aim did not materialise. Whilst the two open-minded composers from Vienna saved their and their spouses' lives, their new careers did not succeed for several reasons and, tragically, both died before the Second World War was over.

The émigré conductor, pianist, repetiteur, and coach Peter Gellhorn from Berlin was well known in London's musical life from his time at Sadler's Wells, at the Royal Opera House, Glyndebourne, and at the BBC. Less known are his own compositions, chamber music, Lieder and cantatas, written mainly for the desk-drawer. NORBERT MEYN surveys Gellhorn's life and his compositions, and his contribution to this volume is based on interviews and research into Gellhorn's estate. Drawing on his own pioneering premieres of Gellhorn's music with students at the Royal College of Music, as part of the project 'Singing a Song in a Foreign Land', of which he was initiator and artistic director, Meyn discusses their structure, compositional intentions, interpretative approach, and public reception.

The song composer and lawyer Max Kowalski from Frankfurt fled to London in 1938. Rounded up by the SS during 'Kristallnacht', he was released from Buchenwald concentration camp only after he agreed, under Gestapo pressure, to leave Germany. NILS NEUBERT's essay about Kowalski's Lieder for voice and piano focuses on Kowalski's family visits to four cities, and draws on personal interviews with Kowalski's nephew Michael Kowal in New York, who still remembers his uncle's visits in the 1950s. Neubert, an experienced singer and vocal coach, here demonstrates the connections between Kowalski's compositions and the details of each of the private visits.

Both an arranger of songs and a practical musician, the émigré Ferdinand Rauter from Klagenfurt, pianist and accompanist of the Icelandic singer Engel Lund, acted as mediator between Austrian and British musicians and composers in difficult political times after 1938. Arriving in London already in 1935, he made his living as a pianist, teacher, and coach. After the war, he left the war-worn city and went for one and a half years to Camphill near Aberdeen. His aim was to be part of the Camphill project founded by the Austrian refugee Karl König and his colleagues. Rauter worked there for the first time as a music therapist for 'seelenpflege-bedürftige Kinder' ('children in need of spiritual care'). JUTTA RAAB HANSEN's essay explores his experiences there, drawing on various archival materials including Rauter's hitherto unpublished Camphill-diaries, a remarkable source held in the Rauter Collection at Salzburg University.

The refugee Mischa Spolianky, one of the most successful song-, cabaret- and film-composers from Berlin, was much welcomed by the London film-industry. The movie *Mr. Emmanuel* (1944) is based on a story by Louis Golding about a Jewish Englishman who went to Nazi-Germany to search for the mother of a boy refugee from Germany to England. In this volume, JÖRG THUNECKE, whose scholarly interests cover German realism of the 19th century and German-speaking exile literature, analyses Spoliansky's film underscore, and particularly how he chooses to set and arrange the 'Hatikvah' melody, later chosen as the Israeli National Anthem, at dramaturgically important places within the plot. In this essay devoted to British exile film music, he highlights how music could serve as a moral and emotional support for refugee cinema-going audiences of the period.

It is striking how many of the wide-ranging topics of the essays gathered here display potential for inter-connections. For instance, in his Berlin days, Berthold Goldschmidt was acquainted with Mischa Spoliansky, who played piano at cabarets on Kurfürstendamm. Later in Britain, the Hamburg composer directed rehearsals and played the piano at the performance of Spoliansky's play *Rufen Sie Herrn Plim! (Send for Mr Plim!)* at the London Austrian Centre. Readers may find their own cross connections and inter-texts, and we hope that the collection, as a whole, will stimulate new ideas and fresh avenues of research to explore.

As the generation of musicians in exile recedes into history, it is reassuring that there are still those who retain direct links with the living memory of that period. Sadly, we note the recent loss of the eminent Austrian-born British composer Joseph Horovitz (1926–2022), who found refuge in Britain after the *Anschluss* in 1938. Horovitz's music reflects a synthesis of Viennese style with the English and European influences of his education at Oxford University, the Royal College of Music, and in Paris with Nadia Boulanger. His varied, prolific oeuvre, coloured by a unique jazz-classical synthesis, includes such popular hits as *Captain Noah and his Floating Zoo* (1970) and the autobiographical String Quartet no.5 (1969), composed for the Amadeus Quartet on the occasion of the sixtieth birthday of the art historian Sir Ernst Gombrich. The recipient of numerous awards both in Britain and from his native Austria, Horovitz, mentioned in Rachel Dickson's essay, was friend and younger colleague to several of the émigré musicians also featured in the present volume, including Berthold Goldschmidt, Franz Reizenstein, Peter Gellhorn and others. It is to all their memories that we dedicate this book, as a salute to the contribution they made to the world of culture and the arts both internationally and in their adopted homes.

In conclusion, we would like to offer thanks to those involved in producing this volume, and who showed us support and interest in the process of editing. We are grateful to the entire committee of the Research Centre for German and Austrian Exile Studies, in particular the Chair Anthony Grenville, and to Stephanie Homer, our copy editor, for her conscientious professionalism. We would like to express our gratitude to the Martin Miller and Hannah Norbert-Miller Trust for financial assistance, as well as thanks to our editors Wendel Scholma and Alessandra Giliberto, and the publisher Brill for their continued support and expertise as the Yearbook proceeds through its third decade.

We appreciate very much the interest and advice of distinguished academic colleagues including Gerold Gruber, Thomas Schinköth, Alexander Knapp, Golan Gur, and Benjamin Wolf. To all those who have shared interviews and materials, including relatives of émigrés, archivists, and librarians, and those who have given permission to reproduce illustrative material, we are deeply grateful.

Finally, we would like to express appreciation to all the authors featured here for their contributions and for sharing their expertise in a volume which, as a whole, we hope represents a significant contribution to the continuing development of the intertwining fields of exile studies and musicology. As an editorial team, we have been enriched with many stimulating hours of enjoyable discussions (on Zoom) during the period of production. In that spirit, we wish all our colleagues and readers equally vivifying conversations and enjoyment in delving into a musical and historical field whose importance is borne out by numerous musical performances, widening repertoires and ever-growing academic research.

1
The Musical Identity of the Austrian Exile

Michael Haas

Abstract

Before 1918, there were two Austrian identities, the German-Austrian and the Austrian who hailed from the non-German speaking regions of the Habsburg realm. Their self-identification as 'Austrian' was distinct from German-Austrians, many of whom were disappointed at Bismarck's view that Austria was not a German nation. With Habsburg Austria reduced to a small Alpine republic made up of Greater Austria's German speaking provinces in 1918, Austrian self-identification became yet another question. Many who hailed from the distant corners of the Empire still regarded themselves as Austrian. Yet, this self-identification took another blow with the annexation of Austria in 1938 when all Austrians, with the exception of Jews, became German citizens. This development left Jewish composers who considered themselves Austrian in limbo, particularly if they had fled abroad. Many felt no connection with the new republics of Poland and Czechoslovakia and did not speak the national languages or identify with their cultures. In exile, there continued a search for a return to a lost Austrian identity – even if the country itself no longer existed.

‚Hinter mir stehen keine Consulate und keine Propaganda Maschine. In dem Lande wo ich (glücklich übrigens) lebe, bin ich ein not-Native.'[1] The composer Karol Rathaus wrote these lines to his friend, the conductor, Jascha Horenstein in a letter in 1950 from his home in New York, where he had taken a position in 1939 as a music lecturer at Flushing's newly established Queens College. Rathaus was only expressing the frustration of countless former Austrians born in the empire prior to 1918. In his case, he came from Ternopol where he was born in 1895. Until 1938, he never thought of himself as anything other than Austrian, though his career was established in Berlin where his operas and ballets were performed at the Staatsoper 'Unter den Linden' and where he began a successful career as the first serious composer to be commissioned a film score

---

1 Undated letter from 1950: Karol Rathaus to Jascha Horenstein, held at Queens College's Rathaus Collection. English translation: 'Backing me there are no consulates and no propaganda machine. In the country where I live (happily, by the way), I am a non-native.'

for 'sound cinema'.² The success was such as to lead to countless subsequent commissions and a dizzying commute between Paris and Berlin before moving permanently to London in 1934. In 1937 the Royal Opera House commissioned and performed his ballet *le lion Amoreux*, and he was even offered an important position at the BBC which was rescinded when it emerged he was not a British citizen.³ He struck out for Hollywood too late to have found work as anything other than a hack orchestrator, and he obtained a Polish passport upon Austria's annexation, thus allowing him to bypass American quotas on German immigration. With the outbreak of war threatening, he had no choice but to take the only job going. Queens College had been established no more than a few years earlier. The Austrian composer Ernst Toch, then working in Hollywood, had sneered to Rathaus that he too had been offered the job but turned it down because the pay was pitiful.⁴

After the war, Rathaus became aware of friends in Hollywood being hunted down, hauled in front of Congressional kangaroo courts and deported. If the composer Hanns Eisler, who had fled Europe and lived in the United States since 1938, returned first to Vienna before eventually taking up residence in East Berlin, Rathaus could potentially have found himself left in the cold. Ternopol was now part of the Ukraine and an integral part of Stalin's Soviet Union. He had no home to which he could be deported. His life-long Austrian identity was now no more than an historic oddity. It cost him dear after the war, and it continues to cost his legacy dear today as no country claims him as its native son. Prior to leaving for America, and up until 1933, he always returned to Ternopol. If Ternopol was 'his' city, Austrian was his identity until he had no choice but to yield to circumstances. In 1942, he wrote to his friend Soma Morgenstern: 'Opportunist that I am, now that Poland no longer exists, I'm absolutely bursting with ardour for something that must always have resided until now deep within: the Polish question!'⁵

Rathaus's near contemporary, Hans Gál, born outside of Vienna in 1890 offers a very contradictory view. With the fall of the Habsburgs, he saw himself as first and foremost Viennese and after that, as culturally German. Like Rathaus, his enormously successful career post-1920 was in Germany, not in

---

2 Rathaus's ballet *der letzte Pierrot* premiered by Georg Szell at Berlin's Unter-den-Linden on 7 May 1927; his opera *Fremde Erde* was premiered at the same house, conducted by Erich Kleiber on 31 October 1930; and his score for UFA-Berlin's *Der Mörder Dmitri Karamasoff*, directed by Fedor Ozep, was first shown in Berlin's Capital cinema on 6 February 1931.
3 *Le Lion Amoreux* premiered at the Royal Opera House for the Colonel Basel's Russian Ballet Company on 10 October 1937.
4 Martin Schüssler, *Karol Rathaus* (Frankfurt a. Main: Peter Lang, 2000), 335.
5 Letter, Rathaus to Soma Morgenstern: 7 December 1942, Queens College's Rathaus Collection.

the tiny Austrian Republic. One needs only to refer to Joseph Roth, to be made aware of the fact that the singularity of Austrian identity was more acutely felt by those not born within the geographical borders of what was formerly called 'Deutsch-Österreich'.[6]

Franz Schreker, a Viennese composer born while his parents were on a visit to Monte Carlo in 1878, finished his opera *Der Schatzgräber* on the day Austria became a republic. It was a work that by 1922 would become the most performed German opera by a living composer. In the margin of the final page, he wrote the following: 'Ende der Oper: 12. November 1918, am Tag der Ausrufung der Republik Deutsch Österreich und der Anschluß an das Deutsche Reich!' Twenty years later, the annexation would become a reality with catastrophic consequences for all of them.[7]

The cultural identification with 'German' would result in even greater conflicts for Hans Winterberg, born in Prague in 1901. As a Prague Jew he spoke German at home, but after the founding of Czechoslovakia in 1918, he identified as Czech. At least this is what one can infer from his 1930 census form, when the Czech government attempted to assess the country's ethnic make-up. To Winterberg, German was a linguistic marker, not an ethnic one.

A number of German speaking composers, born Austrian in what became Czechoslovakia after 1918, chose to remain Austrian. This was the case with Viktor Ullmann who was subsequently murdered in Auschwitz in October 1944. It was also the case with Ernst Krenek who, though not Jewish, was born to Czech parents in Vienna. He suffered Nazi persecution following the success of his jazz-opera *Jonny spielt auf!* and fled to America. Ullmann's Jewish family had converted to Catholicism before he was born; Krenek was born into a military family but became more devoutly Catholic with the establishment of Dollfuss's *Ständestaat* in 1933.[8] Catholicism as a marker of Austrian musical identity is something we shall return to.

Winterberg, unlike Ullmann, survived Theresienstadt and, in 1947, travelled to Germany in order to collect the manuscripts he entrusted to his ex-wife and

---

6 Hans Gál's views were passed to the author in a conversation following the opening of the exhibition 'Continental Britons' at Vienna's Jewish Museum, 2003; the reference to Joseph Roth refers to his most famous novel *Radetsky March*.
7 Manuscript held at the Austrian National Library.
8 The most common definition of Austria's *Ständestaat* (which lasted from 1933 until Austria's annexation in 1938) has been 'the corporative state'. As G.E.R. Gedye points out in his articles filed for the British and American press at the time (and published in 1939 as *Fallen Bastions*), Austria had essentially become a 'clerical dictatorship' with the Catholic Church responsible for determining the status and standing of individuals and professions within society. The most accurate description of Austro-Fascism from 1933 to 1938 is still heavily contested among Austrian historians.

daughter, both of whom had been deported in 1945 as 'German-Czechs' under the Beneš Decrees.[9] Perhaps for private reasons, or out of fear of returning to Prague following the Communist coup in 1948, or possibly out of fear of being exposed as a Czech spy during the first years of the Cold War, Winterberg did something few (if any) Czech Jews dared to do. He decided to remain in Germany, giving an impression that he, like other Sudeten Germans, had been forced to emigrate. It was a daring, possibly dangerous step to take given the large number of disaffected Sudeten Germans who would have known him from earlier days. His situation became even more precarious when Bavarian Radio, along with its leading orchestras, conductors and soloists proceeded to record many hours of his symphonies, concertos, ballets, chamber music and assorted orchestral works – far more than any of the 'genuine' Sudeten German composers. His dissembling appears to have paid off, but, after his death in 1991, the Sudeten German Music Institute (SMI) acquired his musical estate and instantly embargoed performances or access to scores until 1 January 2031. A condition of acquiring the estate, meant to be held in perpetuity, was that no mention was ever to be made of the fact that Winterberg was Jewish. The contract that accorded the estate to the SMI was signed in 2002.

What becomes evident from these brief biographies, is that to Karol Rathaus and Hans Winterberg, two German-speaking Austrians born outside of what would become the Republic of Austria in 1918, German was a language, not an identity. To the Viennese composers Hans Gál and Franz Schreker, German was not a linguistic marker; it was a cultural identity. To add to the complication: to Rathaus being Austrian was his identity, while Winterberg initially identified as Czech before circumstances forced him to change to identifying as German. The convergent yet different threads of language and culture wove a complex fabric after 1918 that ripped apart with the arrival of Adolf Hitler, who added the pseudo-scientific concept of 'race' to that of language and culture. Like Gál and Schreker, he too was an Austrian who identified as German, though for him, it was racial rather than cultural. For Jews such as Rathaus, Gál, Winterberg and Schreker, whose father was Jewish, German as language and culture were markers of assimilation and acceptance, of belonging and thus of entitlement to contribute. With such confusion and potential for misunderstanding, it's worth taking a closer look at the music written once composers

---

9 Beneš Decrees were a system of laws enacted by Edvard Beneš's government in exile and ratified following the Nazi defeat. One of the decrees, based on Article 12 of the Potsdam Agreement, meant that Czechs who had declared themselves 'German' on the 1930 census were to be deported as presumed Nazi collaborators. Individual cases were rarely, if ever, considered and resulted in the deportation of some three million Czech Germans and Hungarians.

were thrown out of their native cultural environments. What is telling is that exile would unleash a sense of cultural return that more than anything would force the identity crises of these musicians to the surface.

The question of Austrian identity, in general, was often a matter of debate. As early as 1815, Carolina von Humboldt wrote to her husband regarding the singular concept of Austria:

> Österreich ist so verschiedenartig und heterogen in seinen Kräften gemischt, in den Nationalitäten, aus denen es besteht, daß ich alles wetten möchte, daß Es noch in diesem Jahrhundert aufhören wird, eine deutsche Macht zu sein. Die nationelle Deutschheit ist offenbar noch im Wachsen und damit hält Österreich nicht Schritt. Den Geist der Zeiten anzuhalten, dazu ist offenbar keine Macht stark genug.[10]

As Golo Mann goes on to point out in his 19th and 20th century history of Germany, the Viennese playwright Franz Grillparzer (1791–1872) could claim never to have been performed or published in '*Ausland*' by which he meant, outside of Austria's sphere. If Grillparzer, who only wrote in German, saw Austria solely within its Habsburg boundaries, Metternich saw German as a mere linguistic utility on behalf of the monarchy, the civil service, and the military. All of the other Austrian nations were free to develop their own languages and cultures.[11] With the 1918 loss of the Empire and its reduced state as a republic that included its historic German-speaking regions (minus German-speaking South Tyrol) and largely the German border regions of newly established Czechoslovakia, the need to differentiate Austrian identity became flexibly plastic, if not to say downright artificial.

Darwinian misinterpretations had opened a Pandora's box of half-cocked science that saw 'race' where previously 'culture' or 'language' were understood. The empirical evidence that proved the blood of German speakers superior to that of Slavs or Jews had not yet been found. Nevertheless, any number of questionable circumstantial elements was brought to bear that supposedly supported this hypothesis, thus pandering to the worst of Austrian Pan-German anxieties.

The fall of Habsburg Austria left the Republic in a position that must seem oddly familiar to the British: a former imperial power, with centuries of tradition, is confronted with a larger, richer and more powerful linguistic cousin,

---

10   Golo Mann, *Deutsche Geschichte des 19. und 20. Jahrhunderts* 11 Auflage (Frankfurt a. Main: Fischer Verlag, 2008), 120.
11   Ibid.

whose rise has been sudden and relatively fortuitous. A view of 'our brains and their brawn' can be implied reading Austria's interwar newspapers and literature. Austria had the apparatus of an empire, even if the empire itself was gone. Heimito von Doderer makes the ridiculousness of this sense of entitlement the defining element in his cast of characters in his novel *Die Strudlhofstiege*.[12] The momentum of deluded privilege continued until Pan-German ambitions to unite Austria's brains with the German Reich's brawn required a new set of Austro-definitions. These were helpfully supplied by Dollfuss's clerical dictatorship from 1933, when Catholicism and folk-culture were seized upon. Dollfuss's purge of Socialists, Communists, and anyone to the left politically, would leave Austrian identity in the hands of conservative Catholics and the former, largely supranational aristocracy. One need only recall the figure of Baron von Trapp in the Hollywood film *The Sound of Music*: Captain von Trapp engages a novice Catholic nun as a nanny for his children. He is intolerant of the German 'Heil Hitler!' greeting following the *Anschluss* and refuses to fly the Nazi flag from his villa. He ultimately evades his posting to the German Navy in Bremerhaven by escaping after performing a programme of Austrian folk music. The historic Georg Ludwig Ritter von Trapp was from Zara in Yugoslavia and was a U-Boat captain in the First World War with the Austrian navy based in the Dalmatian port of Pola.[13] Both the fictional and historic figures represent the sense of Austrian exceptionalism as Catholic, supranational, and deeply rooted in its unique folkloristic music. For Austria's Jewish musicians forced into exile, this was quite a flimsy basis for maintaining a national and cultural identity abroad.

The delineations between Austrian musicians born in *Deutsch-Österreich*[14] and those from *Groß-Österreich*[15] start to become clearer post-1918. For *Groß-Österreicher* like Rathaus, Ullmann, Winterberg or indeed Joseph Roth and Soma Morgenstern, Austrian was supranational and European. As with Metternich, German was a linguistic tool, not an identity. For those born in *Deutsch-Österreich*, German became a national, cultural identity. Indeed, most could

---

12   Heimito von Doderer, *Die Strudlhofstiege* (Munich: Deutscher Taschenbuch Verlag, 1978) – recently translated by Vincent King as *The Strudlhof Steps* (New York: New York Review of Books, 2021).
13   See, Georg v. Trapp's *To the Last Salute, Memories of an Austrian U-Boat Commander* (University of Nebraska, 2007).
14   'German-Austria' (*Deutsch-Österreich*) referred to the German-speaking regions of the Habsburg realms and most specifically, to what is largely present-day Austria, including South Tyrol. Formerly, it also included the German-speaking border regions of what became Czechoslovakia.
15   'Greater-Austria' (*Groß-Österreich*) means the wider Habsburg holdings that spread across much of Central Europe.

FIGURE 1.1   Map taken from the https://www.xn--sterreich-ungarn-lwb.de/demografie.html page which goes on to breakdown the linguistic make-up of Austria-Hungary, with German being the first language of only 23.36%, and c.45% speaking one of several Slavic languages

not conceive of an Austrian 'nation', only a German one. For them, Austria itself was an historic anachronism. As one may deduce from Schreker's note at the bottom of his final page of *Der Schatzgräber*. If national self-determination was truly to be the guiding principle of postwar Europe, leaving German-Austria outside of the German Reich was seen as an injustice. The treaty of Saint-Germain-en-Laye from 1919 agreed to review the 'annexation question' again in twenty years: Nineteen years later, Hitler marched unopposed into Vienna and only Mexico protested that the annexation was illegal.[16]

It is not clear to what extent an Austrian musical identity was being concocted during the *Ständestaat* years. Ernst Krenek and Egon Wellesz both joined in the Catholic renewal of Austria's clerical dictatorship.[17] It's nevertheless striking how open the *Ständestaat* appeared to new music initiatives. Wellesz composed two masses, while Krenek opened his contemporary music

16   There are many historic references to the position of Mexico following the annexation of Austria in March 1938. For an eye-witness account, see Mark Wischnitzer, 'Jewish Emigration from Germany 1933–1938', *Jewish Social Studies*, vol. 2 (Jan. 1940), 23–44.
17   Wellesz, Egon and Emmy, ed. Franz Endler: *Memoiren* (Vienna: Zsolnay, 1985), 236.

project, 'Österreichisches Studio', in which he hoped to profile the works Nazis were banning as *Kulturbolschewismus* in neighbouring Germany.[18] Paul Pisk, another Jewish Schoenberg pupil, founded a similar organisation called Musik der Gegenwart.[19] The antisemitism of the Dollfuss/Schuschnigg *Ständestaat* was in line with the Christian Social Party's view that Judaism was a religious confession and not a race or even a nation. If a Jew converted, he or she was no longer a Jew. Nevertheless, the effects wealthy, ambitious Jews were having on Austrian Catholic society did not go unnoticed. Krenek offers the anecdote of explaining his Austrian Studio project to Dr Joseph Lechthaler, the head of music in Austria's Catholic Church. Lechthaler denounced atonality as 'Musik doch ausschließlich von Juden für Juden komponiert [...] und daher bestenfalls die Angelegenheit einer exotischen Minderheit'. Krenek points out that the only important Jewish composer 'der verdächtigeren Art' he can think of who composed the sort of atonal music Lechthaler disliked was Arnold Schoenberg. Lechthaler then goes on to mention a list of Austrian composers from Schoenberg's circle, leaving Krenek to point out that actually all of them, like himself, Alban Berg and Anton von Webern, came from Austrian Catholic families.[20]

Despite such efforts, it was also clear that Austrian musical identity, whether Jewish or not, was not to be viewed through the lens of atonality or Arnold Schoenberg's 'Zweite Wiener Schule'. Whatever efforts Krenek and Pisk made were nothing compared with the prominence of Joseph Marx and Franz Schmidt. More conventional Jewish composers, many of whom returned to Austria from Germany after 1933, were forced into keeping a lower profile. Egon Wellesz's composition of Catholic masses may have been the result of genuine religious fervour. They should, in any case, also be seen in the context of the *Ständestaat*'s purge of Social Democrats, of which Wellesz had been a prominent supporter. If questions of Austrian musical identity had been left to Marx, he would have moved it southwards towards Italy. Marx was half-Italian, and his music offers a similar sound-world to that of his Italian contemporary Ottorino Respighi. If the question of Austria's musical identity had been put to Franz Schmidt, it would have headed north to Germany. Schmidt, like his

---

18 Ernst Krenek, *Im Atem der Zeit* (Munich: Diana Verlag, 1998), 1015.
19 Paul Pisk, 'Kann der Arbeiter ein inneres Verhältnis zur Zeitgenössischen Musik finden?', *Kunst und Volk. Mitteilungen des Vereines 'Sozialdemokratische Kunststelle'*, 2 (Februar 1927), 2e Jahrgang, 4f. Available online, http://roteswien.com/ [accessed: 11.08.2022].
20 Krenek, *Im Atem der Zeit*, 1017f; It is also worth noting that Krenek's opera *Karl V* – a work that aspired to Christian unity under Habsburg Catholicism – was blacklisted by the Vienna State Opera Orchestra for performances in 1933, possibly owing to Krenek's performance ban in Nazi Germany and the work's twelve-tone composition. *Karl V* did not receive its premiere until 1938 in Prague, where it was conducted by Karl Rankl.

half-Jewish contemporary Franz Schreker, saw Austria's future as part of the German Reich. Korngold struck out for Hollywood, with promises of his opera *Die Kathrin* being premiered at Vienna's Staatsoper in the spring of 1938. As an opera, it owed more to Lehár and Puccini than nationalist traditions coming out of either Italy or Germany. Its plot was a bastardisation of Heinrich Eduard Jacob's novel *die Magd von Aachan*, which Korngold, with an almost pathological instinct to remain apolitical, had translocated from the occupied Saarland to Switzerland, at a stroke neutralising the political frisson, which was the basis of the novel.[21]

Physical translocation post-1938 would create enormous identity issues for Austria's exiled composers and musicians. Post-*Anschluss*, Austria no longer existed officially, and it was left to the Soviet Union to finance separate Austrian refugee centres in so-called 'transit countries' that allowed for specifically Austrian initiatives. Another issue was that countries such as Great Britain, out of fear of home-grown antisemitism, had gone out of their way to play down the fact that most refugees from Germany (or Austria) were Jews.[22] This created the problem of Great Britain going to war with Germany while at the same time having to accommodate thousands of German refugees. In Britain, as in most countries of refuge, employment possibilities were restricted or denied. In Great Britain, France and Switzerland, nearly all refugees were interned as 'enemy aliens'. This combination of displacement, loss of prestige and homeland, along with the subsequent Second World War, provided an important catalyst in creating a musical identity that was effectively a return to a culture that existed long before Hitler.

The most striking manifestation of this was a return to the ultra-Austrian form of the 'Symphony'. Though Gustav Mahler redefined the Symphony with a synthesis of tone-poems strung together as symphonic movements, the following generation of composers had largely dropped concepts of classical form altogether unless recycled within the context of neoclassicism or German *Neusachlichkeit*, a movement that defined interwar Germany more than Austria. Interwar Austria offered a musical plurality that would be difficult to imagine existing today. Schoenberg's 'Zweite Wiener Schule' may be the most noted strand, though traditionalists such as Joseph Marx, Julius Bittner, Emil Nikolaus von Reznicek, Wilhelm Kienzl and Franz Schmidt, the only prominent Austro-German symphonist, dominated. Interwar neoclassicists liked

---

21 Heinrich Eduard Jacob (1889–1967), *Die Magd von Aachen* (Vienna: Zsolnay,1931).
22 For further information, please refer to Louise London's *Whitehall and the Jews* (Cambridge: Cambridge University Press, 2000); another excellent reference is Jutta Raab Hansen's *NS-verfolgte Musiker in England* (Bockel Verlag, 1996).

writing suites and 'Serenades' but rarely toyed with the idea of symphonies and sonatas.[23] Karl Weigl's four symphonies prior to his exile were largely dismissed as less inventive when compared with Schmidt's, which at least seemed to move forward from Mahler. Another traditionalist, Hans Gál won Austria's first State Prize in 1915 with a Symphony that he instantly withdrew afterwards. He later composed a 'First Symphony' that he initially billed as a 'Sinfonietta'. Franz Schreker's star pupils, Ernst Krenek and Karol Rathaus, both wrote first symphonies that consisted of single, rambling movements. They then returned with second Symphonies showing obvious Mahlerian influences. Rathaus withdrew his after a single performance while Krenek managed a third symphony before largely abandoning the concept. Both returned to composing symphonies in exile. More striking are the symphonies by modernists who had never considered writing one while still in their homelands. Egon Wellesz and Ernst Toch both felt compelled to compose symphonies the moment the war was over and relate very similar stories as to what suddenly drew them to a concept they had hitherto dismissed as empty Romanticism. Wellesz was drawn by physical homesickness and missed Austria's landscape, while Toch was drawn to the Austro-German cultural identity of the Symphony. Wellesz's first Symphony offers a Mahlerian melancholy, while Toch's is a study in German Tonsatz consisting of extended fugal passages and dense counterpoint. Ultimately, Wellesz would compose nine symphonies and a Symphonic Epilogue. Toch would compose seven. Wellesz was sixty when he composed his first symphony in 1945. Toch was sixty-three when he composed his first symphony in 1950. Rathaus returned to the symphony in 1942, Krenek in 1947. Korngold wrote his only symphony in 1953.

If the Symphony was the urform of Austro-German music, it had also been a highly successful export. Russian, British and American composers were quicker to exploit the symphony's potential than those closest to the original source, who, with the exception of Franz Schmidt, had largely abandoned it as superseded. Nevertheless, Czechs, too, had a degree of entitlement to the form, and thus Bohuslav Martinů, like Toch, would also turn to the symphony in American exile, writing six between 1942 and 1953. Martinů's symphonies are frequently referred to as 'American works'. This is ambiguous: the fact that they were composed in America cannot be disputed, but the implication has often

---

23   Emil Nikolaus von Reznicek (1860–1945) is an exact contemporary of Gustav Mahler. His five symphonies are largely from before and just after the First World War, and, like Felix Weingartner's symphonies, remain wedded to the 19th century, unlike Franz Schmidt and Karl Weigl who attempted to build on Mahler's wider positioning of symphonic form and scope. Reznicek did advance with other works such as *Ritter Blaubart* and his *Tanzsymphonie*.

been that the complex polyrhythms and syncopations are the 'Americanisation' of Martinů. It ignores the Janáček provenance of these presumed national markers, which can be heard in the music of Pavel Haas, Hans Krása, Erwin Schulhoff and Hans Winterberg. In my opinion, Martinů symphonies are less an outward display of American assimilation and more a statement of cultural remigration.

Karl Rankl, the Schoenberg pupil and political friend of Bertolt Brecht and Hanns Eisler, would also turn to the Symphony following his departure from Berlin, Vienna and latterly Prague.[24] Unlike his compatriots, his first symphony was composed almost as soon as he left. Its composition took place as early as 1938 and was premiered with critical success in Liverpool in 1953. Given the near universal opprobrium heaped on Austro-German composers in Great Britain at this time, we can assume that Rankl was making cultural concessions and had started to realise that even if the symphony *per se* was uniquely Austrian, its export to England would require adaptation.

To what extent this 'return' to the Austro-German concept of classical form dominated the idea of returning to a more abstract ethos of identity needs to be investigated when comparing other contemporary symphonic composers active in countries that had taken in Austro-German refugee composers. American influences are obvious even in the strict Teutonic language of Toch's first symphony and Korngold's only symphony. Wellesz, on the other hand, remained firmly wedded to his Viennese identity in both his tonal and atonal symphonic works, compressing even the most abstract musical ideas into crypto-classical structures.

There is no predefined shape or universal form for Austria's exile-symphonies. Hanns Eisler's *Deutsche Sinfonie* is more oratorio pageant than classical four movement concept. Indeed, it seems a hybrid between Mahler's *Sinfonie der Tausend* and a Bach Passion, using political texts set as secular cantatas, which, in place of movements, make up the constituent units of the work. Wellesz's first four symphonies are tonal and classical. His symphonies five to nine are atonal while remaining structured to a point that allows near-instant coherency for the passive listener, despite the wide intervals he often uses for his thematic material. Toch's symphonies often have the feel of extended tone-poems, which, despite his oft stated dislike of Mahler, are works that without Mahler as his template, would not have been possible. What joins all of these disparate works together is the Austro-classical sense of structure within well-defined

---

24   For further information on the relationship between Rankl and Eisler, see Nicole Ristow, *Karl Rankl: Leben, Werk und Exil eines österreichischen Komponisten und Dirigenten*, Band 20: Musik im 'Dritten Reich' und im Exil (Neumünster: Bockel Verlag, 2017).

individual, interrelated units. The same applies to Arnold Schoenberg's two concertos composed in American exile. Though Schoenberg did not see the Symphony as a statement of Austrian identity, it's noteworthy that his concertos, one for violin written in 1936 and the other for piano in 1942, recall Viennese classicism in the same manner.

The true 'music of identity', however, is usually deposited in the desk-drawer. These are commonly works for chamber ensemble or voice. They frequently lack performance indications or interpretative directions such as tempo, mood or dynamic. This is music that yearns to return to its original homeland and, in a way, complements the much more frequently debated concept of *innere Emigration*, meaning works by composers who could not, or would not, leave Nazi Europe but composed in secret and did not allow their works to be performed. The name most often mentioned in this context is Karl Amadeus Hartmann, who composed copiously during the Nazi years but remained unemployed and, given his political views, unemployable. His father-in-law supported him and his family. But *innere Emigration* is in many cases a double-edged sword. Composers who joined the Nazi party, or composed marches for the *Hitler Jugend*, composed works at home confined to desk-drawers only to be pulled out during de-Nazification hearings in order to prove they had been composing twelve-tone music all along. To postwar de-Nazification committees, twelve-tone was perceived as 'anti-fascist' and customarily viewed as inner resistance. Not many questions were asked and composers such as Hermann Heiß, Hugo Hermann and Wolfgang Fortner were generally absolved of charges of collaboration. Numerous other composers were genuinely estranged politically from Nazism, though either joined the Party in order to keep conducting, performing or teaching, (Felix Petyrek and Eduard Erdmann) or withdrew as inwardly as possible, such as Heinz Tiessen and Max Butting. Others such as Ernst Pepping and Joseph Haas seem to have managed to comply only as much as possible, while occasionally taking personal risks. These grey zones of *innere Emigration* can, on closer observation, only claim qualified verification as inner resistance. Nevertheless, composers who confined their works to the desk-drawer, either in Nazi Europe or in exile, were in search of some form of identity. All of them were looking back to a pre-Hitler age of plurality and creative freedom.

'Wenn ich komponiere, bin ich wieder in Wien' is not only the title of the exhibition running at the Exilarte Centre at Vienna's University of Music and Performing Arts and offering a visualisation of the purge that took place at Vienna's Music Academy in March 1938, it is also the answer given by the composer Robert Fürstenthal to the question as to why, in the 1980s and 1990s, he composed in a similar manner to Gustav Mahler and Hugo Wolf. 'I return to Vienna when I sit down to compose' is an approximation of the above but reflects what he meant. Fürstenthal (1920–2016) was born and grew up in a Vienna that had, with few exceptions, progressed beyond the late Romanticism of the above composers. Following his ejection from high school, unable to complete his Matura, he went to England for a year working as a gardener before immigrating to the United States. Had he been allowed to remain in Vienna, he would have studied composition. He was enormously talented, playing the piano, composing, and improvising to the delight of friends at parties. Once in the United States, he joined the army, served as a translator, and after the war studied accounting, eventually working his way up to head the audit department of the US Navy in San Diego. A failed marriage, followed by the reacquaintance and marriage with his first great love from Vienna, brought him back to music. After forty years of not touching the piano, music poured out including hundreds of Lieder along with orchestral and chamber works. Nearly everything was in the style of Vienna's *fin de siècle*. The Vienna he wished to return to was in fact the Vienna he could never have known.

Adding to the confused ambiguity of displacement, Fürstenthal frequently set the poetry of Josef Weinheber, a poet who made no secret of his own Nazi sympathies. Weinheber appears to have represented to Fürstenthal the enigma of Austrian identity: simplistic and timeless beauty as a venire to a complex sense of cultural frustration. After the defeat of Austria in 1918, German nationalism in what had been known as *Deutsch-Österreich* was rife. As so often with nationalism, it began to define itself by exclusion rather than inclusion. In retrospect, it is very difficult to untangle the pseudo-Darwinian antisemitism of the Nazis, with the exclusionary antisemitism of Pan-German nationalists and the confessional antisemitism of the established Christian churches. No doubt Fürstenthal admired Franz Schmidt as well, who, like Weinheber, welcomed Austria's annexation by Germany. Whatever Pan-German ambitions Weinheber harboured, his poems resonate with echoes of Habsburg-Austrian singularity rather than Bismarck-Prussia. An example of this can be heard in Fürstenthal's setting of the following Weinheber text: 'Liebeslied – Love Song'.

> Wenn Gott, den ich so schmerzvollwerbend suchte,
> plötzlich gemordet wär' in meinem Herzen
> oder betrunken läg' vor meiner Schwelle:
> Ich würde weinen, aber weiter werben

This is the second verse to his 'Liebeslied', in which every verse expresses another example of Austria's fatalistic *Weltanschauung*, seemingly confirming the famous aphorism that in Prussia, a situation is 'serious but not fatal', while in Austria it is the other way around.[25]

Likewise, Walter Arlen, born Walter Aptowitzer 1920 in Vienna, eventually settled into an apparently successful life in Southern California. It seems odd that Arlen and Fürstenthal never met. Arlen was a month younger than Fürstenthal and, though he, too, could not complete his high school Matura examinations, he did manage to study music in the United States with Leo Sowerby in Chicago before spending four years as the amanuensis of Roy Harris. Fürstenthal, in comparison, was self-taught, though his best compositions would never suggest this. Arlen is a child of the 20th century, even if his musical language is gentler than most of his contemporaries. His countless songs recall the musical language of clapboard houses and picket fence in rural America as heard in the songs of Samuel Barber or Aaron Copland. The lyrics he sets, however, could hardly be less American. The texts of Czesław Miłosz's cycle *Poet in Exile* sit alarmingly with the musical simplicity of Arlen's understated Americana, creating a disjunctive sense of both 'here' and 'there':

> Certainly we have much in common,
> We who grew up in the baroque cities
> Without asking what king has founded a church
> We passed every day, what princesses lived
> In the Palace, what were the name of architects, sculptors,
> Where they came from and when, what made them famous.
> We preferred to play football in front of ornate porticoes

Arlen also composed for his desk-drawer. His manuscripts lack tempo, mood or dynamic indications. The impulses to write for the desk-drawer were quite different for the two composers. Fürstenthal composed out of a certain sense of homesickness and nostalgia, trying, through music, to recreate the Vienna that ought to have been rather than the one he confronted in 1938. Arlen composed to numb all memories of Vienna, including the expropriation of the family business, the humiliation of his family being thrown out of their home, his father's deportation to Buchenwald and his mother's chronic depression and eventual suicide. Arlen's family certainly fell further than Fürstenthal's and the humiliation heaped on one of Vienna's wealthiest

---

25   The texts for Fürstenthal and subsequent Walter Arlen songs are taken from scans of manuscripts held at the Exilarte Center at Vienna University of Music and Performing Arts.

families clearly stung deeply.[26] Both Arlen and Fürstenthal had to leave Austria as seventeen-year-olds, abandoning parents and siblings, not knowing if they would ever see each other again. Arlen left on one of the last ships to leave Trieste for America.

Later, when I had to deal with these desk-drawer works as a recording producer, I was confronted with the enigma of only notes on staves, beautifully executed and highly legible, but lacking any and every expressive and interpretative indication. Arlen, who was present during the recordings was somewhat indignant and stated that 'any competent musician would know' what he intended. As we happened to be recording with musicians of the highest calibre, it was sobering for Arlen to recognise that the subtleties of his imagination were not sub-consciously transferable. It seemed selfish that Arlen's works were only intended as an inner dialogue with himself and not meant for public consumption. Fürstenthal was more practical and assumed that he would be the only musician ever to perform his works and would therefore be able to impart his intentions to other musicians or singers involved. It was all the more tragic that Fürstenthal was on his death bed during our recording. All of us puzzled over the works' ambiguities and the only solution was to record takes of one tempo and expressive idea only to change to another. Eventually, we settled on what we believed he intended. He heard the first edit days before he died. According to his wife, we had not always been successful in realising his intentions.

As part of Arlen's inner dialogue, he addressed the additional hardship of his homosexuality. The challenges of fitting in to a new homeland were made all the more complex at a time when homosexuality was criminalised. Even in the music world of Los Angeles in the late 1940s and 1950s homosexuality was secretive, and making contacts was fraught with the dangers of entrapment and blackmail. At this point, he was not only the principal music critic for the *Los Angeles Times*, but he also headed the music department of the Jesuit Loyola Mary Mount University in Los Angeles, and exposure would have been professional suicide. Not until decades later, when in a secure relationship with his partner (now husband) Howard Myers, did he turn to the texts of St. John of the Cross, a Catholic saint who was a Jew who converted and whose poetry, though apparently addressed to Jesus, can also be understood as homo-erotic with one of the songs entitled 'Ah, who can cure me?' while each of the

---

26 Arlen's mother was the daughter of Leopold Dichter, who in 1890 founded Kaufhaus Dichter, one of Vienna's largest department stores in the city's working-class Ottakring district.

other five settings in the cycle offer any number of unambiguous homoerotic references:

> Upon a night of darkness
> Inflamed with love and yearning, kindling,
> I entered where I did not know.

In addition to both coming from Vienna, having been born only a month apart, and both finding refuge in Southern California, there is another remarkable similarity between Arlen and Fürstenthal: they both set extracts from the Old Testament 'Song of Songs'. Their selections rarely coincide, and the end results could hardly be more different. Arlen took an English translation, whereas Fürstenthal took Weinheber's reworking of *das Hohe Lied* in German from 1916, when Weinheber presented it as Austrian propaganda during the First World War. Arlen's setting is for three soloists (mezzo-soprano, tenor and bass) with full orchestra and chorus. It is a work of the twentieth century. Fürstenthal, true to his Hugo Wolf provenance, uses the format of the *Italienisches Liederbuch* and divides the songs between baritone and soprano with piano accompaniment. It is a work of *fin de siècle* Vienna. Arlen and Fürstenthal were not observant Jews, but in the case of Arlen, his setting is a recognition of his identity as a Jew in America. With Fürstenthal, the effect is different: with Weinheber's adaptation of the Old Testament text, Fürstenthal is not only identifying as a Jew, but as an Austrian, German-speaking Jew. When Arlen arrived in America, he put every effort into becoming American. He lost his Austrian accent when speaking English and, as principal critic of the *Los Angeles Times*, his journalism was fluent, idiomatic and American. He maintained close contact with Los Angeles's Austrian émigré population, allowing him to keep his Ottakring Viennese. Fürstenthal remained Austrian to the last with no self-reinvention, other than abandoning his boyhood plans of studying music. He never attempted to lose his accent and preferred speaking German if offered the opportunity.

Though Arlen never really stopped composing, Fürstenthal stopped the minute he was forced to leave Austria. Fürstenthal's Vienna, as expressed in music, was one that did not feature Hitler or even the prospect of Hitler. Arlen's music is an attempt to defeat the demons he confronted as a youngster following the *Anschluss*. Arlen even set Rilke poems in English. His excuse was an inability to find copies of Rilke in German in Los Angeles. Given his position within the enormous émigré presence, this seems feeble, even disingenuous. The only German texts Arlen chose to set were as a seventeen-year-old, after the Gestapo had taken his father away, as well as after the war when he received news that his favourite cousin had committed suicide. Following his father's arrest, he set Eichendorff's 'Es geht wohl anders' (Things Turn out Differently):

> Es geht wohl anders, als du meinst,
> Derweil du rot und fröhlich scheinst,
> Ist Lenz und Sonnenschein verflogen,
> Die liebe Gegend schwarz umzogen.
>
> Und kaum hast du dich ausgeweint
> Lacht alles wieder, die Sonne scheint,
> Es geht wohl anders, anders, anders!
> Es geht wohl anders als man meint.

Following the news of his cousin Michi's death, a relative he had spent happy summers with at the family villa on the Hungarian border, he set 'Wiegenlied' by Paul Heyse:

> Singet leise, leise, leise,
> Singt ein flüsternd Wiegenlied,
> Von dem Monde lernt die Weise,
> Der so still am Himmel zieht.
>
> Singt ein Lied so süß gelinde,
> Wie die Quellen, auf den Kieseln,
> Wie die Bienen, um die Linde,
> Summen, murmeln, flüstern, rieseln

For Arlen, it was clear that German was for expressing sorrow when terrible things happen. Fürstenthal never set English until the very end of his life when he began to break away from the late Romanticism of Wolf and Strauss and attempted a style more identifiable with the later years of the twentieth century. For these works, he unsurprisingly chose James Joyce.

Hanns Eisler's well-known collection of songs composed in exile, later published as *das Hollywooder Liederbuch* is perhaps the best-known example of exiled Austrians composing for the desk-drawer. Eisler explained to Hans Bunge in a series of interviews that 'die größte Inspiration in der Emigration ist [...] die quälende Langeweile eines Emigranten, der zwölf Stunden nur sich betrachten kann'.[27] Unlike Fürstenthal and Arlen, he offers performance

---

27 Hanns Eisler, *Gespräche mit Hans Bunge – Fragen Sie mehr über Brecht* (Berlin: Deutscher Velag für Musik, 1975), 72.

indications. By his own admission, the works were always consigned to his desk-drawer, and his often drastic reworking of texts by his friends Bertolt Brecht and Berthold Viertel suggests that these songs were initially meant for his eyes only. Other texts, with which he was equally cavalier, are by Hölderlin, Mörike, Pascal, Rimbaud, and from the Bible. There are even several songs for which Eisler himself provided the words. The songs vary in length and style, changing from popular to twelve-tone, to Expressionist, to agitprop, to salon, to classical. His most remarkable settings are of Brecht's *Hollywood Elegies*, haiku-like settings that respond with bitter parody to what was the very essence of capitalism, where even Bach and Dante have to walk the streets like prostitutes in the hope they attract a punter.

> Unter den grünen Pfefferbäumen
> Gehen die Musiker auf den Strich,
> zwei und zwei
> Mit den Schreibern. Bach
> Hat ein Streichquartett in Täschchen.
> Dante schwenkt
> Den dürren Hintern.

Identity as a European, where the arts are not subject to crass commercialisation, is sensed via the intended parody of capitalism. But Eisler's Lieder are not just aimed at Hollywood's ability to turn creativity into an assembly line. He also sets images of childhood and family, nightmares, and the fear of being caught by his political persecutors.

Eisler's other proclamation of identity is his invention of the secular cantata based on the Lutheran template of Bach and Telemann. These not only make up many of the constituent 'movements' of his *Deutsche Sinfonie* but are also stand-alone works that express any number of largely political polemics. Later, after his deportation from the United States and eventual return, first to Vienna and then to East Berlin, it became clear that his flight from what he viewed as the totalitarian right led him into the arms of what, after 17 June 1953, could only be viewed as the totalitarian left. Despite composing East Germany's National Anthem and a villa provided by the GDR in East Berlin, he retained his Austrian citizenship and never joined the Communist Party. In view of this, Walter Ulbricht, General Secretary of the East German Central Committee, made a point of referring to him as 'Herr' rather than 'Genosse' Eisler. The actress and chanteuse Gisela May, with whom he had worked closely, recalled Eisler as being almost clownishly Viennese in Berlin. Ultimately Eisler's deskdrawer works, to which can be added his monumental *Deutsche Sinfonie*, were intended for a public that either no longer existed, or did not yet exist. Just as

Fürstenthal projected himself into a Vienna that was before his time, Eisler projected himself into a society that was believed to exist only in the future, yet his societal template was the Vienna in which he grew up.

For the purposes of this survey, I've not covered the sense of identity experienced by interpretive musicians, though it is worth pointing out that conductors such as Otto Klemperer, Fritz Stiedry, Wilhelm Steinberg, among others who prior to emigration had been active as new music protagonists, became bastions of classical conformity in exile. Felix Galimir, whose quartet in Vienna had premiered Ravel and *The Lyric Suite* by Alban Berg, was happy to instruct young American chamber musicians in Haydn, Beethoven, Schubert, and Brahms. Rudolf Kolisch was brother-in-law to Arnold Schoenberg and leader of the Kolisch Quartet, which made the first recordings of Schoenberg quartets. In America, he became leader of the Pro Arte Quartet in Madison, Wisconsin, with whom he recorded Haydn, Mozart, Schubert, and Brahms. Nor did it ever occur to the pianists Rudolf Serkin or Artur Schnabel to stop performing the canon of Austro-German repertoire only because the 'Free World' was at war with the Nazis. Indeed, if anything, the war provided an incentive to prove that even if all Nazis were German, not all Germans were Nazis. For Serkin, Schnabel and the conductors Klemperer, Steinberg, Stiedry, Leinsdorf as well as Kolish, Galimir and the violin virtuoso Fritz Kreisler, it became a mission to show that there was indeed another Germany and another Austria. Most importantly, they wished to show that German culture was not Nazi culture.

2

An Ambiguous Story – Austrian Music Exile in the Netherlands

Primavera Driessen Gruber

Abstract

Occupied by Nazi-Germany in May 1940, the Netherlands was not the safe haven that over 300 Austrian music professionals had hoped for when fleeing their country after the *Anschluss*. For about one hundred musicians with an Austrian background, who did not succeed to move on to the Netherlands' neighbouring countries or overseas in time, it meant being stranded, sharing the tragedy of Dutch Jewry. In spite of resistance and rescue, the history of the Netherlands under German occupation is also a history of naivety, indifference, collaboration and betrayal, resulting in the highest number of Jews (in relation to the Jewish population) in Western Europe being deported and murdered during the Second World War. As little attention has thus far been paid to the specific areas of exile from Austria in the Netherlands – and to Austrian music exile in particular, the story of these musicians, who permanently or for a longer period found refuge in the Netherlands during the Second World War has, with a few exceptions, remained untold. In this very first article on Austrian music exile in the Netherlands, three categories will be examined more deeply, covering a wide range of professions and music scenes: musicians from Austria who already lived or worked in the Netherlands before the *Anschluss*; the vast group of transmigrants; and music exiles who were trapped in the Netherlands after May 1940.

1 Introduction

The story of the Austrian music exile[1] in the Netherlands before and during the Second World War has thus far remained untold. So, in this very first research

---

1 In this article, 'music exile' is used to describe the forced displacement of musicians, musicologists, stage directors, music writers, impresarios, dancers and other professionals in the field of music with an Austrian background during Nazism. As through the ages crossing borders was part of the working conditions for music professionals, in music historiography the term 'exile' is still being discussed, *cf.* Claudia Maurer Zenck, 'Einige Überlegungen zur musikwissenschaftlichen Exilforschung', in Hartmut Krones (ed.), *Geächtet, verboten, vertrieben: Österreichische Musiker 1934-1938-1945* (Wien, Köln, Weimar: Böhlau, 2013), 252-58; Horst

article the experience of musicians from Austria, persecuted by Nazism and seeking refuge in the Netherlands,[2] who as a result partly had to share the tragedy of Dutch Jewry,[3] is framed by a short retrospective of the historical events and cultural ties between these countries.

Although they did not have common borders, strong cultural ties existed between the Netherlands and Austria in the first decades of the 20th century. But whilst during the Great War the Netherlands had remained neutral, Austria

---

Weber, 'Exilforschung und Musikgeschichtsschreibung' in Krones, *op. cit.* 259–84; Primavera Driessen Gruber, 'Leistungen und Desiderata der Exilforschung in Österreich auf dem Gebiet der Musik', in Evelyn Adunka, Primavera Driessen Gruber, and Simon Usaty (eds.), *Exilforschung:Österreich. Leistungen, Defizite und Perspektiven* (Wien: Mandelbaum, 2018), 428–58.

2   For German-speaking exile in the Netherlands see Kathinka Dittrich and Hans Würzner (eds.), *Nederland en het Duitse Exil 1933–1940* (Amsterdam: Van Gennep, 1982); Bob Moore, *Refugees from Nazi Germany in the Netherlands 1933–1940* (Dordrecht, Boston, Lancaster: Martinus Nijhoff Publishers, 1986); Ursula Langkau-Alex and Hans Würzner, 'Niederlande', in Claus-Dieter Krohn, Patrik von zur Mühlen, Gerhard Paul and Lutz Winckler (eds.), *Handbuch der deutschsprachigen Emigration 1933–1945* (Darmstadt: Primus Verlag, 1998), 321–33; Veit J. Schmidinger and Wilfried F. Schoeller, *Transit Amsterdam: Deutsche Künstler im Exil 1933–1945* (München: Allitera, 2007); Debórah Dwork and Robert Jan van Pelt, *Flight from the Reich: Refugee Jews 1933–1946* (New York, London: W.W. Norton & Company, 2009). For an in-depth comparative study of West-European immigration policies see Frank Castaecker and Bob Moore (eds.), *Refugees from Nazi Germany and the Liberal European States* (New York: Berghahn, 2010). For German-speaking music exile see Marius Flothuis, 'Duitse musici in Nederlandse ballingschap', in Dittrich and Würzner, 250–57; Rainer Licht, 'Warten – Widerstehen – Untertauchen: Musiker-Exil in den Niederlanden', in Hanns-Werner Heister, Claudia Maurer Zenck and Peter Petersen (eds.), *Musik im Exil: Folgen des Nazismus für die internationale Musikkultur* (Frankfurt am Main: Fischer Taschenbuch Verlag, 1993), 235–54.

3   Jacob Presser, *Ashes in the Wind. The Destruction of Dutch Jewry* (London: Souvenir Press, 1968, reprint 2010); Nanda van der Zee, *Om erger te voorkomen: De voorbereiding en vernietiging van het Nederlandse jodendom tijdens de Tweede Wereldoorlog* (Amsterdam: Meulenhoff, 1997, 5th ed. 2001), available in German translation: *Um Schlimmeres zu verhindern* (München: Carl Hanser, 1999); Bob Moore, *Slachtoffers en overlevenden: De nazi-vervolging van de joden in Nederland* (Amsterdam: Bert Bakker, 1998), in English: *Victims and Survivors. The Nazi Persecution of the Jews in the Netherlands 1940–1945* (London: Hodder Education Publishers, 1997); Marnix Croes and Peter Tammes, *'Gif laten wij niet voortbestaan'. Een onderzoek naar de overlevingskansen van joden in de Nederlandse gemeenten 1940-1945* (Amsterdam: Aksant, 2004); Saul Friedländer, *Die Jahre der Vernichtung: Das Dritte Reich und die Juden 1939-1945* (München: C.H. Beck, 2006); Katja Happe, *Viele falsche Hoffnungen: Judenverfolgung in den Niederlanden 1940-1945* (Paderborn: Ferdinand Schöningh, 2017), in Dutch translation: *Veel valse hoop. De Jodenvervolging in Nederland 1940-1945* (Amsterdam, Antwerpen: Atlas Contact, 2018).

had lost the war. After 1918 the newly proclaimed Republic of Austria had to overcome the loss of the largest parts of the former Austro-Hungarian Empire. It had to deal with a strong migration movement from its former territories in the East and, suffering from poverty and famine, was struggling to find a new identity. In these postwar years, relief organisations in the Netherlands invited over 150,000 undernourished children from Austria and Hungary for a holiday, sometimes fostering them for up to a year and nurturing them back to health.[4] This often resulted in lasting relationships with the foster families.

In the field of music, the Concertgebouw Orkest under its chief conductor Willem Mengelberg had championed Gustav Mahler, who in turn engaged Dutch musicians for the Vienna Court Opera. At the start of the 20th century, violin virtuosos Oskar Back (1879 Vienna–1963 Anderlecht) and Carl Flesch (1873 Mosonmagyaróvár–1944 Lucerne), both educated in Vienna, were teaching at Belgian and Dutch conservatories. In 1906, Flesch had married Bertha Josephus Jitta from a prominent Dutch-Jewish family, whilst Back married a Dutch non-Jewish woman, whom he later divorced. During the First World War he served in the k.u.k. Army, returning in 1917 to the Royal Conservatory of Brussels. Two years later he switched to the Conservatorium of the Vereeniging Muzieklyceum in Amsterdam, whilst Flesch had returned to Berlin, but continued to concertise in the Netherlands. At the Amsterdam Mahler Festival in 1920, Back and Flesch performed as additional players in the first violin section of the Concertgebouw Orkest. Among the guests of the Festival were many prominent Austrian music professionals.[5] Between October 1920 and March 1921, upon the invitation of Mengelberg, Arnold Schoenberg (1874 Vienna–1951 Los Angeles) gave classes for Dutch musicians at the seaside resort Zandvoort.[6] During this period, the pianist and composer Vally Weigl, née Pick (1894 Vienna–1982 New York), the sister of Austrian economist and women's activist Käthe Leichter, was living in the Netherlands. She worked as a foreign language secretary for Edo Fimmen, Secretary General of the International Transport Workers Union, which from 1933 would support political exile organisations and

---

4 Isabella Matauschek, *Lokales Leid – Globale Herausforderung: Die Verschickung österreichischer Kinder nach Dänemark und in die Niederlande im Anschluss an den Ersten Weltkrieg* (Wien, Köln, Weimar: Böhlau, 2018), 127–81; https://acceptatie.vijfeeuwenmigratie.nl/migratiebeweging/pleegkinderen-uit-oostenrijk [accessed: 07.09.2022].
5 Mahler Festival 1920 Amsterdam, https://mahlerfoundation.org [accessed: 19.12.2020].
6 Leo Samama in collaboration with Hylke van Lingen, *Nederlandse muziek in de 20-ste eeuw: Voorspel tot een nieuwe dag* (Amsterdam: Amsterdam University Press, Salomé, 2006), 79f; Arnold Schoenberg Center Vienna, https://schoenberg.at/index.php/en/schoenberg-2/biographie [accessed: 19.12.2020].

play an important role in resistance activities.[7] The savings on her Amsterdam account in 1938 enabled the escape of the Weigl family from Austria, including her husband, the composer Karl Weigl (1881 Vienna–1949 New York) and their young son.[8] In 1935, the Dutch pianist and composer Rosy Wertheim (1888 Amsterdam–1949 Laren) studied for a while with Karl Weigl, whilst the pianist, composer and music journalist Julius Hijman (1901 Almelo–1969 New York) had studied with Austrian pianist Paul Weingarten (1886 Brno–1948 Vienna) and in 1926 married Margarete Safir in Vienna. As a member of the Vereeniging voor Hedendaagsche Muziek (Society for Contemporary Music) he organised exchange concerts with Austria.[9]

Before, during or shortly after the Great War, a group of younger musicians from the (former) Habsburg Empire had settled in prosperous and peaceful Dutch society. The composer Ignace Lilien (1897 Lemberg/Lviv–1964 The Hague), then a piano student at the Ludwig Marek School of Music in Lviv, came on a bicycle tour in 1914. Pianist Franz Weisz (1893 Budapest–1944 Auschwitz) remained in the Netherlands after a concert tour in 1920, while the violinist Zoltán Székely (1903 Kocs–2001 Banff) arrived in 1922 in Nijmegen with a Children's Transport Train from Hungary.[10] In 1926, the Austrian pianist and composer Stefan Bergmann[11] (1903 Vöslau–1983 Bussum) a former student of the Vienna Music Academy, settled in the Netherlands. In 1932 he still appeared as a soloist with the Berlin Philharmonic Orchestra under George Szell (1897 Budapest–1970 Cleveland), but one year later his career in Nazi-Germany ended.

---

7   Langkau-Alex and Würzner, 'Niederlande', 326f.
8   Primavera (Driessen) Gruber, 'Was geht uns das an? / Is this our business?', in Elena Fitzthum and Primavera (Driessen) Gruber, *Give Them Music: Musiktherapie im Exil am Beispiel von Vally Weigl* (Wien: praesens, 2003), 19.
9   For these and other persecuted Dutch composers see Carine Alders and Eleonore Pameijer, *Vervolgde componisten in Nederland* (Amsterdam: Amsterdam University Press, 2015). In German translation: *Verfolgte Komponisten in den Niederlanden* (Berlin: Hentrich & Hentrich, 2020).
10 Joop Leijendeckers: Székely als solist in Nijmegen, https://www.noviomagus.nl/Gastredactie/Leijendeckers/Szekely.htm [accessed: 08.09.2022].
11 Information by Standesamts- und Staatsbürgerschaftsverband Bad Vöslau. When no other sources are mentioned, biographical data are based on the research database of the author, 'Forschungsdatenbank BioExil Primavera Driessen Gruber', in preparation of a 'Austrian Biographical Dictionary of Music Professionals, persecuted during Nazism', to be published in the years to come.

2   1933. ‚Die Situation ist fürchterlich. In Deutschland werde ich als Jude ausgestoßen, im Ausland als Deutscher' (Paul Pella)

From 1932 onward, the political developments in Germany, with Hitler coming to power, had been given extensive coverage by the Dutch media, including the music press. In particular, the Dutch left-wing political parties (not part of the government until 1939), artists and intellectuals were very much aware of the increasing threat.[12] When Mahler's former assistant at the Vienna Court Opera, Bruno Walter (1876 Berlin–1962 Beverly Hills), whose concerts in Leipzig and Berlin had been impeded by the Nazis, arrived at the Amsterdam Central Station on 23 March 1933, he was welcomed by an enthusiastic crowd, with the choir 'The Voice of the People' singing *Brüder zur Sonne, zur Freiheit*. Schoenberg's former pupil, composer, teacher and music writer Paul Amadeus Pisk (1893 Vienna–1990 Los Angeles), who was regularly heard on Dutch Radio Hilversum and who wrote for daily papers and journals, reported in his 'Letter from Vienna' in the Dutch music journal *De Muziek* from May 1933 on antisemitic riots in Vienna that were targeted against Walter, and the crisis relating to the stage director of the Vienna State Opera, Lothar Wallerstein (1882 Prague–1949 New Orleans).[13]

With the German Law on the Restoration of the Civil Service of 7 April 1933, a legal instrument had been created for dismissing Jews and 'non-Aryan' artists with one Jewish parent or grandparent. It affected numerous opera singers, conductors, orchestra members and teachers. Austrian music professionals working in Germany also lost their positions and tried to flee to the neighbouring countries. In this first period, the Dutch borders were still open to refugees. The government tried to find a balance between the Dutch tradition of granting asylum to oppressed persons and fear for competition on the labour market, striving not to irritate its powerful German neighbour and trading partner.[14] But already by July 1933, the Dutch Ministry of Justice prohibited refugees to work or to take part in political actions and organisations under penalty of expulsion.[15] Two months later, the German Law on the Creation of a

---

12   Van der Zee, 43f.
13   Pauline Micheels, *Muziek in de schaduw van het Derde Rijk. De Nederlandse symfonieorkesten, 1933–1945* (Zutphen: Walburg Pers, 1993), 51f., 56f.
14   Moore, *Refugees from Nazi Germany*, 2f. For commercial ties with Germany see Chris van der Heijden, *Grijs verleden: Nederland en de Tweede Wereldoorlog* (Amsterdam: Olympus, 10th ed. 2009), 97.
15   Dan Michman and Ursula Langkau-Alex, 'Het Nederlandse vluchtelingenbeleid 1933–1940. Chronologie', in Dittrich and Würzner, 274–77 (274).

Reich Chamber of Culture made it impossible for Jewish or politically undesirable musicians to perform in Germany. In 1935, they were definitively excluded from membership.

The German-speaking refugees in the Netherlands were welcomed by relief organisations from diverse humanitarian, political or religious backgrounds. In April 1933, prominent members of the Dutch Jewish community, amongst them David Cohen and Abraham Asscher, the future Presidents of the Jewish Council of Amsterdam, created the Comité voor Joodsche Vluchtelingen (Committee for Jewish Refugees (JRC)), a department of the Comité voor Bijzondere Joodsche Belangen (Committee for Special Jewish Interests).[16] It was allowed to take care of the refugees, but it had to guarantee that the refugees would not become a burden on the Dutch economy and that the JRC would do their utmost to enable further emigration overseas.[17] By the end of April, around 4,000 Jewish refugees had registered with the JRC.

One of the first Austrian musicians to arrive in the Netherlands in 1933 was Paul Pella,[18] born Morgenstern (1892 Vienna–1965 Enschede). After holding positions in Prague, Lübeck and Dortmund, Pella, a former student of Arnold Schoenberg and the Vienna Music Academy, had become *musikalischer Oberleiter* at the Stadttheater Aachen. After the Aachen premiere of Alban Berg's opera *Wozzeck* under his baton in 1930, Pella conducted its Dutch premiere in Amsterdam that same year. Antisemitic attacks by Aachen's music director Peter Raabe, who in 1935 was to become president of the Reich Chamber of Music as Richard Strauss' successor, forced him to leave Germany. In 1933 Pella opened a small opera studio in Amsterdam, founded a class for music drama training at the Amsterdam Conservatory of the Vereeniging Muzieklyceum, and taught at the Rotterdam Community College. In a letter to Alban Berg, however, he complained: ‚Die Situation ist fürchterlich. In Deutschland werde ich als Jude ausgestoßen, im Ausland als Deutscher.'[19]

3   1934–1938. ‚... gutwillig aber zu langsam' (Bruno Walter)

In February 1934, a brief civil war in Austria ended with the defeat of the SDAP (Social Democratic Workers' Party) and the ban of the Unions, resulting in a

---

16   Prof. Dr. D.(avid) Cohen, *Zwervend en dolend. De Joodse vluchtelingen in Nederland in de jaren 1933–1940* (Haarlem: De Erven F. Bohn, 1955), 60ff.
17   Van der Zee, 91f.
18   Willem Bruls (ed.), *En route: De geschiedenis van opera Forum Filharmonisch* (Zutphen: Walburg Pers, 2006), 39–52.
19   Letter from Paul Pella to Alban Berg, cited after Willem Bruls.

Catholic corporate state under Chancellor Dollfuss ('Austrofascism'). After his assassination by the Nazis in July (known as the *Juli-Putsch*), he was succeeded by Kurt Schuschnigg. A great admirer of Bruno Walter, Schuschnigg envisioned Austria as a conservative alternative to Nazi-Germany, using the Salzburg Festival as its (anti-Bayreuth) artistic figurehead with the participation of numerous Jewish artists who had been expelled from Germany, and Bruno Walter as its music director.[20] For a short period Austria became a stopover on the way to a safer country of refuge.[21]

Although by 1 January 1934 the greatest part of the first wave of refugees in the Netherlands had left for overseas, the Dutch government under Prime Minister Hendrik Colijn further hardened its immigration policy. Police and border surveillance were instructed not to allow German and Austrian refugees to cross the border. In particular Jews with an Eastern European background should be refused admittance because of their 'aberrant mentality', which was felt as a threat to Dutch society.[22] Due to the citizenship laws of the newly founded states, by 1920 millions of residents of the former Austro-Hungarian Empire had lost their citizenship and were stateless, which represented an additional obstacle for Austrian refugees, often of East-European origin.[23] Like everywhere else in Europe, nationalism, xenophobia and antisemitism were on the rise in the Netherlands, intensified by the global financial crisis that had struck the Netherlands heavily. In 1935 the Dutch National Socialist Party (NSB) reached its high point of eight per cent, but although in 1936 the unemployment rate stood at thirty-five per cent, it dropped to four per cent of the vote two years later.[24] The government initiated measures against poverty and unemployment in the entertainment world. Theatre and cabaret ensembles were obliged to employ a certain number of Dutch artists,[25] while restaurants and cafés were ordered to engage no more than ten per cent of foreigners

---

20   Primavera Driessen Gruber, 'Mimi Gruder-Guntram's Autograph Album. Sidelight on exiled Salzburg Festival musicians and opera performers persecuted by the Nazis', in Marcus G. Patka and Sabine Fellner im Auftrag des Jüdischen Museum Wien (eds.), *Jedermanns Juden: 100 Jahre Salzburger Festspiele / Everyman's, Jews: 100 Years Salzburg Festival* (Salzburg: Residenz, 2021), 204–19.
21   Ursula Seeber, *Asyl wider Willen: Exil in Österreich 1933–1938* (Wien: Picus, 2003).
22   Dan Michman, 'De joodse emigratie en de Nederlandse reactie daarop tussen 1933 en 1940 en 1940', in Dittrich and Würzner, 93–108 (95f.); Michman and Langkau-Alex, 'Chronologie', 274–77 (275).
23   Dwork and van Pelt, 58.
24   Ian Kershaw, *To Hell and Back: Europe 1914–1949* (London: Penguin Books, 2016), 2, 234f.
25   Ben Albach and Jacques Klöters, 'Exiltheater in den Niederlanden', in Frithjof Trapp, Werner Mittenzwei, Henning Rischbieter and Hansjörg Schneider (eds.), *Handbuch des deutschsprachigen Exiltheaters 1933–1945*, Vol. 1 (München: K.G. Saur, 1999), 222.

in their orchestras.²⁶ But even musicians with a position in one of the eight Dutch symphony orchestras were in dire financial straits. The Federatie van Nederlandse Toonkunstenaars, an organisation of Dutch musicians, protested against performances of ensembles from abroad and lobbied with the government for protective measures and a privileged treatment of Dutch soloists and conductors.²⁷

In spite of the economic crisis, the entertainment centres of Amsterdam, The Hague and its seaside resort Scheveningen continued to flourish. In 1935, the violinist and saxophonist Alfred Cecil, born Abraham (1907 Lviv–1965 San Mateo), a former student at the Vienna Music Academy, came to the Netherlands to work as a bar musician. A year later his colleague from the Academy, pianist and violinist Franziska/Fanny Kreiter (1906 Lviv–2009 Enschede) also found employment in the Dutch entertainment scene.²⁸ Some dancers, operetta singers and members of touring cabaret and revue ensembles (such as Ping-Pong, Pfeffermühle, Nelson Revue), amongst them several Austrians, also managed to obtain working permits.²⁹ But applications for residence and working permits were being delayed or not extended, and the employment of exiled musicians was becoming ever more complicated. Even in the case of Bruno Walter the Dutch authorities were not too cooperative. Appointed as music director of the Vienna State Opera and the Salzburg Festival after his escape from Berlin to Vienna, Walter followed Pierre Monteux as guest conductor of the Concertgebouw Orkest. In spite of being honoured as Officer in the Order of Oranje Nassau, his attempts to have his siblings

---

26 Jacques Klöters, ‚Amusement in de dagen van Olim', in Joost Groeneboer and Hetty Berg (eds.), ... *Dat is de kleine man ... 100 jaar joden in het Amsterdams amusement, 1840–1940* (Amsterdam, Joods Historisch Museum, Zwolle: Waanders, 1995), 83–114 (95); Kees C.A.T.M. Wouters, *Ongewenschte muziek: De bestrijding van jazz en moderne amusementsmuziek in Duitsland en Nederland 1920–1945* (Den Haag: Sdu, 1999), 55f.

27 Micheels, 16ff.

28 Gemeentearchief Den Haag; Archive of the University of Music and Performing Arts Vienna (Archiv mdw); Historische Meldeunterlagen der Stadt Wien, Wiener Stadt- und Landesarchiv (WrSuLA).

29 On Jewish singers and cabaret artists from Austria who were exiled in the Netherlands, see Albach and Klöters; Katja B. Zaich, *'Ich bitte dringend um ein Happyend'. Deutsche Bühnenkünstler im niederländischen Exil 1933–1945* (Frankfurt am Main: Peter Lang, 2001); Hilde Haider-Pregler, 'Theaterwissenschaft und Exilforschung', in Evelyn Adunka and Peter Roessler (eds.), *Die Rezeption des Exils: Geschichte und Perspektiven der österreichischen Exilforschung* (Wien: Mandelbaum, 2003), 187–99; Kay Weniger, *Zwischen Bühne und Baracke. Lexikon der verfolgten Theater-, Film- und Musikkünstler 1933 bis 1945* (Berlin: Metropol 2008).

admitted to the Netherlands were in vain: 'Ich hatte mich an mehrere Stellen in Holland gewandt, die sich gutwillig aber zu langsam erwiesen.'[30]

The pianist, composer, conductor and music teacher Felix Hupka (1896 Vienna–1966 Amsterdam), a pupil of the renowned music theorist Heinrich Schenker,[31] had come from Paris, where he had worked as a composer and film conductor, to The Hague as a guest conductor of the Residentie Orkest. As was the case for Georg Szell, who was until 1937 the General Music Director of the German Opera House in Prague, a permanent position with the orchestra was out of reach for foreigners.[32] In 1938, Hupka settled in Amsterdam, where he worked as a music teacher and accompanist for the tenor Joseph Schmidt (1904 Davydivka–1942 Girenbad), who had gained enormous popularity in the Netherlands by singing 'Ik hou van Holland' (I love Holland) on Radio Hilversum in the Dutch language.

In 1934, the violinist and conductor Alma Rosé (1906 Vienna–1944 Auschwitz), daughter of the concertmaster of the Vienna State Opera and the Philharmonic Orchestra Arnold Rosé (1863 Jassy–1946 London), toured the Netherlands with her ladies' band, the Wiener Walzermädel. One of her singers, Hildegard/Mady Meth[33] (1908 Innsbruck–1988 Amsterdam) succeeded in obtaining a permanent residence permit for herself and her mother thanks to her brother, an engineer at the Fokker airplane factory. She appeared in productions of the Fritz Hirsch Operetta in The Hague, the successful ensemble of German singer, actor and director Fritz Hirsch (1888 Mannheim–1942 Mauthausen).[34] It provided a network for German-speaking exiles, with a huge concentration of Austrian singers. Hirsch's greatest star was Austrian tenor Richard Tauber[35] (1891 Linz–1948 London), who had become immensely popular as a singing film star. After his subsequent dismissals from the opera in

---

30   Bruno Walter, *Thema und Variationen: Erinnerungen und Gedanken* (Stockholm: Bermann-Fischer, 1947), 494.

31   Felix Hupka, in Schenker Documents Online, https://schenkerdocumentsonline.org/profiles/person/entity-000399.html [accessed: 19.12.2020].

32   Micheels, 27f.

33   Österreichisches Staatsarchiv (ÖstA)/Archiv der Republik (AdR), Hilfsfonds 21730 (Hildegard Meth).

34   Katja B. Zaich, ‚Fritz Hirsch', in Claudia Maurer Zenck, Peter Petersen and Sophie Fetthauer (eds.), *Lexikon verfolgter Musiker und Musikerinnen der NS-Zeit* (Hamburg: Universität Hamburg, 2014), https://www.lexm.uni-hamburg.de/object/lexm_lexmperson_00004336 [accessed: 19.12.2020].

35   Jutta Raab Hansen, *NS-verfolgte Musiker in England. Spuren deutscher und österreichischer Flüchtlinge in der britischen Musikkultur* (Hamburg: Von Bockel, 1996), 467; Evelyn Steinthaler, *Morgen muss ich fort von hier. Richard Tauber. Die Emigration eines Weltstars* (Wien: Milena, 2011).

Berlin and Vienna in 1938, Tauber settled in London, which served him as a starting point for his guest appearances and tours all over the world.

The support of the JRC for less fortunate refugees was based mainly on contributions from the Joint Distribution Committee and HICEM. Private funding from the Netherlands included the proceeds from benefit events. One of its patrons was the art dealer Jacques Goudstikker, who used his country estate Kasteel Nijenrode as a venue for charity concerts with star violinist Bronislaw Huberman (1882 Częstochova–1947 Corsier-sur-Vevey), the Concertgebouw Orkest under Willem Mengelberg and the singer Dési Halban-Kurz (1912 Vienna–1996 Bilthoven), whom he would marry shortly after.[36]

4 1938–1940. „… aber die schwierigkeiten bei den behörden sind hier größer als überall sonst' (Hugo Kauder)

In an interview with *The New York Times* in Amsterdam, published on 2 March 1938, Bruno Walter confirmed his intention not to abandon the Salzburg Festival, which, he said 'would stay exactly as it was'.[37] But on the evening of 11 March 1938, Austrian Chancellor Schuschnigg announced his forced resignation on the Austrian radio, and, in the early morning of 12 March, German troops crossed the Austrian border. Walter's daughter, the singer Charlotte Lindt (1903 Vienna–1970 Colorado Springs) was arrested in Vienna. Walter had been premiering Egon Wellesz' (1885 Vienna–1974 Oxford) *Prospero's Beschwörungen* and Ernst Krenek's (1900 Vienna–1991 Palm Springs) second *Piano Concerto* with the Concertgebouw Orkest.[38] Both composers were present but left the country immediately afterwards. Walter cancelled his contract with the Vienna State Opera and the Salzburg Festival in order to avoid being dismissed. He eventually managed to have his daughter released from prison two weeks later. Meanwhile, the Austrian lawyer Arthur Seyss-Inquart was temporarily appointed *Reichsstatthalter* of the incorporated Austrian Republic. Nazis raided the streets, Jews were terrorised, and, on 1 April, the first deportation of prominent Austrians (Jews and non-Jews) to the concentration camp at Dachau took place.

Although the Netherlands was not among the main destinations for Austrian refugees, some of the routes to overseas required Dutch harbours.

---

36 Cohen, 74, 77–90, 97; Presser, 9; Licht, 237.
37 'Walter in Amsterdam' in *The New York Times*, 02.03.1938.
38 Claudia Maurer Zenck, „Eduard Erdmann im „Dritten Reich"", in *mr-Mitteilungen 100*, February 2020, 25–42.

The JRC was flooded with requests, asking for help and information. Many of these letters held a reference to an earlier stay in the Netherlands as a foster child after the Great War. One of the petitioners was the conductor and composer of popular music Kuno Cesoli, born Konrad Holzstein (1906 Siret–1993 Beaumont-sur-Oise), living at the time in Amsterdam. On 2 April 1938, he wrote to the Board of the JRC:

> Als Kapellmeister seit 1.1.1938 im ersten Haus Amsterdams tätig, wurde ich auf Grund meines Namens und Könnens 4 Mal prolongiert und verbleibe bis 30. auf diesem Posten. An diesem Endtage erlischt auch meine hiesige Arbeits- und Verbleibserlaubnis. Mein ständiger Wohnort ist Wien 9, Alserstraße 39, wo ich eine eigene Wohnung besitze. Durch den Umsturz ist mir die Möglichkeit eines Zurückgehens genommen.[39]

Cesoli probably did not remain in the Netherlands. Apart from his death in France, information on his life and career after 1938 is still missing.

The Austrian singer, composer, lyricist and milliner Emilie/Mimi Grossberg née Buchwald[40] (1905 Vienna–1997 New York) also asked the Jewish Community in Amsterdam for help, imploring them to rescue her parents.[41] As in so many other cases, the JRC answered with a standard letter, explaining that the Dutch borders had been closed for foreigners without a transit visa, and that it was not possible to obtain working permits. While Mimi Grossberg managed to escape to the USA, her parents had to stay behind. They were murdered in Maly Trostenets near Minsk.

In reaction to the *Anschluss*, the Dutch government – fearing uncontrolled immigration, increasing antisemitism and tensions towards German speaking refugees – decided to close the borders. In internal circulars of 23 March and 7 May referring to the admission of (ex-) Austrians, the Catholic Minister of Justice Goseling ordered that in future (and retroactively applicable to 1 March) refugees were only to be admitted at the border when in possession of a passport and an official declaration stating that they could return to the German Reich unimpeded. This measure de facto prohibited any further immigration of Jewish refugees.[42] During the night of 9/10 November 1938 in a planned orgy

---

39 Letter, Kuno Cesoli to the Board of the JRC, 02.04.1938 Amsterdam, NIOD, Comité voor Joodsche Vluchtelingen 181b/14 I (spelling and grammar slightly adapted by the author).
40 Susanne Blumesberger (ed.), *Mimi Grossberg (1905–1997). Pionierin – Mentorin – Networkerin: Ein Leben zwischen Wien und New York* (Wien: Praesens, 2008).
41 Letter, Mimi Grossberg-Buchwald to the Jewish Community Amsterdam, 24.06.1938, NIOD, Comité voor Joodsche Vluchtelingen, 181b/14 III.
42 Cohen, 188; Michman and Langkau-Alex, 275f.

of violence in Vienna (known as the 'November pogroms'), over 4,000 Jewish shops, eighteen synagogues and over sixty prayer houses, as well as thousands of Jewish residences were stormed, plundered and destroyed by Austrian SS- and SA-troops and civilians.[43] This caused another stream of refugees from Austria to the Netherlands.

Since 1936, Dutch intellectuals and artists had intensely warned against Nazism, amongst others with a Comité van Waakzaamheid (Vigilance Committee). In its brochure *De gesloten grens* (The closed border) from November 1938 it strongly condemned the immigration policy of the government. In reaction to parliamentary interrogations and public pressure on 15 November 1938, the government decided to admit 2,000 'German' refugees, increasing the number to 7,000 refugees with papers in the following days, under the condition that the refugees would be interned in camps. To offset the expenses, the government required a security deposit of one million guilders from the JRC, later extending this requirement to other relief organisations for smaller sums. In that week alone, the JRC received 6,000–7,000 enquiries for admission to the country. By the end of December, the maximum quota had almost been reached. 1,400 children had been admitted on legal grounds; allegedly some 1,500 refugees had crossed the borders illegally. In October 1939, the first German and Austrian refugees were assigned to the (Dutch) Central Refugee Camp Westerbork. Systematic internment started in the first months of 1940.[44] One of the first Austrian musicians to be interned was Joachim Kerker[45] (1913 Kolomea–1995 Dade, Fl.), a laureate violin graduate of the Vienna Music Academy. After sixteen months of internment, he was able to escape to the USA, where, in 1943, he joined the US Army in order to fight Nazi-Germany.

Paul Pella had returned to the Netherlands in 1938 after a tour in the USSR and a position as guest conductor at the Tbilissi opera house. In the following year he was appointed chief conductor of the Nederlandse Operastichting (Dutch Opera foundation). His debut took place on 11 December 1939 with a performance of *Die Zauberflöte* under the stage direction of Lothar Wallerstein

---

43 Gerhard Botz, Ivar Oxaal, Michael Pollak and Nina Scholz (eds.), *Eine zerstörte Kultur. Jüdisches Leben und Antisemitismus in Wien seit dem 19. Jahrhundert* (Wien: Czernin, 2nd ed. 2002); Eveline Brugger, Martha Keil, Albert Lichtblau, Christoph Lind and Barbara Staudinger (eds.), *Geschichte der Juden in Österreich* (Wien: Ueberreuter, 2006), 519ff.

44 Michman and Langkau-Alex, 277. On Westerbork and other Dutch camps see also Dirk Mulder, *Buitengewone transporten. Deportaties van Joden, Roma en Sinti uit Nederland, 1940–1945* (Zwolle: Wbooks, 2022).

45 ÖStA/AdR, Hilfsfonds 40.350/8 B, 37.386 (Joachim Jacob Kerker).

at the Groote Schouwburg in Rotterdam,[46] one of the venues that were to be destroyed during the German bombardment of the city in May 1940.

Wallerstein, dismissed by the Vienna State Opera, had arrived in Amsterdam after the November pogroms. Bruno Walter had invited him to direct *Figaro's Hochzeit* with the Wagner Vereeniging, which had its premiere on 17 November 1938 in Amsterdam. In April 1939, upon the invitation of director Sem Dresden (1881 Amsterdam–1957 The Hague), Wallerstein started the first class for opera direction in the Netherlands at the Koninklijk Conservatorium, The Hague.[47] He was most likely supported by his sister, the concert singer and voice tutor Laura/Lotte Bunzel (1876 Prague–1962 Vienna). With the announcement on 4 September 1940 that German and stateless Jews had to be evacuated from the seashore, Wallerstein had to leave his residence in The Hague,[48] but even after being dismissed by the Conservatorium in November, he continued to give classes for his Dutch students in a small village on the outskirts of The Hague. He managed to escape to the USA,[49] where he worked as a stage director at the Metropolitan Opera New York, cooperating again with Bruno Walter, who had left Europe in 1939.

The composer, music theorist and teacher Hugo Kauder[50] (1888 Tovačov–1972 Bussum) arrived in the Netherlands in December 1938. His songs on 'Twaalf Gedichten' (Twelve Poems) by the prominent Dutch writer and lyricist Albert Verwey, whose admiration for Stefan George Kauder shared, had resulted in a warm relationship with the Verwey family, eventually leading to a publishing contract. It provided him with a temporary entrance permit to the Netherlands. He stayed at the home of Verwey's widow in Santpoort, translating Verwey's letters into German. Some of his compositions were performed by musicians of the Residentie Orkest. Kauder felt welcome in the Netherlands, but in a letter to his friend, the philosopher Rudolf Pannwitz, he wrote:

---

46 Theater Instituut Nederland in cooperation with Nederlandse Opera (eds.), *Annalen van de Opera Gezelschappen in Nederland 1886–1995* (Amsterdam: Theater Instituut Nederland, 1996), 585.

47 John Kasander, *150 Jaar Koninklijk Conservatorium* (Den Haag: Koninklijk Conservatorium, 1976), 76–81.

48 On the evacuation of German-speaking refugees from the seashore see Presser, 222.

49 Lotte Bunzel-Wallerstein, *Dr. Lothar Wallerstein. Eine biographische Skizze* (Wien 1950, unpublished typescript, Archiv der Gesellschaft der Musikfreunde Wien), 20f.

50 Karin Wagner, *Hugo Kauder (1888–1972). Komponist-Musikphilosoph-Theoretiker: Eine Biographie.* (Wien, Köln, Weimar: Böhlau, 2018), 96ff.

ja gewiß wäre von allen überhaupt in betracht kommenden möglichkeiten die schönste und beste die, in Holland bleiben zu können; aber die schwierigkeiten bei den behörden sind hier größer als überall sonst.[51]

In April 1939, with Pannwitz's help, Kauder was able to move to London, where he was reunited with his wife and son. In February 1940, the family finally arrived in New York.

On 1 September 1939, the German *Wehrmacht* crossed the border to Poland. Three days later England was at war with Germany and the Second World War II had commenced. About 250,000 Jews were still living in Germany and former Austria, many of them stateless and becoming more and more impoverished. In October 1939, the first Jews from Vienna, Ostrava and Katovice were deported to Nisko.[52]

5 1940–1942. ,Was uns allen in Holland angetan worden ist, ist unbeschreiblich.' (Bertha Flesch)[53]

During the night of 10 May 1940, German armed forces invaded the Netherlands. Three days later the Dutch Royal family and the government escaped to England. The bombing of Rotterdam led General Winkelman to surrender; the capitulation was signed on 15 May. One of the last ships to leave the harbour of IJmuiden for Southampton, the SS Bodegraven, enabled a narrow escape for some 200 Dutch- and German-speaking Jews, among them a group of refugee children and the family of Dési Halban-Kurz. She had assisted Gertruida/Truus Wijsmuller-Meijer, who rescued over 10,000 Jewish children from Austria, Germany and Czechoslovakia, bringing them on 'Kindertransports' to England.[54] Her husband was to die on-board, but Dési and their little son, Edo, arrived safely in England, from where they managed to reach the USA.

The German occupiers installed a civil administration in the Netherlands under Arthur Seyss-Inquart as *Reichskommissar*. Four *Generalkommissare* were supervising the Dutch ministries, three of them (former) Austrians. During

---

51 *Ibid.*, 101.
52 Friedländer, 60.
53 Copy of an undated, unaddressed and unsigned letter by Bertha Flesch, Lucerne, to Karl-Ulrich Schnabel, written after the death of Carl Flesch, Nederlands Muziek Instituut (NMI), archief Carl Flesch; cf. Kathinka Rebling (ed.), *Carl Flesch: Die hohe Schule des Fingersatzes* (Frankfurt am Main et al.: Peter Lang, 1995), 18.
54 Cohen, 336; The Unknown Dutch Holocaust Hero Who Saved Over 10,000 Children, https://fozmuseum.com/blog/dutch-holocaust-hero/ [accessed: 18.09.2022].

the first months of the occupation, the Nazi administration strived to show a friendly face in order to win over the Dutch population for National Socialism, exposing its real character only gradually. General Winkelman and Dutch high officials called upon the population to remain calm amid the new situation. Even former Prime Minister Colijn, who in a national appeal on Radio Hilversum before the invasion had raised a sum of 473,000 Dutch guilders to support Jewish refugees, argued in his leaflet *Op de grens van twee werelden* (At the border between two worlds) for adjustment.[55] In June 1940, De Nederlandsche Unie was established, a political party with the objective of preserving Dutch culture and identity by cooperating with the occupying forces. It was dissolved by Seyss-Inquart in the following year. In October 1940, Dutch officials, university professors, schoolteachers and orchestra musicians, with only very few exceptions, voluntary completed a form with a declaration of their 'Aryan' descent. One month later, Jewish officials, professors, teachers and musicians were discharged.

At the moment of the invasion some 26,000 non-Dutch Jews were living in the Netherlands, amongst them approximately 20,000 German-speaking refugees.[56] As many of them had already experienced Nazi terror, they were struck with panic, and during the first years of the occupation they indeed turned out to be more exposed.[57] Dutch Jewry, on the other hand, had lived in peace for the last centuries, partially becoming part of the Dutch economic and intellectual elites, or merging into the socialist and communist labour movements. But the fragmentation along religious and political lines of Dutch society ('pillarization'), in which most people used to restrict professional and social contacts to members of their own groups according to religion, political party or class, prevented a clear insight in the distant relationship between the non-Jewish majority and the Jewish population. In the years to come, this would limit the networking possibilities of Jews and gentiles alike. The general strike in February 1941 (known as the *Februaristaking*), organised by the banned Communist Party, ultimately was to remain the only major public protest against the German anti-Jewish measures in the Netherlands.[58]

Two weeks earlier, Hans Böhmcker, the representative of the German Reich for the City of Amsterdam, had ordered the establishment of the Joodsche Raad (Jewish Council) for Amsterdam, controlled by the Zentralstelle für Jüdische

---

55 Hendrik Colijn, *Op de grens van twee werelden* (Amsterdam, 1940), cited from van der Heijden, 132; Castaecker and Moore (eds.), 275.
56 Moore, *Slachtoffers en overlevenden*, 313; Michman and Langkau-Alex, 277; Cohen, 157. On the correct numbers see also Mulder, *Buitengewone transporten*, 219–24.
57 Dwork and van Pelt, XII.
58 Croes and Tammes, 601.

Auswanderung, and modelled after Eichmann's Zentralstelle in Vienna. With this office, Eichmann was overseeing the forced emigration of some 150,000 Jews from Austria, robbing them to the last cent.[59] From August 1941 onwards, the Zentralstelle was responsible for the deportations to the extermination camps. Upon Eichmann's orders, the executive director of the reorganised Jewish Community Council in Vienna, Josef Löwenherz, father of exiled musicologist Sigmund Levarie (1914 Lviv–2010 New York), visited Asscher and Cohen in Amsterdam to 'help organise the emigration of Austrian Jews'.[60] Like Löwenherz in Vienna, Asscher and Cohen soon were 'inextricably involved in a *danse macabre*, with Satan playing the tune':[61] forced to cooperate with the Nazis whilst trying to save the life of as many persons as possible.

Although the lives of Carl Flesch and Alma Rosé are fairly well documented,[62] newer findings shed more light on their unintended exile in the Netherlands and exemplify the perilous, ever narrowing trap in which German-speaking exiles were caught. Both had come for professional reasons. Flesch, who had moved his residence from Germany to London, arrived in September 1939 in the Netherlands for concerts and masterclasses at the Conservatorium in The Hague. Like many of his Dutch friends who believed the country would remain neutral,[63] the German invasion came as a surprise and impeded his return to England.[64] Already in June 1940, in anticipatory obedience, and before being legally obliged, Flesch's contract as a soloist at the Kurhaus in Scheveningen was cancelled for racist reasons by his long-time 'friend' Adama Zijlstra.[65] Flesch had helped Alma Rosé to secure the safety of her father in London

---

59   Dwork and van Pelt, 191.
60   Cohen, 188.
61   Presser, 165. For Löwenherz see Doron Rabinovici, *Instanzen der Ohnmacht. Wien 1938–1945. Der Weg zum Judenrat* (Frankfurt am Main: Jüdischer Verlag, 2000).
62   For Carl Flesch see a.o. Hans Keller (ed.), *The memoirs of Carl Flesch*. Translated by Hans Keller and edited by him in collaboration with C.H. Flesch. Foreword by Max Rostal (London: Barrie & Rockliff, 1957); Kathinka Rebling: ‚Carl Flesch', in Maurer Zenck and Petersen (eds.), *Lexikon verfolgter Musiker und Musikerinnen der NS-Zeit* (Hamburg: Universität Hamburg, 2006), https://www.lexm.uni-hamburg.de/object/lexm_lexmperson_00001449 [accessed: 19.12.2020]. For Alma Rosé see Richard Newman and Karen Kitley, *Alma Rosé: Vienna to Auschwitz* (Pompton Plains, Cambridge: Amadeus Press, 2003); Michaela Raggam-Blesch, Monika Sommer and Heidemarie Uhl (eds.), *Nur die Geigen sind geblieben / Only the Violins Remain. Alma & Arnold Rosé*. Exhibition catalogue of Haus der Geschichte Österreichs (Wien, 2019), 134ff.
63   Katja Happe, *Veel valse hoop*, 373.
64   Letter, Bertha Flesch, Lucerne, to Karl-Ulrich Schnabel, NMI, archief Carl Flesch.
65   Letter, Carl Flesch to [Anthony Adama] Zijlstra 25.06.1940, NMI, archief Carl Flesch 254/659.

by sending a circular letter to his friends and colleagues, asking for financial help.[66] To support her father, in the fall of 1939 Alma also travelled to The Hague on a contract with the Grand Hotel Central. For a while living with the Meth family in The Hague, she appeared in solo recitals, performed on Radio Hilversum and went on tour with the Fritz Hirsch Operetta. After the German invasion she too found herself stranded. Moving to the house of Ed and Millie Spanjaard, she became part of an illegal circuit of house concerts for musicians who were banned from concert life, impeded or refusing to become a member of the Muziekgilde (the Dutch equivalent of the Reich Chamber of Music). She appeared in house concerts all over the Netherlands, often accompanied by Géza Frid (1904 Sighetu Marmaţiei–1989 Beverwijk) at the piano.

When in May 1942 Jews were being ordered to wear a yellow star, and a general ban on travelling for Jews was issued one month later, she could no longer perform. In July 1942, massive raids against the Jews started. Alma Rosé was arrested and taken to the 'Joodsche Schouwburg' in Amsterdam (the gathering place for deportation), only to be released because of her marriage of convenience with the non-Jew, Constant van Leeuwen Boomkamp. A relative of the Spanjaards, the Dutch composer and conductor Martin Spanjaard (1892 Borne–1942 Auschwitz) was among the first musicians to be deported to Westerbork, together with his Austrian wife, the harpist Eleonore Okladek (1901 Vienna–1942 Auschwitz), who was educated at the Vienna Music Academy. They both perished in Auschwitz in September 1942.[67] Since for Ed and Millie Spanjaard danger was increasing too, Alma had to find other hosts to live with, amongst them her feminist friend Marie Anne Tellegen, a member of a resistance network (and, after the war, the director of the cabinets of both Queen Wilhelmina and Juliana of the Netherlands).[68]

In October, Alma Rosé was ordered to report at the Zentralstelle für Jüdische Auswanderung, but she was rescued again, this time by Tellegen, who eventually organised an escape route to neutral Switzerland. In a letter to Carl Flesch from 7 August 1942, Alma said goodbye:

---

66 Letters Alfred Rosé to Carl Flesch 1938 NMI, archief Carl Flesch 254/467–469; letters Carl Flesch to Alma Rosé 09.02.1941 and 09.07.1942, NMI 254/471–472.
67 Carine Alders, ‚Martin Spanjaard', in Alders and Pameijer (eds.), 249–255; Historische Meldeunterlagen der Stadt Wien, WrSuLA; Archiv mdw.
68 W.H. Weenink, *Vrouw achter de troon. Marie Anne Tellegen 1893–1976* (Amsterdam: Boom, 2nd ed. 2015); Doris Hermans, ‚Marie Anne Tellegen', https://www.fembio.org/biographie.php/frau/biographie/marie-anne-tellegen [accessed: 19.12.2020].

> Es gibt keinen anderen Weg von Ihnen Abschied zu nehmen – damit wissen Sie alles! Ich gehe – versuche in die Freiheit zu kommen – sonst gehe ich zu Grunde. ... Werde ich Sie im Leben wiedersehen?[69]

The escape route was blown up and Alma Rosé was arrested in France. From there, she was deported to Auschwitz, where, as a conductor of the women's orchestra, she saved the lives of Jewish women by accepting and tutoring them as members of the orchestra.

In the meantime, Carl Flesch had to move from his noble residence in The Hague to a sublet in Scheveningen. In spite of an affidavit provided by the Curtis Institute of Music in Philadelphia and entrance visa for the USA, the German authorities were not willing to issue an exit permit.[70] Like Ed Spanjaard[71] and Oskar Back[72] he had sent a request to Hans Calmeyer, the representative of the German Department of Justice at The Hague, to have his 'Aryan' origins investigated, in order to be exempted from anti-Jewish measures.[73] Spanjaard and Back succeeded in proving their non-Jewish descent with the help of forged papers and false 'witnesses'; they both survived. According to the historian Presser, Flesch also had a special stamp of exemption from deportation as a so called 'blue knight',[74] but it did not protect him from being arrested various times. One night, Flesch and his wife were taken to the 'Oranjehotel', the notorious Scheveningen prison, only to be miraculously released by showing a letter from Wilhelm Furtwängler, which had been written on a different occasion. Ultimately, with the help of Dutch and Hungarian friends, Flesch was able to revive his Hungarian citizenship and, in December 1942, the couple could leave the Netherlands for Budapest, eventually arriving in Switzerland in April 1943. Among Flesch's many Dutch pupils were Jo Juda (1909 Amsterdam–1985 Laren), Sam Swaap (1888 Amsterdam–1971 The Hague), Samuel Tromp (1902 Groningen–1987 Amsterdam) and Hungarian-born Gabriella/Mili Lüps (1901 Szatmár–1991 Rheden). Honoured as a 'Righteous Among the Nations' by Yad Vashem, Mili Lüps played a role in reobtaining Flesch's Hungarian citizenship.

---

69 Letter, Alma Rosé to Carl Flesch, Utrecht 07.08.1942, NMI, archief Carl Flesch 254/470.
70 Letter, Bertha Flesch, Lucerne, to Karl-Ulrich Schnabel, NMI, archief Carl Flesch.
71 Paul Denekamp and Hans Schogt, 'Mr. Ed Spanjaard, schaker en pleiter op meesterniveau', in Eduard Spanjaard, oudzuylenutrecht.nl/eduard-spanjaard [accessed: 22.09.2022].
72 Theo Olof, *Oskar Back en veertig jaar Nationaal Vioolconcours* (Bussum: Theo Olof en uitgeverij Thoth, 2005). For Presser on Hans Calmeyer see Presser, 296–311.
73 Matthias Middelberg, *'Wer bin ich, dass ich über Leben und Tod entscheide?' Hans Calmeyer, 'Rassereferent' in den Niederlanden 1941–1945* (Göttingen: Wallstein, 2015).
74 Presser, 111.

She also might have supported Paul Pella and relatives of Bertha Flesch in hiding in and around Velp.[75]

In The Hague, Lotte Bunzel and her husband, the former Austrian Minister of Finance Julius Bunzel, had been marked as being Jewish with the forced name 'Sara' and a handwritten 'J' in the residence register.[76] In 1941, they returned to Vienna, where Julius Bunzel passed away. One month later, his widow and daughter were deported to Theresienstadt. In February 1945, Lotte Bunzel was liberated, together with a group of prominent Dutch-Jewish musicians such as Sam Swaap and Samuel Tromp, and was brought to Switzerland as part of an exchange action.[77] Her daughter perished in Auschwitz.[78]

6   1942–1945. „… bis auf Weiteres'

In July 1942 the mass deportations of Dutch Jewry in Amsterdam started. Jews were rounded up from the streets and taken out of their houses in violent raids. The Jewish Council was involved in preparing the deportation lists. This caused a run on jobs with the Council, since working there meant being exempt from deportation for a while – 'bis auf Weiteres' (until further notice).[79] In 1943, some 15,000 stamps of exemption existed,[80] but soon enough most stamps proved to be without value. German-speaking Jews had the advantage of understanding the language and mentality of their oppressors. In this way, some of the refugees were able to obtain influential positions at the Council, like the Viennese lawyer Eduard Sluzker, who, as head of the *Expositur* (the liaison with the Zentralstelle), saved other Jews from being deported and managed to survive the war.[81]

Although some Dutch musicians, writers, artists, physicians, lawyers, students and others (many women amongst them) took part in resistance and

---

75   Correspondence Carl and Bertha Flesch with Mili Lüps, NMI, archief Carl Flesch 254/266–291; Yad Vashem, https://righteous.yadvashem.org/?search=Goswin%20Lups&searchType=righteous_only&language=en&itemId=4044644&ind=0 [accessed: 19.12.2020].
76   Gemeentearchief Den Haag, Verblijfsregister. For the registration of Jews and the letter 'J' on Dutch registration cards see Presser, 273.
77   Emil Wennekes, '"Some of the Jewish musicians are back at their desks". A case study in the remigration of European musicians after World War II', in Erik Levi (ed.), *The Impact of Nazism on Twentieth-Century Music* (Wien, Köln, Weimar: Böhlau, 2014), 323–36 (324).
78   Historische Meldeunterlagen der Stadt Wien, WrSuLA; Personenstandsblatt Lotte Bunzel, Archiv mdw.
79   Presser, 166.
80   Van der Heijden, 217.
81   Presser, 245ff.

rescue activities (in Yad Vashem's database of 'Righteous among the Nations' the Netherlands has the largest number of 'Righteous' per capita), too many others looked the other way or sought to benefit from the anti-Jewish measures. For most Jews, help arrived too late.[82] In September 1943, with the liquidation of the Jewish Council and the deportation of its remaining functionaries, the annihilation of Dutch Jewry was almost complete. Only some 25,000 people in hiding, some living in mixed marriages, so called 'quarter Jews', persons on the 'Calmeyer-list,' or people enjoying other forms of protection, were left.[83]

7 Westerbork

The first generation of internees in the Central Refugee Camp Westerbork was made up of German-speaking refugees, sent there by the Dutch authorities. In agreement with the JRC and the Dutch administration, the prisoners organised the camp life autonomously. When, in July 1942, the German administration took over, Westerbork became a transit camp for Theresienstadt, Auschwitz, Sobibor and Bergen-Belsen. The first Dutch Jews to arrive in Westerbork found themselves in a difficult position, fearing to be prioritised for further deportation by the German-Jewish camp 'elite'. As a result, the existing tensions between Dutch and German-speaking prisoners worsened ever more.[84] Arthur Pisk, a former officer in the Austrian Army, head of the dreaded *Ordedienst* in Westerbork, became one of the most hated persons of the camp. German-born Kurt Schlesinger, as *Oberdienstleiter* supervising the transports to the extermination camps, was accused of collaboration with the Germans after the war.[85] The cabaret ensembles in Westerbork, who typically presented their new programs on the eve of the transports to 'the East', for the main part consisted of German and Austrian refugees. Playing for time, they, too, were 'bis auf Weiteres', temporarily exempt from deportation. But although some artists, like Camilla Spira (1906 Hamburg–1997 Berlin)[86] and Josef Baar (1894 Vienna–1951 Andernach)[87] managed to be released in 1943 after having their 'Aryan'

---

82 For rescue networks and the role of German-speaking refugees in these networks see Moore, *Slachtoffers en overlevenden*, 207–29.
83 Presser, 213.
84 Moore, *Slachtoffers en overlevenden*, 264ff. In Mulder, *Buitengewone transporten*, the role of the German-speaking refugees is only mentioned occasionally.
85 *Ibid.*, 266.
86 Middelberg, 64, 102f., 113.
87 Katja B. Zaich, „Ich bitte dringend um ein Happyend', 223; Stadsarchief Amsterdam, Gezinskaart.

descent 'confirmed', the exemptions did not last, and, by September 1944, most of the artists and musicians were sent to Theresienstadt and Auschwitz. At least twenty-six music professionals from Austria perished in the extermination camps.

Among those deported to Westerbork and murdered in Auschwitz were Fanny Kreiter's sister Antonia/Toni Bettelheim (1903 Lviv–1942 Auschwitz) and her son Heini. Toni had studied piano at the Vienna Music Academy. In March 1938 she joined her sister in the Netherlands. Her sons Dolf (1921 Vienna–1996 Amsterdam) and Heini (1924 Vienna–1943 Auschwitz) arrived before the end of that year. The boys, studying violin and piano, moved to the Lloyd Hotel in Amsterdam to enable talented Dolf to visit the Muzieklyceum and continue his violin lessons. In October 1940 they were placed in a home for boys in Arnhem, while the sisters were still able to earn a living playing in cafés and restaurants. But during the summer of 1942 they all had to go into hiding. Dolf stayed with his aunt Fanny in Wassenaar; Heini with his mother in The Hague. Toni and Heini were arrested, betrayed by members of the NSB; Dolf and Fanny survived.[88]

8 Liberation – a New Start?

During 'Operation Market Garden' in September 1944, the southern parts of the Netherlands were liberated by the Allies. The Dutch population in the other parts had to survive a 'winter of famine' until the liberation of the Netherlands on 5 May 1945. Of the 140,000 Jews who had been living in the Netherlands in 1940, 107,000 had been deported to the extermination camps. Only 5,200 returned.

Stefan Bergmann, who before the German invasion of the Netherlands had performed with the Concertgebouw Orkest and the Concertgebouw Trio, in 1941 still appeared as a soloist with the Joodsch Symphonie Orkest at the 'Joodsche Schouwburg'.[89] After the liberation he emerged from hiding and performed again in concerts and on Dutch radio.[90] Dési Halban-Kurz returned to the

---

88 Primavera Driessen Gruber, '(Vor)Schule der Geläufigkeit', in Susana Zapke, Oliver Rathkolb, Kathrin Raminger, Julia Teresa Friehs and Michael Wladika (eds.), *Die Musikschule der Stadt Wien im Nationalsozialismus. Eine ‚ideologische Lehr- und Lerngemeinschaft'* (Wien: Hollitzer, 2020), 207–232 (223, 226); information by Jacques Bettelheim 06.06.2020.
89 Micheels, 187.
90 Composers' Classical Music, http://composers-classical-music.com/b/BergmannStefan.htm [accessed: 19.12.2020].

Netherlands, working as a voice tutor and occasionally appearing in concerts. Alfred Cecil survived an unidentified concentration camp and in 1949 emigrated to the USA, where he started a career as a sales representative.[91] Mady Meth survived in hiding, and after 1945 she appeared again with the Hoofdstad Operette and the KRO-radio orchestra. Also Felix Hupka, who had worked as a music teacher at the Jewish Lyceum in Amsterdam until its closure in 1943,[92] survived in hiding. After the liberation, he became head of the orchestra and opera classes of the Amsterdam (Sweelinck) Conservatory. Among Hupka's many pupils were the Dutch conductor Bernhard Haitink, the singer Christine Deutekom and Simon C. Jansen, cantor and organist of the Westerkerk in Amsterdam. Oskar Back, who had helped his pupil, the violin prodigy Theo Olof (1924 Bonn–2012 Amstelveen), to hide in Brussels during the war, continued to work as an outstanding teacher for several generations of Dutch violinists. Fanny Kreiter became a violinist in the Overijssels Philharmonisch Orkest, whereas Dolf Bettelheim from 1950 until his retirement in 1984 was a member of the Concertgebouw Orkest. Paul Pella was appointed co-director of the revived Stichting De Nederlandse Opera after the war. He worked as a conductor with the Holland Festival, for the Dutch radio and abroad, sometimes in cooperation with Lothar Wallerstein. The last years of his life he spent as co-founder and music director of an opera company, Opera Forum Enschede, in the eastern provinces of the Netherlands. Right after the war, Wallerstein took over the opera classes in The Hague and Amsterdam for some months, later returning from the USA to Europe every now and then to direct opera productions in the Netherlands, at the Salzburg Festival and for European opera houses. After his death, his former Dutch pupils created a 'liber amicorum' *Lothar Wallerstein in Memoriam*[93] and performed Cimarosa's opera *L'impresario in angustie* in Wallerstein's Dutch translation in homage to their beloved teacher.[94]

9 'Perhaps Some Day Someone Will Give Them the Particular Attention They Deserve' (Jacob Presser)

With these words Presser, in his monumental work on the destruction of Dutch Jewry, *Ashes in the Wind*, regretted that he was not able to give enough

---

91 Historische Meldeunterlagen der Stadt Wien, WrSuLA; Stadsarchief Amsterdam.
92 Dienke Hondius, *Absent. Herinneringen aan het Joods Lyceum Amsterdam 1941–1943* (Amsterdam: Vassalucci, 2001), 290.
93 Leerlingen en vrienden van Lothar Wallerstein, *Lothar Wallerstein In Memoriam*, November 1949, archief NMI.
94 Bunzel, 20.

attention to the fate of the German-speaking refugees.[95] To understand the situation of music exiles from Austria in the Netherlands during and after the war, it is necessary to relate it to the suffering of the Dutch (Jewish and non-Jewish) population. The burden of the German occupation weighed heavily on Dutch society. The country was terrorised and plundered; numerous Dutch citizens had lost relatives or friends. After May 1945, people had to cope with their own war trauma. They were not interested in the story of the Jewish survivors, and even less in that of German-speaking refugees. It took many years before the remaining survivors from Austria, now mostly stateless, were naturalised as Dutch citizens. With the postwar implementation of the Decree on Enemy Property (E-133) issued by the Dutch government-in-exile in October 1944, the Dutch state was entitled to confiscate all assets of 'enemy citizens', depriving them of their social rights and their prewar residence and working permits. It included former German-Jewish refugees and political refugees from German-controlled territories such as Austria or former parts of the Habsburg Empire. Although they could object against their status as 'enemy citizens' and submit a request for a 'declaration of de-enemisation' in order to recover their assets and qualify for Dutch citizenship by proving their behaviour during the German occupation as 'politically correct', this procedure could take many years.[96] Felix Hupka, who with the *Anschluss* had become a German citizen, had been denaturalised because of his Jewish background and was stateless since then. A victim of German persecution himself and without any assets, he too had to be 'de-enemised' after the liberation. It took until 1950 until he became a Dutch citizen.[97]

10 Conclusion

The ruptures in music life in 1933, 1934, 1938 and 1940–45 also had an impact on the research situation after 1945. In the Netherlands, the end of the war was followed by intensive debates on collaboration and resistance,[98] ultimately resulting in a strong wish to look forward, not backwards, accompanied by a long-lasting distrust against anything 'German'. In Germany, exile research began in the late 1970s, in Austria even later, but whilst in the following years

---

95 Presser, 222.
96 Marieke Oprel, *The Burden of Nationality: Dutch citizenship policies towards German nationals in the aftermath of the Second World War (1944–1967)* (Amsterdam: VU University Press, 2020), 15, 119–35.
97 Nationaal Archief, Nederlands Beheersinstituut (NBI) 95117 (Felix Hupka), with many thanks to Marieke Oprel for making Hupka's file available to the author.
98 Samama, 194ff.; Micheels 329ff.

in German-speaking and Anglophone countries exile studies were flourishing, in the Netherlands research on music exile during Nazism – with few exceptions[99] – has remained a desideratum. In his article on German-speaking music-exiles in the Netherlands, the Dutch composer, musicologist and music writer Marius Flothuis (1914 Amsterdam–2001 Amsterdam), who was active in Dutch resistance and a survivor of concentration camps, concluded that the influence of German-speaking music exiles in the Netherlands was negligible, since only a few composers had been able to establish themselves in this country. He nevertheless conceded that some conductors (in particular Bruno Walter), instrumentalists and singers had exerted some influence due to their performances and teaching activities.[100] Because of the lack of biographical information, in this period no distinction was made between German musicians and musicians with an (ex-)Austrian background. Although survivors and contemporary witnesses have now passed away, after almost fifty years of exile studies and biographical research on Austrian music exiles, the research situation has improved. So, whilst in 1993 the German scholar Rainer Licht mentioned about fifty German-speaking music professionals exiled in the Netherlands,[101] by now the number of *Austrian* music exiles in the Netherlands documented by this author has doubled and might still increase.

Due to the limits of space, in this very first essay on Austrian music exile in the Netherlands, many aspects could only be discussed cursorily; some issues had to be left out. Since only a small selection of biographies could be presented, many musicians still remain in the dark. To avoid premature conclusions, and in order to eventually analyse the impact of Austrian music exiles on music life in the Netherlands, continuing research will be necessary. The ambiguous story of the Netherlands under German occupation will remain a point of discussion for future generations of scholars, but other research questions are more likely to be clarified in the near future. Extensive examination of existing archival sources in the Netherlands and abroad, together with in-depth biographical, historical and musicological studies may help to fill the gaps and contribute to a common European commemorative culture.[102]

---

99   Dick Verkijk, *Radio Hilversum 1940–1945* (Amsterdam: De Arbeiderspers, 1974); Micheels, *ibid.*; Wouters, 55; Emanuel Overbeeke, 'Vervolgde componisten in Nederland', in Emanuel Overbeeke and Leo Samama (ed.), *Entartete muziek* (Amsterdam: Amsterdam University Press, 2004), 147–60; Alders and Pameijer. The groundbreaking recovery work by oboist and conductor Werner Herbers with The Ebony Band and by flutist Eleonore Pameijer with the Leo Smit Stichting should be mentioned here too.
100   Flothuis, 257.
101   Licht, 236.
102   Aleida Assmann, *Der europäische Traum: Vier Lehren aus der Geschichte.* (München: C.H. Beck, 3rd ed., 2018).

3
Vom Kitchener Camp in australische Wüstenlager: Der Weg jüdischer Exil-Musiker über Großbritannien nach Down Under

Albrecht Dümling

Abstract

When, after the November pogrom, German Jews desperately searched for ways to leave their country, the Central British Fund for Germany Jewry persuaded the British government to allow the rescue of children and adult men. An old First World War base known as Kitchener Camp was rented and transformed into a transit camp. Already by the end of January 1939 the first refugees had arrived. Among the about 4,000 men, who in the end found a temporary home here, were the violinist and conductor Majer Pietruschka, born in 1901 in Russia, who had lived in Berlin; and the nineteen-year-old violinist Otmar Silberstein from Graz, Austria. They became members of the newly created Kitchener Camp Orchestra und appeared in concert. From May 1940, all Jewish refugees in Great Britain were regarded as 'enemy aliens'. Consequently, these musicians were deported aboard the ship *Dunera* to Australia. The present article describes the road of life of these and other refugees, who contributed to the cultural life in internment camps in Britain and Australia.

1 Die Situation der deutschen und österreichischen Juden 1938/39

Nach dem Scheitern der Konferenz von Evian wurde die Suche nach Aufnahmeländern für jüdische Flüchtlinge aus Deutschland und Österreich immer verzweifelter. Die Besetzung des Sudetenlandes im Oktober 1938 und die Festnahme von ca. 30.000 jüdischen Männern nach der ‚Reichskristallnacht' steigerte noch die Dringlichkeit. Am 15. November 1938 besuchten Mitglieder des Central British Fund for German Jewry den britischen Premierminister Neville Chamberlain und appellierten an ihn, eine gemeinsame Lösung zu finden. So kam es zunächst zur Rettung von 10.000 unbegleiteten Kindern durch den Kindertransport. Außerdem wurde festgestellt, dass die Eröffnung von Flüchtlingslagern die einzige Möglichkeit biete, deutsche Juden aus den

Konzentrationslagern zu entlassen. Am 2. Januar 1939 beschloss das britische Innenministerium, das Home Office, männlichen Juden unter der Bedingung die Einreise zu gestatten, dass sie innerhalb eines Jahres in ein anderes Land weiterziehen würden. Vorgesehen war ein Durchgangslager für bis zu 5000 Männer im Alter von siebzehn bis fünfundvierzig Jahren.[1] Für diesen Zweck wurde ein ehemaliges Armeelager aus dem ersten Weltkrieg, das Kitchener Camp in Richborough bei Sandwich, zur Verfügung gestellt. Es lag in der Grafschaft Kent unweit des Hafens von Dover, wo die Flüchtlinge ankamen.

Die britische Regierung übergab die Verantwortung für das neue Lager einschließlich der Finanzierung dem Central Fund for German Jewry. Mit Mitteln des Lord Baldwin Fund for Refugees wurde daraufhin das ehemalige Militärlager angemietet und in ein Durchgangslager verwandelt. Obwohl dieses Lager, wo einst 40.000 Soldaten untergebracht waren, zweiundzwanzig Jahre lang unbewohnt geblieben war, befanden sich achtundvierzig Baracken noch in einem relativ guten Zustand.[2] Der Architekt Ernest Joseph, der das Camp mitentworfen hatte, half bei den Renovierungsarbeiten. Wie schon beim Kindertransport sollten die Reichsvertretung der Juden in Berlin und die Israelitische Kultusgemeinde in Wien geeignete männliche Bewerber auswählen. Das britische Innenministerium sah ein, dass die verfolgten Juden so schnell ihre endgültige Emigration nicht organisieren konnten, und ließ sie vorübergehend ins Land, wenn sie dort keine bezahlte Arbeit annahmen und sich um die Weiterreise bemühten. Entsprechend hieß es auf dem Visums-Stempel ‚For transit only, Richborough Camp, pending emigration'. In der Zwischenzeit übernahm das Jewish Refugees Committee die nötigen Garantien.[3]

Ob der Geiger und Orchesterleiter Majer Pietruschka nach der Reichspogromnacht verhaftet wurde, konnte bisher nicht nachgewiesen werden. Am 17. Februar 1901 war er als das vierte von acht Kindern im damals russischen Opatow als Sohn des Pelzhändlers Alter Pietruschka und dessen Ehefrau Rachel geb. Kurlander zur Welt gekommen. Seine Musikalität wurde früh entdeckt, so dass er bald nach Lodz übersiedelte, dort Geigenunterricht bei dem Joachim-Schüler Wieniecki erhielt und im Symphonieorchester mitspielte. 1919 zog Pietruschka nach Berlin, wo er seine Musikausbildung bei hervorragenden Lehrern fortsetzte: bis 1924 bei dem aus Odessa stammenden Issay Barmas

---

1 Clare Ungerson, *Four Thousand Lives: The Rescue of German Jewish Men to Britain, 1939* (Cheltenham: The History Press, 2019), 37.
2 *Ibid.*, 32, 67.
3 Vgl. Herbert Freeden, 'In Transit. Reminiscences of Kitchener Camp', in *Dispersion and Resettlement: The Story of the Jews from Central Europe* (London: Association of Jewish Refugees in Great Britain, 1955).

(1872–1946), einem Violinlehrer am Klindworth-Scharwenka-Konservatorium, danach bis 1928 bei dem in Kiew geborenen Ševčík-Schüler Alexander Fiedemann (1878–1940), der zuletzt am Sternschen Konservatorium unterrichtet hatte. Pietruschka war mehrere Jahre lang als Kapellmeister in diversen Berliner Kinos tätig (etwa im Filmpalast Puhlmann, Schönhauser Allee 148, oder dem 1100 Plätze umfassenden Welt-Kino, Alt-Moabit 99), bis sich 1930 nach Einführung des Tonfilms die Filmorchester auflösten.[4] Danach gründete er ein eigenes Salon-Orchester, das Caféhaus-Musik spielte, im April 1933 aber seine Tätigkeit einstellen musste. Da er wegen seiner jüdischen Herkunft nicht in die Reichsmusikkammer aufgenommen wurde, blieb er von nun an auf Auftritte vor jüdischen Zuhörern beschränkt. Zur weiteren Sicherung seines Lebensunterhalts entschloss sich Pietruschka zum Berufswechsel und besuchte dazu im Winter 1935/36 einen Lehrgang als Damenschneider.[5] Das 1936 erschienene Handbuch *Judentum und Musik* nannte als seine Berliner Adresse die Linienstrasse 121.[6] Ab Sommer 1938 bemühte er sich beim Hilfsverein der Juden in Deutschland um die Ausreise nach China, trat aber die ihm angebotene Orchesterstelle in Harbin nicht an.[7] Die Berliner Gedenkdatenbank verzeichnet für Majer Pietruschka als letzte Adressen die Auguststrasse 33 und Große Hamburger Straße 38 und gibt an, er sei am 2. April 1939 nach England entlassen worden.

Der Pianist und Unterhaltungsmusiker Siegfried Salomon Cohn war nach dem Novemberpogrom ins KZ Sachsenhausen eingeliefert worden. Am 13. Oktober 1907 war er in Lübeck geboren, wo seine Eltern eine Kunst- und Antiquitätenhandlung betrieben. Mit der Mittleren Reife hatte er 1923 die Oberrealschule verlassen und ein Jahr später ein Caféhaus-Trio gegründet, in dem er Klavier und Akkordeon spielte und für das er auch komponierte; als Komponist verwendete er das Pseudonym ‚Fred Köhn'.[8] Ab 1933 erhielt er wegen seiner jüdischen Herkunft kaum noch Engagements, 1935 verhängte die Reichsmusikkammer ein Berufsverbot. Siegfried Cohn verdiente seinen Lebensunterhalt seitdem in einem Warenhaus. In Sachsenhausen erlitt er

---

4 Albrecht Dümling, *Die verschwundenen Musiker: Jüdische Flüchtlinge in Australien* (Köln, Weimar, Wien: Böhlau, 2011), 26f.
5 *Ibid.*, 85f.
6 Christa Maria Rock und Hans Brückner (Hg.), *Judentum und Musik. Mit dem ABC jüdischer und nichtarischer Musikbeflissener*, 2. Auflage (München: Brückner, 1936), 179.
7 Personenakte Majer (Max) Pietruschka der Organisation DALJEWCIB (Sign: The Archives of the Far Eastern Jewish Central Information Bureau (DALJEWCIB) Harbin-Shanghai, RG-68.114M, DAL/224 Majer Pietruschka, Film-Nr. 158, Bild-Nr. 1029–1055).
8 Theo Stengel und Herbert Gerigk (Hg.), *Lexikon der Juden in der Musik. Mit einem Titelverzeichnis jüdischer Werke. Zusammengestellt im Auftrag der Reichsleitung der NSDAP auf Grund behördlicher, parteiamtlich geprüfter Unterlagen* (Berlin: Bernhard Hahnefeld, 1940), 49.

schwere gesundheitliche Schäden; man hatte ihm einige Sehnen herausgezogen, so dass er als Musiker stark behindert war. Im Frühjahr 1939 wurde Cohn aus dem KZ entlassen. Er suchte in Lübeck ärztliche Hilfe, bis er noch kurz vor Kriegsbeginn am 23. August die Möglichkeit erhielt, ins Kitchener Camp nach England auszureisen.[9]

Der Komponist und Kapellmeister Hans Werner Katz, am 30. Dezember 1898 in Danzig geboren, hatte nach dem Militärdienst von 1919 bis 1922 an der Berliner Hochschule für Musik Komposition (bei Paul Juon) und Dirigieren (bei Rudolf Krasselt und Julius Prüwer) studiert. Seinen Lebensunterhalt verdiente er als Komponist von Kammer-, Tonfilm- und Unterhaltungsmusik sowie als Pianist und Klavierlehrer. Das Handbuch *Judentum und Musik* verzeichnete ihn unter der Adresse Grätzwalde, Wittstockstraße.[10] In Grätzwalde, einem kleinen Vorort östlich von Berlin, lebte Katz mit seiner Frau Margarete geb. Petersen, einer Nichtjüdin. 1925 war ihre gemeinsame Tochter Brigitte zur Welt gekommen. Angeblich nach der Denunziation eines regimetreuen Nachbarn war Katz geflohen[11] und Anfang April 1939 nahe der holländischen Grenze von der Gestapo bzw. der Grenzpolizei verhaftet und ins Gefängnis Kleve geworfen worden.[12] Am 3. Mai 1939 wurde er ins KZ Dachau eingeliefert. Dort wurde Katz unter der Häftlings-Nummer 33057 als jüdischer Musiker registriert und am 1. Juni wieder entlassen.[13] Um ihm die Flucht nach England zu erleichtern, taufte ihn wenig später, am 15. Juni, der evangelische Pfarrer von Schöneiche-Grätzwalde. Pfarrer Joachim Heinrichs, der die Taufe vollzog, stand als Mitglied der Bekennenden Kirche im Widerspruch zur Mehrheit der Deutschen Christen in seiner Gemeinde; er musste den Juden Hans Werner Katz deshalb heimlich in dessen Wohnung taufen.[14] Über Hamburg floh dieser daraufhin nach England. Seine nichtjüdische Frau und die kleine Tochter ließ er in Deutschland zurück. Katz selbst bezeichnete sich später in amtlichen Unterlagen als Lutheraner und Mitglied der Church of England.[15]

---

9   Stolpersteine für Siegmund und Ida Cohn in Lübeck, *Initiative Stolpersteine für Lübeck*, https://www.stolpersteine-luebeck.de/main/adressen/bismarckstrasse-12.html [Letzter Zugang: 20.03.2010].
10 Rock/Brückner, 122.
11 Auskunft der Tochter Brigitte Goldstein, Albuquerque. Vgl. Dümling, *Die verschwundenen Musiker*, 123f.
12 Mitteilung des Entschädigungsamts Berlin vom 5.09.1966 an den Internationalen Suchdienst Arolsen (Reg.Nr. 12 198/III F).
13 Auskunft der KZ-Gedenkstätte Dachau.
14 Jani Pietsch, ‚Ich besaß einen Garten in Schöneiche bei Berlin'. Das verwaltete Verschwinden jüdischer Nachbarn und ihre schwierige Rückkehr (Berlin, New York: Campus, 2006), 9f.
15 Internee Werner Katz, National Archives of Australia, MP1103/1, E39899.

Otmar Silberstein war am 16. August 1920 als Sohn der Eheleute Markus und Salka Silberstein im österreichischen Graz zur Welt gekommen.[16] Seine Eltern waren polnische Staatsbürger und besaßen das Modehaus Markus Silberstein in der Mariahilferstr. 3. Otmar wechselte nach dem Besuch der jüdischen Volksschule ins Gymnasium und dürfte gleichzeitig Musikunterricht erhalten haben. Nach dem Anschluss Österreichs ans Deutsche Reich musste er im Mai 1938 die Schule verlassen. Als das Geschäft der Eltern unter kommissarische Verwaltung gestellt wurde, weigerte sich der Vater, den ‚arischen' Verwaltern die Ladenschlüssel zu übergeben und wurde daraufhin in ‚Schutzhaft' genommen. Im Oktober beantragte er für sich und seine Familie die Ausreise in die USA, wo bereits eine Verwandte lebte. Aber noch bevor die Ausreisepapiere eintrafen, musste er mit seiner Familie die geräumige Wohnung in der Conrad-von-Hötzendorfstr. 3 verlassen und in die kleinere Behausung seines Bruders Robert Silberstein (Neutorgasse 8) ziehen.[17]

Zum Zeitpunkt der Reichspogromnacht befand sich Markus Silberstein offenbar in Haft. Die Familie seines Bruders Robert wurde am nächsten Morgen verhaftet und ins nächste Polizeigefängnis gebracht. Beide Silberstein-Brüder hatten je einen Sohn namens Otmar. Während der Sohn von Markus Silberstein im August 1920 zur Welt gekommen war, wurde der Sohn Robert Silbersteins acht Monate später, am 18. April 1921, geboren. Der Jüngere von beiden wurde zusammen mit seinem Vater Robert nach Dachau deportiert. Der Ältere, der Sohn von Markus Silberstein, konnte sich der Verhaftung entziehen und in einem Versteck überleben. Von hier aus bemühte er sich um die Ausreise.

2   Musikleben im Kitchener Camp

Am 20. Januar 1939 wurde das Kitchener Camp eröffnet. Die ersten Flüchtlinge, die schon am Monatsende eintrafen, waren Handwerker, welche das Lager für weitere Neuankömmlinge vorbereiteten. Jede Baracke (‚Hut' genannt) wurde in zwei Abteilungen unterteilt, wo jeweils doppelstöckige Schlafkojen für 35–40 Personen zur Verfügung standen. Wie beim Militär gab es gemeinsame Waschräume und einen Speisesaal. Zusätzlich wurden Klassenzimmer für Sprachkurse eingerichtet. Das Lager wurde geleitet von den Brüdern Jonas und Phineas May, die aus einer orthodox jüdischen Familie

---

16   Dümling, *Die verschwundenen Musiker*, 402.
17   Vgl. Grazer Stolpersteine für die Familie Silberstein, *Verein für Gedenkkultur: Stolpersteine in Graz*, http://www.stolpersteine-graz.at/stolpersteine/silberstein-otmar/, [Letzter Zugang: 20.3.2020].

aus Nord-London stammten. Ihr Vater war aus Deutschland nach England gekommen. Die May-Brüder hatten im Rahmen der Jewish Lads Brigade, einer Art Pfadfinderorganisation, bereits Sommerlager für junge Männer organisiert und konnten nun auf dieser Erfahrung aufbauen.[18]

Bei der Auswahl der Flüchtlinge, die ins Kitchener Camp kommen sollten, wurden die Reichsvertretung der Juden in Deutschland und die Kultusgemeinde Wien durch den Börsenmakler Julian David Layton beraten. Er besaß über seine Eltern, die 1893 von Frankfurt nach England ausgewandert waren, ausgezeichnete Verbindungen nach Deutschland, nicht zuletzt zur Rothschild-Familie, die sich für die Rettung der europäischen Juden einsetzte. Im Auftrag des Home Office, Aliens Department, reiste Layton 1939 nach Berlin und Wien, um zusammen mit Reichsvertretung und Kultusgemeinde geeignete Kandidaten auszusuchen. Vorgesehen war, dass die Kultusgemeinde 1000 Männer auswählen sollte, die Reichsvertretung 2000.[19]

Da in Berlin sehr umfangreiche Fragebögen beantwortet werden mussten, gab es Verzögerungen, so dass die dort ausgewählten Flüchtlinge langsamer als erwartet im Kitchener Camp eintrafen. Unter dem Druck Adolf Eichmanns ging in Wien die Auswahl schneller vonstatten. In begleiteten Gruppen wurden die Männer mit der Eisenbahn ins belgische Ostende geschickt, von wo ein Fährschiff sie nach Dover brachte. Im Kitchener Camp wurden sie bei ihrer Ankunft registriert.[20] Die Berliner Reichsvertretung hatte auf einem Merkblatt mitzubringende Gegenstände aufgelistet; dazu gehörten neben Essbesteck und Arbeitskleidung auch Schreibmaterial, Sprachführer und Musikinstrumente („Violinen, Gitarren etc.').[21] Phineas May, der seine Funktion im Camp als die eines ‚Entertainment and Welfare Officers' beschrieb,[22] hat ein ausführliches Tagebuch hinterlassen, welches eine wichtige Quelle darstellt.[23] So berichtete er am 27. März 1939 von der Ankunft von 127 Flüchtlingen aus Wien, darunter Musiker mit ihren Instrumenten. Um den Zollbeamten zu beweisen, dass sie wirklich Musiker waren und nicht etwa Schmuggler, hatten sie unmittelbar nach ihrer Ankunft ein kurzes Konzert geben müssen.[24]

---

18 Ungerson, 41f.
19 *Ibid.*, 70.
20 Vgl. zur Ankunftsprozedur *Kitchener Camp Review* (KCR) 1, 5. Die Ausgaben der Lagerzeitschrift sind auf der Webseite http://www.kitchenercamp.co.uk/ einzusehen.
21 Ungerson, 81.
22 *Ibid.*, 61.
23 Das Tagebuch steht auf der erwähnten Webseite zum Kitchener Camp zur Verfügung. Für weitere Hilfe dankt der Autor Clare Weissenberg, der Betreuerin dieser Webseite.
24 Ungerson, 82.

Möglicherweise befand sich unter diesen Neuankömmlingen auch der siebzehnjährige Otmar Silberstein, dem die Wiener Kultusgemeinde die Flucht nach England ermöglicht hatte. Um ihr die Dringlichkeit seiner Situation zu demonstrieren, hatte er Postkarten vorgelegt, die sein gleichnamiger Vetter aus dem KZ Dachau an seine Eltern geschickt hatte. Indem dieser Otmar Silberstein vorübergehend die Identität seines jüngeren Namensvetters annahm, erhielt er tatsächlich die nötigen Ausreise-Papiere. Wann genau er mit seiner Violine im Kitchener Camp eintraf, konnte bislang nicht festgestellt werden. Majer Pietruschka hatte Berlin Anfang April verlassen und dürfte wenig später im Lager eingetroffen sein; er war achtunddreißig Jahre alt und trug ebenfalls eine Geige mit sich. Der fast drei Jahre ältere Hans Werner Katz wurde am 1. Juni aus Dachau entlassen und kann deshalb erst nach diesem Termin ins britische Camp gekommen sein.[25]

Jeder Lagerinsasse hatte täglich zwei Englischstunden zu absolvieren, ergänzend dazu gab es Vorträge, Diskussionen und eine Bücherei. Ab März erschien eine monatlich vervielfältigte Zeitung, *The Kitchener Camp Review*, für die Phineas May verantwortlich zeichnete. In ihrer April-Nummer berichtete sie über ein Orchester aus der benachbarten Ortschaft Sandwich: ‚Auf Einladung von Mr. Max Burwood, dem enthusiastischen Dirigenten des Sandwich String Orchestra, wurden einige begabte Flüchtlinge, denen ihre Musikinstrumente fehlten, zum Mitspielen in diesem Orchester aufgefordert und gehen nun an jedem Donnerstag zu Proben. Wenn wir genügend Musiker im Lager haben, wird Mr. Burwood herkommen und ein Kitchener Camp Orchestra heranbilden.'[26] Dieses Lagerorchester bildete sich sehr rasch, denn schon am 4. April dirigierte es Burwood bei einem ersten erfolgreichen Konzert.[27] Zu diesem Programm trug auch der aus Wien geflohene liberale Lagerrabbiner Dr. Werner van der Zyl[28] bei. Wenig später wurde eine neue Darbietungsform ausprobiert, wie May am 16. April notierte: ‚Am Abend um 9.30 hatten wir das erste einer Reihe von zehnminütigen Konzerten mit klassischer Musik – mit der Idee, dass es angenehm ist, mit etwas guter Musik zu Bett zu gehen.' Weitere abendliche Kurzkonzerte folgten am 17., 22., 24. und 26. April, wobei jeweils die *Schöne blaue Donau* von Johann Strauss besonders beliebt war.

In der Lagerzeitung beschrieb ein Orchestermitglied ein klassisches Konzert in einer provisorischen Halle, die bis auf den letzten Platz besetzt war.

---

25 Dem Berliner Entschädigungsamt zufolge ist Katz erst ‚ca. August 1939' ausgewandert.
26 'Sandwich String Orchestra', in *KCR* 2 (April 1939), 3.
27 Tagebuch Phineas May 4.4.1939.
28 Vgl. Wikipedia-Artikel 'Werner van der Zyl'.

Während die Zuhörer in ihrer besten Sonntagskleidung erschienen waren, trugen die Orchestermitglieder Arbeitszeug und schmutzige Gummistiefel, hatten sie doch bis zuletzt noch draußen arbeiten müssen. ‚Wir hatten nur anderthalb Stunden Probe unmittelbar vor dem Konzert, aber die deutliche Leitung von Mr. Burwood half uns über alle Schwierigkeiten.' Der Auftritt begann mit der Nationalhymne *God Save the King* und wurde mit einer Haydn-Symphonie fortgesetzt.[29] Ein Streichquartett von Joseph Haydn eröffnete das zweite Konzert am 22. April, gefolgt von britischen Werken, Edward Elgars *Pomp and Circumstance*, Edward Germans *Morris Dance* und Henry Purcells *The virtuous wife*, während die *Schöne blaue Donau* von Johann Strauss den Abschluss bildete. Wie schon am ersten Abend unterstützte Anneliese van der Zyl, die Gattin des Lagerrabbiners, auch dieses Konzert mit Klaviereinlagen.

Angesichts des starken Interesses an Musik war der Wunsch nach einem eigenen Konzertsaal entstanden, der tatsächlich am 29. April mit einer Show eingeweiht wurde.[30] Zur weiteren Förderung des Musiklebens beschloss die Lagerleitung am 10. Mai, alle Berufsmusiker von sonstigen Arbeitsverpflichtungen zu befreien, damit sie sich ganz auf ihre Kunst konzentrieren konnten; vorgesehen war sogar eine Musikakademie.[31] Der neue Konzertsaal wurde auch für Schallplattenabende und Gastkonzerte genutzt; am 16. Mai traten hier vierzig Chormitglieder der Ramsgate Philharmonic Society auf.[32] Einige Tage zuvor hatte es eine ‚Show for our Friends' gegeben: ‚An einem wunderbaren sonnigen Mai-Nachmittag versammelten sich 700 Engländer in unserem großen Konzertsaal zur ersten Unterhaltungsshow speziell für die englischen Freunde des Lagers. Keine gedruckten oder geschriebenen Einladungen waren verschickt worden, es gab auch keine Plakate außerhalb des Lagers, nur durch Mundpropaganda hatte man von dieser Show erfahren.' Nach Elgars *Pomp and Circumstance* folgte ein Varieté-Programm mit Jazzsängern, Saxophonisten, Akrobaten und Akkordeonisten. Den Schluss machte wiederum die *Schöne blaue Donau*.[33]

Die Mai-Ausgabe der *Kitchener Camp Review* zitierte eine Zeile aus einem Lagerlied, zu dem die Frau von Camp Leader Jonas May den Text verfasst hatte[34] und das auf die Melodie des *Lambeth Walk* gesungen wurde:[35]

---

29 'Classical Concert', in KCR 3 (Mai 1939), 11f.
30 Dieser Konzertsaal lag außerhalb des Stammlagers im ehemaligen Haig Camp, vgl. KCR 6 (Aug. 1939), 1.
31 Tagebuch, Phineas May, 10.05.1939.
32 KCR 4 (Juni 1939), 2f.
33 *Ibid.*, 5, sowie Tagebuch, Phineas May, 07.05.1939.
34 Ungerson, 57.
35 KCR 3 (Mai 1939), 11.

Any time you're Richboro' way,
Any evening, any day,
You'll find us all
Working the English way, Oi!

Every man and every boy
Helps to make the Camp a joy,
You'll find us all
Working the English way, Oi![36]

In seinem Tagebuch erwähnte Phineas May am 16. Mai einen Musiker im Camp, der als erfahrener Liedkomponist eine Melodie geschaffen hatte, die sich für ein neues Lagerlied eignen könnte. Den Namen des Komponisten überging er. Eine Musikerdelegation hatte May gebeten, sich die Melodie vorspielen zu lassen. Eine Liste der Lagerinsassen aus dem Jahr 1939[37] enthält siebenundzwanzig Personen mit der Berufsbezeichnung Musiker; unter ihnen befanden sich nur zwei Komponisten: Friedrich Graff und Hans Werner Katz. Katz hielt sich zu diesem Zeitpunkt noch in Dachau auf. Hatte also Graff, über den keinerlei Informationen vorliegen, die Melodie komponiert? Diese Frage bleibt offen und auch die Melodie ist unbekannt. Überliefert wurde jedoch der Text, den Phineas May dazu ergänzte:

We're far away from home
Only hope we bring;
Waiting before we roam,
And every day, stouter of heart all of us sing:

From afar we're come over to Richborough
Under England's Flag for a while:
Working happy we are all free men,
In our freedom now we smile.

When we take one day leave from Richborough
Our hearts remain over here,
And we never can forget these days
Friendships that we've made so dear.

---

36 Zitiert nach Ungerson, 86f.
37 Auf der Webseite zum Kitchener Camp.

May bezeichnete seinen eigenen Text als kitschig. ‚Schwache Verse, aber sie passen zur Melodie.'[38] Am 24. Mai, einem sonnigen Tag, sang man bei einem Freiluftkonzert neben bekannten englischen Songs gemeinsam auch das neue Lagerlied. Phineas May notierte befriedigt, das Lied sei gut angekommen.[39] Den Komponisten erwähnte er auch hier nicht.

Da sich unter den Neuankömmlingen immer wieder auch Musiker befanden, wurde nun stärker auf ihre künstlerische Qualität geachtet und eine Jury eingesetzt, welche Personen mit dieser Berufsbezeichnung begutachtete.[40] Neben regulären Orchesterkonzerten und einem ‚Musikfestival' Anfang Juni[41] wurden im Lager auch die 10-Minuten-Konzerte fortgesetzt.[42] Bei einem gemeinsamen Singen, das als Wunschkonzert (‚Do-as-you-please-Concert') gestaltet wurde, entdeckte man als neue Talente einen guten Sänger und einen ausgezeichneten Mundharmonikaspieler (‚fast ein Larry Adler').[43] Zu dem Musikfestival vom Monatsanfang hatte ein ‚Konzert für die englischen Freunde' gehört, welches 800 Besucher anzog. ‚Am Abend hatten wir den ersten Auftritt unserer eigenen Tanzband, und es war ein erstaunlicher Erfolg – absolut erstklassig und wir werden vermutlich noch mehr davon hören – sie werden sicher sehr gefragt sein. Sie hatten es irgendwie alle geschafft, sich ähnlich anzuziehen – rote Pullover und graue Flanellhosen und das war sehr wirkungsvoll.'[44] Nach dem Erfolg dieses Wochenendes erhielten die Musiker leihweise Trommeln und andere Instrumente.

Wie alle Lagerinsassen erhielten auch die Orchestermitglieder für ihre Arbeit keinen Lohn. Das Lager-Orchester, das im Juli schon fünfundvierzig Mitglieder umfasste,[45] trat also kostenlos auf, weshalb es gern und immer häufiger zu Wohltätigkeitsveranstaltungen außerhalb des Camps eingeladen wurde.[46] Auch der Bürgermeister von Sandwich bat die Lagerleitung um Musiker, die im ortseigenen Musikpavillon auftreten könnten.[47] Dieses Freiluftkonzert fand am 16. Juli vor einer großen Menschenmenge statt; ‚es war ein reizender Abend und die Musiker wurden herzlich begrüßt.'[48] Ohnehin gehörten auch

---

38 Tagebuch, Phineas May, 16.05.1939.
39 *Ibid.*, 24.5.1939.
40 *Ibid.*, 7.6.1939.
41 *Ibid.*, 3.6.1939.
42 *Ibid.*, 7.6.1939.
43 *Ibid.*, 10.6.1939.
44 *Ibid.*, 4.6.1939.
45 Ungerson, 86.
46 Tagebuch, Phineas May, 03.06.1939.
47 *Ibid.*, 7.6.1939.
48 *Ibid.*, 16.7.1939 sowie KCR 6 (Aug. 1939), 3.

zum Sandwich String Orchestra inzwischen überwiegend Camp-Musiker.[49] Bald darauf war das Lagerorchester in einer benachbarten Mädchenschule[50] sowie beim Ramsgate Carnival zu hören.[51] Bei einigen ortsansässigen Musikern riefen diese unbezahlten Auftritte allerdings Unmut hervor; sie schrieben der Lokalzeitung: ‚Während wir Engländer diesen unglücklichen Kollegen gerne Gastfreundschaft anbieten, ist recht viel verlangt, wenn ihnen gestattet wird, bezahlte oder unbezahlte Engagements im Wettbewerb mit existierenden Ensembles anzunehmen.'[52] Enttäuschend verlief der Auftritt einiger Musiker in der Residenz des Earl of Whaincliffe, der seine Gäste schlecht behandelte. Phineas May registrierte: ‚Sie gingen nicht mit einer guten Meinung über die englische Aristokratie.'[53] Auch die Londoner BBC hatte von den Konzerten im Kitchener Camp gehört und bot eine Sendung mit klassischer Musik aus dem Lager an.[54]

Am 1. Juli stieß zu den inzwischen schon 2000 Lagerinsassen ein ungewöhnlicher Musiker,[55] den die Lagerzeitung als einen der weltweit nur achtundzwanzig Personen vorstellte, welche auf der zwölfsaitigen Viola d'amore spielen können. ‚Dieser Herr ist ein Kenner der Blasmusik des 17. Jahrhunderts und hat bei sich einige schöne alte Militärmärsche vom 17. bis zum 19. Jahrhundert.'[56] Es handelte sich um den Dirigenten und Musikwissenschaftler Karl Haas, der bis 1933 im Stuttgarter Sender gearbeitet hatte.[57] Nach der Reichspogromnacht war er durch die Stuttgarter Gestapo verhaftet und ins KZ Welzheim gebracht worden. Von hier wurde er am 27. Januar 1939 entlassen unter der Auflage, sich jeden Tag auf dem zuständigen Polizeirevier zu melden, bis ihm schließlich die Ausreise nach England gelang.

Da sich besonders viele Männer aus Wien im Camp befanden, hatte es am 24. Juni ein Konzert ausschließlich mit Musik Wiener Komponisten gegeben. Phineas May entwarf dazu einen eigenen Liedtext.[58] Am 1. Juli wurde dieses Konzert, ergänzt durch Projektionen von Wien-Bildern, wiederholt.[59] Ganz ohne Konflikte lief das Kulturleben allerdings nicht ab. So musste May am

---

49 *Ibid.*, 8.6.1939.
50 *Ibid.*, 15.6.1939.
51 *Ibid.*, 20.7.1939.
52 *East Kent Mercury*, 17.6.1939, 5, zitiert bei Ungerson, 114.
53 Tagebuch, Phineas May, 29.07.1939.
54 *Ibid.*, 18.08. und 21.08.1939.
55 *Ibid.*, 01.07.1939.
56 KCR 6 (Aug. 1939), 2.
57 Vgl. Matthias Pasdzierny, ‚Karl Haas', in Claudia Maurer Zenck, Peter Petersen (Hg.), *Lexikon verfolgter Musiker und Musikerinnen der NS-Zeit* (Hamburg Universität, 2009).
58 Tagebuch, Phineas May, 18.06.1939.
59 *Ibid.*, 1.7.1939.

5. Juli Streitigkeiten zwischen den Leitern des Orchesters und der Jazzband schlichten.[60] Im August wurde erneut eine ‚Show for our English Friends' vorbereitet. Ein Zeitungsreporter besuchte die Proben und machte Fotos. Phineas May hob den von Simon Hochberger verfassten englischen Text hervor.[61] Hochberger, ein sprachbegabter Wiener Journalist und Werbefachmann, befand sich seit dem 30. März im Lager.[62] Von ihm hatte die *Kitchener Camp Revue* bereits in ihrer Juni-Nummer einen Beitrag abgedruckt. Den von Hochberger verfassten Sketch ‚Illustrated Phrase Book' aus der neuen Revue – er handelt auf witzige Weise vom praktischen Nutzen eines Reise-Sprachführers im Alltag – empfand May als besonders wirkungsvoll, weshalb er ihn in der nächsten Ausgabe der Lagerzeitung abdruckte.[63] Zur Premiere kamen etwa 1000 Besucher, darunter mehrere Kinder, obwohl für die Show wiederum nur ein einziges Plakat geworben hatte.[64] Hochberger hatte das ganze Programm zusammengestellt, das er auch moderierte. Die Presse lobte neben der hervorragenden englischen Aussprache aller Mitwirkenden die musikalische Qualität des Orchesters, das zur Eröffnung fünf Kontratänze von Mozart spielte. Einige Musiker, so hieß es, seien Mitglieder der Berliner Philharmoniker gewesen – eine Angabe, die wohl nicht zutreffen dürfte.[65]

Wie Phineas May am 23. August (dem Tag des Stalin-Hitler-Pakts) notierte, war inzwischen von einem drohenden Krieg die Rede: ‚Alle Radios und Nachrichtenblätter sind umgeben von Männern mit sorgenvollen Gesichtern, und man kann die Spannung spüren.'[66] Am folgenden Tag trafen weitere einhundert Flüchtlinge ein, womit sich die Zahl der Lagerinsassen auf 3000 erhöhte. Unter den Neuankömmlingen dürfte sich auch der Pianist und Komponist Siegfried Cohn befunden haben, dem noch im letzten Moment die Flucht aus Deutschland gelungen war. Am Abend jenes 24. August holten Armeefahrzeuge die Mitwirkenden der ‚English Show' nach Canterbury ab, wo sie vor 500 Soldaten auftraten. Phineas May war begeistert: ‚Wir erhielten einen wunderbaren Empfang und es war die beste Show, die wir jemals gegeben haben. [...] Es war eine ganz einzigartige und interessante Erfahrung.'[67]

---

60 *Ibid.*, 5.7.1939.
61 *Ibid.*, 19.8.1939.
62 Kitchener Camp: Refugees to Britain in 1939, http://www.kitchencamp.co.uk/documents/simon-hochberger-documents/, [Letzter Zugang: 18.04.2020].
63 *KCR* 7 (Sept. 1939), 13f.
64 Tagebuch, Phineas May, 20.08.1939.
65 'Rich In Musical Talent. Refugees' Concert for British Legion', in *Thanet Advertiser and Echo*, 23.08.1939, 9.
66 Tagebuch, Phineas May, 23.08.1939.
67 *Ibid.*, 24.08.1939.

Obwohl am nächsten Tag zahlreiche Gasmasken in Sandwich eintrafen,[68] blieben die Lagerinsassen ‚erstaunlich ruhig'. So wurde am 26. August die Wiederholung der ‚Show for our English Friends' wiederum zu einem großen Erfolg.[69] Insgesamt fanden vier Aufführungen dieser Revue statt. Die BBC sagte allerdings ihre geplante Live-Aufnahme von einem Orchesterkonzert im Camp ab.

3   Kriegsbeginn 1939

Nachdem am 29. August im Kitchener Camp die Verwendung von Gasmasken demonstriert worden war,[70] überschlugen sich plötzlich die Ereignisse. Am 1. September begann mit dem deutschen Überfall auf Polen der Zweite Weltkrieg. Zwei Tage später erklärten Großbritannien und Frankreich dem Deutschen Reich den Krieg. Das Kitchener Camp musste nun nachts verdunkelt werden, die Insassen durften sich nicht weiter als fünf Meilen vom Lager entfernen. Ab dem 26. September wurden alle in Großbritannien befindlichen Flüchtlinge in drei Kategorien eingeteilt. Auch ins Kitchener Camp kamen nun die Mitglieder eines Tribunals, das in den Klassenräumen der Lagerschule die 3500 Insassen auf ihre politische Zuverlässigkeit überprüfte.[71] Die meisten wurden als ‚friendly aliens' der Klasse C zugeordnet und erhielten den Stempel ‚Refugees from Nazi Oppression' in ihren Reisepass.

Um männlichen Flüchtlingen der Klasse C die Möglichkeit zu geben, sich am Krieg gegen Hitler-Deutschland zu beteiligen, wurde Ende Oktober ein militärisches Pionier-Hilfskorps eingerichtet. Schon im November meldeten sich fünfundachtzig Lager-Insassen freiwillig zu diesem Korps und das Camp erhielt einen Militärkommandanten. Damit beendete die bisherige Lagerleitung ihre Tätigkeit. Im November erschien die letzte Ausgabe der *Kitchener Camp Review*. Sie berichtete vom aktiven Beitrag der Männer zur nationalen Verteidigung, indem sie Sandsäcke füllten, Gräben aushoben und Luftschutzräume herstellten. Große Aufmerksamkeit erhielt im Oktober der Besuch des Erzbischofs von Canterbury im Lager.[72] Am 29. Oktober traten zwanzig Streicher des Orchesters vor Schülern der King's School in Canterbury auf; einige ältere Angehörige dieser Anstalt hatten regelmäßig das Camp

---

68   *Ibid.*, 25.08.1939.
69   *Ibid.*, 26.08.1939.
70   *Ibid.*, 29.08.1939.
71   KCR 9 (Nov. 1939), 8ff.
72   *Ibid.*, 3–5.

besucht, um dort die Flüchtlinge bei der englischen Konversation zu unterstützen. Sogar die Londoner *Times* erwähnte das Konzert in Canterbury,[73] bei dem unter anderem das d-Moll-Doppelkonzert von Johann Sebastian Bach erklang, gespielt von den beiden Geigensolisten Max Jekel und Majer Pietruschka.[74] Außerdem standen auf dem Programm ein Rondo für Solovioline und Streicher von Franz Schubert,[75] das *con sordino* gespielte *Lyrische Andante* (*Liebestraum*) von Max Reger sowie die viersätzige *Serenade* in F-Dur von Karl Goldmark. Nach dem Konzert unterhielten sich die Flüchtlinge in englischer Sprache mit Angehörigen der Schule. Die Lagerzeitung berichtete auch über ein gutbesuchtes klassisches Konzert des Lagerorchesters mit Orgel am 2. November in der alten, aus dem 12. Jahrhundert datierenden St. Clement's Church in Sandwich: ‚Die sakrale Atmosphäre dieses Orts verlieh der Musik zusätzliche Schönheit.'[76]

Informationen über weitere Konzerte im Kitchener Camp in den folgenden Monaten liegen nicht vor. Obwohl sich schließlich etwa 1900 Männer zum Militärdienst meldeten, blieben Siegfried Cohn, Hans Werner Katz, Majer Pietruschka und Otmar Silberstein weiter im Lager. Katz meldete sich vermutlich deshalb nicht zum Militär, weil er seine in Deutschland verbliebene Ehefrau nicht gefährden wollte. Cohn, Pietruschka und Silberstein waren alleinstehend, aber Silberstein noch zu jung für das Militär. Pietruschka dürfte, wie auch später in Australien, aus gesundheitlichen Gründen als nicht diensttauglich gegolten haben. Aus den gleichen Gründen meldete sich Siegfried Cohn nicht. Andere Männer besaßen Visas und hofften auf eine baldige Weiterreise, so dass sich insgesamt noch etwa 1200 Männer als Zivilisten im Lager aufhielten.[77] Deshalb gab es weiterhin ein kleiner besetztes Kitchener Camp Refugee Orchestra, das unter Leitung von Karl Haas beispielsweise am 10. Dezember bei einer Rotary-Veranstaltung in Margate[78] und am 25. Januar 1940 bei einem ‚Carnival Dance' in Ramsgate auftrat.[79]

---

73   Anonym, 'Entertainments: Concert by Refugee Orchestra. A Visit to Canterbury', in *The Times*, 2.11.1939, 6.
74   Vgl. Jutta Raab Hansen, *NS-verfolgte Musiker in England. Spuren deutscher und österreichischer Flüchtlinge in der britischen Musikkultur* (Hamburg: von Bockel, 1996), 259. Die Autorin nahm damals an, bei ‚M. Pietroushka' handele es sich um eine Frau, eine Österreicherin oder Tschechin. Jekel war später Mitglied des Covent Garden Orchestra.
75   Vermutlich das Rondo A-Dur für Violine und Orchester D 438.
76   *KCR* 9 (Nov. 1939), 2.
77   Ungerson, *Four Thousand Lives*, 161.
78   'Musical Refugees Provide Rotary Hampers', in *Thanet Advertiser*, 12.12.1939, 2.
79   *Thanet Advertiser*, 12.01.1940, 8.

St. Clement's Church,
SANDWICH.

AN
ORCHESTRAL CONCERT
- with ORGAN

will be given in Church by the

KITCHENER CAMP ORCHESTRA

. ON .

Thursday, Nov. 2nd, 1939,
3 p.m.

ALL WELCOME.

T. F. PAIN & SONS, SANDWICH & DEAL

ABBILDUNG 3.1 Plakat zum Konzert des Kitchener Camp Orchestra am 2. November 1939 in der St. Clement's Church Sandwich
QUELLE: TANYA MAKIN, MELBOURNE

Nach dem Rücktritt von Neville Chamberlain übernahm der erklärte Hitler-Gegner Winston Churchill am 10. Mai 1940 das Amt des Premierministers. Schon zwei Tage später befahl er – im Widerspruch zu früheren Entscheidungen – die vorübergehende Internierung aller männlichen Deutschen und Österreicher im Alter zwischen sechzehn und sechzig Jahren, die sich in Küstennähe aufhielten.

Betroffen waren auch Personen mit dem anerkannten Status als ‚Flüchtlinge vor Nazi-Unterdrückung'. Als Konsequenz wurden auch die im Camp verbliebenen Musiker Siegfried Cohn, Hans Werner Katz, Majer Pietruschka und Otmar Silberstein am 12. bzw. 26. Mai aufgegriffen und verhaftet.[80]

4 Deportiert nach Australien

Da die Verhafteten auch auf dem britischen Festland noch als Sicherheitsrisiko galten, wurden mehrere von ihnen – darunter Siegfried Cohn, Hans Werner Katz, Majer Pietruschka, Otmar Silberstein und Simon Hochberger – mit dem Truppenschiff *Dunera* nach Australien deportiert. Dieser ferne Kontinent hatte vielen Insassen des Kitchener Camp bis dahin als Traumziel gegolten. Drei Männer, die am 3. Mai 1939 dorthin ausgereist waren, hatten für die Lagerzeitung einen ausführlichen Bericht über ihre Überfahrt geschrieben. Die Rede war dort von bequemen Liegestühlen an Deck, von denen aus man in einen klaren blauen Himmel blickte.[81] Die Überfahrt auf der *Dunera*, die am 10. Juli 1940 in Liverpool begann, war dagegen alles andere als ein Vergnügen – die Männer wurden von der britischen Wachmannschaft wie Verbrecher behandelt.[82] Nicht wenige Insassen erkrankten auf der fünfwöchigen Reise. Nachdem das Schiff schließlich am 6. September im Hafen von Sydney angekommen war, musste Otmar Silberstein sofort ins dortige Krankenhaus eingeliefert werden. Als er am 18. September endlich zu den anderen Männer im siebenhundert Kilometer entfernten Wüstenlager Hay stieß, gab er in einem ‚Report on Internees' die Namen seiner Eltern in ihrer ursprünglich polnischen Form an, nicht mit der sonst in Graz verwendeten österreichischen Namensform; er wollte sich damit offenbar von Großdeutschland so weit wie möglich distanzieren. Neben zwei Koffern hatte er diesem Bericht zufolge eine wertvolle Violine aus England mitgebracht.[83]

Trotz des sehr ungünstigen Klimas in Hay entwickelte sich in den beiden dortigen Camps 7 und 8 ein Kulturleben, welches in vielen Einzelheiten an dasjenige im Kitchener Camp erinnert. Simon Hochberger, dessen englischsprachige Revue in Richborough so erfolgreich gewesen war, übernahm in Camp 7 die Leitung des Recreation Department. Bereits im November

---

80   Beim Verhaftungstermin 25.6.1940, der in den Papieren von Siegfried Cohn (National Archives of Australia: MP1103/1, E39285) angegeben wurde, handelt es sich vermutlich um einen Schreibfehler.
81   'Life afloat. Impressions of a Voyage to Australia', in *KCR* 5 (Juli 1939), 9f.
82   Vgl. Paul R. Bartrop u. Gabrielle Eisen (Hg.), *The Dunera Affair. A Documentary Resource Book* (Melbourne: Jewish Museum of Australia, 1990).
83   Internee Otmar Silberstein, National Archives of Australia, MP1103/2, E40656.

ABBILDUNG 3.2 Einladung zur Show ‚Hay-Fever' aus dem australischen Internierungslager Hay vom November 1940
QUELLE: DEUTSCHES EXILARCHIV 1933–45 FRANKFURT/MAIN

präsentierte er ein Stück *Hay-Fever* (Heuschnupfen), dessen Titel sich ironisch auf den Ortsnamen bezog. Für die Musik zeichneten die ihm aus Richborough vertrauten Experten Siegfried Cohn und Hans Werner Katz gemeinsam verantwortlich.[84] Cohn ließ sich auf dem Akkordeon hören, er begleitete auch Majer Pietruschka beim berühmten *Csárdás* von Vittorio Monti. Zum Programm gehörte nicht zuletzt der bereits im Kitchener Camp erfolgreiche Sketch ‚The Illustrated Phrase-Book'.

Wie im Kitchener Camp war auch in Hay Hans Werner Katz der erfahrenste Komponist. Seine *Jewish Rhapsody* erklang am 10. Dezember bei einem Konzert des vierköpfigen Orchestra Petroushka, das bei dieser Gelegenheit außerdem bekannte Stücke von Ludwig van Beethoven, Carl Loewe, Antonín Dvořák und Pablo de Sarasate spielte. Da im Lager damals noch kein Klavier vorhanden war, sprang Siegfried Cohn mit seinem Akkordeon ein.

Leiter des kleinen Ensembles, zu dem auch Otmar Silberstein gehörte, war Majer Pietruschka. Er trat bei weiteren Lagerveranstaltungen, etwa bei einer *Show without a name*, auch als Solist auf. Katz schuf die Musik ebenso zur Revue *Wir reisen um die Welt*, bei der ein neunköpfiges Orchester mitwirkte.[85] Der schon grauhaarige Komponist, der gerne eine Baskenmütze trug, gab im Lager außerdem Unterricht in Harmonielehre, während Pietruschka Stunden im Geigenspiel gab. Zu seinen Schülern gehörte Otmar Silberstein, der gemeinsam mit seinem Mentor Johann Sebastian Bachs d-Moll-Doppelkonzert zur Aufführung brachte.

Im Mai 1941 durften die Männer von Hay ins klimatisch günstigere Internierungslager Tatura im Norden des Staates Victoria umziehen. Dort befanden sich seit September unter anderem auch jüdische Flüchtlinge, die aus Singapur nach Australien deportiert worden waren. Die aus Hay transferierten ‚Dunera Boys' veranstalteten sechs Wochen nach ihrer Ankunft ein von Majer Pietruschka arrangiertes und geleitetes Programm mit leichter Musik. Als Gitarrist wirkte der 1910 in Wien geborene Gebrauchsgrafiker und Musiker Alfred Landauer mit, der ebenfalls vom Kitchener Camp nach Australien gekommen war.[86] Im September war in Tatura *Die Geschichte vom braven Soldaten Schweyk* mit einer von Katz arrangierten Bühnenmusik, gespielt vom Pietruschka-Orchester, zu erleben. Im November kam eine englische Fassung der zuvor in Hay gezeigten Revue *Reise um die Welt* zur Aufführung, zu Weihnachten eine von Kurt Sternberg konzipierte Schneewittchen-Revue, und im Januar 1942 ein großes, von Pietruschka geleitetes Unterhaltungskonzert,

---

84 Dümling, *Die verschwundenen Musiker*, 219.
85 *Ibid.*, 219f.
86 *Ibid.*, 232, 394. Vgl. www.kitchenercamp.co.uk/list-of-names/ [Letzter Zugang: 23.12.2022].

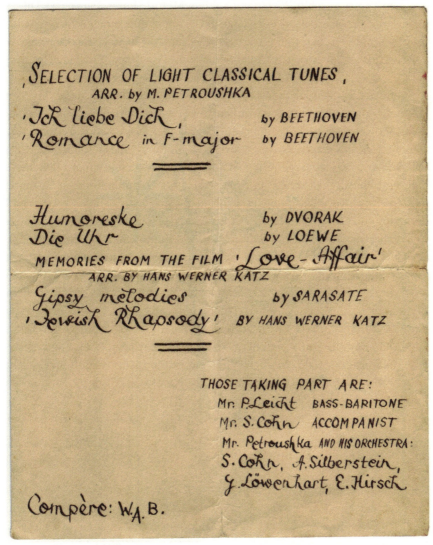

ABBILDUNG 3.3 Handgeschriebener Programmzettel für ein Konzert mit unterhaltsamer Klassik aus Hay
QUELLE: TANYA MAKIN, MELBOURNE

zu dem verschiedene Kompositionen von Hans Werner Katz gehörten, darunter ein Potpourri *Von Heidelberg bis Richborough*.[87] Nachdem dieser vielseitige Musiker noch an weiteren Auftritten mitgewirkt hatte, durfte er im August 1942 die Rückreise nach Europa antreten. In Kapstadt stieg Katz am 8. Oktober

---

87 *Ibid.*, 234.

von dem Transportschiff *Westerland* auf den Motorfrachter *Abosso* um. Dieser wurde am 29. Oktober in der Nähe der Azoren durch deutsche Torpedos getroffen und versenkt. Dabei starben insgesamt 362 Menschen, darunter der junge Schriftsteller Ulrich A. Boschwitz[88] und der Komponist Hans Werner Katz.

Nachdem im Februar 1942 Singapur, die stärkste Festung des britischen Empire, an die Japaner gefallen war, beschloss das australische Parlament angesichts der wachsenden Bedrohung, auch Ausländer an der Landesverteidigung zu beteiligen. Zu den in Tatura internierten Männern, die sich freiwillig zum Militärdienst meldeten, gehörten Majer Pietruschka und Otmar Silberstein. Während Pietruschka schon im August 1942 aus gesundheitlichen Gründen wieder ausschied, blieb Silberstein bis 1946 Mitglied der 8th Employment Company, die überwiegend aus ehemals Internierten bestand. Angesichts der vielen Künstler in ihren Reihen konnte diese Kompanie 1943 die Revue *Sgt. Snowhite* auf die Bühne bringen, welche die Märchenfigur Schneewittchen in eine Soldatenuniform steckte.[89] Als ein Höhepunkt dieses erfolgreichen Programms galt das von dem Schauspieler Sigurd Lohde vorgetragene Gedicht ‚Sounds of Europe' von Simon Hochberger, das eindringlich die Zerstörung Europas durch barbarische Armeen, aber auch den Widerstand der Opfer beschrieb. Der aus Berlin geflohene Musiker Werner Baer, der im September 1940 aus Singapur nach Australien deportiert worden war, vertonte das Gedicht und gewann damit 1944 einen Kompositionswettbewerb der australischen Rundfunkanstalt ABC.[90]

5   Schicksale nach 1945

Bei Kriegsende erfuhren die Musiker von den zahlreichen Angehörigen, die viele von ihnen im Holocaust verloren hatten. So waren die Eltern von Siegfried Cohn 1941 aus Lübeck nach Riga deportiert worden, wo sie ein Jahr später ums Leben kamen. Fast alle Verwandten von Majer Pietruschka waren ermordet worden. Er selbst hatte überlebt, erhielt aber nach der Entlassung aus dem Militärdienst zunächst keine Stelle als Musiker und musste sich seinen Lebensunterhalt als Bügler in einer chemischen Reinigung verdienen. 1946

---

88   Sein Roman *Der Reisende*, 1939 in englischer Sprache veröffentlicht, kam 2018 zum ersten Mal im deutschen Original heraus.
89   Dümling, *Die verschwundenen Musiker*, 236–53.
90   *Ibid.*, 252.

heiratete er in einer anglikanischen Kirche die australische Konzertpianistin und Komponistin Phyllis Batchelor. Aus dieser Ehe gingen zwei Kinder hervor. Nachdem er 1946 australischer Staatsbürger geworden war, war Pietruschka von 1949 bis 1951 Geiger im 3DB-Konzertorchester Melbourne und danach bis 1967 Mitglied der 2. Violinen im Victorian Symphony Orchestra.[91] Seinen beiden Kindern spielte er gerne Solopartiten von Johann Sebastian Bach vor, ohne jemals seine Verfolgung als Jude anzusprechen. Am 24. Dezember 1979 ist er in Melbourne gestorben.

Für Otmar Silberstein endete der Militärdienst erst im Februar 1946. Nach der Einbürgerung im April 1948 wurde er Bratschist im Victorian Symphony Orchestra. Diese Stelle gab er schon bald auf, um in die USA zu übersiedeln, wo sein Vater, eine Tante und sein Cousin inzwischen lebten.[92] Um Verwechslungen mit seinem ebenfalls in die USA geflohenen Cousin auszuschließen, nannte er sich nun Otto Silverstein. Er wurde als Geiger Mitglied des Kansas City Symphony Orchestra, das bis 1971 von dem aus Deutschland stammenden Hans Schwieger geleitet wurde.[93] 1976 verließ Silverstein dieses Orchester und zog zu Verwandten nach Daytona Beach (Florida), wo er am 9. Juni 1986 starb.[94] Zwei Jahre zuvor war in Melbourne Siegfried Cohn gestorben. Er war hier unter dem Namen Sid Conny als Unterhaltungsmusiker tätig gewesen und hatte außerdem Musikunterricht gegeben.[95]

Simon Hochberger setzte seine journalistische Laufbahn in Australien fort, zunächst als Mitarbeiter der jüdischen Zeitschrift *The Zionist*. Im gleichen Jahr veröffentlichte er in einem kleinen jüdischen Verlag die epische Dichtung *Warsaw Ghetto – Tale of Valor* (Warschauer Ghetto – Geschichte des Heldenmuts), welche die Thematik seines Gedichts ‚Sounds of Europe' weiterführte.[96] Im Sommer 1947 übersiedelte Hochberger in die neuseeländische Hauptstadt Wellington, wo ihm die Redaktion der Zeitschrift NZ *Jewish Chronicle* angeboten worden war. Nur wenige Monate später erlag er am 13. Dezember 1947 einer Herzthrombose.[97]

Die in Deutschland verbliebene Ehefrau von Hans Werner Katz, die für diesen noch einen Entschädigungsantrag eingereicht hatte, starb ca. 1978

---

91   Ibid., 290, 397.
92   Ibid., 290, 402.
93   Vgl. Peter Lange, *Ein amerikanischer Europäer: Die zwei Leben des Dirigenten Hans Schwieger* (Berlin: Metropol, 2015).
94   Vgl. Grazer Stolpersteine für die Familie Silberstein.
95   Stolpersteine für Siegmund und Ida Cohn in Lübeck, https://www.stolpersteine-luebeck.de/main/adressen/bismarckstrasse-12.html, [Letzter Zugang: 18.4.2020].
96   Simon Hochberger, *Warsaw Ghetto – Tale of Valor* (Melbourne: Oyfboy Publishing, 1946).
97   Vgl. Wikipedia-Artikel ‚Simon Hochberger'.

in Berlin. Ihre Tochter Brigitte, Abkömmling eines jüdischen Vaters und einer christlichen Mutter, war 1938 in Grätzwalde von Pfarrer Heinrichs getauft worden. Nach dem Krieg hatte sie den in Deutschland stationierten US-Soldaten Merton Goldstein geheiratet, mit dem sie in die USA zog.[98] Dort studierte sie an der Universität von Albuquerque die Fächer Spanisch und Soziologie und promovierte 1988 in einer soziologischen Arbeit über jüdische Identität.[99] Danach übernahm sie zusammen mit ihrem Mann, der ebenfalls der lutherischen Kirche angehörte, die Leitung eines Lagerhauses für Arbeits- und Wohnungslose. Außerdem sorgte Brigitte Katz Goldstein für eine Aufführung des 1937 entstandenen 2. Streichquartetts ihres Vaters Hans Werner Katz.[100] Dessen Kompositionen aus den Internierungslagern in Großbritannien und Australien sind leider nicht überliefert.

---

98   Mitteilung von Karin Butchard, der Tochter von Brigitte Goldstein.
99   Brigitte Katz Goldstein, *Jewish Identification Among the Jews of Albuquerque, New Mexico: The Maintenance of Jewishness and Judaism in the Integrated Residential Setting of a Sunbelt City* (Albuquerque: University of *New Mexico*, 1988).
100 *Dunera News*, 40, Okt. 1997, 4.

4

Creation of Jobs, Union Work and Cooperation: The Institutionalisation of Musical Life by the European Jewish Artist Society, the Shanghai Musicians Association, and the Association of Jewish Precentors in the Shanghai Exile, 1938–49

Sophie Fetthauer

Abstract

From 1938, about 18,000 mainly Jewish refugees fled to Shanghai from the German Reich. They included more than 450 musicians. In this treaty port, economics and politics had priority. Musical life was not at the centre of interest and differed from what the refugees were used to. Hardly any urban subsidies and no professional organisations existed. Thus, in order to prevail economically, socially and culturally, the refugees founded several organisations modelled after those they had known before. The Artist Club, and later the European Jewish Artist Society, wanted to create jobs and strengthen the cultural heritage of the refugees. This turned out to be difficult in view of a shortage of funds and small audiences. The Shanghai Musicians Association was a union and campaigned for better working conditions, fee controls and reduced competition in the entertainment venues. It was rather successful, but it had to adapt constantly to changing political and economic conditions. The Association of Jewish Precentors was a professional association for Jewish synagogue cantors. It worked in relative isolation and developed into a kind of cooperative for liberal and conservative cantors. In addition to social and cultural objectives, it also sought to balance economic interests.

The political, cultural and social situations in the countries and cities in which the refugees from the Third Reich sought refuge after 1933 differed considerably. Some had democratic structures, others did not. In some places, the living conditions were safe; elsewhere, whether in Europe or East Asia, the refugees had to face a situation of war and occupation. Culturally, exile offered musicians opportunities for integration provided there was a European-style cultural life. Sometimes this was the case, but often only to a limited extent. After all, there were differences in terms of social and economic structures, including professional organisation, provision for healthcare and old age as well as legal protection.

In 1938, Shanghai became a refuge for thousands of mostly Jewish refugees. Conditions were different from what they were used to. Despite being a metropolis, the city turned out to have very limited options. The refugees could not settle in the periphery, and due to the Japanese occupation, the European war and restrictive visa regulations, only a few were able to travel to other Chinese cities, let alone abroad. In addition, the urban area was fragmented politically and topographically. Since the Opium Wars in the mid-19th century, and based on the 'unequal treaties' that had been signed afterwards, Shanghai consisted of foreign settlements, i.e. the French Concession and the International Settlement, as well as the Chinese-administered suburbs, which were controlled by the Japanese army since 1937, including the eastern part of the International Settlement. Furthermore, there were inner-Chinese conflicts between nationalists and Communists as well as gang crime. This triggered restrictions. For instance, according to the aid organisations' instructions, the refugees were not allowed to be politically active.[1] The proclamation of the 'designated area' by the Japanese occupiers in 1943 implemented the hardest restrictions. Until the end of the Pacific War, the refugees needed special passes to leave the so-called Hongkou ghetto. It was set up in the district of Hongkou where most of the refugees had lived from the beginning. Because of the proclamation, they were not able to escape the poor supply situation there.[2]

At the same time, other aspects of life were not regulated in Shanghai. This applied to the free immigration in 1938/39, a result of the suspension of immigration controls due to the Second Sino-Japanese War.[3] And this also applied to taking up a job. The newcomers could work in any profession. Even doctors and lawyers did not require special qualifications.[4] The population of Shanghai was too cosmopolitan for such regulations. In addition, the treaty powers possessed extraterritorial rights, meaning the right to be judged according to the laws of their own respective countries. Because of this, musicians could work,

---

1 See Georg Armbrüster, Michael Kohlstruck and Sonja Mühlberger, 'Exil Shanghai. Facetten eines Themas', in Georg Armbrüster, Michael Kohlstruck, Sonja Mühlberger (eds.), *Exil Shanghai 1938–1947: Jüdisches Leben in der Emigration* (Teetz: Hentrich & Hentrich, 2000), 12–19 (16).
2 See David Kranzler, *Japanese, Nazis & Jews: The Jewish Refugee Community of Shanghai, 1938–1945* (New York: Yeshiva University Press, Sifria, 1976), 521–77.
3 See Irene Eber, *Wartime Shanghai and the Jewish Refugees from Central Europe: Survival, Co-Existence, and Identity in a Multi-Ethnic City* (Berlin: de Gruyter, 2012), 85–87.
4 See Kranzler, 302, 422.

too. For them, certificates and diplomas generally were not too important. But unlike in the United States, Canada and Australia, no musicians' union existed that prevented them from working in order to protect long-established practitioners from competition.[5] The musicians in Shanghai came from Russia, Western Europe, the United States and the Philippines. Especially in the entertainment sector, their composition was too international and their fluctuation too intense for any restrictions to be feasible. Therefore, in Shanghai an opportunity existed for the professional integration of musicians. At the same time, the refugee group was so large that it could only survive if it built up its own infrastructure with shops, restaurants, and all kinds of economic, social, cultural and religious organisations. This process of institutionalisation also affected the refugees' musical life.

Musical life in Shanghai was different from that with which the refugees from Germany and Austria were familiar. Since, with respect to the majority of the population, it was a Chinese city, there was a traditional Chinese musical life. It took place especially in theatres, but it was hardly accessible to the refugees, neither as audience nor as performers.[6] The Western-style entertainment sector was huge. Numerous ballrooms, night clubs, restaurants and bars needed live music and thus offered work. But not all musicians were able to adapt to the multiple, especially Chinese, tastes of the audience. There was also a Western classical musical life with concerts and productions of musical theatre, but, in relation to population figures, it rather resembled the musical life of a small town.[7] Besides, it was predominantly organised privately. On the whole, there was no comprehensive urban funding for theatres, stage ensembles and orchestras. Only the Shanghai Municipal Orchestra received subsidies from the International Settlement, in part supplemented by grants from the French Concession and the Italian government. But these were highly controversial among the ratepayers of the International Settlement.[8] As a consequence, many companies, such as the Shanghai Opera Company and the Grand Opera Shanghai, were unable to work continuously or, like the

---

5   See Regina Thumser, *Vertriebene Musiker. Schicksale und Netzwerke im Exil 1933–1945*, Universität Salzburg, Ph.D., 1998 (Salzburg: self-publishing, 1998), 55–57; Paul Helmer, *Growing with Canada: The Émigré Tradition in Canadian Music* (Montreal: McGill-Queens's University Press, 2009), 161; Albrecht Dümling, *Die verschwundenen Musiker: Jüdische Flüchtlinge in Australien* (Köln: Böhlau, 2011), 163–83.
6   See Kurt Lewin, 'Shanghai-Streiflichter. Chinesisches Theater in Shanghai', *Shanghai Journal. Die neue Zeit*, vol. 1946: 27 (2 February 1946), 4.
7   See Anonymous, 'Music as a Part of One's Life. Talk by M. [Monsieur] Grosbois at Rotary Luncheon; "Kind Friend" at Lyceum', *The North-China Daily News*, 14 October 1938, 7.
8   See e.g. Shanghai Municipal Council, *Report for the Year 1938 and Budget for the Year 1939* (Shanghai: North-China Daily News & Herald, 1939), 9–20.

British, French and German Amateur Dramatic Clubs, which staged theatre productions, were run by amateurs. Religious musical life was even more limited. Some churches had choirs and organised concerts, but it is not known whether, during this period, the same was the case in synagogues of Sephardic and Orthodox Ashkenazi Jewish communities. In any case, they offered few working opportunities since most of the refugees belonged to Reform Judaism. After all, there were no professional associations or unions for musicians in Shanghai, as had been the case in Germany and Austria since the 19th century and in a different form after the Nazis came to power in 1933 when these organisations were incorporated into the professional structures of the new regime. Thus, there was no protection in case of litigation, illness and old age.

Among the approximately 18,000 refugees in Shanghai were more than 450 individuals with professions related to music.[9] When it came to integration, the disproportionately high number of musicians[10] proved to be both a disadvantage and an advantage. On the one hand, considerable competition arose; on the other hand, the large human resources made the development of an independent musical life feasible in the first place. Soon, questions of institutionalisation emerged. As non-profit companies, the Artist Club and its successor organisation, the European Jewish Artist Society, organised theatre and operetta productions, concerts, and variety shows in order to create employment and to support the refugees with a familiar cultural programme. The Shanghai Musicians Association, on the other hand, was a trade union primarily for entertainment musicians, and the Association of Jewish Precentors was a professional organisation for synagogue cantors. With regard to their organisational structures and objectives, they were based on models from German and Austrian musical life. The way they adjusted to Shanghai's musical life indicates the specific problems of musicians' exile in Shanghai.

---

9   Funded by the Deutsche Forschungsgemeinschaft, the author has carried out a research project about 'Musicians' exile in Shanghai 1938–1949' at the University of Hamburg from 2014 to 2019. As a result, a monograph has been published which focuses on several professional musical fields, including popular music, concert, musical theatre, synagogue music, and music education (Sophie Fetthauer, *Musiker und Musikerinnen im Shanghaier Exil 1938–1949* (Neumünster: von Bockel, 2021)). In this context, the biographies of 450 musicians were examined. Resulting biographical information has been and will be published in: Claudia Maurer Zenck, Peter Petersen, Sophie Fetthauer (since 2014), Friedrich Geiger (since 2020) (eds.), *Lexikon verfolgter Musiker und Musikerinnen der NS-Zeit* (Hamburg: Universität Hamburg, since 2005), https://www.lexm.uni-hamburg.de.

10 See Sophie Fetthauer, 'Das Far Eastern Jewish Central Information Bureau in Harbin und Shanghai. Nachrichtensteuerung und individuelle Beratung für NS-verfolgte Musiker und Musikerinnen mit dem Fluchtziel Shanghai bzw. Ostasien', in Wolfgang Gratzer and Nils Grosch (eds.), *Musik und Migration* (Münster: Waxmann, 2018), 51–65.

Sources related to the subject are available in various archives. The Leo Baeck Institute's 'Jews in Shanghai Collection' in New York City keeps records of the Shanghai Musicians Association, as does the YIVO Institute for Jewish Research's 'Shanghai Collection' in New York City for the Association of Jewish Precentors. There are also scattered items related to the Artist Club and the European Jewish Artist Society in the 'Shanghai Collection', but, on the whole, the archives of these organisations must be considered lost. At least, newspaper clippings, collected by their secretary Alfred Dreifuß, have been preserved in the 'Alfred Dreifuß Archiv' of the Akademie der Künste in Berlin.[11] In addition, there are references in the Shanghai press, especially in newspapers issued by the refugees themselves. Only few researchers have already addressed these organisations. David Kranzler has done this rather briefly; Tang Yating has looked at the Association of Jewish Precentors and Michael Philipp at the European Jewish Artist Society in more detail.[12] A synopsis and comparative consideration are not yet available.[13]

1   Artist Club and European Jewish Artist Society

The Western classical musical life of Shanghai included a municipal orchestra, opera, operetta and ballet ensembles shaped by Russian musicians, further instrumental ensembles, military bands and choirs, as well as concert initiatives in cinemas, clubs and private houses. Only in individual cases were the refugees able to maintain long-term positions, for example in the Shanghai Municipal Orchestra, the Russian Light Opera or at the Conservatory, but it was hardly possible for anyone to make a living from just giving concerts in the settlements. Thus, soon, the question came up of how employment opportunities could be created for the musicians and also for actors whose limited language

---

11 See Jews in Shanghai Collection, AR 2509, Box 1, folder 10, New York (NY): Leo Baeck Institute (LBI); Shanghai Collection, RG 243, folders 32, I–V, 58, 67 I–II, New York (NY): YIVO Institute for Jewish Research (YIVO); Alfred Dreifuß Archiv, folder 449, 453, 467–471, 474–482, 485, 499–500, 510, Berlin: Akademie der Künste (AdK).

12 See e.g. Kranzler, 375, 426–27; Tang Yating, 'Reconstructing the Vanished Musical Life of the Shanghai Jewish Diaspora: A Report', *Ethnomusicology Forum*, vol. 13:1 (2004), *Silk, Spice and Shirah: Musical Outcomes of Jewish Migration into Asia c. 1780–c. 1950*, 101–18 (107–109); Michael Philipp, *Nicht einmal einen Thespiskarren: Exiltheater in Shanghai 1939–1947*, Hamburger Arbeitsstelle für Exilliteratur (ed.), (Hamburg: Hamburger Arbeitsstelle für deutsche Exilliteratur, 1996), 58–73.

13 For a general overview of the development of Chinese and Western research on musicians' exile in Shanghai, see Fetthauer, *Musiker und Musikerinnen im Shanghaier Exil 1938–1949* (Neumünster: von Bockel, 2021), chapter 2.

skills made integration even more difficult. Many artists were inspired by the example of the Jewish Cultural League (Jüdischer Kulturbund) in Germany, which had given them work after they had been dismissed from their positions in Germany in 1933. For this reason, in the spring of 1939, the idea to establish a central cultural organisation arose.

The Artist Club was founded in March 1939 by a group of musicians, actors, cabaret artists and journalists: Hans Baer, Ossi Lewin (its first presidents), Martin Jacobi, Alfred Wittenberg (its first treasurers), Heinz Ganther, Robert Rosé, and Fritz Schnitzer. During the first months of its existence, the Artist Club realised a few events with music, cabaret and dance, but did not generate any earnings of note. The situation changed after it had merged with the Group of Hongkou Artists (Gruppe Hongkewer Künstler) under the direction of Walter Friedmann in the summer of 1939.[14] Like the Jewish Cultural League, the Artist Club now had a directorate, that is a president (Ossi Lewin) and a director's secretary (Heinz Ganther). When, a little later, the dramaturg, stage director and critic Alfred Dreifuß, who had been active in the Communist Party, became secretary, a stage ensemble was formed, and a series of stage productions of theatre and operetta (mainly light entertainment) was released. In the case of Gotthold Ephraim Lessing's *Nathan der Weise* and Ferenc Molnár's plays, the Artist Club's repertoire partially copied the programme of the Jewish Cultural League.[15] However, ambitious plans for a theatre building and a schedule, which included new productions of drama, operetta and opera every week,[16] could not be realised. The Artist Club lacked donations. Furthermore, there was not a large enough audience and, what is more, the audience could not afford to pay much for tickets. The organisation was therefore unable to provide its approximately 150 members[17] with work. Finally, a conflict regarding Dreifuß' objectives emerged. He had worked for the Jewish Cultural League

---

14 See Hans Baer, '10 Monate juedische Musik in Shanghai', *Shanghai Jewish Chronicle*, vol. 2:19 (20 January 1940), 4, Sindorf: private collection Axel Schüttauf; Artist Club: *Concert, Shanghai Jewish Club*, 15 June [1939], Nachlass Wolfgang Fraenkel, Ana 496, box 5, folder: Programme, München: Bayerische Staatsbibliothek; Alfred Dreifuss [Dreifuß], '"Wir vom Theater". Zur Versanstaltung [recte Veranstaltung] des Artist Club am 15. Aug. im Broadway Theater', in [title unknown], 14 August 1939, Alfred Dreifuß Archiv, folder 481, fol. 12, Berlin: AdK.

15 See Stephan Stompor, *Jüdisches Musik- und Theaterleben unter dem NS-Staat*, Andor Izsák (ed.) (Hannover: Europäisches Zentrum für jüdische Musik, 2001), 26, 35, 41, 56.

16 See Anonymous, 'Artist Club Opens Season Tonight', *The North-China Daily News*, 2 November 1939, 3.

17 See Guenther [Günther] Lenhardt, 'Besuch bei Oedipus', in [title unknown], 2 November 1939, Alfred Dreifuß Archiv, folder 481, fol. 36, Berlin: AdK.

in Berlin[18] and, like some other representatives of this organisation,[19] he preferred a schedule that resembled the legacy of 'German culture' to a decidedly Jewish-oriented programme, especially Yiddish theatre.[20] This ignored the heterogeneous composition of the group of Jewish refugees from Germany and Austria, many of whom, or at least their parents, had migrated from Eastern Europe and thus had links to Yiddish culture. Ossi Lewin, who was also the editor of the *Shanghai Jewish Chronicle*, for instance, came from Galicia. Aside from that, he had Zionist interests.[21] In the end, Dreifuß resigned as secretary, and the Artist Club terminated its work.[22] In early 1940, the Chamber Orchestra of 1939 ('Kammerorchester 1939'), which had been founded in conjunction with the Artist Club, also ceased operations after its third concert.[23]

A little later, a new organisation was created, again with Ossi Lewin as president, Alfred Dreifuß as secretary and, from March 1941 on at the latest, the pianist and conductor Henry Margolinski as vice president.[24] The European Jewish Artist Society continued to organise productions of drama and operetta, variety shows, and an increasing number of concerts. In the beginning, it had grants from wealthy Shanghai businessmen, including Victor Sassoon, Michel Speelman and Paul Komor.[25] But the problems remained. The European Jewish Artist Society did not have its own theatre and had to use the small stages of the cinemas in Hongkou for its productions. Still, there was not a sufficient audience for subscriptions, and the funds were used up at some

---

18   See Dreifuß, *Ensemblespiel des Lebens. Erinnerungen eines Theatermannes* (Berlin: Der Morgen, 1985), 127.
19   See Lily E. Hirsch, *A Jewish Orchestra in Nazi Germany: Musical Politics and the Berlin Jewish Culture League* (Ann Arbor: University of Michigan Press, 2010), 39f.
20   See Alfred Dreifuss [Dreifuß], 'Das Erbe', *Shanghai Jewish Chronicle*, 26 November 1939, Alfred Dreifuß Archiv, folder 481, fol. 60–61, Berlin: AdK; Dreifuss [Dreifuß], 'Der Spielplan. Eine Betrachtung', *Die Tribüne*, no. 2, 3rd week of February 1940, 1–4. – Dreifuss [Dreifuß], 'Sapiro', *Die Tribüne*, no. 12 (4th week of April 1940), 401–405.
21   See Wilfried Seywald, 'Der vergessengemachte Zeitungsmacher Ossi Lewin und seine Zeit im Exil in Shanghai', in *IWK. Mitteilungen des Instituts für Wissenschaft und Kunst*, vol. 44:3 (1989), 22–27 (22, 24).
22   See G.L. [Günther Lenhardt], 'Zur Erklaerung des Artist Club', in [title unknown], [1940], Alfred Dreifuß Archiv, folder 481, fol. 85, Berlin: AdK.
23   See 'Das Kammerorchester 1939. 3. Konzert [advertisement]', *Gelbe Post*, vol. 2:7 (21) (27 January 1940), 1.
24   See E.P., 'Geburtstag der EJAS', *Shanghai Jewish Chronicle*, vol. 3 (15 March 1941), 5, Shanghai Collection, 1924–1950, RG 243, folder 67, I, fol. 724, New York (NY): YIVO.
25   See A.R. [Alfred Robitschek], 'The European Jewish Artists' Society. Development and Aimes [sic]', in *EJAS Operatic Concert* [programme], 10 Mai 1941, 1–2, Alfred Dreifuß Archiv, folder 478, Berlin: AdK.

point, meaning that the performers' salaries had to be cut.[26] In May 1941, the European Jewish Artist Society consequently gave up its expensive theatre division. In this context, it claimed that private initiatives would take over this field of activity. As a non-profit organisation, the European Jewish Artist Society from then on focused on music only.[27] This narrowed the organisation's artistic aims and objectives in terms of job creation. But even the plans made after the reorganisation[28] could only be put into practice to a small extent or had to be abandoned altogether, such as the planned choir[29] and the university courses to be given by Dreifuß in cooperation with the University of Shanghai.[30] The political situation after the Japanese occupation of Shanghai at the time of the attack on Pearl Harbor in December 1941 was the main reason for this development. Soon it was no longer Dreifuß but Margolinski, together with the engineer Alfred Robitschek, who managed the organisation. Various competitive projects, the Shanghai Art Club,[31] the Pro Arte Artist-Agency[32] and a concert initiative by Fritz A. Kuttner,[33] which were launched in response to the change of programme in 1941, also had limited options of development at this time.

Throughout the proclamation of the 'designated area' between spring 1943 and summer 1945, the European Jewish Artist Society only sporadically organised chamber music concerts and song recitals.[34] The main event was a benefit concert given by the Shanghai Philharmonic Orchestra (formerly

---

26   See W. [Wolfgang] Fischer, 'Broadway-Gefluester', *8 Uhr Abendblatt*, vol. 2: 292 (23 November 1940), 3.

27   See Anonymous, 'Das Privattheater hat das Wort! Die "Ejas" stellt ihre Theateraufführungen ein', *Shanghai Jewish Chronicle*, 9 May 1941, 6, Shanghai Collection, 1924–1950, RG 243, folder 67, I, fol. 857, New York (NY): YIVO.

28   See Anonymous, '"EJAS" und ihre Plaene', *Shanghai Jewish Chronicle*, 3 August 1941, *ibid.*, fol. 1007.

29   See Anonymous, '"EJAS" gruendet Chorvereinigung', *Shanghai Jewish Chronicle*, 28 July 1941, *ibid.*, fol. 998.

30   See Alfred Dreifuß Archiv, folder 499, Berlin: AdK.

31   See Chair of the Shanghai Art Club, 'Aus unserem Kulturschaffen', *Die Laterne*, vol. 1941:1 (14 June 1941), 9.

32   See Walter Lewens, 'Zum Geleit', in Pro Arte Artist-Agency, *Sonderveranstaltung in der S.J.Y.A. School* [programme], 7 June 1941, Ferdinand Adler-Album, Kufstein: private collection Christina Adler.

33   See Fritz A. Kuttner in connection with the Committee for the Assistance of European Jewish Refugees in Shanghai: *Miriam Magasi in Aid of the European Emigrants*, 25 November 1941 [programme], *ibid.*

34   See Erwin Felber, 'Das erste EJAS-Konzert', *Shanghai Jewish Chronicle*, vol. 6: 27 (28 January 1944), 2; Felber, '"Ejas-Konzert"', *Shanghai Jewish Chronicle*, vol. 6:52 (22 February 1944), 3.

Shanghai Municipal Orchestra) in Hongkou in May 1944.[35] During this time, the European Jewish Artist Society occasionally cooperated with the Jewish Community of Central European Jews,[36] which was the only institution accepted by the Japanese to represent the refugees.[37] However, the sources do not indicate that the European Jewish Artist Society was supervised directly by the occupation force. Presumably to curry favour with the Japanese administration, in 1943 Henry Margolinski organised a concert in aid of the Foreign Pao Chia, an organisation for the self-administration of the refugees that served the Japanese.[38] But it appears as if the European Jewish Artist Society was not involved in this concert.[39]

After the end of the war, only one event on behalf of the European Jewish Artist Society took place. This was a performance of Johann Strauss' operetta *Die Fledermaus* as a note of thanks to the Allied Nations and the city of Shanghai. Afterwards, a debate arose in the press, because the music critics Martin Hausdorff and Erwin Felber had published contradicting reviews.[40] An open letter by the conductor Carl Maximilian Winternitz now made it clear that some regarded the European Jewish Artist Society only as an instrument of protection for a small group of artists.[41] Obviously, it had failed in its original aim to create work for a large number of artists, and it does not seem to have existed after that. In any case, the number of concerts and stage productions declined from the summer of 1946 onwards, because the refugees began to leave the city.

---

35 See Jewish Community of Central European Jews in connection with the cultural department of the European Jewish Artist Society, *Symphonie-Konzert des Shanghaier Philharmonischen Orchesters*, 30 May 1944 [programme], Ferdinand Adler-Album, Kufstein: private collection Christina Adler.
36 See Felber: 'Das erste EJAS-Konzert', 2.
37 See Heinz Ganther, 'Das religioese Leben', *The Shanghai Herald. German Language Supplement*, special issue (April 1946), 3f (3).
38 See Kranzler, 493–95.
39 See *Gala Concert in Favour of Foreign Pao Chia*, 27 November 1943 [programme], Shanghai Collection, 1924–1950, RG 243, folder 57, fol. 35, New York (NY): YIVO.
40 See Hff. [Martin Hausdorff], '"Die Fledermaus". Auffuehrung der EJAS im Lyceum Theater', *China Daily Tribune. German Language Supplement*, vol. 1946:11 (60), (1 May 1946), 3; Felber, 'Die Fledermaus im Lyceum', *Shanghai Echo*, vol. 1:120 (2 May 1946), 3; Felber, 'Kunstpflege und Emigration', *Shanghai Echo*, vol. 1:123 (5 May 1946), 7f.
41 See C.M. [Carl Maximilian] Winternitz, 'Die freie Meinung. Die Fledermaus oder Das Mirakel der Kritik', *China Daily Tribune. German Language Supplement*, vol. 1946:18 (67) (8 May 1946), 3.

2 Shanghai Musicians Association

Hundreds of solo entertainers and bands worked in Shanghai's entertainment venues. Their repertoire of popular music was shaped by US swing music, but at the same time it took into account all possible tastes. Gypsy swing was just as much a part of this scene,[42] as well as dance music specially adapted to Chinese tastes.[43] With this repertoire on offer, and also because of strong connections to gambling, drug trafficking and prostitution, the entertainment venues involved large audiences and opportunities to earn money. For this reason, it became the object of political conflicts. Chinese nationalists repeatedly committed terrorist attacks in ballrooms and night clubs in order to denounce the waste of people and funds on Western entertainment in times of war with Japan.[44] In addition to long working hours, low fees and a mixed audience including seafarers and military personnel, it was not easy to work in these places. The bars and restaurants that were founded by the refugees in the Hongkou district offered a more familiar environment, among other reasons, because the musicians knew the hit songs and dance music which were in demand there. But the competition was fierce, and the audience in Hongkou had hardly any money.

Since the musicians were not able to enforce their interests individually, in 1940 they developed the idea of creating a union. This had been discussed in Shanghai for a long time but had never been put into practice.[45] After a musicians' meeting organised by the violinist Oskar Leisten, they founded the International Musicians Association. Its members soon included over 140 refugees, including one Filipino and one Russian musician. After a further meeting of all Shanghai musicians, they set up another, now indeed 'international', association in the summer of 1940: the Shanghai Musicians Association. Its board of directors and members, in addition to the refugees, included Russian, US, Filipino and Chinese musicians. Initially, it had 300 members,[46] which

---

42   See Paul French, *Destination Shanghai* (Hong Kong: Blacksmith Books, 2019), 277–91.
43   See Andrew David Field, *Shanghai's Dancing World: Cabaret Culture and Urban Politics, 1919–1954* (Hong Kong: Chinese University Press, 2010), 43–47.
44   See Frederic Wakeman, Jr., *The Shanghai Badlands. Wartime Terrorism and Urban Crime, 1937–1941*, (Cambridge: Cambridge University Press, 2002, first edition 1996), 65–69.
45   See e.g. P. Soboleff, C. Meloni, A. Antropoff and D. Sposito, 'Unemployed Musicians. An Appeal [letter to the editor]', *The North-China Herald and Supreme Court & Consular Gazette*, 29 April 1936, 202; Observer, 'Poor Musicians: A Plea for Assistance [letter to the editor]', *The North-China Daily News*, December 1938, 2.
46   See E.P., 'Emigranten gruenden internationalen Musikverband. Vor einer Organisierung aller Angestellten der Nachtbetriebe', *Shanghai Jewish Chronicle*, 13 October 1940, RG 243, folder 67, II, fol. 281, New York (NY): YIVO.

increased to 600 members a little later on.[47] Like the refugees, US and Russian musicians also supported the foundation of the Union,[48] which soon campaigned for economic and social issues, i.e. standard wages, legal protection, fair treatment, mediation of jobs, and protection in case of illness or death.[49] Funds were obtained from membership fees and fundraising events.[50] In 1941, the officiating president of the Union, José Contreras articulated artistic aims, such as adapting the musical level to US standards,[51] but such ideas were not at the centre of the activities. According to the drummer Herbert Löwy, who initially was a member of the body of delegates assigned to the board, the model for some of the association's objectives was the International Artists' Lodge ('Internationale Artisten-Loge'), founded in Berlin in 1901 for artists working in variety shows, circuses and cabarets.[52] Until 1933, this organisation had dedicated itself to similar areas of work. It, too, had been internationally oriented.[53]

After the proclamation of the 'designated area' in 1943, the Shanghai Musicians Association came under Japanese control. The musicians were now forced to organise a new association in the ghetto district.[54] The Shanghai Musicians Association of Stateless Refugees continued work under harsh conditions. Unemployment increasingly played a role among its more than 180 members, who mainly worked as entertainment musicians and, in addition, as music educators.[55] Many tried to work as street musicians under precarious conditions.[56] The union had to provide individual support through

---

47 See José Contreras, 'Message', *Shanghai Musicians Associations Grand Midnight Ball* [programme], 23 May 1941, AR 2509, Box 1, folder 10, New York (NY): LBI.
48 See Anonymous, 'Interned Pootung Hep-Cats Form "Hottest" Dance Band', *The Shanghai Evening Post and Mercury*, 4 February 1944, 7; Stroy, 'In the Russian Colony', in *The North-China Daily News*, 7 June 1940, 2.
49 See E.P., 'Emigranten gruenden internationalen Musikerverband'.
50 See e.g. Anonymous, 'Musicians' Ball', *The North-China Daily News*, 31 May 1940, 3.
51 See José Contreras, 'Message', *Shanghai Musicians Associations Grand Midnight Ball* [programme], 23 May 1941, AR 2509, Box 1, folder 10, New York (NY): LBI.
52 See E.P., ‚Emigranten gruenden internationalen Musikerverband'.
53 See Max Berol-Konorah, *25 Jahre Internationale Artisten-Loge. Freigewerkschaftlicher Zentralverband der Spezialitätenkünstler vom Varieté, Zirkus und Kabarett. Ihr Werden, Wachsen und Wirken 1901–1926* (Berlin: Programm, [1926]); Birgit Peter, 'Zirkus und Artistik unter der NS-Herrschaft', in Brigitte Dalinger and Veronika Zangl (eds.), *Theater unter NS-Herrschaft: Theatre under Pressure* (Göttingen: V & R Unipress, 2018), 161–80 (165f).
54 See K.M. [Kurt Meyer], 'Die erste Musiker-Versammlung im Distrikt. Plaene und Beschluesse auf dem General-Meeting der "Shanghai Musicians Association of Stateless Refugees"', *Shanghai Jewish Chronicle*, vol. 5 (19 November 1943), 2, AR 2509, Box 1, folder 10, New York (NY): LBI.
55 See 'Members of the Shanghai Musicians Association of Stateless Refugees' [register of members], 20 May 1944, *ibid.*
56 See K.M. [Kurt Meyer], 'Die erste Musiker-Versammlung im Distrikt', 2, *ibid.*

grants and loans.⁵⁷ In order to raise funds, it organised benefit concerts.⁵⁸ But, above all, the union served as a link to the Bureau of Stateless Refugees Affairs. Often under harassment, its employees Ghoya Kano and Okura issued the special passes for the exit from the ghetto.⁵⁹ Since many musicians worked outside the 'designated area', it was vital for them that the union helped them with the applications and that it took over the responsibility towards the Japanese.⁶⁰ Despite these circumstances, compulsory membership was not introduced. In order to reassure the Japanese officials, the union granted Ghoya, Okura and others the status of honorary supporting members and, in May 1944, awarded them honorary diplomas.⁶¹

After the war, the union regained independence and the original state of an international organisation was restored, at least partially. The union, now known as Shanghai Musicians Association of Central European Musicians,⁶² cooperated with the associations of Russian, Filipino and Chinese musicians as part of the umbrella organisation, Federation of Shanghai Musicians.⁶³ New tasks arose in the postwar period. As Shanghai now belonged without restrictions to the Chinese state, which was ruled by the nationalists ('Guomindang') from Nanjing, special rights for foreigners were reduced. This, for example, applied to tax returns, for which there were now only Chinese forms. The musicians were finally allowed to handle their tax matters in English through the union.⁶⁴ Unemployment and a rapid inflation were still the main problems. In order to limit the tasks of the union in this situation, the union imposed an

---

57   See K.M. [Kurt Meyer], 'Refugee-Musiker-Verband unter neuer Leitung. Vorstandsneuwahl beim General-Meeting der Shanghai Musicians Association', *Shanghai Jewish Chronicle*, [vol. 6 (Mai 1944)], *ibid.*

58   See Shanghai Musicians Association of Stateless Refugees: *1. Sommer-Konzert des SMA-Orchesters*, 15 July 1944 [programme], *ibid.*; Shanghai Musicians Association of Stateless Refugees: *2. Sommer-Konzert des SMA-Orchesters*, 2 August 1944 [programme], *ibid.*

59   See Kranzler, 496–500.

60   See Anonymous, 'Die Reorganisation des Refugees-Musiker-Verbandes', *Shanghai Jewish Chronicle*, vol. 6 (4 June 1944), 3, AR 2509, Box 1, folder 10, New York (NY): LBI.

61   See *ibid.*

62   See Anonymous, 'Reorganisation unserer Berufsmusiker', *The Shanghai Herald. German Supplement*, vol. 1946:1 (2 March 1946), 3.

63   See N. [Nick] Korin, Federation of Shanghai Musicians, to the Shanghai Musicians Association of Central European Musicians, 9 March 1946, AR 2509, Box 1, folder 10, New York (NY): LBI; José Contreras, Federation of Shanghai Musicians, to [Walter] Kamm, Shanghai Musicians Association of Central European Musicians, 10 January 1949, *ibid.*

64   See Anonymous, 'An alle Musiker, Kellner, Gasthausangestellte u. Bardamen [advertisement]', *Shanghai Journal. Die neue Zeit*, vol. 1946:15 (20 January 1946), 7; Anonymous, 'Steuerabgabe von Musikern und Gasthaus-Angestellten', *Shanghai Journal. Die neue Zeit*, no. 15 (20 January 1946), 8.

admission ban in 1946.[65] Nevertheless, a financial crisis occurred in 1947. The situation deteriorated as some musicians were without a job, while the number of members decreased in consequence of emigration or re-migration.[66] Nonetheless, work continued to be carried out. The main tasks were the mediation of jobs, the implementation of a procedure to divide jobs between those who had contracts and those who had not, as well as the raising of fees.[67] By 1948, the inflation had driven the fees for the engagement of bands up to ten figures.[68] Ultimately, since inflation continued after a currency reform that year, the union tried to link the fees to the prices of drinks and food offered in the entertainment venues.[69]

After the Communists came to power in Shanghai in May 1949, the refugee musicians continued to operate the union. For example, its managing director Walter Kamm announced new fee regulations based on so-called 'basic units'. These were connected to the wholesale price of five important goods required daily.[70] However, members were also asked to register with the Chinese union. This way, they could obtain working permits, which were now necessary if they wanted to work.[71] In August 1949, the Shanghai Musicians Association of Central European Musicians and its members were required to join the CCMU's Foreign Section, probably the abbreviation for Central Chinese Musicians' Union.[72] Presumably, this was the music section (Yin yan ye gonghui) of the All-China Federation of Trade Unions (Zhonghua quanguo zonggong hui). Thereby, the independence of the Shanghai Musicians Association of Central European Musicians came to an end.

---

65   See Kurmey [Kurt Meyer], 'Mitglieder-Versammlung des Musikerverbandes', *The Shanghai Herald. German Supplement*, vol. 1946:43 (13 April 1946), 3.
66   See K.M. [Kurt Meyer], 'Unsere Musiker fuer weitere Aufrechterhaltung ihrer Organisation', *Shanghai Echo*, vol. 2: 217 (9 August 1947), 5.
67   See K.M. [Kurt Meyer], 'Eine wichtige Musiker-Versammlung', *Shanghai Echo*, vol. 1:165 (16 June 1946), 5; Kurmey [Kurt Meyer], 'Mitglieder-Versammlung des Musikerverbandes', 3; Leo, 'Wichtige Berufsprobleme unserer Musiker', *Shanghai Echo*, vol. 1:102 (13 April 1946), 4.
68   See Federation of Shanghai Musicians, 'Minutes of the Meeting of the Working Committee', 19 July 1948, AR 2509, Box 1, folder 10, New York (NY): LBI.
69   See Federation of Shanghai Musicians, 'Minutes of the Working Committee Meeting', 2 November 1948, *ibid.*
70   See Walter Kamm to all members of the Shanghai Musicians Association of Central European Musicians, 19 July 1949, *ibid.*
71   See *ibid.*
72   See Foreign Section to [Walter] Kamm, 22 August 1949, *ibid.*

3   Association of Jewish Precentors

In addition to the classical and the light entertainment sector, the refugees also developed the religious sector as an independent musical area in Shanghai. This could happen because, alongside the long-established Orthodox Baghdadi-Sephardic and Russian-Ashkenazi communities, the refugees developed their own community structures in Hongkou. In 1939, the Jewish Community of Central European Jews (Jüdische Kultusgemeinde, later renamed Jüdische Gemeinde) was founded. Its objectives were diverse. Births had to be registered and bar mitzvahs, weddings and funerals organised. In addition, community life had to be furthered through events. Above all, services had to be held. After the first major services in Broadway Theatre in Hongkou in May 1939, so-called unitary services were organised for 'liberal' and more traditional adherents alike. In the following year, the 'liberal' community (Jüdisch-liberale Gemeinde) split off. In addition, the services of the Jewish Community of Central European Jews were separated into 'liberal' and more traditional services. All of this happened because the 'liberal' worshippers did not feel well enough represented in the unitary services, which also showed consideration for the Orthodox traditions of the long-established Jewish communities of Shanghai.[73] The 'liberal' services differed musically in that they used mixed choirs and instrumental music, while the more traditionalist services which were designated as '*konservativ*' in the newspaper advertisements engaged male choirs.[74] The services took place partly in the Sephardic synagogues Ohel Rachel and Beth Aharon, but also in the Ashkenazi synagogue Ohel Moishe in Hongkou, as well as in cinemas, schools and other secular halls. In the beginning, permanent places of worship only existed in the refugee homes. It wasn't until 1941 that the Jewish Community of Central European Jews set up the synagogue Emet v'Shalom[75] in a residential building on MacGregor Road as a permanent prayer room.[76]

Like the majority of the refugees, the cantors who had fled to Shanghai also mainly belonged to either 'liberal' or more traditional Judaism, but they

---

73   See Managing Board of the Jewish Community of Central European Jews, 'Unsere Juedische Gemeinde', *Shanghai Jewish Chronicle*, special issue, March 1940, 18–19; Lutz Wachsner, 'Die Aufgaben des Kultusdezernates', in *Jüdisches Nachrichtenblatt*, vol. 1:1, 2 August 1940, 8; Anonymous, 'Juedisch-liberale Gemeinde', *8 Uhr Abendblatt*, vol. 2:231 (11 September 1940), 4; Ganther, 3–4.
74   See e.g. 'Die Bethaeuser der Juedischen Gemeinde fuer die Hohen Feiertage [advertisement]', *Jüdisches Nachrichtenblatt*, vol. 1:3 (30 August 1940), 3.
75   Spelling in the Shanghai newspapers: Emes w'scholaum.
76   See Ganther, 3.

included very few distinctly Orthodox cantors. They were not only prayer leaders, but also music directors who had more or less developed skills as choir directors, singers, pianists, composers and music teachers. There was a need for them in the newly established community life. But with almost forty cantors, the professional group was too large, so that no more than half of them could find long-term employment. For some, changing the job was necessary. But even those who were involved in religious life did not find it easy to get along as fees were not high. Most of them additionally worked as preachers, teachers, circumcisers and kosher butchers, just as they had done back in Europe. However, even before their exile some of them had practiced their profession as a part-time job.

Apart from economic difficulties, the cantors had to deal with comparatively powerful institutions, namely the Jewish communities and the aid organisations, which were active in the refugee homes. Because of this, a plan to set up professional representation for the cantors soon emerged. In April 1940, Rudolf Glahs, Jacob Aschendorff and Max Ehrenberg put it into action. Similar to the General German Cantors Association ('Allgemeiner Deutscher Kantoren-Verband') and the Austrian Cantors Association ('Österreichischer Kantorenverein'), the newly founded Association of Jewish Precentors ('Gemeinschaft Jüdischer Kantoren' or 'Chewrath Chasonim') chose a board of directors with a chairman, a deputy chairman, a treasurer and a secretary. The cantor Rudolf Glahs, a former theatre director who had gained experience within the German Stage Association ('Deutscher Bühnenverein'),[77] became the first and only chairman. The other positions were also relatively stable with Jacob Aschendorff, Max Ehrenberg, Leopold Fleischer and Mendel Lewkowitz. During the years of its existence, the professional association consisted mostly of no more than twenty cantors.[78]

The Association of Jewish Precentors had ambitious aims which concerned the cantors' economic, social and cultural interests. In economic terms, the objective was to raise the fees for the services in the Jewish communities and

---

77　See Frithjof Trapp, Werner Mittenzwei, Henning Rischbieter and Hansjörg Schneider (eds.), *Handbuch des deutschsprachigen Exiltheaters 1933–1945*, vol. 2: *Biographisches Lexikon der Theaterkünstler* (München: Saur, 1999), part 1, 316.

78　See Association of Jewish Precentors to the managing board of the Jewish Community of Central European Jews, 16 March 1942, RG 243, folder 32 III, fol. 88, New York (NY): YIVO; Anonymous, 'Die Feier des 5 Jaehrigen [sic] Bestehens der Gemeinschaft juedischer Kantoren', *Jüdisches Nachrichtenblatt*, vol. 6: 19 (17 May 1945), 2; Anonymous, '"Die Gemeinschaft Juedischer Kantoren"', *Shanghai Echo*, vol. 1:123 (5 May 1946), 13; Association of Jewish Precentors: minutes of a general meeting, 7 May 1946, RG 342, folder 32 V, fol. 149, New York (NY): YIVO; Anonymous, 'Association of Jewish Precentors Shanghai', in Ossi Lewin (ed.), *Almanac Shanghai 1946/47* (Shanghai: Shanghai Echo, 1947), 58.

the refugee homes. It was, as the Association of Jewish Precentors claimed, difficult to make a living even though the cantors did not have high demands.[79] The cantors achieved some success therein. But, in times of inflation, this had only limited effect. In order to compensate for economic hardship, the Association of Jewish Precentors also pursued a social programme. It created a fund to support sick and needy colleagues.[80] The money came from monthly membership fees as well as special fees in case the costs could not be covered.[81] In addition, the association accepted donations[82] and generated an income through concerts and other events, which were carried out by the cantors as soloists and choir singers.[83] Some donations were received in the form of food and distributed among the cantors.[84] The Association of Jewish Precentors campaigned in individual cases to ensure that the cantors were provided with free meals, but it was not always successful in this regard.[85] Finally, the association tried to compensate for the precarious situation by dividing the income from funerals and services in the refugee homes among the participating cantors.[86] The reason for this was that the income differed from service to service so that it had to be balanced.[87] This way, in economic and social terms, the Association of Jewish Precentors acted as a kind of professional cooperative. It was, therefore, more than just a representative of interests.

---

79   See Association of Jewish Precentors to the Committee for the Assistance of European Jewish Refugees, 8 April 1941, RG 243, folder 32 II, fol. 58, New York (NY): YIVO.

80   See invitation to a ceremony on 9 May 1945 at Emes w'scholaum, RG 243, folder 32 I, fol. 18, *ibid.*; YIVO: Questionnaire: Association of Jewish Precentors, Shanghai (Hevrath Hasanim), o. J., RG 243, folder 5, fol. 19–21, *ibid.*; Anonymous, 'Association of Jewish Precentors Shanghai', in Lewin (ed.), *Almanac Shanghai 1946/47*, 58.

81   See Rudolf Glahs to the members of the Association of Jewish Precentors, 11 May 1946, RG 243, folder 32 V, fol. 150, New York (NY): YIVO.

82   See e.g. Jüdisches Wissenschaftliches Lehrhaus to the die Association of Jewish Precentors, 23 February 1942, RG 243, folder 32 III, fol. 84, *ibid.*; M. [Meir] Birman, Far Eastern Jewish Central Information Bureau, to R. Glass [Rudolf Glahs], 11 May 1945, RG 243, folder 32 IV, fol. 110, *ibid.*

83   See Association of Jewish Precentors to unknown receiver, 18 January 1941, RG 243, folder 32 II, fol. 45, *ibid.*

84   See Rudolf Glahs to the members of the Association of Jewish Precentors, 18 April 1946, RG 243, folder 32 V, fol. 147, *ibid.*

85   See Association of Jewish Precentors to the Committee to Captain Herzberg, Assistance of European Jewish Refugees in Shanghai, 19 November 1941, RG 243, folder 32 II, fol. 78, *ibid.*

86   See Association of Jewish Precentors to Feldstein, management of the religious cult in the refugee camps, 17 September 1941, RG 243, folder 32 II, fol. 72, *ibid.*; Statement of the Association of Jewish Precentors, 11 August 1941, RG 243, folder 28 II, fol. 21, *ibid.*

87   See Rudolf Glahs, Association of Jewish Precentors, to Fischel, president of the Jewish Community of Central European Jews, 16 September 1946, RG 243, Folder 32 IV, Bl. 112, *ibid.*

The cantors, who, with some exceptions, mostly followed the 'liberal' rite, were unable to find work in the Sephardic and Orthodox Ashkenazi Jewish communities of the city. Their scope of activity was limited to the refugee community. Among other things, this had to do with the musical tradition. Female voices and instruments were taboo in Orthodox worship. Furthermore, the Orthodox Jews rejected 19th century choral synagogue music because of its proximity to customs of Christian church music. The Shanghai Rabbinate Court even passed a judgment in 1940 stating that those who violated the sacred tradition by participating in such services should not hope for support from the old-established communities.[88] However, nothing is known about sanctions ever being enacted. Rather, the services of the refugees continued according to the well-known pattern. In fact, the cantors tried to make their musical point of view clear by means of concerts. 'Jewish concerts' or 'Jewish evenings', which were organised by the cantor's professional association over the years, presented works of choral synagogue music, above all by Louis Lewandowski, Salomon Sulzer and Samuel Naumbourg, but also by a younger generation of composers. Usually, the programmes were combined with Yiddish songs. This expressed an assimilatory as well as a traditional approach to 'Jewish music' that was closely linked to the history of the Jews in Europe.[89] Over the course of time, all kinds of musicians from the refugee group were invited to perform at these concerts – yet no Orthodox cantors, neither from their own ranks nor from those of the old-established Jewish communities.

The Association of Jewish Precentors maintained its objectives over the years. This included the permanent distancing from the old Orthodox communities as well as pushing back newcomers who, like the Viennese choir singer Josef Fruchter, had no formal training as a cantor.[90] The association, which did not change significantly during the proclamation of the 'designated area', was probably active until most of the cantors left in around 1947.

4   Conclusion

The Jewish refugees from Germany and Austria had been used to a highly organised musical life, that is state and city funding for theatres and orchestras,

---

88   See Beth-Din, Rabbinate Shanghai, 'Harmonium-Gottesdienst und Frauenchor religionsgesetzlich unzulaessig', *Gelbe Post*, 5 July 1940, 4, RG 243, folder 67 II, fol. 2, *ibid.*
89   See Heidy Zimmermann, 'Was heißt "jüdische Musik"? Grundzüge eines Diskurses im 20. Jahrhundert', in Eckhard John and Heidy Zimmermann (eds.), *Jüdische Musik? Fremdbilder – Eigenbilder* (Köln: Böhlau, 2004), 11–32 (14–17).
90   See Association of Jewish Precentors to the Committee for the Assistance of European Jewish Refugees, 4 September 1941, RG 243, folder 28 II, fol. 26, New York (NY): YIVO.

as well as protection by unions and professional associations. After the Nazis came to power, the refugees had to learn that music organisations controlled by the state could also turn against them. Nevertheless, the Jewish Cultural League, which finally led to the Jews' cultural ghettoisation, was rated favourably by parts of the Jewish population,[91] and the Reich Chamber of Music ('Reichsmusikkammer') initially was not viewed only unfavourably, because it sometimes correlated with long cherished ideas of a well-regulated music market. Besides, in the beginning, the professional bans issued by the Reich Chamber of Music, from the summer of 1935 onwards, could not have been foreseen. The General German Cantors' Association, for example, in 1934 decided to join the Reich Chamber of Music.[92] However, this obviously did not conform to the interests of the Nazis. The plan was not carried out. In Shanghai, the refugees ignored the ambivalence of musical organisation in the Third Reich and started a process of institutionalisation mainly with a view to the difficult living and working conditions and the large numbers of musicians in the city. The aim was to find or create jobs, raise fees, improve working conditions and represent the refugees' culture. Depending on their objectives and working methods, the initiatives were successful in different ways and had to struggle with a broad range of problems.

Despite their high activity at times, the objectives of the Artist Club and the European Jewish Artist Society proved to be the most difficult ones to realise. Their role model, the Jewish Cultural League, had been created under coercion that initially did not exist in Shanghai. In the Chinese port city, neither the artists nor the public could be forced to join the organisation. In addition, there were no subsidies or long-term patronages. When the secretary Alfred Dreifuß used his position to enforce his concept of German high culture, thereby ignoring the heterogeneous cultural backgrounds of the refugees, the Artist Club collapsed. Due to the lack of audiences and money the European Jewish Artist Society later had to narrow down its range of activities to concerts. But these concerts involved fewer artists than the drama and operetta productions had before, and they were often presented to an international audience and only from time to time to the refugees. The fact that the Japanese occupiers did not control the European Jewish Artist Society directly shows the minor

---

91 See Eike Geisel, 'Premiere und Pogrom', in Eike Geisel and Henryk M. Broder, *Premiere und Pogrom: Der Jüdische Kulturbund 1933–1941: Texte und Bilder* (Berlin: Siedler, 1992), 7–35 (9–14).
92 See Leon Kornitzer and Bernhard Alt, 'Bericht über die IX. Mitgliederversammlung am 26. Dezember 1933 in Leipzig', *Der Jüdische Kantor*, vol. 7: 6 (February 1934), 1–4 (1–2).

importance of this organisation at that time. The hostilities in the postwar period underline the fact that the organisation's extensive claim for representation was not generally recognised by the refugees. Ultimately, the political situation, economic problems and disagreement within the refugee community prevented a permanent operation. The trade union approach of the Shanghai Musicians Association and its successor associations, however, met a rather positive response due to the deficiency of musical organisation in Shanghai. This becomes clear by the rapid internationalisation of the association. The member-based work and the constant adaptation to economic and social changes benefited a relatively large number of musicians. But it also made the union significant for those in power. The Japanese occupiers used the union as a contact point, as did the nationalists, until in 1949 the organisation, including those members still present, was incorporated into the Communist Chinese union. The Association of Jewish Precentors somehow united the objectives of the European Jewish Artist Society and the Shanghai Musicians Association since its work was designed to be economic, social and cultural in nature. This was only feasible because the members of the association formed a relatively small group and had fairly homogeneous interests. Presumably due to the continuous staffing and the isolating approach, there were only minor conflicts. This way, the Association of Jewish Precentors did not significantly change its orientation in matters of structure and objectives and was never of significant interest to those in power until its liquidation after the war.

Shanghai offered the musicians extensive opportunities of labour and self-organisation. This worked out best, even during politically difficult times, when the focus was on member-oriented interests, as with the Shanghai Musicians Association and the Association of Jewish Precentors. However, the enforcement of individual cultural interests in connection with the creation of jobs in the field of theatre and music proved to be difficult due to the heterogeneity of the refugees, low audience numbers and lack of funds. Although the situation in Shanghai was very different, some mechanisms that had determined developments in Germany also occurred in Shanghai, but in an adapted way. The Artist Club and the European Jewish Artist Society struggled with the fact that they did not have a monopoly such as that which had influenced the Jewish Cultural League's work. The Shanghai Musicians Association had good working conditions, but for this reason it was like all the unions and professional organisations in the Third Reich, controlled and finally absorbed by those in power, and the Association of Jewish Precentors was just not important enough to be of interest. Ironically, for this reason it could continue its work with only the smallest degree of interference from outside.

5

'A State of Crass Ideological Confusion': Avant-Garde Music and Antisemitism in the Free German League of Culture

Florian Scheding

Abstract

The article deals with the musical activities of the exile organisation Free German League of Culture that was active in the UK during the time of the Second World War, focusing in particular on Ernst Hermann Meyer's role in these activities. The history of the League (especially its musical dimension) has received rather scant attention from scholars, in part because of the lack of access to the materials that were transferred to East Germany after the war. I offer several explanations for the focus of the musical events of the League on the Austro-German musical canon at the expense of modernist music, much of which was written by Jewish composers who were forced into exile. Particularly significant was the communist core of the League in advancing ideological positions that foreshadowed debates about nationalism and race in postwar East Germany.

In 1989, the East German Academy of the Arts staged an exhibition in East Berlin, the capital of the dying GDR. Entitled 'Free German League of Culture, 1938/39–1946,' it commemorated the half-centenary of one of the Second World War's largest migrant organisations. The League had been founded by German refugees in 1938 as a centre for migrant artists and intellectuals. Based in London with branches throughout Britain, its goal was to promote an image of German culture in opposition to Hitler. Musical events were a frequent feature of the League's cultural activities. Yet, the avant-garde was largely absent from programmes – a paradoxical omission given that many of the avant-garde's foremost protagonists were refugees from Nazi Germany and annexed Austria, where large numbers of progressive composers and works were banned as 'degenerate music'. In this chapter, I identify several reasons for this. First, as a spearhead of progressive thinking, avant-garde music was ill-equipped as a vehicle for nostalgia. Second, dominant sections in the League deemed avant-garde music to alienate the more conservative forces of British society, threatening to hinder integration of Austrian and German refugees. Third, the avant-gardes of Schoenberg, Stravinsky, and others were difficult to reconcile with the beliefs of the League's powerful Communist core.

Even more striking than the omission of the avant-garde is the apparent antisemitism evident among parts of the League. In 1943, around forty Jewish migrants left the League in protest of a pamphlet they considered Judeophobic. After the war, the League was absorbed into the East German Kulturbund, which significantly influenced the cultural and political life of the nascent GDR. In the emerging Cold War, antisemitic undertones became more vociferous. As I show in this chapter, League members accused Jewish circles of conspiring in the West's 'reactionary' ideology, a sentiment that culminated in an internal League document in 1946: 'The Jews are in a state of crass ideological confusion.'

While the exodus of many of Europe's foremost figures during the era of European fascism has been richly documented, the League and its legacy have received scant attention. As the case of the League exemplifies, far from presenting a united front, migrants were increasingly entrenched in ideological battles that cut to the heart of debates concerning race, and the relationship between art and politics. The League's complex history reflects the heterogeneity of the migrant community and moves us beyond monolithic aggressor-victim notions of exile toward a more nuanced understanding of Europe's musical migrants.

1   Beginnings of Exile

Following Hitler's rise to power in February 1933, few Germans predicted the eruption of the Second World War six years later, and fewer still the Holocaust. Even Adorno, not widely known for owning up to misapprehensions, admitted 'the outbreak of the Third Reich took my political judgment by surprise.'[1] In 1934, one year after the initial shock wave of emigration from Germany following Hitler's rise to power, several thousand German-Jewish refugees returned to Germany.[2] Indeed, it was a widespread belief among those opposed to Hitler that his regime was going to be over sooner rather than later. Even those who had been dismissed from their academic and teaching posts due to the

---

1   Theodor W. Adorno, *Minima Moralia. Reflexionen aus dem beschädigten Leben* (Frankfurt am Main: Suhrkamp, 1951), 366.
2   Marion Berghahn, *German–Jewish Refugees in England* (London and Basingstoke: Macmillan, 1984), 72.

so-called Law for the Restitution of the Professional Civil Service, promulgated in April 1933 and that banned all 'non-Aryans' from official positions, were at first reluctant to leave Germany. Up until 1938, comparatively few left Germany and, of those who did, only a handful decided to move to Britain. Everything changed in 1938. In March, Nazi Germany annexed Austria, and hopes that the Third Reich would be short-lived were eradicated. Refugee numbers now skyrocketed. Even though many refugees still chose to migrate to Germany's and Austria's neighbouring countries, especially to the cities of Prague, Amsterdam, and Paris, late 1938 and early 1939 saw over 80,000 Austrian and German immigrants in Britain, 63,000 of them new arrivals.[3]

Given this political context, it seems understandable why no major refugee organisations were established in Britain between 1933 and 1938. However, in 1938, with refugee numbers at their peak, migrants from Germany and Austria began to organise themselves and erected numerous support circles. One of these organisations was the Free German League of Culture. Formed in late 1938 and early 1939 in London as a centre for refugee artists and intellectuals, its primary goal was to promote an image of German culture in opposition to Hitler, to portray a better Germany. Membership numbers soon reached 1,500 and eventually totalled 3,000. Compared to the approximately 40,000 refugees from Germany alone, this number may seem modest, but it still makes the League the biggest refugee organisation of the time on British soil. As entry and participation were not restricted to card-holding members or to Germans, migrants from many displaced continental European communities visited the League. Indeed, attendance numbers at the various activities went far beyond that of full members, especially after the League acquired a large house in Hampstead in north-west London and opened a café and restaurant with continental European cake and cuisine. A Free German University was opened, and between five and six cultural events were held per week, ranging from lectures to exhibitions, readings, theatre productions, concerts, language courses and similar activities. The League became a cultural and social centre of migrant life in London and in the United Kingdom as a whole, once it had established branches in Manchester, Birmingham, Leeds, Oxford, Glasgow, Edinburgh, and Bristol.[4]

---

3   Paul Tabori, *The Anatomy of Exile* (London: Harrap, 1972), 235.
4   Besides archival materials, the main (published) source for a history of the League is Charmian Brinson and Richard Dove (eds.), *Politics by Other Means: The Free German League of Culture in London 1939–1946* (London: Vallentine Mitchell, 2010). The volume is a much-expanded version of a book chapter by the same authors, 'The Continuation of Politics by Other Means: The Freie Deutsche Kulturbund in London, 1939–1946', in Anthony Grenville and Andrea

The League was organised into several sub-sections. Among them were divisions for literature and migrant authors, painters, and also musicians. Honorary members of the League's literature section included Heinrich Mann, Lion Feuchtwanger and Stefan Zweig, and the League specifically promoted contemporary writing, particularly by refugee writers banned in Nazi Germany. Despite a small market, at various points the League published three newspapers (*Freie Deutsche Kultur, Kunst und Wissen* and *Die Zeitung*) and either published under its own auspices or supported the publication of numerous books by exiled writers such as Jan Petersen (*Weg durch die Nacht*) and Max Zimmering (*Der Keim des Neuen*).

2   The Place of Music

Given the League's outspoken aim to focus its promotional efforts on a cultural image of Germany in opposition to Nazi ideology, one might expect that the musical riches of the interwar years and the legacy of the almost feverish spirit of experimentation in the Weimar Republic may have represented an obvious focus. Many of the musical works the Nazis banned and included in the degenerate music exhibition of 1938, for example, could easily have been integrated into the League's concert programmes.[5] The literature section, for example, ran events dedicated to readings of books that were burning on the squares of Nazi Germany. The migrant community, however heterogeneous, included some of the foremost musicians and composers of its time. And even beyond such names as Schoenberg, Bartók, Weill, Stravinsky, Eisler, Krenek, and Wolpe, there is an almost fantastical number of musicians and composers who may today be little known, but who had associated themselves to the avant-garde in one way or another prior to their enforced migration. Numerous highly trained and experienced migrant musicians lived in nearby areas and were eager to find performance opportunities, and the scores were available, too. Erik Levi has counted 400 professional instrumentalists and singers and seventy composers

---

Reiter (eds.), *'I didn't want to float; I wanted to belong to something': Refugee Organizations in Britain 1933–1945*, Yearbook of the Research Centre for German and Austrian Exile Studies, Vol. 10 (Amsterdam: Rodopi, 2008), 1–25. The League also features in Jutta Raab Hansen, NS-*verfolgte Musiker in England: Spuren deutscher und österreichischer Flüchtlinge in der britischen Musikkultur* (Hamburg: von Bockel, 1996).

5   For an exploration of the 'Degenerate Music Exhibition', see Albrecht Dümling, *Entartete Musik: Dokumentation und Kommentar zur Düsseldorfer Ausstellung von 1938* (Düsseldorf: DKV, 1993).

among the Germans and Austrians who escaped to Britain, almost all of them living in London when and where the League was first founded.[6]

It does appear as though the Free German League of Culture was eager to provide platforms for the avant-garde compositions of its members, if only from 1941 onward, when the League's music section, consisting of André Asriel, Ernst Hermann Meyer, Peter Stadlen and Ingeborg Wall, organised 'Modern Chamber Music' programmes. One of these concerts, on 25 March 1942, included (unidentified) works by Ludwig Brav, Berthold Goldschmidt and Mátyás Seiber. Again, given the numbers of migrant composers and musicians in Britain, many of them living in the neighbourhood of the League's base, there would have been ample opportunities to stage further concerts like these. Yet, in the papers of the Free German League of Culture, now mainly housed in the Akademie der Künste in Berlin, I have been able to find a mere six further concerts with programs including contemporary compositions. This makes a total of only seven concerts – one in 1941, four in 1942, one in 1943, and one in 1944. More striking, perhaps, is the tiny pool of names of composers that were represented, totalling no more than a dozen names, and, apart from Hanns Eisler, excluding perhaps more obvious works by canonical modernist composers, such as Schoenberg, Berg or Bartók. Besides Brav, Goldschmidt and Seiber, composers included André Asriel, Gerhard Hadda, Peter Ury, Franz Reizenstein, Erich Katz, Egon Wellesz and Ernst Herman Meyer. Most works were performed only once.

Indeed, any survey of the League's papers and materials cannot fail to reach the perhaps striking conclusion that the largest migrant organisation on British soil seems to have paid little attention to what was, after all, one of Hitler's prime targets in the field of music. Around ninety per cent of the works performed were taken from the German Baroque, classical or Romantic canon, a selection that not only points to a less than adventurous programming policy, but also, in effect, mirrored one of the Nazis' core music policies: the nationalist concentration on the German canon. The League's music section to all evidence did not concert its efforts in providing a platform for 'degenerate' music.

In addition to this repertoire of the Germanic classics, a second area of activity concerns light musical events, especially cabarets. Five new cabaret productions were staged in 1942, for example, and they were successful

---

6   Erik Levi, 'The German Jewish Contribution to Musical Life in Britain', in Werner Mosse, Julius Carlebach, Gerhard Hirschfeld, Aubrey Newman, Arnold Paucker and Peter Pulzer (eds.), *Second Chance: Two Centuries of German-speaking Jews in the United Kingdom* (Tübingen: Mohr, 1991), 279; The figure is endorsed in Raab Hansen, NS-*verfolgte Musiker in England*, 19.

enough to allow the League to purchase a building especially to house cabaret performances.[7] Many numbers in cabaret programmes were designed as sing-along events to strengthen communal spirits, and gatherings to sing folksongs were also a favourite. In addition to the many hundreds of concerts dedicated to Schubert songs, Mozart string quartets and Beethoven piano sonatas, then, there were dozens of cabarets and sing-alongs. Even during the internment crisis of 1940 and 1941, when the British authorities imprisoned numerous Austrian, German and Italian migrants as enemy aliens and thus deprived the League of many of its musicians, the League managed to initiate about forty different musical events per year, just under one per week.[8] In comparison, the seven concerts featuring a handful of works by Asriel, Brav, Seiber, Goldschmidt, and others, seem almost to pale into insignificance.

What reasons might there have been for this reluctance to support avant-garde music? On a surface level, two points are important in this context. First, rather than representing a homogeneous collective, migrants were a highly heterogeneous group, and not all of them embraced the avant-garde. As a spearhead of progressive thinking, avant-garde music was ill-equipped as a vehicle for nostalgia and homesickness for the migrants themselves and did not easily fulfil desires for escapism. As Johann Fladung, chairman of the League from 1941, explained in 1944, 'Classical music, as heard in great concerts, encourages us and gives us strength for our actions.'[9] Like the Free German League of Culture, the Hungarian migrant societies, the Society of Free Hungarians in Great Britain, the Free Hungarian House, and the Hungarian Club in London, for example, put considerable efforts into the London Pódium, which staged performances of three cabaret programs in 1943 and 1944 in front of an audience totalling nearly a thousand Hungarian exiles, but performed a piece by

---

7   Unlike in the case of the League more generally, there are several publications dedicated to the League's cabaret programmes. See, for example, Reinhard Hippen, *Satire gegen Hitler: Kabarett im Exil* (Zurich: Pendo-Verlag, 1986), 107–23; Hugh Rorrinson, 'German Theatre and Cabaret in London, 1939–45', in Günther Berghaus (ed.), *Theatre and Film in Exile: German Artists in Britain, 1933–1945* (Oxford: Berg, 1989), 47–77; and Jörg Thunecke, '"Das hübscheste sind die Lieder": Allan Gray's Contribution to the FDKB Revue *Mr Gulliver Goes to School*', in *Theatre and Film in Exile*, 79–97. See also Stephan Stompor, *Künstler im Exil: In Oper, Konzert, Operette, Tanztheater, Schauspiel, Kabarett, Rundfunk, Film, Musik- und Theaterwissenschaft sowie Ausbildung in 62 Ländern*, 2 vols. (Frankfurt/Main: Lang, 1994).

8   For a history on internment of 'enemy aliens', see Peter and Leni Gillman, *"Collar the Lot!" How Britain Internet and Expelled its Wartime Refugees* (London: Quartet Books, 1980); François Lafitte, *The Internment of Aliens* (London: Libris, 1988); and Richard Dove (ed.), *"Totally un-English"? Britain's Internment of "Enemy Aliens" in Two World Wars* (Amsterdam and New York: Rodopi, 2005).

9   Johann Fladung, 'Ein Schritt ins Freie', *Freie Deutsche Kultur*, October 1944, 1.

Bartók only once during its existence.¹⁰ Adorno highlighted the need for nostalgia and escapism in his *Minima Moralia*, written during the same years, when he quipped, in an almost cabaret-ish one-liner, 'In the memory of emigration, every German venison roast tastes as if it was freshly felled by the *Freischütz*.'¹¹

3   Antimodernist Voices

A second reason for the reluctance to stage progressive music more prominently stems from fears that avant-garde music could alienate the more conservative forces of British society instead of motivating them to assist the fight against Hitler. Antimodernist voices were not, of course, restricted to Britain. Reporting from a concert held during the festival of the International Society for Contemporary Music (ISCM) in the New York Public Library in May 1941, which included works by Anton Webern, Viktor Ullmann, Paul Dessau, Artur Schnabel and Mátyás Seiber, leading US music critic Olin Downes posed the rhetorical question, 'Is it any wonder that the culture from which [these works] emanate is even now going up in flames?'¹² Despite the efforts of younger composers like William Walton and Benjamin Britten, antimodernist feelings were arguably even stronger in Britain. Elgar's late-romantic pathos and the Celtic nationalism of Arnold Bax still largely epitomised British musical style at the time the Nazi refugees began arriving in the late 1930s. Amidst an atmosphere of anti-German hostility that had been bubbling away in British musical life since the First World War, in 1934, one year after Hitler's takeover, Constant Lambert published his book *Music Ho!*, subtitled '*a study of music in decline*,' a highly acclaimed and scathing attack on all musical things modernist.

In 1938 the ISCM festival was held in London. At the so-called 'Music and Life Conference', which accompanied the festival, the conference organisers decided to assign all the non-British speakers to the same session and entitled it 'Problematic Tendencies in Contemporary Music.' (Hanns Eisler spoke on the 'Twelve Note System,' Franz Reizenstein on 'Hindemith's New Theory,' Mordecai Sandberg on the 'Micro-tonal System,' Alois Hába on 'Non-thematic Composition,' and Mátyás Seiber on 'Swing.') In its conference report, *The*

---

10   See my text '"I Only Need the Good, Old Budapest": Hungarian Cabaret in Wartime London,' in Pauline Fairclough (ed.), *Twentieth-century Music and Politics: Essays in Memory of Neil Edmunds*. (Farnham: Ashgate, 2012), 211–30.

11   Theodor W. Adorno, *Minima Moralia. Reflexionen aus dem beschädigten Leben* (Frankfurt/Main: Suhrkamp, 1951), 78.

12   Olin Downes, 'Chamber Program Heard at Library', *The New York Times*, 22 May 1941, 24.

Musical Times ridiculed the migrants' contributions as implicitly pretentious, incompetent and unintelligible:

> One session of the Congress was devoted to 'Problematic Tendencies (what a phrase!) in Contemporary Music.' Here were expounded the Twelve-Tone System; Hindemith's New Theory; the Micro-Tonal System (Dr Sandberg, the expounder, played a harmonium whose keyboard must have measured four or five feet, and whose compass was precisely a fourth!); Non-Thematic Composition (Mr Alois Haba's pet – its intention, so we were told, is to reflect the spirit of the new brotherhood of mankind), and so on. [Only] Mr. Seiber [...] understood his subject thoroughly and was able to express himself intelligibly and unpretentiously.[13]

Press coverage of the ISCM festival that followed the 'Music and Life' conference, in June 1938, was likewise dismissive of the musical avant-garde. As the *Guardian* put it:

> One after another [...] composers exhibited poverty of thought, clumsiness of technique, deformity of style, and everything else that we commonly typify as amateurish. [...] The music was intelligible to the point of superficiality, and its prevailing mark was that very concealment of ordinariness under the cloak of vehemence of which we have in the past acquitted the leaders of the movement.[14]

The Times went one further and described progressive music as essentially alien and foreign, with London portrayed as 'the ancient City which they have come from all quarters of Europe to conquer with their modernity.'[15] Vaughan Williams responded to the ISCM festival by discrediting the avant-garde as 'this wrong-note stuff', urging immigrant musicians to refrain from constructing a 'little Europe' in Britain and to abandon the avant-garde styles they brought with them from the continent if they wished to integrate into British musical life.[16]

---

13   Alan Frank, 'Music and Life, 1938', *The Musical Times*, 79 (1938), 461.
14   William McNaught, 'Modern Music: Festival at Queen's Hall', *The Manchester Guardian*, 18 June 1938, 19.
15   'Modern Music: Festival at Queen's Hall', *The Times*, 18 June 1938, 12.
16   Ralph Vaughan Williams, 'Nationalism and Internationalism', *National Music and Other Essays* (Oxford and New York: Oxford University Press, 1987), 154–59.

4   Communist Influences

In the case of the Free German League of Culture, migrant nostalgia and British antimodernism were not the only reasons for the relative silence of avant-garde music. Even though the League was first established by a number of migrants with very different political views and backgrounds, united only by their fate of being exiled, it always had a strong Communist core. It is difficult to assess with any certainty whether the League was, in effect, an offshoot of the Communist Internationale and supported directly or indirectly by Stalin. Of the eight founding members (Fred Uhlman, Hans Flesch, Hans Schellenberger, Fritz Gottfurcht, Gerhard Hinze, Oskar Kokoschka, Ernst Hermann Meyer and Berthold Viertel), only three (Hinze, Meyer and Schellenberger) had Communist credentials. However, it is clear that the League became increasingly more Communist throughout its existence. Soon after the League's foundation, those with Communist sympathies found themselves in the difficult situation that the government that had driven them out of their country had suddenly become an ally of Stalin's Soviet Union. Before this context of the Hitler–Stalin pact of June 1939, it made sense to keep one's Communism to oneself. Jürgen Kuczynski, for example, recalled thirty-five years later that the League was set up at the instigation of the Communist party and that he had received the first membership card but that, for conspiratorial reasons, it bore not the membership number 1 but 251.[17] Recruited for the GRU (Soviet military intelligence), Kuczynski provided intelligence for the Soviet Union throughout the Second World War.[18]

This attitude of covert Communism changed in June 1941 with Nazi Germany's attack on Soviet Russia. With Stalin and Hitler now enemies, the defence of the Soviet Union became a prominent campaigning issue. Language courses supported by the League were now reduced to Russian tuition. More significantly, the makeup of those in powerful positions in the League changed. Already in 1939, theatre critic and vice chairman Alfred Kerr had left the League in protest of the small but powerful Communist group that, in his opinion, made all the crucial decisions.[19] By 1941, the Austrian-Jewish author and founding member Hans Flesch was edged out as chairman and replaced by Communist Manfred Uhlman. In the same year, an article appeared in the *Daily Herald* alleging that

---

17   See Brinson and Dove, *Politics by Other Means*, 13.
18   See Jefferson Adams, 'Kuczynksi, Jürgen (1904–1997)', in Jefferson Adams, *Historical Dictionary of German Intelligence* (Lanham, Md.: Scarecrow Press, 2009), 250–1. See also Charmian Brinson and Richard Dove, *A Matter of Intelligence: MI5 and the Surveillance of Anti-Nazi Refugees, 1933–50* (Manchester: Manchester University Press, 2014).
19   See Brinson and Dove, *Politics by Other Means*, 26–7.

Communists controlled the League. It can be traced back to Social Democrat refugee Victor Schiff.[20]

In the music section, which was co-founded by the apolitical Ludwig Brav and Ernst Hermann Meyer, the influence of Communist members was strong from the beginning. Meyer, a pupil of Hanns Eisler, friend of Alan Bush, and a staunch Communist, soon took control and relegated Brav to a passive member. Throughout its existence, Meyer played a crucial role as Head of the Music Section and was a central figure in the organisation of the League as a whole, serving as Vice-Chairman, Chairman and Executive Member. After the war, Meyer was to exert a significant influence upon the musical life of the GDR.

As I have mentioned, the Communist members of the League often acted covertly and conspiratorially, especially during the early war years. Open proclamations of Communism are extremely rare, and indeed words such as Communism or Socialism are hardly ever mentioned in the League's publications. This is where a look at the music section is instructive. In 1940, Meyer established a women's choir, which soon grew to become a mixed choir. And even though the opening concert included works of Schumann, Brahms and Verdi, the choir soon took on an increasingly political function, singing at worker's events and supporting the League's cabaret performances. In an explanatory article, Meyer again avoids words such as Communism or Socialism directly, but the nods to Communist rhetoric are nonetheless apparent, for example in the reference to the labour movement:

> The use of music in the battle for freedom is as old as the battle itself. Ever since mankind began to fight for human rights, human progress and happiness, against tyrants, homebred and foreign, people were roused by singing. The singing of the songs of liberty has always assisted those who have been in this struggle. [...] Singing, and again singing has played its part in the growth of the great Labour movements of this century and the one before. It plays its part now, in the struggle of the free countries against the dark forces of destruction.[21]

In addition to these musical activities, Meyer's writings on music, published in the biggest of the League's newspapers, *Freie Deutsche Kultur*, reveal unequivocally the politico-aesthetic policy of the League. One of the first articles Meyer published was an appraisal of Hanns Eisler, who, besides Meyer himself,

---

20   Ibid., 158–62.
21   Ernst Hermann Meyer, 'The Call to Freedom', *Freie Deutsche Kultur*, October 1941, 6.

was the only living composer who received a signature concert in the League's history. Writing in 1941, Meyer claims:

> Among the musicians of our time, Hanns Eisler is undoubtedly the most distinctive and boldest personality. [...] Arnold Schoenberg, the main exponent of the 'ultra-modern' school of the 1920s, was his teacher. [...] It is fascinating to see how Eisler tore himself away from this atmosphere of unproductive cynicism and tired scepticism. [...] It was the socialist idea, the notion of the way out as a political fighter, which he joined passionately.[22]

This set the tone for many of Meyer's future comments on contemporary music. Strikingly, while attacking a fellow migrant composer, Arnold Schoenberg, Meyer failed to write articles against Nazi sympathisers like Hans Pfitzner or Richard Strauss, for example. Instead, his main targets were the avant-gardes represented by other migrants. His favourite target throughout remained Schoenberg.

At the same time, Meyer aimed to construct the German musical canon, particularly Bach, Mozart and Beethoven, as predecessors of the Communist cause. In March 1941, he wrote:

> The spirit that is alive in all of Bach's works was the real novelty in his time: It is an independence, a 'new humanity', that bursts out here in a fundamental way for the first time in Germany. [...] Only the doctrines of the French Revolution leveraged this humanist individuality.[23]

And in 1944:

> Throughout their lives, Mozart and Beethoven were passionate believers in the ideas that formed the basis for the French Revolution. [...] The hallmark of the 1920s was the infinite number schools, trends, and '-isms'. There was a lot of dogmatism, abstraction, dilettantism, and irresponsible experiments. And yet out of this confusion a few tendencies stand out that aimed to re-unite the composer and the people, to connect a new joy of life, clarity and intelligibility with a modern compositional idiom. Yet again, the close observer will notice that these tendencies, which are connected with the names of Hindemith, Eisler and Weill [...] who are

---

22 Meyer, 'Hanns Eisler', *Freie Deutsche Kultur*, February 1941, 2–3.
23 Meyer, 'Johann Sebastian Bach', *Freie Deutsche Kultur*, March 1941, 6.

linked more or less consciously with the socially progressive movement of the time.²⁴

Meyer's song 'Berolina', set to a text by Rolf Anders and written for the cabaret *In den Sternen stehts geschrieben / What the stars foretell*, illustrates that Meyer's preferred idiom was that of agitprop.²⁵ In a review of a concert with Meyer's music at the League, reviewer 'S.Z.' wrote:

> The composer of the people's movement and of the collective society will utilize all the skills and techniques he has inherited from the past to write not luxurious music for the few, but music which shall be for and about the many. His is the task of breaking down the age-old division between learned or art music on the one hand and folk or popular music on the other. [...] One of the most progressive composers in this sense is Ernst H. Meyer [...] one of the most versatile and gifted composers among the German émigrés. [...] Ernst Meyer thanked the enthusiastic audience in his usual modest manner and spoke of his aim to write for the people, and 'not sterile academicism or irresponsible experiment' as Alan Bush put it.²⁶

5 Music between Nationalism and Antisemitism

While the Nazi attack on Soviet Russia in 1941 had meant that the Communists among the migrants could now voice their support for Stalin more openly and could call on the Western allies to do the same, the year 1943 showed a further shift. After the Red Army won the battle of Stalingrad, many Communists – and, indeed, many migrants of whichever political conviction – became more optimistic that Hitler would lose the war. On the part of the Communists among the migrants, voices now became increasingly triumphalist. Many refugees felt the time had come to discuss what was to happen after Hitler's eventual defeat. As far as the League was concerned, any Germany after Hitler could only be Socialist. And music was to play a major part in this. As Meyer put it in October 1944:

---

24 Meyer, 'Der Leidensweg der deutschen Musik' [The Ordeal of German Music], *Freie Deutsche Kultur*, October 1944, 4f.
25 The song is in the Akademie der Künste Berlin, Archiv Darstellende Kunst: Exil-Sammlung, Rep. 101/Exil Großbritannien, III.1.–III.9. Kabarettrevuen des FDKB.
26 S.Z., 'E.H. Meyer-Konzert', *Freie Deutsche Kultur*, May/June 1944, 11.

a rebirth of German music is only possible after the destruction of the Fascist poison by the German people. [...] A resurrection of Germany's musical greatness can only be imagined in a true democracy. [...] There is no progress in music without the inspiring factor of progressive ideas in the social realm. [...] But the German artist (and the *entire* German people with him) have to earn this new democratic tolerant attitude; this will only be possible through systematic and uncompromising self-discipline and self-education. ... In musical production itself we need realism, not escapism to cloud-cuckoo-land; simplicity and truth, no more false sentimentality; clear, logical development of thought, not opportunism and chaos – and no more of the empty, meaningless insistence on method and this abstract, dogmatic construction, that has been so typical for German intellectuals and artists for the last 100 years.[27]

Apart from the customary attack on the interwar avant-garde and the assertion, here voiced for the first time, that realism was to be the approach of choice, Meyer's statement introduces a new aspect to the discourse: that of nationalism. Rather than outsiders, it was the German people who were to re-educate themselves. Moreover, the title of Meyer's article, 'The Ordeal of German Music', presented Germans not as aggressors, but as victims, including those that had not migrated – not as collaborators of Hitler, but as a suppressed people.

Meyer's article responded to an earlier article published by Johannes Becher in 1943 in Moscow. Becher had fled Nazi Germany in 1935 to the Soviet Union, where he became editor-in-chief of the German migrant magazine there and a member of the Central Committee of the Communist Party. Following the battle of Stalingrad, Becher had written the so-called German lesson (or doctrine), in which he aimed to set out his plan for a new Germany. Even more so than Meyer's article, Becher's was marked by outspoken nationalism. According to Becher, Germany's current situation had been caused by its failure to unite as a nation earlier than it had. If anything, Germans had not been nationalist enough. This failure, he felt, had been caused by the aristocracy, the bourgeoisie, and foreign influences. Becher describes the Third Reich and the war as an 'incomparable self-sacrifice and a holy passion of the whole German people.' The only way to get out of this mess, Becher argued, was for the German workers – and them alone – to rise and achieve Germany's national utopia.[28]

---

27   Meyer, 'Der Leidensweg der deutschen Musik'.
28   Johannes R. Becher, *Deutsche Lehre*, in *Volk und Vaterland. Schriften zur deutschen Erneuerung*, Vol. 1 (1945) (Paris: CALPO). The League published its own edition in 1943.

Such attitudes were met with little enthusiasm among parts of the migrant community. Becher's article was widely advertised by the Free German League of Culture in Britain, including directly below Meyer's article on 'The Ordeal of German Music'. The Jewish members of the League were particularly offended, not only because they felt that those responsible for the Third Reich and its atrocities should be punished after the war, an issue Becher avoided, but also because the factor of antisemitism was omitted by Becher and Meyer. More to the point, many Jewish members of the League felt that they were increasingly excluded from the debate and considered Jewish instead of German. In late 1943, Hans Flesch, one of the League's founding members, left the League with some forty other Jewish members in protest. As Johann Fladung remembered in 1975, several members disagreed with Becher's 'Deutsche Lehre' and left the League,

> which led to a number of League members, amongst them Rehfisch, Wolff, Unger, to found a far smaller cultural circle of about forty people, Club 43. [...] The members of Club 43 were all Jews.[29]

The particular arguments were not carried out publicly, and written evidence is scarce. Again, music can help shed some light. Shortly after the German capitulation, in May 1945, Johanna Metzger and Paul Lichtenstern organised a concert of Jewish folk songs at the Manchester branch of the League, the first and only one of its kind. The programme notes make for an almost apologetic reading, in which Metzger and Lichtenstein seem to feel the need to defend why Jewish music should be heard in the first place:

> Jewish songs have much in common with folk songs from other nations, especially with regard to a number of themes which appear, in more or less similar form, in the folklore of all countries. But their peculiar aspect is the preponderance of religious, philosophical, sometimes even mystical elements, and the fact that again and again we hear of longing for deliverance and freedom – nothing to wonder at considering the Jewish history. [...] There was a time when the Jewish folk song seemed to fall into oblivion. But the cruel present, with the sufferings of Jews and all mankind, has awakened it again. *However one may, as a Jew or Gentile, think of Jewish matters* – everybody can enjoy, and find interest in, those

---

29   This quote is taken from a long 'Protokoll über ein Gespräch mit Dr Johann Fladung am 16.4.75 in Gundernhausen', written by Ulla Hahn and held in the Bundesarchiv Berlin, Stiftung Archiv der Parteien und Massenorganisationen der DDR, shelfmark SAPMO ZPA DY/27/1505. The quote is on page 6.

folk songs. For they are genuine treasures of culture, like all other folk songs. – If we succeed to create, with these concerts, pleasure, interest, and meditation, we, as Jewish artists, will be happy!³⁰

Following the end of the war, the League decided to dissolve so that its Communist members could return to Germany. Again, the Jewish members felt differently. As Hans Fladung put it:

> The largest part of the Jewish émigrés in England did not return to Germany after the German liberation. Of the non-Jewish German émigrés, on the other hand, no more than 10% did not return to Germany [...] Most comrades went straight to the Soviet sector.³¹

It seems that the leadership of the League did not feel that there was much point in persuading them otherwise, and that Germany was best reconstructed without them. In early 1946, the so-called Council for German Democracy in the UK held a conference in London on the reconstruction of Germany after Nazism. Shortly afterwards, in early February, the League sent a long report to Johannes R. Becher, who had just been appointed President of the Kulturbund in the Soviet Zone and was eventually to serve as minister of culture of the GDR. The report makes for antisemitic reading:

> The latent and open risks of fascism and reactionism – especially in the western zones – and the necessity of full support of the progressive forces in Germany are often not recognized. We find [...] a lot of disbelief and reservations regarding the successes of democratic reconstruction in the Soviet Zone. [...] We had hoped to get some support from cultural circles in France and America. Unfortunately we have failed. [...] There are in America influential and powerful circles that are dominated by Jewish-Zionist Americans and the Jewish émigrés. [...] These demand far too draconian actions by the allies. [...] The Jews are in a state of crass ideological confusion.³²

---

30 Johanna Metzger, Paul Lichtenstern Concert of Jewish folk songs, programme notes, Manchester, 5.-6.5.45, held in Bundesarchiv Berlin, Stiftung Archiv der Parteien und Massenorganisationen der DDR, shelfmark SAPMO ZPA NY4266/4.
31 See 'Protokoll über ein Gespräch mit Dr Johann Fladung am 16.4.75 in Gundernhausen', 6.
32 The seven-page report was posted on 2 February 1946. It is held in the Bundesarchiv Berlin under the archive number DY/27/1501. Hans Fladung, Heinz Willmann and other League members sent frequent letters reporting to Becher, often about specific individuals, during this time.

Becher's reply was brief: 'It is certainly unfortunate if friends in America think they must make clever suggestions.'[33]

6 The East German Heritage

Intellectual discussions in the GDR mirror such antisemitic attitudes with surprising accuracy. The somewhat dubious opinion prevailed throughout the existence of the GDR that Jewish migrants should not be categorised as exiles, because they had not been politically but ethnically persecuted. The more highly charged term 'exile' remained reserved to the Communist activists among the migrants. For example, the prestigious seven-volume East German encyclopaedia, *Kunst und Literatur im antifaschistischen Exil* (Art and Literature in Antifascist Exile), published between 1979 and 1981, excluded most Jewish refugees. Published and sanctioned by the state-run Academy of the Sciences and the Arts in East Germany, the encyclopaedia can be seen as the official party line. As the editors state on the first page of the first volume:

> We do not conceive the various centres of exile as places of escape but as meeting points in the fight against fascism. [...] First and foremost, we want to portray lives, fight, desperation, and sighs of relief of those German artists and writers that pursued the liberation of their fatherland from the fascist yoke in their exile, those who persisted with their fight, those who perished and those who were victorious.[34]

Writing on the League in 1977, East German scholar Ulla Hahn took a similar approach, arguing for a focus in exile studies on those she described as political exiles:

> the proportion of racially persecuted émigrés was 90%; no more than 2% were political refugees. [...] England was therefore sociologically a centre of bourgeois emigration – of Jewish mass emigration, to be

---

33   Becher replied on 4 May 1946. The reply is in the Bundesarchiv Berlin, Stiftung Archiv der Parteien und Massenorganisationen der DDR, shelfmark SAPMO ZPA DY/27/1501.

34   Mittenzwei, Werner, *et al.* (eds.), *Kunst und Literatur im antifaschistischen Exil 1933–1945*, 7 vols. (Leipzig: Reclam, 1979–81). For an overview of the entanglement of German exile studies and politics, see my article '"The Splinter in your Eye": Uncomfortable Legacies and German Exile Studies,' in Erik Levi and Florian Scheding (eds.), *Music and Displacement: Diasporas, Mobilities and Dislocations in Europe and Beyond*, Europea: Ethnomusicologies and Modernities, Vol. 10 (2010) (Lanham, Md.: Scarecrow Press), 119–34.

precise. [...] Even so, those persecuted for political reasons were [...] the crucial factor for the achievements of German emigration not only in the political, but also in the social and cultural sense. The Communists in Britain therefore had to work in a conspiratorial way, which they preferred anyway. [...] There were two main aspects in all programs: the preservation of the bourgeois humanist heritage and the fighting spirit of the antifascist artists.[35]

Even though they constituted the majority among the migrants, the Jews, then, were not only all bourgeois, but also considered politically, socially, and culturally useless.

It seems ironic in this context that artists such as Hanns Eisler and even Ernst Herman Meyer were Jewish. And yet, their Jewishness is never mentioned in official GDR literature. Instead, they are described as Communist freedom fighters who had to escape due to their political beliefs alone. The fact that many migrants had escaped because their lives were threatened was not considered a sufficient reason to include a record of their biographies. Only those among the persecuted who had followed a calling to active resistance and had joined the international underground fight were deemed worthy of inclusion in the documentation of 'antifascist exile,' thus phrased in the encyclopaedia's title. Only Communists could be antifascist. This focus on political activists led to an exclusion of the social-democratic, conservative, and, indeed, Jewish victims of persecution. In effect, this avoidance of the issue of antisemitism is therefore precisely tantamount to antisemitism. The precise reasons behind this Eastern denial of the centrality of antisemitism in the Nazi state and ideology are surely manifold and may have been partly born out of the ideological aim of Socialist ideology to exclude the role of religious beliefs or institutions.

---

35   Ulla Hahn, 'Der Freie Deutsche Kulturbund in Großbritannien. Eine Skizze seiner Geschichte', in Lutz Winckler (ed.), *Antifaschistische Literatur: Programme, Autoren, Werke*, Vol. 2 (1977) (Kronberg/Taunus: Scriptor), 133f. Similar attitudes permeate other publications by GDR scholars about the League. See Ursula Adam, *Zur Geschichte des Freien Deutschen Kulturbundes in Großbritannien (Ende 1938–Mai 1945)*, PhD thesis (Akademie der Wissenschaften der DDR, Berlin, 1983); Adam, 'Das Echo auf die Gründung des Kulturbundes zur demokratischen Erneuerung Deutschlands in Großbritannien und dessen geschichtliche Voraussetzungen', in *Weimarer Beiträge*, Vol. 5 (1985), 743–54; Adam, '"Antinazi Germans help Russia". Freier Deutsche Kulturbund und Solidarität mit der UdSSR in Großbritannien (1941–1943)', in: *Militärgeschichte*, Vol. 6 (1985), 499–505; and Birgit Leske and Marion Reinisch, 'Exil in Großbritannien', in Autorenkollektiv der Akademie der Wissenschaften der DDR/Zentralinstitut für Literaturgeschichte und der Akademie der Künste der DDR, *Kunst und Literatur im antifaschistischen Exil 1933–1945. Band 5: Exil in der Tschechoslowakei, in Großbritannien, Skandinavien und Palästina* (Leipzig: Reclam, 1980 and 1987), 157–293.

But my intention here is not so much to speculate on the reasons as to reveal a continuous strand from the Free German League of Culture right through to the last decade of the GDR's existence. Rather than solely a dutiful response to Stalin's antisemitic purges of the postwar years, a strand of antisemitism therefore predates Stalin's postwar actions, and stood at the core of GDR cultural policies even before its foundation.

In 1988, East German scholars Ursula Adam and Ulla Hahn successfully lobbied the GDR authorities to stage an exhibition about the Free German League of Culture, on the occasion of the fiftieth anniversary of its foundation. As their concept reveals, attitudes had changed little, and non-Communists – including Jewish refugees – were now even described as antifascist.

> The real antifascists among the émigrés were fully aware that the Communist Party's political concept for the fight against fascism could essentially only be fought with the ideological means of cultural work under the circumstances of the host country. [...] Leading members of the organization were above all Communists. [...] The FGLC forms part of the humanist and antifascist democratic traditions of the history of the GDR; it forms part of the historical conditions of its cultural fabric.[36]

One year after the exhibition, the GDR ceased to exist.

7 Conclusion

The history of the League has scarcely been researched. The papers of the League were transferred to East Berlin soon after the war, effectively putting them out of reach for Western researchers. But even in former East German scholarship, only very little was ever written on the League. What few writings there are, are dominated by an aim to present the League through the socialist lens as a cell of Communist freedom fighters preparing in exile the socialist postwar society. None of them place particular emphasis on the musical activities of the League. In September 2010, over seventy years after its foundation, Charmian Brinson and Richard Dove published the first book-length study on the League, which provides a welcome insight into the League's history and is based on an extensive wealth of archival material. But they are more

---

36 Ursula Adam, 'Konzeption zur Ausstellung "Freier Deutscher Kulturbund in Großbritannien 1938/39–1946"', 13.4.88, Bundesarchiv Berlin, Stiftung Archiv der Parteien und Massenorganisationen der DDR, shelfmark SAPMO ZPA DY27/3862.

focused on the non-musical activities of the League. As I have mentioned, the League's Communist core acted mostly covertly and avoided making explicit any links that may have existed to the Internationale or the Communist Party in the Soviet Union, even though it seems likely that these links existed. An investigation of the League's musical policy is instructive and revealing against this background. The musical activities and, maybe even more so, the musical silences that form part of the League's history can tell us a great deal about underlying ideologies and ideological struggles. An aesthetic programme of real socialism marks the activities of the League's Music Section and of its Head, Ernst Herman Meyer. In so doing, the musical activities of the League pre-empt the musical policy that became crucial for the fledgling GDR. In other areas, too, did the League discursively foreshadow debates. For example, the *Historikerstreit* ('historians' quarrel') of 1990s Germany, during which German intellectuals argued about whether the Third Reich was solitarily evil or comparable to other terror regimes, and also whether the German people could in fact be seen as victims of the war, mirrors debates of the late years of the Second World War among the German migrant community.[37] They cut to the heart of ideological clashes concerning not only aesthetic beliefs, but nationalism and race, too. This suggests that the insights that can be gained from an investigation into the history of the Free German League of Culture far exceed the particular historical narratives or circumstances of the few years during which the League actually existed.

---

37 Led by left-wing and right-wing intellectuals between 1986 and 1989, the 'quarrel' centered on the questions as to whether the Holocaust should be regarded as a uniquely evil event in history or whether it ought to be compared to other crimes, particularly those of Stalin's Soviet Russia, other genocides, such as the Khmer Rouge genocide in Cambodia, or even the suffering of those Germans displaced as a result of the Second World War. Initially played out between the philosophers Ernst Nolte and Jürgen Habermas in the national West German press, the debate soon attracted widespread interest and was characterized by a highly aggressive tone and frequent personal attacks on either side. The dispute is summarised and documented in Rudolf Augstein (ed.), *'Historikerstreit': Die Dokumentation der Kontroverse um die Einzigartigkeit der nationalsozialistischen Judenvernichtung* (Munich: Piper, 1987).

6
'Almost as Impressive as Its Legacy in the Visual Arts': Ben Uri Art Society and Music in Exile, 1931–60

Rachel Dickson

Abstract

Although there has been much research regarding Ben Uri's important role as exhibition platform and cultural nexus for émigré artists fleeing National Socialism, to date little attention has focused on its lesser-known contribution, supporting émigré musicians, singers and composers. This aspect of its history was first revealed in 2015, when Ben Uri presented the exhibition 'Arts in Harmony: An Art Gallery's Musical Heritage' at the Royal College of Music's Museum, inspired by rediscoveries from its archives, together with the RCM's research and performance project 'Singing a Song in a Foreign Land'. Alongside its programme of open exhibitions, which welcomed émigré participation from 1934 onwards, Ben Uri organised regular recitals and formed its own orchestra, chamber orchestra, choir and opera appreciation circle – unique even today within the context of an art gallery. Drawing primarily on archives from Ben Uri, the *Jewish Chronicle* and the Association of Jewish Refugees (AJR), this chapter explores the émigré contribution to this musical output, both secular and religious, highlighting both well-known and little-known names, including Engel Lund, Paul Hamburger, Franz Reizenstein, Paul Lichtenstern, Jenny Sonnenberg, Marianne Mislap-Kapper, Norbert Brainin, Brigitte Loeser and Carola Grindea. Finally, the chapter acknowledges Ben Uri's unusual role in bringing both émigré art and music together.

1 Emigré Musicians at Ben Uri to the End of the Second World War

When[1] the Ben Uri Art Society was founded in London's Whitechapel, the city's de facto Jewish ghetto, in July 1915, in the midst of war,[2] it was to act as a support mechanism for newly arrived *Ostjuden* artists and craftsmen – Yiddish

---

1 Quotation in title is from Norbert Meyn https://www.meer.com/en/14945-arts-in-harmony [accessed: 27 February 2020].
2 David Mazower, 'Lazar Berson and the origins of the Ben Uri Art Society', in Gillian Rathbone (ed.), *The Ben Uri Story from Art Society to Museum* (London: Ben Uri Gallery, The London Jewish Museum of Art, 2001), 37–58.

speaking, orthodox immigrants from eastern Europe, who were unable to access the cultural bastions of assimilated Anglo-Jewry. The society's original, and ambitious, aims, as stated in its first constitution, included the creation of a gallery for Jewish art, the celebration of broad Jewish artistic endeavour, and the organisation of art lectures and tours to various museums and exhibitions.[3] Ben Uri's first decade, therefore, saw much varied activity prior to the acquisition and display of any actual artworks.[4] A rich calendar of social and fundraising initiatives included dances, talks, a garden party and, from the outset, art and music were, on occasion, presented together. A programme printed in Yiddish from 11 March 1916 records a soirée and ball held at Crown Hall, 40 Redmans Road, E1, with a festive speech by founder and Russian émigré Lazar Berson and 'Mr Guzman singing, violin, piano and cello solos, poetry and declamations' along with 'Living pictures' of works by 'Hirschenberg, Lilien and Pilichowski'.[5]

Two decades later, the society once again found itself cast in the role of exhibition platform and cultural nexus for the second wave of newly arrived, mainly German-speaking émigrés, now fleeing Nazi persecution. Simultaneously, its geographical focus shifted from the East End towards central, and beyond, to north-west London, with its lingua franca now English rather than Yiddish, as the first generation of émigrés became more prosperous and integrated. At this point, music seems to have been rather an ad hoc addition to the programming of the Ben Uri Art and Literary Society, but as the second wave of émigré participation grew via its engagement with the visual arts, so did the Society's musical profile. Not surprisingly, Yiddish and Jewish folksongs were a material of transition, engaged with by both the earlier *Ostjuden* émigrés and by later central Europeans.

On 17 May 1931, world-renowned Danish-born soprano Engel Lund (1900–1996) gave a recital at the progressive Whitechapel Art Gallery[6] under the auspices of the Ben Uri Jewish Art & Literary Society, performing folk songs in Yiddish and Hebrew. The eye-catching flyer, illustrated with her portrait photograph, announced: 'Great Singer to give concert for Ben Uri Society in the heart of Jewry.'[7] Although Lund was non-Jewish, she remained committed

---

3 Translation from original Yiddish in Ben Uri Archives.
4 Ben Uri's first exhibition of its permanent collection opened on 17 May 1925 at 68 Great Russell Street, WC1. See *Programme for the official opening of gallery and club at Great Russell Street*, Ben Uri Archives, Box 11.
5 Illustrated flyer, Ben Uri Archives, Box 26.
6 Opened in 1901 by Canon Samuel and Henrietta Barnett, the Whitechapel Art Gallery was designed to bring art to the East End masses.
7 Ben Uri Archives, Box 25.

to a repertoire of Jewish and Yiddish songs and refused to perform in Nazi Germany once such material was banned. Lund became celebrated for her performances of the *Book of Folk Songs*, a collection of forty-nine pieces from fourteen countries, developed in the interwar years, each sung in its native language (first published in English by Oxford University Press in 1936), accompanied by Austrian émigré composer and pianist Ferdinand Rauter (1902–1987), whom Lund had met in 1929, several years before his immigration in the mid-1930s to England.[8]

With the outbreak of war, Lund chose to remain in England and, together with Rauter, they became frequent performers at the National Gallery's lunchtime concerts organised and directed by Myra Hess. Performances for various charities also brought Lund into contact with Professor Gilbert Murray (1866–1957), the eminent classical scholar, public intellectual and humanist, who helped raise aid for refugees from Nazism and other wartime causes.[9]

Following the mass internment of enemy aliens in Britain from late spring 1940,[10] Rauter was interned for a few months on the Isle of Man with fellow Austrians, Norbert Brainin (1923–2005) and Peter Schidlof (1922–1987), whom he encouraged to form what would become the Amadeus Quartet after their release. Post-internment Rauter himself became a key participant in developing Austrian music in exile, co-founding the Refugee Musicians Committee in 1941, the Austrian Musicians Group (which he chaired) in 1942, to provide practical help for refugee musicians (affiliated to the umbrella organisation Free Austrian Movement (FAM), though without its political leanings), and the Anglo-Austrian Music Society.[11]

In September 1933, Ben Uri's secretary, Marcus Lipton, published a strongly worded statement in the *Jewish Chronicle*, the mouthpiece of Anglo-Jewry, entitled 'Jewish Artists will be lost to Jewry without Jewish Support',[12] reminding the community to support its own. Although primarily directed at visual artists, this admonishment became altogether more urgent and broader in its implication as the situation deteriorated in Europe, and it became increasingly

---

8   Marietta Bearman, Charmian Brinson, Richard Dove, Anthony Grenville, Jennifer Taylor (eds.), *Out of Austria: The Austrian Centre in London in World War II* (London: Tauris Academic Studies, 2008), 154–57. Also, see Nimbus Records N15813/14, 2008 and *Engel Lund Book of Folk-Songs* (Nimbus Music Publishing NMP1009, 2014).

9   Janus Paluda, *Obituary: Engel Lund*, https://www.independent.co.uk/news/people/obituary-engel-lund-1327474.html [accessed: 26.02.2020].

10 David Cesarani and Tony Kushner (eds.), *The Internment of Aliens in Twentieth Century Britain* (London: Frank Cass, 1993).

11 Bearman et al., 154–57.

12 *Jewish Chronicle*, 29 September 1933, 13.

apparent that the Society's duty was to assist the growing number of émigrés, across a range of cultural endeavours. Eighteen months later, Mrs Israel Sieff, wife of the Society's president, stated: 'The important principle – and it was in this direction that the Ben Uri was making its cultural contribution – was the free and unfettered expression of individual creative forces. This kind of self-expression was only possible in an atmosphere of liberty.'[13] Henceforth, the Society's 'Annual Exhibitions of Works by Jewish Artists' began to be enriched by émigré participation, and a programme of music – both classic and contemporary, religious and secular, Jewish and Gentile – began to develop. 'The Nazi Philosophy', her husband further noted, 'was not merely an attack on Jews as Jews but on Jewish culture. It was therefore of the utmost importance [...] to focus attention on Jewish achievement in the modern world, as illustrative of the eternal truths and values.'[14]

Ben Uri, as with many commercial galleries, museums and sites of entertainment, was closed with the outbreak of war (the Society had occupied a succession of temporary London homes in both the East End and West End until this point).[15] However, the efforts of Cyril Ross, the Society's treasurer and owner of the world's largest furrier, Swears and Wells, not only facilitated the safe wartime storage of the art collection in the store's central London vaults, but also secured rent-free premises in a Georgian townhouse in Portman Street, near Marble Arch, which Ben Uri had occupied by January 1944, while many other galleries and museums remained closed. Here, the Society was simultaneously able to show selected works from its permanent collection (which now numbered some 150 pieces) alongside temporary loan exhibitions and – most relevant to this chapter and volume – to have sufficient space for a piano, enabling a variety of musicians and singers to perform against a changing backdrop of artworks, and to host a lecture programme that embraced various musical topics.

Just before the unveiling of the new premises (with its high-profile re-opening exhibition), late 1943 saw the appointment of Ben Uri's first salaried secretary/curator, former internee, Berlin-born émigré Fritz Solomonski (1899–1980, later Rabbi Frederick Solomon).[16] Both a qualified art historian with a PhD from Berlin under Adolph Goldschmidt and a painter of biblical themes who had been a pupil of the Expressionists Eugen Spiro and Willy

---

13   *Jewish Chronicle*, 24 May 1935, 21.
14   *Jewish Chronicle*, 26 June 1936, 38.
15   See Rachel Dickson, 'Jewish Artists will be lost to Jewry without Jewish Support: The Ben Uri Art Society and émigré artists 1933–51', in Burcu Dogramaci and Karin Wimmer (eds.), *Netzwerke des Exils: Künstlerische Verflechtungen, Austausch und Patronage nach 1933* (Berlin: Gebruder Mann Verlag, 2011), 313–332.
16   'Guide to the Rabbi Frederick Solomon Papers, 1927–1977', https://www.library.unh.edu/find/archives/collections/rabbi-frederick-solomon-papers-1927-1977 [accessed: 27.02.2020].

Jaeckel, and championed in exile by Samuel Courtauld, Solomonski was also musically-inclined. German émigré, Klaus Hinrichsen (1912–2004), chronicler of art in internment,[17] waspishly noted of their shared time in Hutchinson camp on the Isle of Man, that Solomonski 'was a cantor [...] a singer in a synagogue, beautiful voice, and indeed I think he was a much better singer than artist. But he was one of those people who can do almost anything'.[18] Hinrichsen also recalled in his oral testimony for *Refugee Voices* that Solomonski 'was unhappy with Ben Uri, because they always wanted him to arrange *kleine Tänzle*, 'little dances' – little social events',[19] a task clearly not relished by the academically-trained and religiously-inclined German. Nevertheless, although Solomonski left Ben Uri around 1945 in unclear circumstances, replaced by Sadie Buchler as secretary (c.1946–48), he may have participated in fostering musical activity.

2 Musical Performance in the Postwar Period, 1940-50s

Certainly, the immediate postwar period saw significant émigré participation in Ben Uri's contemporary 'open' exhibitions and a rapid increase in the number of refugees who sang, played or composed for its audiences, formed of Society paid-up members and their guests. Archive materials indicate that the musical programme began in earnest in late 1946, with five recitals taking place between October and December. The previous April, a plaintive advert in the *Jewish Chronicle* had requested:

> Piano Wanted for Chamber Concerts first Sunday evening of every month. [...] This is part of a scheme to make the gallery a centre where those interested in the artistic life of the community can foregather. Unhappily we have no piano, without which it is impossible to arrange concerts.[20]

Four years later, a similar plea was repeated by Sadie Buchler: 'Grand Piano needed for Ben Uri Art Gallery Chamber Concerts', with the reassuring qualifier that 'it will not be overused and will be frequently tuned.'[21]

---

17   Klaus Hinrichsen, 'Visual Art Behind the Wire', in Cesarani and Kushner (eds.), *The Internment of Aliens in Twentieth Century Britain* (London: Frank Cass, 1993), 182–209.
18   Undated typescript of oral testimony between Klaus Hinrichsen and 'MAB', Reel 7, Hinrichsen Family, London.
19   Typescript transcript of an interview for AJR Refugee Voices (The Testimony Archive of the Association of Jewish Refugees) with Klaus Hinrichsen (RV43). Interview conducted on 20 November 2003 in Highgate, London by Anthony Grenville.
20   *Jewish Chronicle*, 19 April 1946, 13.
21   *Jewish Chronicle*, 14 April 1950, 19.

Unfortunately, however, scant archival material remains to illuminate any discussions behind this shift in programming. Committee minutes mainly record formal outcomes – the events themselves – and the dull but necessary bureaucracy, along with related expenditures, such as recital and venue fees and instrument hire,[22] but not the steps taken to secure the services of any given performer. There is little personal correspondence to suggest how these individual émigrés were involved with Ben Uri; in contrast to the organisation of exhibitions and artwork acquisitions, there is virtually no paper trail, although personal contacts clearly played a key role, as is evidenced by the networks linking many of the émigré performers with the artists who gathered under Ben Uri's wing, as indicated throughout this chapter.

Furthermore, although wider institutional links may have been limited, many performers at Ben Uri were also connected with the AJR, founded in 1941 and whose journal (founded in 1946) regularly recorded their musical activities. In addition, correspondence from 1953 between Ben Uri and the Jewish Institute (under the auspices of the United Synagogue and located in the Jewish Free Reading Room and Institute Library in Adler Street, Whitechapel) records the Institute canvassing for financial support towards its concerts to be held on alternate Sundays, organised by émigré Paul Hamburger (1920–2004) with Esther Salaman (1914–2005), youngest child of the distinguished Anglo-Jewish botanist, Redcliffe Salaman. The letter states that the concerts 'are patronised to a large extent by people who are not very fortunately placed and no entrance charge is made' and, furthermore, that 'efforts to introduce a little culture and happiness to many Jewish people in the East End, and your contribution, however small, would be most welcome.' A stiff reply from Ben Uri's then secretary, Barry (Baruch) Fealdman, confirmed that the Society was hampered with its own 'financial difficulties' but was happy to display the programme in the gallery. This exchange suggests that there was little awareness between the two organisations of their shared activities or of their mutual challenging circumstances.[23]

The earliest documented émigré contribution to music after the war was a pianoforte recital given by Franz Reizenstein (1911–1968) at Portman Street on 6 October 1946,[24] the venue considered by the *Jewish Chronicle* to have 'both its advantages and disadvantages',[25] its intimate size meaning that some of the audience was rather too close to the pianist, particularly in the *forte* sections. The programme featured Reizenstein's own compositions (including

---

22   Ben Uri accounts ledger for 19 December 1952 records: 'recital fee £1.1 – (petty cash).' This was less than the amount paid to the cleaner. Ben Uri Archives, Box 61.
23   Two typescript letters dated between 23 November and 28 December 1953, Ben Uri Archives, Box 25.
24   Concert flyer, Ben Uri Archives, Box 3.
25   *Jewish Chronicle*, 11 October 1946, 20.

his Sonata in B major, Op.19 [1944]),[26] as well as pieces by Bach, Beethoven, Mendelssohn, Schumann and Mozart. Reizenstein himself had a specific link with Ben Uri via his artist sister Lotte Reizenstein (1904–1982), who had followed him into exile in London, in 1936, to continue her studies at St. Martin's School of Art. She subsequently exhibited in Ben Uri's re-opening exhibition in January 1944 and several later shows.[27] Reizenstein's connection with Ben Uri continued over the next decade, with his wife Margaret writing to Barry Fealdman in autumn 1954, asking him to publicise Franz's forthcoming concert at the Wigmore Hall. She reminded Fealdman that Ben Uri had performed this service previously and that 'it is a great help and much appreciated'.[28]

Three weeks later, on 31 October 1946, émigré Tatjana Magid gave an 'International Song Recital' at Portman Street[29] (accompanied by fellow émigré Melitta Heim (1888–1950), featuring arias, Lieder, French, Russian, Hebrew and Yiddish compositions, a 'cultured rendering in many languages'.[30] Also known as Tatjana Riester,[31] Magid and her non-Jewish husband Wilhelm Friedrich Riester, an engineer and businessman, had emigrated to England in 1936. Though there are few records of Magid in Germany, a striking portrait entitled 'Tatjana Magid-Riester' (1928), by the German *Neue Sachlichkeit* painter Ulrich Neujahr (1898–1977), is recorded on exhibition and in the collection of Frank Brabant.[32] Magid certainly had some professional success in exile, as she was listed in *Radio Times* during the late 1940s and early 1950s, including on 13 December 1949 when she sang soprano with Ralph Elman and his Bohemian Players in 'Melody Hour (Music For the Housewife)' at 3pm on the Light Programme,[33] and was accompanied by the Aeolian String Quartet in a chamber music concert on the Third programme on Sunday, 12 August 1951.[34]

---

26 *Ibid.*
27 Lotte Reizenstein had studied at the Nuremberg School of Applied Arts and the Reimann School in Berlin. She continued to show in group exhibitions at Ben Uri through the 1950s, participated in a three person show with fellow émigrés Erich Dotich and Fritz Kraemer in 1956, and had her own solo exhibition in 1959. Her work is also represented in Ben Uri's permanent collection.
28 Letter from Margaret Reizenstein dated 15 October 1954, Ben Uri Archives, Box 25.
29 Invitation to the recital, Ben Uri Archives, Box 3.
30 *Jewish Chronicle*, 29 November 1946, 24.
31 *AJR Information*, August 1946, 63.
32 The portrait, now in the Frank Brabant Collection, featured in an exhibition held at the Kunsthalle Jesuitenkirche, Aschaffenburg, from 28 September 2013–26 January 2014, https://kultur-online.net/inhalt/eiskalte-emotionen [accessed: 28.02.2020].
33 'Light Programme, Issue 1365, Television', 11–17 December 1949, https://genome.ch.bbc.co.uk/page/a46055f1fb1643f3a9f32a2157d93f75 [accessed: 27.02.2020].
34 'Chamber Music, Third Programme', 12 August 1951, https://genome.ch.bbc.co.uk/bd34e2dfc6114c87bc00a54a610fc3a4 [accessed: 27.02.2020].

Magid gave a further recital at Ben Uri on 18 October 1951, as reviewed in the *Jewish Chronicle* by 'P.Z.A.':

> Tatiana Magid, soprano, divided her programme into two parts: the first half devoted to French, German, and Russian songs, the second to Hebrew and Yiddish folk songs. When Miss Magid sings these latter, one is aware that Jewish folk music as an art form is as important as any other. She does not condescend to sing them, she seems to want to sing them, and her interpretations give an unusually moving experience.[35]

1947 saw at least nine recitals, with several émigré participants. On 2 March 1947, a 'Lieder Recital'[36] was given by German-born, Jewish singer Jenny Sonnenberg (date of birth unknown-1978), who had grown up in South Africa before studying for two years in London at the Royal College of Music, then in Paris and finally in Berlin, where she had settled in the mid-1920s. In 1925 she featured in a recording of Schubert songs and, in early 1928, participated in Germany's celebration of Beethoven's Centenary as a contralto in Deutsche Grammophon's first electric recording of the *Ninth Symphony*, with conductor Oskar Fried, the Berlin State Opera Orchestra and the Bruno Kittel Choir. Sonnenberg also had a distinguished recording and touring career in Europe and South Africa during the 1920s (including performing in London at the Aeolian Hall in 1922)[37] and in the early 1930s.[38] *Radio Times* listed her concerts on the National Channel in 1930 and 1935, and she was still performing in Europe until at least February 1938. However, under the National Socialist regime's antisemitic legislation, Sonnenberg was identified and included in the *Lexikon der Juden in der Musik* (Encyclopaedia of Jews in Music), first compiled for the *Reichsleitung* by Theo Stengel and Herbert Gerigk in 1940, to provide a comprehensive list for the authorities.[39] Despite her postwar appearance at Ben Uri, it is unclear whether she escaped to Britain permanently.

---

35 *Jewish Chronicle*, 26 October 1951, 23.
36 Concert flyer, Ben Uri Archives, Box 3.
37 F. Gilbert Webb, 'Current Vocalism', *Musical News and Herald*, 2 December 1922, 506, https://books.google.co.uk/books?id=t262J2y8HSMC&pg=RA4-PA507-IA1&lpg=RA4-PA507-IA1&dq=jenny+sonnenberg+singer&source=bl&ots=ahOugvNCJ3&sig=ACfU3Uo8_tO7uTBYWtPY2TXDJYrvHQiDZw&hl=en&sa=X&ved=2ahUKEwiF9qnBhIjyAhUPgVwKHYmTAPM4ChDoATAJegQIDhAD#v=onepage&q=jenny%20sonnenberg%20singer&f=false [accessed: 29.07.2021].
38 *The Zionist Record*, a Johannesburg newspaper, featured an interview with Sonnenberg during her South African tour in 1931 (*The Zionist Record*, 9 October 1931, 16).
39 Theo Stengel and Herbert Gerigk (eds.), *Lexikon der Juden in der Musik* (Berlin: Bernhard Hahnefeld Verlag, 1940).

Sonnenberg's performance at Ben Uri was followed three weeks later by 'Love Songs Through the Ages' (13th–20th century), a lecture-recital by Marianne Mislap-Kapper (1900–1978),[40] accompanied by Paul Hamburger. Described as having been one of 'Vienna's busiest artists',[41] a decade later, on Sunday, 13 October 1957, she performed 'Folk Songs of Many Lands' (which were 'mostly unfamiliar')[42] in Portman Street.

One of the final concerts of 1947, which took place on 3 November, was a 'Sonata Recital' by Shula Doniach, featuring the aforementioned Norbert Brainin. A gifted young Viennese violinist, Brainin had emigrated to London in 1938 after the *Anschluss* and had studied with distinction at the Guildhall School of Music, including with noted émigré Max Rostal (1905–1991). *AJR Information* noted, in December 1946, that Brainin, who had acted 'as the leader in previous AJR Concerts', had been awarded the prestigious Carl Flesch Medal.[43] In 1947, Brainin became one of the founder members and first violinist of the renowned Amadeus Quartet (originally named the Brainin Quartet), which, remarkably, retained its founding three-quarter émigré line-up throughout its forty-year history. Brainin had encountered Peter Schidlof (another Viennese Jew) initially in 1940, when both were interned in Prees Heath transit camp on the British mainland, before being transferred to the Isle of Man. After Brainin's release, Schidlof met violinist Siegmund Nissel in the camp. Ben Uri's permanent collection now holds a striking charcoal portrait of Nissel by Eva Albrook – formerly Eva Urbach – herself an émigré,[44] providing one of many links between music and the visual arts that run through Ben Uri's first century. In 1947, the British cellist Martin Lovett completed the quartet.

---

40   *Jewish Chronicle*, 21 March 1947, 22.
41   Malcolm Cole and Barbara Barclay, *Armseelchen: The Life and Music of Eric Zeisl* (Westport: Greenwood Press, 1984), 23.
42   *Jewish Chronicle*, 18 October 1957, 24.
43   *AJR Information*, December 1946, 4.
44   Painter, illustrator, and costume designer Eva Albrook was born Eva Mehl in Hamburg, Germany, in 1925. Immigrating to the UK with her family in 1938, she attended Bunce Court – a progressive boarding school in Kent for Jewish refugee children – for one year, where she met her future husband Alexander Urbach (the name later changed to Aldbrook), a Viennese refugee. After training as a classical dancer (using the name Eva Melova), she studied fashion and costume design under Muriel Pemberton at St. Martin's School of Art, becoming a highly successful fashion illustrator in the 1950s and 1960s. Aldbrook was celebrated for her elegant, confident designs, and received commissions from the fashion house Dior and publications including *British Vogue*, *The Evening Standard* and *The Sunday Times*. Latterly, she turned to portraiture and landscapes of the Tuscan countryside, where she spent time with her husband, later returning to England.

Brainin performed again for Ben Uri on 1 February 1948, accompanied on the piano by fellow Viennese émigré, Paul Hamburger; the archives retain the receipt for the hire of a Bechstein grand piano for this auspicious occasion.[45]

Early 1948 saw the formation of Ben Uri's Studio Group Music Circle, an offshoot of the Studio Group of artists, which tended to appeal to a younger cohort. This amateur group gathered regularly to practice chamber music in Portman Street on weekday evenings, and to host lectures on musical topics, continuing in parallel with the programme of more formal recitals. Musical commitment took a further step forward in early January 1950 when the *Jewish Chronicle* announced the Music Circle's 'Hope of forming a Jewish Chamber Orchestra'.[46] The following year these aspirations were furthered with the founding of the Ben Uri orchestra, conducted by Bernard Jacob under the leadership of Hans Geiger, and reviewed with enthusiasm by the *Jewish Chronicle* after its first public performance in spring 1952:

> The Ben Uri Orchestra, which made its debut at the Adolph Tuck Hall on Sunday afternoon, is, one hopes, a permanent addition to Jewish musical life. Led by Hans Geiger and consisting of amateurs with a stiffening of professional players, it has been developed by its conductor, Bernard Jacob, to a high degree of efficiency. It is vigorous yet clean in attack, and its upper strings especially have a fine bite and precision. Ensemble work is of a high quality already, and if other departments are not so outstanding as the strings, that is more a question or balance than material [...] The programme, in addition to Haydn and Mozart and Honegger's *Pastorale d'Ete*, included Matyas Seiber's *Besardo Suite No. 2* and Schoenberg's [sic] arrangement of Monn's *Concerto for Cello and Strings with Continuo*, in which Brigitte Loeser and Paul Hamburger were the soloists.[47]

It is clear from this account that émigré participation was embedded from the outset. Hans Geiger, orchestra leader, was the son of Isy Geiger, former concertmaster of the orchestra at the Viennese Carl Theatre, where many successful Viennese operettas had their premieres. His first orchestra became one of Vienna Radio's most frequent and popular broadcasters, often relaying to foreign radio stations. In March 1938, following the *Anschluss*, Geiger senior fled to Poland and subsequently to Britain, eventually forming his own orchestra in exile, Isy Geiger and his Viennese Music, and he successfully auditioned for

---

45 Ben Uri Archives, Box 25.
46 *Jewish Chronicle*, 27 January 1950, 20.
47 *Jewish Chronicle*, 4 April 1952, 27.

the BBC in 1951 at the age of sixty-five. His brother Josef had a small orchestra at Claridge's hotel.[48]

During this period, from the late 1940s to early 1950s, Ben Uri provided a significant platform for émigré performers, both regulars and those who made only limited appearances. The pianist Paul Hamburger, in the former category, performed as both soloist and accompanist between 1947 and 1952, and his first documented appearance was on 1 June 1947, for a 'Piano and Song Recital', accompanying Esther Salaman. Hamburger had studied at the Vienna State Academy before emigrating to England in 1939, receiving a scholarship to the Royal College of Music two years later. From 1945, he developed a celebrated international career as an accompanist, chamber musician and teacher, featuring in many recordings with instrumentalists and vocalists.[49]

Hamburger subsequently opened Ben Uri's 1950 season of recitals, playing pieces by classical and contemporary composers, mainly Jewish, including Handel, Mendelssohn, Frankel, Copland (*Four Piano Blues*), Boskovich (all six movements of his *Semitic Suite*), and Bloch.[50]

The following winter, the *Jewish Chronicle* praised Hamburger's performances at Ben Uri on 4 November 1951 as both accompanist to baritone, Ernest Frank, and as a soloist 'in some "Inventions for Piano" by Timothy Moore and Beethoven's 'Waldstein' sonata, which he approached with a virile attack. His playing was authoritative, with finely controlled dynamics'.[51] The aforementioned Ernest Frank was also an émigré; born in Calcutta to a British mother and a German father, he had then lived in Germany and performed opera and Lieder until he fled to England in 1936, taking British nationality shortly thereafter.[52]

---

48   *Radio Times*, schedule for Regional Programme London, 19 January 1938, https://genome.ch .bbc.co.uk/schedules/service_rt_regional_london/1938-01-19 [accessed: 22 December 2022].
49   Hamburger performed in Britain and abroad, accompanying artists such as Dame Janet Baker, Elisabeth Söderström, Max Rostal and Pierre Fournier. He coached variously for the English Chamber Group and Glyndebourne Opera and was official accompanist at the BBC for twelve years, later producing the 'Artists of the Younger Generation' series. He taught at the Guildhall School of Music and Drama, London, where he became a Fellow. He was awarded the Austrian Cross of Honour for Science and Art in 1991, upgraded to 1st class in 2000.
50   *Jewish Chronicle*, 13 October 1950, 20. Alexander Uriyah Boskovich (1907–1964) was a Romanian émigré responsible for much of the early development of Israeli music.
51   *Jewish Chronicle*, 16 November 1951, 27.
52   Ernest Frank (dates unconfirmed) also recorded with the BBC just before and after the war and performed in a National Gallery Concert in 1941. He sang with the Carl Rosa Company and appeared as Monostatos at Glyndebourne in 1937. Thanks to Jutta Raab Hansen for this information.

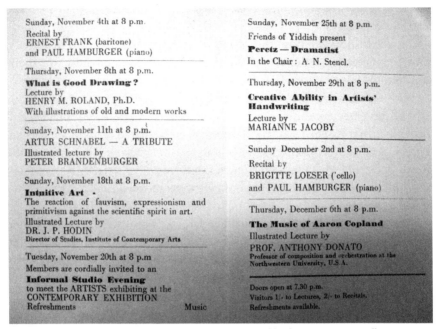

FIGURE 6.1   'Lectures and Recitals, Nov.–Dec. 1951' printed leaflet, Ben Uri Art Gallery
COURTESY OF BEN URI ARCHIVES

On 2 December, Hamburger was again performing at Portman Street, this time accompanying émigré cellist, Brigitte Loeser (later Brigitte Eisner, 1923–2012).[53] Berlin-born Loeser had emigrated with her medical family to Britain in 1935, when her father was no longer able to work, in the wake of the Nuremberg Laws which restricted Jews within the professions. On this occasion, Hamburger and Loeser's repertoire included works by Eccles, Beethoven, Brahms, Fauré, Granados, Ravel, and the premiere of a piece by a young émigré composer from Vienna, Joseph Horovitz (1926–2022). Horovitz was the son of Hungarian-born Béla Horovitz, founder of the renowned art book publishing house Phaidon Press, in Vienna in 1923, and which he had re-established in exile in London in 1938 with fellow émigré Ludwig Goldscheider.[54] Horovitz had arrived in England in 1938, studied music at New College, Oxford, then for a period in Paris with Nadia Boulanger, eventually returning to England where, in 1951, he composed

---

53   *Jewish Chronicle*, 30 November 1951, 7.
54   Anna Nyburg, *Émigrés: The Transformation of Art Publishing in Britain* (London: Phaidon Press Ltd., 2014).

his ballet *Alice in Wonderland* for the Festival of Britain, while Music Director of the Bristol Old Vic.

Horovitz would forge a distinguished compositional career, his works including the String Quartet no.5 of 1969, composed for the Amadeus Quartet and dedicated to the émigré art historian Sir Ernst Gombrich (1909–2001). The early cello sonata of 1951 (still unpublished), performed by Loeser and Hamburger, was highlighted in an unidentified press cutting in Ben Uri's archives:

> A new sonata by the young Jewish composer, Josef Horowitz [sic], was an interesting item in the cello-piano recital [...] It is a short work and sensibly the composer has not sought to go very deeply into emotional expression, but rather to provide the 'cello with a pleasant, engaging addition to its repertoire.[55]

Hamburger also accompanied Hungarian émigré, violinist Suzanne Rosza (1923–2005) at Ben Uri in late 1952 – she was a frequent partner to his playing and yet another link to the Amadeus Quartet. Rosza was married to cellist Martin Lovett for over fifty years, and it was through Suzanne that Lovett made the important connection with Brainin, meeting him at the home of a fellow refugee, and enabling the three émigrés, Brainin, Nissel and Schidlof, to find their fourth player.[56]

In July 1950, the *Jewish Chronicle* reviewed a Lieder recital by Hanna Lowen (Johanna Löwenstein), with the comment that Ben Uri was pursuing its 'policy of encouraging Jewish arts'.[57] Certainly during the early 1950s Ben Uri provided a platform for many émigrés (both male and female) to perform, at a time when the émigré contribution to British culture was becoming particularly visible through the 1951 nationwide Festival of Britain. 27 January 1951, at the beginning of the year-long Festival, saw a recital by George Isserlis (1917–2012, violin) and Elaine Hugh-Jones (piano) given at Ben Uri under the auspices of the London Jewish Graduates Association.[58] Born in Odessa, George was the son of Julius Isserlis (1888–1968) a renowned Russian pianist, who had studied in Paris in 1907 and performed at Carnegie Hall in New York,

---

55 *Jewish Chronicle*, 7 December 1951, p. 26, For various reasons this early cello piece was omitted from Horovitz' catalogue.
56 Anne Inglis, 'Suzanne Rosza: Fine violinist key to the founding of the Amadeus Quartet', *The Guardian*, https://www.theguardian.com/news/2005/nov/17/guardianobituaries.art sobituaries1 [accessed: 27.02.2020].
57 *Jewish Chronicle*, 14 July 1950, 20.
58 Listed in the *Jewish Chronicle*, 26 January 1951, 7.

before his appointment in Russia as professor at the College of the Imperial Philharmonic Society.

Post-revolution Isserlis senior was employed by the Soviet regime to play the piano for factory workers, among others, often in difficult conditions, and in 1922 he was one of a dozen musicians selected by Lenin to travel abroad as musical ambassadors for the newly formed Soviet Union; none of the twelve returned, and, in 1923, Isserlis arrived in the Austrian capital with his wife and young son. George studied the violin in Vienna but had to abandon professional ambitions due to a medical condition. Nevertheless, he remained a committed and accomplished amateur musician throughout his life. In 1938, his father was fortuitously on his first tour of Britain, just a week before the *Anschluss*, and was thus able to remain and to obtain visas for George and his mother to follow. Briefly interned on the Isle of Man, George established key friendships with Norbert Brainin and Peter Schidlof in the camp. On his return to London, he studied metallurgy, leading to a scientific career, but he remained a keen performer, particularly in émigré circles. His son Stephen Isserlis (b. 1958) continues the musical dynasty as an internationally renowned cellist.

Sunday 4 February 1951 saw a recital at Ben Uri by Margaret Haes (soprano), accompanied on the piano by Erna Gál (1899–1995), which included biblical songs, Ravel's Kaddish and 3 Psaumes by the Swiss composer Honegger from 1943.[59] Erna (Ernestine), herself a gifted pianist, was the sister of the Austrian composer Hans Gál (1890–1987) who had fled to London immediately after the *Anschluss*, initially intending to continue to America, but who then settled in Edinburgh instead.[60] Immigrating to Norway in 1938, Erna had arrived separately in Britain as a refugee in 1940, having studied piano with her brother in Austria under the renowned teacher Anka Landau, and having performed as piano partner of the eminent violinist Rudolf Kolisch for seven years. In exile, Erna taught piano at various schools, including Summerhill, the progressive Suffolk establishment founded by A.S. Neill; she was also a member of the Glyndebourne Ensemble as a piano coach.[61]

On 6 July 1951, the *Jewish Chronicle* reviewed a recital at Ben Uri by Hilde Beal (1922–2009), which included German, Flemish, Norwegian, Yiddish, Hebrew,

---

59   Typed recital programme, Ben Uri Archives, Box 25.
60   Gál was invited to Edinburgh where he was Reid Professor of Music at the University, moving to Scotland permanently in 1939. In 1940, he was held in Huyton transit Camp near Liverpool, before being interned on the Isle of Man; there, he wrote the Huyton Suite for flute and two violins, which remained unpublished until 1970.
61   See Herbert Arthur Strauss, Werner Röder, Hannah Caplan, Fred Bilenkis, Belinda Rosenblatt et al. (eds.), *International biographical dictionary of Central European émigrés 1933–1945*, vol. 2, The arts, sciences and literature (Munich: K.G. Saur, 1999), 354.

and English folk songs. Beal – like so many émigrés – had grown up in a Berlin household steeped in music and recalled her father 'whistling *Fidelio* and my mother singing German folk songs'.[62]

Beal immigrated to Britain in 1939 and worked as a market gardener in Shropshire, while her mother was in domestic service. After the war, she became a noted singer, teacher and one of the first German language coaches at the Guildhall School of Music, Royal Opera House, and at Morley College, an adult education college in south London, where Michael Tippett was Director of Music and which counted many émigrés amongst its teaching staff.[63] Notable in the music department was the German émigré composer and conductor Walter Goehr (1903–1960), a Berliner who studied with Schoenberg and who had come to Britain before the war to work in the fledgling recording industry. During the war, continuing to work at Morley and the BBC, Goehr moved with his wife, Russian émigré, Laelia, and son, Alexander, to the relative safety of Amersham, outside London. Both mother and son would find respective exposure through the various efforts of Ben Uri.

Laelia Goehr (1908–2004), an accomplished musician herself, had performed as a child in Russia, before leaving for Berlin at the age of fourteen. She remained in Germany until she and Walter fled at the end of 1932. In Britain, through contact with émigré photographer Bill Brandt and editor/publisher Tom Hopkinson, Goehr established herself in exile as a respected portrait photographer[64] – particularly of musicians[65] – despite having no previous experience. In May 1952, Ben Uri hosted Laelia's 'Exhibition of Photographs', which included images from Israel, at Portman Street, in conjunction with the *Jewish Chronicle*. Opened by the paper's editor, David Kessler, this was Ben Uri's first exhibition dedicated to photography.

---

62 Daniel Snowman, *The Hitler Émigrés* (London: Pimlico, 2003), 12. Daniel Snowman interviewed Beal in 1997 for the oral history collection at the Imperial War Museum, London, which records much of her early life before and after the rise of National Socialism.
63 Mátyás Seiber (1905–1960) taught musical composition at Morley College from 1942.
64 Laelia Goehr studied with and observed émigré photographer Bill Brandt. After Brandt showed her photographs to Tom Hopkinson at the Hulton Picture Library, Goehr's work was published in *Picture Post*, *Lilliput* and, postwar, in *The Observer*. In the 1950s, she photographed notable Israelis, including cabinet ministers and the philosopher Martin Buber.
65 Laelia Goehr's exhibition 'Stravinsky rehearses Stravinsky' held at the Royal Festival Hall in honour of Stravinsky's eighty-fifth birthday, was publicised in *AJR Information*, July 1967, 16. She also published three books: *Faces* with Vita Sackville-West (recently reissued); *Musicians in Camera* with text by John Amis, and *A Little Tiger* with text by Elspeth Huxley.

Her son Alexander Goehr – in an example of the interconnectedness that is so often a hallmark of émigré narratives – also features in Ben Uri's archives, with a handwritten letter he sent from Tel Aviv in August 1953 concerning arrangements for a concert premiering his new work, *Five Songs from Babel*, to be held under the auspices of Ben Uri in November,[66] along with the concert programme. The recital, held at the Dalcroze Hall, Westbourne Grove, featured June Wilson (soprano) and Margaret Kitchin (piano), with pieces by Mozart, Henry Purcell, Schubert, Smetana, Turina – and Goehr's premiere. An accounts ledger also records the hall fee of £2.2.0.[67] This event represents a fascinating instance of an émigré context impacting on the early premiere of a creative artist who became one of the most prominent British composers of his generation.

On Sunday, 25 April 1957, Romanian-born Carola Grindea (1914–2009) gave a piano recital in Portman Street.[68] Grindea was a piano teacher and became best known as founder of the European Piano Teachers' Association (EPTA) and the International Society for Study of Tension in Performance (ISSTP), an organisation aimed at understanding and treating the musician's physical stress. She was also a member of staff at the Guildhall School of Music. Educated at the Bucharest Conservatory, she arrived in Britain with her husband, the literary editor and writer Miron Grindea (1909–1995), two days before the outbreak of war in September 1939.[69]

As can be seen by the above, a roster of distinguished and little-known émigré names enriched the music programme at Ben Uri into the mid-1950s, whether as performers or, to a lesser extent, as composers, providing fascinating smaller narratives within the wider émigré story. For many, these appearances went hand in hand with performances in mainstream British venues, while, for others, identification with the Jewish community was key, even if the reviews in the *Jewish Chronicle* were often rather waspish in tone. Ben Uri, with its broad approach, was able to host young musicians as well as seasoned performers, and provide an opportunity for the premiering of compositions, alongside well-loved folk, classical, historical, and contemporary works.

---

66 Letter, Ben Uri Archives, Box 25 (see *Jewish Chronicle*, 13 November 1953, 25).
67 Ben Uri Archives, Box 25, Ledger for 10 June–21 Oct 1954.
68 Programme, Ben Uri Archives, Box 25.
69 The Grindeas had a close friendship with Romanian-born émigré artist Arnold Daghani (1909–1985). A Holocaust survivor, Daghani chronicled his experiences in a diary and artwork which were published, first in Romanian, in 1947, and later translated into English as 'The Grave is in the Cherry Orchard', appearing in ADAM International Review, edited for fifty years by Miron Grindea. The ADAM archive is held at King's College, London.

3 Liturgical Music

Much of this chapter has so far focused on classical, folk and contemporary music; however, given Ben Uri's roots as a Jewish art society, Jewish liturgical music also had its place in the postwar repertoire, despite Ben Uri's position as a secular institution.

On Sunday, 12 September 1948, Ben Uri held a reception to meet Polish-born émigré Julius Chajes (1910–1985) and his wife Marguerite Kozenn, 'prima donna at the Vienna Folks Opera'. The event was part of a European tour by the couple, who gave eighteen concerts in England, France, Switzerland, and Italy, featuring African American spirituals, Indian music, Gershwin, and Chajes' own compositions, among other pieces. Chajes had begun his professional career composing and performing as a teenager, and was now a virtuoso concert pianist, conductor and composer of Jewish liturgical and secular music, and his wife, a dramatic soprano. The couple, described in the programme as 'Pioneers of Jewish music in New York'[70] had immigrated to America in 1938 after several years in Palestine, where Chajes had been particularly influenced by Arabic and Hebrew Palestinian folk music, and Jewish scores from antiquity, all of which impacted his later compositions. The *Detroit Jewish News*, in reviewing the tour, described how the couple had been invited 'by the radio stations to broadcast American music but also injected Palestinean [sic] melodies. In all the countries but Italy, they were on their own performing in the latter at request of the Joint Distribution Committee at DP camps. They started their concert in Italy in the former villa and palace of Hermann Goering at Monte Mario. It is now a sanatorium for Jewish people'.[71]

Two of the most significant figures in Jewish liturgical music to participate in Ben Uri's programme were Viennese-born émigré Paul Lichtenstern (1903–1991), organist, pianist, composer, and synagogue music director, and his wife, the singer Hanni Lichtenstern (Joanna Metzger-Lichtenstern, 1916–2012).[72] Paul had the distinction of being the last organist at the Neue Synagogue in Berlin, a post he held from 1937–39.[73] Ironically, this 'cathedral' synagogue survived *Kristallnacht* in November 1938 through the actions of a German police officer, but was later destroyed by Allied bombing in 1943, with only the magnificent facade left intact.

---

70 Invitation card, Ben Uri Archives, Box 3.
71 *Detroit Jewish News*, 24 September 1948, 21.
72 Biographical reference.
73 Tina Frühauf in *The Organ and its Music in German-Jewish Culture* (OUP, 2009), chronicles the history and role of the instrument in Jewish sacred music.

Hanni, a Berlin-born Pole, who had studied with Wilhelm Gutmann and later sang at the Städtische Oper, gave her debut performance in Germany as a mezzo soprano under the auspices of the Nazi-approved Jüdische Kulturbund, following the imposition of antisemitic legislation. Subsequently, like many émigré women who had no other option, she was admitted to Britain in May 1939 on a domestic visa and was later interned at Port Erin on the Isle of Man, where she gave recitals; Paul arrived three months after her. In England she built up her career (with early appearances under the auspices of the Free German League of Culture), often accompanied by her husband, primarily performing Yiddish and Jewish songs in multiple languages.

Both were to play significant roles in establishing music at the centre of activities at Belsize Square Synagogue, the émigrés' *shul* and heart of the *liberale* community in exile.[74] The synagogue is located close to the southern end of *Finchleystraße*[75] (as local bus drivers referred to nearby Finchley Road, the thoroughfare which formed a geographical 'spine' for the German-speaking refugee community, running between Swiss Cottage and Golders Green), and its first Friday evening Service was held on Friday, 24 March 1939. Belsize Square Synagogue became renowned for its music, often provided gratis by previous performers from the great opera houses of Berlin and Vienna. Paul played the synagogue organ from 1950, following retired opera singer, Austrian émigré Melitta Heim, and Hanni subsequently founded the youth choir. Bea Lewkowicz has noted how important Belsize Square Synagogue was in providing community support for the Jewish émigrés gathered around *Finchleystraße*[76] – as did Ben Uri, to a less-formalised and more secular extent.

Both husband and wife were to perform at Ben Uri in the early 1950s. On 2 February 1952, the *Jewish Chronicle* reviewed a piano recital by Paul, which highlighted modern Jewish/Israeli composers, including Ernst Toch (1887–1964), Paul Ben-Haim (born Paul Frankenburger in Munich, 1897–1984) and

---

74 The Lichtensterns and their musical contribution to the community are mentioned in Anthony Godfrey, *Three Rabbis in a Vicarage: The Story of Belsize Square Synagogue* (London: Larsen Grove Press, 2005), 58.

75 See Rachel Dickson and Sarah MacDougall, 'Mapping "Finchleystrasse": Mitteleuropa in northwest London', in Burcu Dogramaci, Mareike Hetschold, Laura Karp Lugo, Rachel Lee and Helene Roth (eds.), *Arrival Cities: Migrating Artists and New Metropolitan Topographies in the 20th Century* (Leuven: Leuven University Press, 2020).

76 Bea Lewkowicz, 'Belsize Square Synagogue: Community, Belonging, and Religion among German-Jewish Refugees', in Anthony Grenville, Andrea Ilse Maria Reiter (eds.), *'I didn't want to float; I wanted to belong to something': Refugee Organizations in Britain 1933–1945*, Yearbook of the Research Centre for German and Austrian Exile Studies, vol. 10 (Leiden: Brill, 2008), 113–36.

Rudolf Walther Hirschberg (1889–1960; born in Berlin, he fled to France after his release from Sachsenhausen in 1938, where he remained in hiding during the war, but returned to Berlin at the end of his life). Three years later, on Sunday, 13 February 1955, both husband and wife performed together under the auspices of Ben Uri in the elegant and elevated premises of the Arts Council, at 4 St James's Square, in London's West End[77] – very much beyond the familiar environs of *Finchleystraße*. Archival correspondence between Barry Fealdman, Ben Uri's secretary, and Ethel Solomon (Mrs Robert Solomon), Chairman of Ben Uri, from October 1954, confirms the welcome news that the Arts Council agreed to 'grant the use of their Great Drawing Room at St James's Square for our recitals. This should greatly enhance the prestige of the Society'.[78]

4   The 1960s and Onwards

Following this period of high-profile musical output, by the end of the 1950s, Ben Uri's change in focus led to a move away from music and a re-concentration on the visual arts and literary activities. Furthermore, with the founding of the State of Israel in 1948, increased support from the Israeli Embassy resulted in a change in emphasis in exhibition programming, with a greater presence of contemporary Israeli artists. And of course, financial issues were never far from the surface. In late 1959, Leon Kossoff (1926–2019), the eminent young Anglo-Jewish painter, criticised what he perceived as Ben Uri's lack of support for living artists. A stern letter from Ethel Solomon was published in the *Jewish Chronicle* as a rebuttal, while issuing a plea for greater community support and confirming that musicians were still very much part of Ben Uri's wider reach: 'Ben Uri is not only concerned with painters and sculptors [...] its activities embrace all the arts. With greater support from the community more practical help could be extended to Jewish artists, musicians and writers.'[79]

Unfortunately, the new decade saw Ben Uri having to move from its spacious Portman Street townhouse, as the lease expired. There was a brief hiatus before activities regrouped in a basement exhibition space at 14 Berners Street, behind Oxford Street. Music received a fillip with the consent of Harriet Cohen, eminent concert pianist, to become Patron of the Society's Music

---

77 Recital flyer, Ben Uri Archives, Box 25.
78 Typescript letter dated 2 July 1954 from Barry Fealdman, Ben Uri Archives, Box 25. The Council charged 5 Guineas per concert.
79 *Jewish Chronicle*, 18 December 1959, 18.

Section, announced under the heading 'New Plans for Ben Uri' in the *Jewish Chronicle* on April Fool's Day, 1960.[80]

However, with a further relocation in 1964 to a top floor space in a synagogue building in Dean Street in Soho,[81] an aging émigré cohort, combined with a new vision for Ben Uri and increasing support and alignment with the Israeli Embassy, émigré participation in gallery activities began to dwindle, although the larger musical picture remained positive. Beyond the confines of Ben Uri itself, October 1960 saw the formation of the Jewish Music Council – increasingly looking towards the newly founded State of Israel for input – and with Ben Uri's Barry Fealdman as Acting Secretary.[82] Furthermore, in December, the *Chronicle* published the suggestion that Jewish Music Week 'may' become Jewish Music Month (the Jewish Music Council met at Ben Uri to discuss this important issue).[83]

Archive material from the early 1970s suggests that the issue of whether, and how, Ben Uri should extend its role within and beyond the visual arts was still a divisive topic. Minutes and a working party report record discussions concerning future activities, with a view to making the Gallery a centre of the arts and especially attractive to younger people. Harvey Chesterman (member of the Music Committee, 1972–73) felt that Ben Uri should be expanded to make it The Arts Council of the Jewish Community in England, with inhouse activities such as exhibitions, lectures, recitals, poetry reading and a café; Ben Uri should sponsor young musicians and artists, foreign Jewish musicians and artists and provide scholarships; it should also provide in-gallery lessons for schools and adults as well as work in schools. Chesterman proposed a structure of committees to run these proposals. However, Barry Fealdman felt that the Dean Street premises was unsuitable for an arts centre and that the separate committees running art, music and activities should be brought together for a trial period to run the Gallery to see how it worked.[84]

Although recitals were given sporadically until 1998, often in other, more suitable, venues, and although a music club was formed in the 1970–80s for young musicians,[85] Ben Uri's orchestra ceased performing in 1972, with music no longer occupying a central part of Ben Uri's programming. Indeed, its overall role in the institution's history remained largely forgotten until the exhibition 'Arts in Harmony: An Art Gallery's Musical Heritage' opened at the

---

80 *Jewish Chronicle*, 1 April 1960, 14.
81 Where Ben Uri remained until 1996.
82 *Jewish Chronicle*, 14 October 1960, 8.
83 *Jewish Chronicle*, 30 December 1960, 9.
84 Ben Uri Archives, Box 25, Minutes from 1971–72.
85 Email to author in June 2021 from Malcolm Miller who attended the club in the 1980s.

Royal College of Music's Museum in April 2015. Organised by Ben Uri's first archivist Clare Jackson, with curator Rachel Dickson, the exhibition formed part of Ben Uri's centenary output.[86] It explored émigré music and its links to the visual arts at Ben Uri, displaying examples of archival ephemera, including photographs, cuttings, correspondence and programmes, along with selected artworks with musical themes at their heart. It also promoted the online project 'Singing a Song in a Foreign Land', created and researched by Royal College of Music professor Norbert Meyn in order to preserve the legacy of émigré musicians who fled from central Europe during the 1930s and 1940s.[87]

The significance of Ben Uri's musical history, and the role of émigrés therein, was acknowledged in the press release issued jointly by Ben Uri and the Royal College of Music, in which Meyn enthusiastically announced:

> Ben Uri's musical history is almost as impressive as its legacy in the visual arts. Hundreds of concerts, performed by first-rate artists in major London venues, [...] give evidence of Ben Uri's importance for classical music, featuring world famous musicians, many of them émigrés from Nazi Europe, as well as emerging composers and performers through the 20th century.[88]

As Meyn suggests, and as I hope to have demonstrated in my historical survey, Ben Uri's hitherto largely unrecognised commitment to émigré music, from composers to performers, ran parallel to its visual arts programming in the immediate postwar years. The result was more than a decade of musical enrichment for its community and the creation of an archive of important refugee names whose contribution has enhanced 20th and 21st century British cultural life immeasurably.

---

86 The exhibition ran from 27 April to 28 August 2015. See 'Arts in Harmony', *Royal College of Music*, https://www.rcm.ac.uk/about/news/all/artsinharmony.aspx [accessed: 27.02.2020].
87 'Singing a Song in a Foreign Land: Online Resource – The Legacy of Migrant Musicians from Nazi-Europe in Britain', *Royal College of Music*, https://www.rcm.ac.uk/singingasong/ [accessed: 27.02.2020].
88 'Arts in Harmony', 23 April 2015, https://www.meer.com/en/14945-arts-in-harmony [accessed: 27.02.2020].

7
Goldschmidt and Hamburg

Peter Petersen

Abstract

Berthold Goldschmidt was born in Hamburg in 1903. He had strong family ties to the city. He studied composition and conducting in Berlin. After 1933 he composed and performed works connected with the Jewish community. In 1935 he fled from the Nazis to England. Much later, after the war he visited Hamburg several times where his works were performed, including a lecture-concert in 1991 featuring an interview with the author. Here they discussed his projected string trio *Retrospectum*, which autobiographically alludes to his prewar life in Hamburg, referred to in his late works as 'HBG'. Hamburg also hosted his ninetieth birthday gala concert in 1993 and was where, in 1996, he gave his last public performance as pianist. He wrote incidental music for W. Borchert's *Draußen vor der Tür*.

When Berthold Goldschmidt died, many people in Hamburg felt that they had lost not only an important musician but also a good friend. His winning personality, keen understanding of his time and culture and, not least, his humour had made him popular with everyone. He was able, moreover, to create that sense of trust so appreciated by the young. Those who were then students and graduates of my working group 'Exilmusik'[1] will not easily forget their meetings with him.[2]

1 Family Ties in Hamburg

Goldschmidt's ancestry can be traced back to the beginning of the 19th century (see Appendix). His great-grandparents were probably born in Hamburg; his paternal grandparents certainly were, at roughly the same time Johannes

---

[1] Further details can be found at www.exilmusik.de.
[2] This chapter is based on material published in Peter Petersen (ed.), *Berthold Goldschmidt – Komponist und Dirigent: Ein Musiker-Leben zwischen Hamburg, Berlin und London* (Hamburg: von Bockel, 2003).

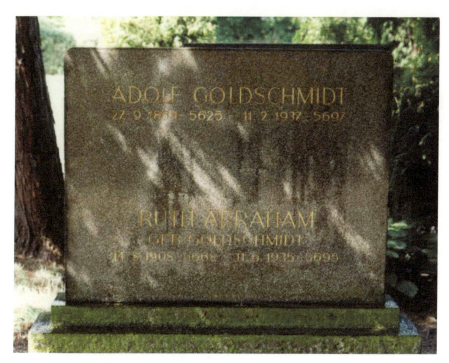

FIGURE 7.1 The Goldschmidts' headstone in the Jewish cemetery in Ohlsdorf
SOURCE: AUTHOR'S OWN

Brahms was born in the Gängeviertel – his grandfather Michael Beer Goldschmidt in 1831 and his grandmother Bertha Beer Goldschmidt, *née* Lewin, in 1832. His father, Adolf Michael Goldschmidt (1864–1937), lived his entire life in Hamburg. Both he and Berthold's much-loved sister, Ruth, who died before her father – in 1935, from pneumonia – are buried at the Jewish cemetery in Ohlsdorf. The gravestone still has a large blank space that Berthold's mother, Henriette Goldschmidt (*née* Wiesner), had intended for her own name; fortunately, Goldschmidt was able to secure her passage to London before the outbreak of the Second World War. She became a British subject and died in 1953 at the age of seventy.

Adolf and Henriette Goldschmidt ran a shop in Alt-Hamburg, which Bertha Goldschmidt had founded in the early 1870s and ran for the next thirty years. Berthold was born on its three-storey premises at Steinstrasse 12 on 18 January 1903 at 9:45, as his birth certificate states. The name of the company was given in a manner typical of tradition-conscious Hamburg: 'Bedding specialists / M. Goldschmidt W^{we} & Söhne', where the M stood for Michael and the W^{we} (*Witwe*: widow) for Bertha; the sons were Gustav, Daniel, Adolf, John and

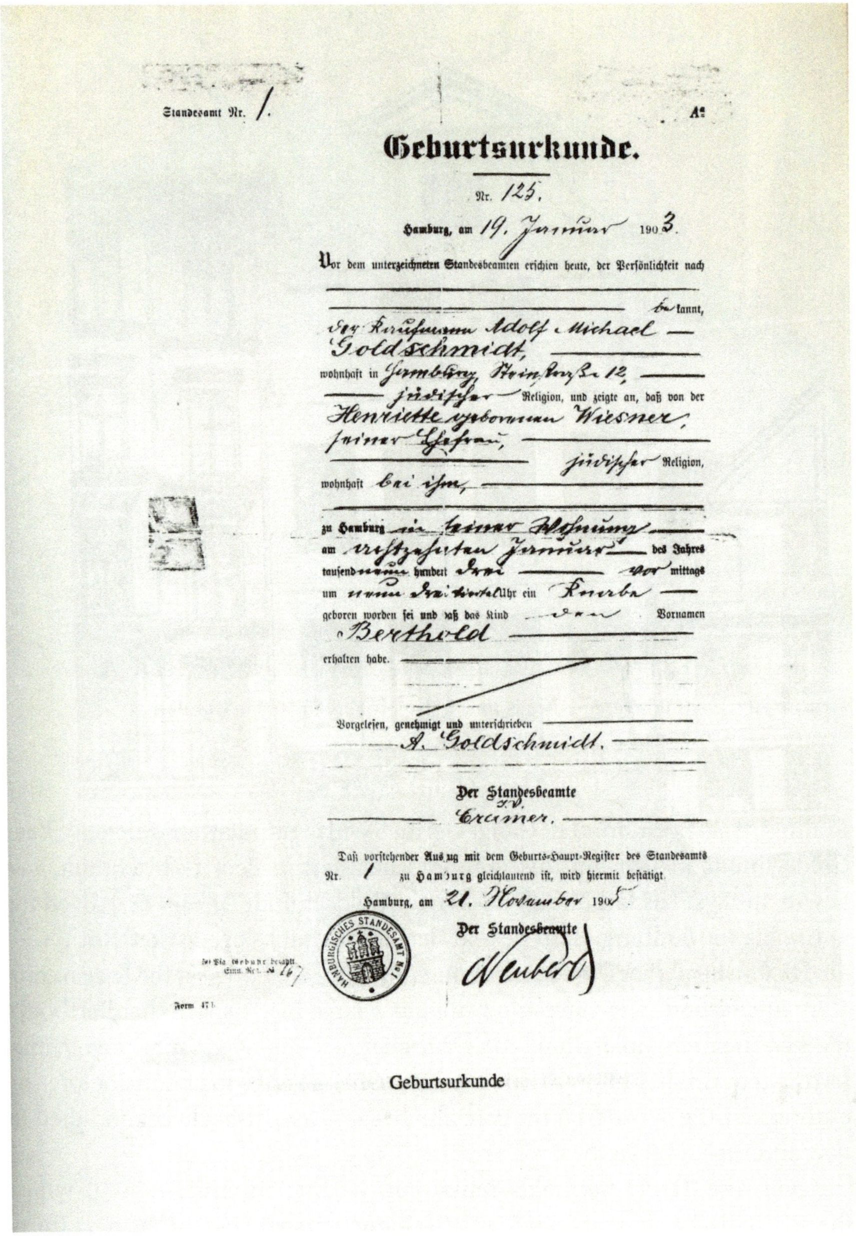
Standesamt Nr. 1.

Geburtsurkunde.

Nr. 125.

Hamburg, am 19. Januar 1903.

Vor dem unterzeichneten Standesbeamten erschien heute, der Persönlichkeit nach bekannt,

der Kaufmann Adolf Michael Goldschmidt,

wohnhaft in Hamburg, Steinstraße 12,

jüdischer Religion, und zeigte an, daß von der Henriette geborene Wiesner, seiner Ehefrau, jüdischer Religion,

wohnhaft bei ihm,

zu Hamburg in seiner Wohnung

am achtzehnten Januar des Jahres tausend neun hundert drei vor mittags

um neun dreiviertel Uhr ein Knabe

geboren worden sei und daß das Kind den Vornamen

Berthold

erhalten habe.

Vorgelesen, genehmigt und unterschrieben

A. Goldschmidt.

Der Standesbeamte

i.V. Cramer.

Daß vorstehender Auszug mit dem Geburts-Haupt-Register des Standesamts Nr. 1 zu Hamburg gleichlautend ist, wird hiermit bestätigt.

Hamburg, am 21. November 1905

Der Standesbeamte

HAMBURGISCHES STANDESAMT No 1

Geburtsurkunde

FIGURE 7.2 Berthold Goldschmidt's birth certificate
SOURCE: FACSIMILE CREATED BY THE AUTHOR

FIGURE 7.3 The house – Steinstrasse 12 – in which Berthold Goldschmidt was born
SOURCE: PHOTOGRAPH COURTESY OF MUSEUM FÜR HAMBURGISCHE GESCHICHTE

Josef Goldschmidt. The entire street was demolished some years later to make way for urban re-building, although a photograph of the street, as it then was, has survived, and we were able to give a copy to Goldschmidt on the occasion of his ninetieth birthday.

Whenever Goldschmidt encountered documentation of his childhood, it often unleashed a flood of memories, which were recounted in a lively manner. When I showed him a postcard of the burning 'Michel' – the steeple of St Michael's church and the true symbol of Hamburg – he remarked: 'Many thanks for the burning Michel. [...] I well remember the moment as my father shouted in horror from the balcony of Gr. Allee 2a "Michel's on fire!"'[3] That was on 3 July 1906. At that point, the Goldschmidts lived in the Große Allee (today the Adenauer Allee). All of the family's addresses in Hamburg were close to the Außenalster, the large body of water that, with the Innenalster, make up much of the character of Hamburg. This district figured highly in Goldschmidt's childhood memories. When for his 93rd birthday we gave him a photograph of the frozen Alster with its skaters and sledgers, he wrote:

> Dear Peter, warmest thanks to you, Marianne and all of the members of the working group [...]. Warm enough, perhaps, to thaw the frozen Alster (unlike the opera house in the Dammtorstr.?). I remember being pulled in a sled by my father over the frozen lake in 1910. Since then, a lot of water has flowed down the Elbe – and in Hanover, I've made the visual acquaintance with the line that's hooked Beatrice.[4]

The playful references to the 'frozen' opera house in the Dammtorstraße and the Magdeburg Opera performances of his opera *Beatrice Cenci* in Hanover (it opened on 10 January 1996, in the composer's presence) were typical not only of his correspondence style but also of his feelings towards Hamburg

---

3 'Danke vielmals für den brennenden Michel. [...] wie ich mich an diesen Moment erinnere, als mein Vater auf dem Balkon von Gr. Allee 2^A Erdbeeren ass u. voller Entsetzen ausrief "der M. brennt"!' – letter to the author, dated 16 February 1993.

4 'Lieber Peter, Dir und Marianne sowie allen Mitgliedern der "Arbeitsgruppe" [...] wärmsten Dank. Der allein würde vielleicht die vereiste Alster auftauen (im Gegensatz zum Opernhaus in der Dammtorstr.?). Ich erinnere mich, von meinem Vater auf einem Schlitten 1910 über die Aussenalster gezogen worden zu sein. Seitdem ist ja recht viel Wasser in die Elbe geflossen – u. in Hannover machte ich die visuelle Bekanntschaft mit der Leine, an die sich nun auch Beatrice angebunden hat' – letter dated 19 January 1996. 'Leine' is the name of a river in the city of Hanover. On the other hand, the meaning of the German word 'Leine' is 'line' which you need to fix an object to another object – in this context: the opera *Beatrice Cenci* cannot run in Hanover because it has been hooked by anyone in the cultural administration of the city.

itself, the city that he felt had ignored his now international reputation. But his opinion had no effect on his love for his native city. Family was important to Goldschmidt, perhaps because several members of his were lost during the Holocaust (see Appendix); he kept himself informed of the smallest details of the fates of his furthest-flung relatives, and Hamburg was the common element in his memories of those closest to him. He would show considerable excitement at the unexpected re-appearance of long-lost relatives, or even snippets of information about them. In spring 1992 he wrote to me:

> Today I'm waiting for a visit from my newly discovered relative, a grandson of the painter Max Weiss (born 1884 in Hbg), my cousin missing since 1920. – Reviews of the concert on 8.3.92 in the Berlin Tagesspiegel were noticed by Michael Weiss and led to our correspondence. The remarkable thing is our near-simultaneous discovery of Max W. at an exhibition of his work in Hbg. I'll send further documentation after M.W.'s visit here.[5]

The painter Max Weiss (1884–1954), who was born and died in Hamburg, was the son of Goldschmidt's aunt Henriette Weiss (*née* Goldschmidt), who was deported from Hamburg to Theresienstadt (Terezín) on 19 July 1942; she died there on 19 October of the same year, at the age of eighty-two.[6] Max Weiss was taken to Theresienstadt, too, but only in the last months of the war and survived until the liberation, although he was not released until 30 June 1945. Back home in Hamburg, he completed a set of sketches of life in Theresienstadt, several of which were shown in the exhibition '400 years of Jews in Hamburg' presented in the Museum of Hamburg History between November 1991 and March 1992 – an exhibition I attended with Goldschmidt.[7] The unexpected encounter with Weiss' grandson unsettled Goldschmidt considerably; in another letter to me, he recounted the many Hamburg relatives murdered by the Nazis, among them his cousin Amely Heymann, *née* Goldschmidt, who was exterminated in a concentration camp along with her husband and two sons.

---

5 'Ich erwarte dieser Tage den Besuch des neu entdeckten Verwandten, eines Enkels von dem Maler Max Weiss (geb. 1884 in Hbg) meinem seit 1920 verschollenen Cousin. Die Besprechung des Konzerts vom 8.3.92 im Berliner Tagesspiegel erregte die Aufmerksamkeit von Michael Weiss u. führte zu unserem Briefwechsel. Das Merkwürdige ist die (fast) Gleichzeitigkeit der Entdeckung von Max W. bei unserm Besuch der Ausstellung in Hbg. Demnächst werde ich weitere Dokumente senden – nach M. W's Besuch hier', letter dated 2 April 1992.
6 *Hamburger jüdische Opfer des Nationalsozialismus. Gedenkbuch*, Staatsarchiv, Hamburg, 1995, 428.
7 See Ulrich Bauche (ed.), *Vierhundert Jahre Juden in Hamburg* (Hamburg: Dölling, 1991); and Arno Herzig (ed.), *Die Juden in Hamburg 1590 bis 1990* (Hamburg: Dölling, 1991).

The same fate befell another Hamburg cousin, Fritz Loew, who was murdered in Auschwitz with his wife and two children. He mentioned fourteen more relatives from the Goldschmidt and Wiesner families – old and infirm, parents and children – who fell victim to the Nazis, and there were many whose flight and survival was only a matter of luck.[8]

It was with his characteristic irony that Goldschmidt approached a question that frequently torments people persecuted in and driven from the place where they grew up – what 'home' actually means:

> I was and am a European first and foremost. It's true that I grew up in Germany, but I don't feel myself to be German. My ambition was always to speak several European languages. Unfortunately I didn't quite manage that. It's more difficult with the concept of 'home'. I could call this apartment here in London, where I've now been living for almost 60 years, and where I've never felt exiled, 'home'. Otherwise, what does 'home' mean? I was born in Hamburg. That's what one calls 'home'. I grew up and received the most, and biggest, influences in my formative years in Berlin, so that's 'home', too. I had enormous pleasure, both spiritual and physical, in Italy, a place I only spent a couple of weeks in, and so it's somewhere I would also like to call a spiritual 'home'. And in Great Britain I have quite simply made myself 'at home' and pay taxes and am labelled 'British', or even 'English composer of German birth', by all the dictionaries.[9]

In spite of all his laconic comments of this type, there can be little doubt that Goldschmidt had a special emotional relationship with Hamburg. Childhood and youth, after all, are the years which have the deepest influence, and everything Goldschmidt experienced there – the large body of relatives, the

---

8   Goldschmidt, 'My mother's family Wiesner', script written in spring 1993; letter from Goldschmidt to Michael Weiss, dated 17 March 1992; documentary material housed in The Berthold Goldschmidt Archive, Akademie der Künste, Berlin. See also Petersen, 2003, 124–28.
9   'Ich war und bin vor allem Europäer. Ich bin zwar in Deutschland aufgewachsen, aber ich fühle mich nicht als Deutscher. Mehr Ehrgeiz war immer, mehrere europäische Sprachen zu sprechen. Leider ist mir das nicht ganz gelungen. Schwieriger ist es mit dem Begriff "Heimat". Ich kann diese Wohnung hier in London, wo ich nun bald 60 Jahre lebe, doch nicht als Exil empfinden, das ist meine – Heimat. Anderseits, was heißt "Heimat"? Ich bin in Hamburg geboren, das nennt man "Heimat". Erwachsen geworden bin ich und die meisten und größten Einflüsse hatte ich in Berlin, also auch "Heimat". Das größte Vergnügen, geistig und körperlich, hatte ich in Italien, wo ich nur ein paar Wochen war, das will ich also – eine ausgesprochen geistige "Heimat" nennen. Und in Großbritannien bin ich ganz einfach "beheimatet" und zahle Steuern und werde in allen Lexika als "British" oder sogar "English composer of German birth" aufgeführt', Goldschmidt, in Petersen, 2003, 113f.

graves of his father and sister in Ohlsdorf,[10] the many trips along the Elbe and by the North Sea and the Baltic coast, his bar-mitzvah in the large Bornplatz Synagogue,[11] his school years in St Georg (a district of Hamburg near the station), the First World War and the military importance of the harbour, the musical life in St Michael's and the music-hall, standing on what today is Johannes Brahms Square – must have left ineradicable impressions on him. Another factor to be taken into account is the particular attitude of the spirit of the citizens of Hamburg, a spirit born of the Hanseatic sense of freedom and a heritage of openness, with a general tendency towards Anglophilia. That Goldschmidt should have chosen England as the land of his exile may well be the result of those early Hamburg influences.

2   Visits to Hamburg after the Second World War

Apart from a trip in 1951, in the unfulfilled hope of interesting North German Radio (NDR) in performing his music, Goldschmidt's first visit to Hamburg took place in 1988, fifty-three years after his flight from Germany, for the opening of an exhibition called 'Burning Songs, Burnt Music',[12] documenting the fate of Hamburg musicians persecuted by the Nazis, to which the city council had invited him.

The exhibition, which lasted for several weeks, was accompanied by four concerts dedicated to the theme of 'Music in Exile'. In the first concert, in the

---

10   In a letter to me, dated 25 January 1993, Goldschmidt wrote: 'I was much moved by your photograph of the headstone of my father and sister. The trees have grown enormously since my visit to Ohlsdorf in 1951! More than 42 years have done nothing to the stone' ('Ganz gerührt war ich über Deine Aufnahme des Grabsteins meines Vaters und meiner Schwester. Die Bäume sind riesig gewachsen seit meinem Besuch in Ohlsdorf 1951! Mehr als 42 Jahre haben dem *Stein* nichts angetan').

11   Goldschmidt distanced himself from religious aspects of Judaism: 'I was born and have stayed a Jew, but I am no practising Jew. I am not close to any religion at all, since I am an atheist. [...] To be honest, I didn't like learning Hebrew because I had to give up my Sundays instead of being able to go out among nature' (quoted in Herlinde Koelbl, *Jüdische Portraits. Photographien und Interviews* (Frankfurt am Main: Fischer, 1989), 78: 'Ich bin als Jude aufgewachsen und Jude geblieben, aber ich bin kein gläubiger Jude. Ich stehe überhaupt keiner Religion nahe, denn ich bin Atheist. [...] Ehrlich gesagt, war mir das Hebräischlernen zuwider, weil ich meine Sonntage opfern mußte, anstatt hinaus in die Natur gehen zu können'. Nevertheless, he always remembered the precise date of his bar-mitzvah, 16 January 1916.

12   The exhibition catalogue was published as Peter Petersen (ed.), *Zündende Lieder – verbrannte Musik. Folgen des Nazifaschismus für Hamburger Musiker und Musikerinnen* (Hamburg: VSA-Verlag, 1988); a completely revised edition appeared in 1995.

FIGURE 7.4   Cover of the book *Zündende Lieder, verbrannte Musik*

Brahms Saal on 15 November 1988, works by the Hamburg composers Robert Müller-Hartmann, Paul Dessau, Goldschmidt, Ilse Fromm-Michaels and Ruth Schonthal were performed, as well as music by Erich Wolfgang Korngold, Hanns Eisler, Stefan Wolpe and Emil František Burian; the works by Goldschmidt, who was present, were the songs 'Ein Rosenzweig', 'Nebelwehen', 'Clouds' and 'The Old Ships'. In the second concert, given in Studio 10 of NDR[13] on 19 November 1988, Goldschmidt's *Ciaconna sinfonica* and *Letzte Kapitel* were performed, as well as the 'Adagio' from Korngold's Symphony in F sharp minor, Op. 40. What gave the concert a special significance was that Goldschmidt conducted the *Ciaconna sinfonica* himself and received a prolonged ovation. It had personal importance, too: it was almost sixty years since he had last conducted in Hamburg, for the first performance of his *Tanz-Suite*, on 30 January 1929, in the Large Hall of the Hamburg Musikhalle, the city's major concert hall. Goldschmidt was also represented in the third concert, on 29 November, a piano recital with his *Variations on a Palestinian Shepherd's Song*, although by now he had already returned to London. (The last concert, on 6 December, was dedicated to resistance songs and songs from the ghetto with works by the Auschwitz survivor Esther Bejarano and performed by the group Siebenschön.)

The exhibition and its concerts at last alerted the citizens of Hamburg to Goldschmidt – a year after Simon Rattle had brought the forgotten composer before the public in Berlin. Each performance drove home, for the cultural authorities and music-lovers alike, the fact that Goldschmidt was a native Hamburger.[14] Yet he was never granted a large-scale concert in the city of his birth – although he would, of course, have been delighted to hear, for example, his two operas performed in the former Hamburg Stadttheater, now the Hamburgische Staatsoper. He was nonetheless granted a *Gesprächskonzert*, a lecture-concert, in the chamber-music hall of the Musikhalle on 25 May 1991, when he heard performances of the Second String Quartet, composed in 1936, the Third Quartet of 1989, and the Clarinet Quintet from 1983. At the end of the pre-concert discussion, during which he had reminisced about his childhood

---

13 Studio 10 (Oberstrasse 120) is now called the Rolf Liebermann Studio. It is in the building that once housed the temple of the Jewish Reform community in Hamburg, built in the Bauhaus style at the beginning of the 1930s and bought by NDR after the Second World War. A plaque and a memorial commemorate the history of the building.

14 The same was true for his fellow Hamburg composer Paul Dessau, who gained local recognition only when his *Deutsches Miserere* was given its west European premiere in the Musikhalle on 1 September 1989.

in Hamburg and his first encounters with the music of Gustav Mahler,[15] I asked what his next work would be. Here is his answer:

> Now that I've successfully recovered from an eye operation two and three weeks ago on each eye I can now see even the smallest notes, and so I've decided to compose a string trio. The biggest effect a string trio has ever had on me, except for, of course Mozart's Divertimento in E flat, was Schoenberg's; it was one his few works truly to impress me. So based on Mozart's work, the peak of all music literature, and Schoenberg's, perhaps the peak of what can be achieved in music, perhaps I can dare to write something. And, of course, that can be done only in a completely different manner, neither Schoenbergian – let alone Mozart.[16]

A year later Goldschmidt's engagement with the music of Gustav Mahler was referred to in the text of an invitation to a reception given by the cultural authorities of Hamburg to mark his eighty-ninth birthday:

> The free Hansa city honours the native Hamburg composer Berthold Goldschmidt with a Senatorial reception on the occasion of his 89th birthday. The Philharmonic Orchestra, conducted by Gabriel Chmura, will perform Mahler's Tenth Symphony, the concert version of which was prepared from the fragments by Deryck Cooke and Berthold Goldschmidt. Goldschmidt conducted the premiere in 1964.[17]

These repeated visits to Hamburg began to awaken in Goldschmidt a sense of being at home there again, with the result that he decided to celebrate his ninetieth birthday there, and so the senator responsible for culture, Dr Christina Weiss, invited him to a banquet on 18 January 1993, with a gala concert on the

---

15   A recording of the occasion and a transcript are in my possession.
16   'Nachdem ich jetzt durch eine doppelte erfolgreiche Augenoperation, gerade vor 14 Tagen oder drei Wochen, wieder im Stande bin, kleine Noten zu Papier zu bringen, werde ich sehen, daß ich ein Streichtrio schreibe. Der größte Eindruck eines Streichtrios, abgesehen von Mozarts Divertimento in Es-Dur, hat mir Schoenbergs spätes Streichtrio gemacht, eines der wenigen Werke Schoenbergs, die mir wirklich enorm imponieren. Also gemessen an dem Mozart–Divertimento, was eines der Gipfelwerke der Musikliteratur ist, und dem Schoenbergschen Streichtrio, was vielleicht ein Gipfelwerk des Erreichbaren in der Musik ist, kann man vielleicht wagen, etwas zu schreiben. Und das kann natürlich nur auf ganz andere Art geschehen, weder Schoenbergisch – let alone Mozart.'
17   Concerning this performance see Jörg Rothkamm, *Berthold Goldschmidt und Mahlers X. Symphonie. Zur Entstehung der Konzertfassung von Deryck Cooke* (Hamburg: von Bockel, 2000), 175f.

following day: 'Your visit to Hamburg for the event of your 90th birthday we view as an honour the value of which, in light of Germany's history and present, we are well aware'.[18] The concert, mounted by the Free Academy of Arts, took place in the NDR Studio 10: the Auryn Quartet performed Goldschmidt's Second and Third Quartets.

If Hamburg became an affair of the heart for Goldschmidt, Berlin was the focus of his late fame. His Hamburg visits became sporadic, the last being on 25 April 1996, only a few months before his death; the occasion being the presentation of a prize to Simon Rattle by the Toepfer Foundation, which is based in Hamburg. The concert to mark the event was presented by Kolja Lessing on the violin and Berthold Goldschmidt at the keyboard – his last public appearance as musician.

On 14 January 1997, three months after his death, the Free Academy of the Arts put on a memorial concert. After a short *in memoriam* address from me, the Mandelring Quartet performed the Fourth and Second String Quartets, and Kolja Lessing played the *Capriccio*, Op. 11, and the *Variations on a Palestinian Shepherd's Song*, Op. 32, both for piano, as well as the work Goldschmidt dedicated to him, the *Capriccio* for solo violin of 1991–92.

3   HBG (Hamburg) and Other Ciphers in Goldschmidt's Late Works

The customary abbreviation for Hamburg is 'Hbg', and Goldschmidt often toyed with it in his letters. In his Third Quartet, he brought these letters into his music, as well as the secondary notes 'Sch-H', an abbreviation for Schleswig Holstein, the state which lies immediately to the north of Hamburg. The decryption of the entire cypher is in his writing on the title page of the autograph (see the facsimile and the transcription on the following pages).[19]

In the programme notes of the premiere, in Rendsburg (Schleswig Holstein) on 6 November 1989, he wrote:[20]

---

18   Original wording of the invitation from Dr Weiss: 'Ihren Besuch in Hamburg anläßlich Ihres 90. Geburtstages betrachten wir als eine Ehre und als eine Geste, die wir, besonders im Blick auf Ihre Lebensgeschichte und die deutsche Vergangenheit und Gegenwart, zu schätzen wissen und würdigen möchten'.
19   Commissioned by the Ministry of Education, Science, Youth and Culture of the State Schleswig-Holstein – with respect of Hamburg.
20   The German original can be found in Petersen, 2003, 136 ('Seit unbeschwerten Besuchen von Norddeutschland waren furchtbare Zeiten und viele Jahre vergangen, im Falle Schleswig-Hosteins mehr als 60. In Verbindung mit meiner Geburtsstadt Hamburg, erschienen nun der Nord-Ostseekanal und Rendsburg und seine weite grüne Umwelt wie eine Fata Morgana von Kindheit und Schulzeit, Eindrücke, die sich in meiner Musik

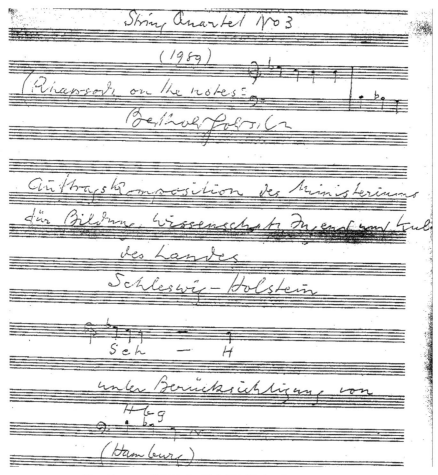

FIGURE 7.5A   The title page of Goldschmidt's *Third String Quartet*
SOURCE: FACSIMILE CREATED BY THE AUTHOR

Since previous carefree visits to North Germany, terrible times and many years had been and gone – more than 60 years in the case of Schleswig Holstein. In connection with the city of my birth, Hamburg, the North Sea-Baltic canal and Rendsburg with its broad green surroundings seemed like a fata morgana of my childhood and school years – impressions that

> naturgemäß reflektieren würden. Wie war die zu schreibende Komposition eindeutig mit dem Auftraggeber zu copulieren? Meine Lösung war im Prinzip keineswegs neu: von Bach bis Berg haben Komponisten die Buchstaben von Eigennamen der Nomenklatur unserer Tonscala aufgepropft und so entschloss ich mich, die Noten SCH-H und als Partnermotiv HBG aus melodischen Keimzellen so zu entwickeln, dass kaum eine Episode ohne diese sieben Töne abläuft').

String Quartet No 3
(1989)

(Rhapsody on the notes:

Berthold Goldschmidt

Auftragskomposition des Ministeriums für Bildung, Wissenschaft, Jugend und Kultur des Landes Schleswig-Holstein

S c h   —   H

unter Berücksichtigung von

Hbg

(Hamburg)

S = E♭, C = C♮, H = B♮, B = B♭

FIGURE 7.5B   Transcription of the title page of Goldschmidt's *Third String Quartet* (by Peter Petersen)

would naturally be reflected in my music. How was the work I had to write to be clearly linked with the commissioner? In principle my solution was in no way new: from Bach to Berg composers have taken the letters of people's names and set them in the nomenclatura of our musical scales, and so I decided to develop the notes SCH–H, with a subsidiary theme HBG, from germinating melodic cells in such a manner that these seven notes are present in virtually every subsequent episode.

Goldschmidt's comments on his use of ciphers describe a superficial characteristic that has hardly any relationship with the actual content of the composition. A quotation from his dark choral work *Belsatzar*, and the 'Chanukka' melody,[21] presented as an optimistic counterpoint, are more important, since they introduce the implicit semantic resonance of the minor third and minor second, the melodic outline of which can be found in Mahler songs ('Oft denk' ich, sie sind nur ausgegangen' from the *Rückert Lieder*, for example) and in Berg (as in 'Ach Marie!' from *Wozzeck*), as well as in the augmented second of certain traditional Jewish modes (in the Ahavah Rabah *steiger*,[22] for instance), often with connotations of suffering and sorrow. Goldschmidt did not use these motifs simply as *objets trouvés*; they are so closely related that their use is obviously deliberate. The only intervals in these groups are the minor third and the minor second, with the HBG (B♮, B♭, G♮) motif being the retrograde inversion of the SCH (E♭, C♮, B♮). Goldschmidt's views on the relationship between Hamburg and Schleswig-Holstein, by contrast, may perhaps be gleaned from his comments: his formulation 'with reference to Hbg' could be either a friendly acknowledgement or a disappointed afterthought – after all, the 'northern lights' of Kiel, capital of Schleswig-Holstein, came to him with commissions, while the 'pepper sacks'[23] of Hamburg could never bring themselves to make concrete gestures of support.

The String Trio, written in 1991 and given the telling title *Retrospectrum*, also uses ciphers. It is a programmatic, single-movement composition that refers directly to Hamburg and his immediate family in the first half of the century.[24] In a letter to me, dated 13 March 1992, Goldschmidt explained the programme:

---

21   *Ibid.*, 136.
22   Hanoch Avenary: 'Jüdische Musik' (western diaspora) in: 2MGG, Sachteil, vol. 4, Kassel 1996, col. 1551.
23   Metaphor for the mercantile character of the upper tens of Hamburg.
24   The dedication reads: 'To the memory of my parents'.

Here is the RSO production[25] of the quasi biographical trio that is built exclusively from my own material, including a quotation from my ballet 'Chronica', not a 'waltz' as reported in the 'Tagesspiegel', but rather a 'barcarolle' with associations that now re-occur – to a punting trip on the Outer Alster during which a thunderstorm suddenly arose, bringing danger for my mother and sister. Moreover, the work reflects 'en miniature' the comings and goings of the 20s, with threatening darknesses, the anagrams [sic] of my parents,
A D F G D Es C H D - - - - - - - H E – G – Dis^{Es} C H D[26]
A d o l f G o l d s c h m i d t   H e n n y G o l d s c h m i d t
tragic events and ultimately the will to survive.[27]

Thus, Goldschmidt's String Trio expresses, as no other work of his does, his relationship with and feeling for Hamburg, mostly as reflected by the happy memories of his life with his parents and sister.

In conclusion, I would like to draw attention to a little *pièce d'occasion* indirectly linked to Hamburg – the unpublished song 'Noble Little Solder's Wife', composed in 1948 for the first performance of Wolfgang Borchert's play, *The Man Outside*.[28]

Borchert's *Draußen vor der Tür* takes place in bombed-out Hamburg in 1946; Goldschmidt's song is sung by Beckmann, a returning soldier, who hopes to

---

25   He is referring to the recording of the first performance, given in Berlin on 23 January 1992 by three members of the Berlin Radio Symphony Orchestra; see also Barbara Busch, *Berthold Goldschmidts Opern im Kontext von Musik- und Zeitgeschichte* (Oldenburgh: BIS, 2000), 387.

26   That is, A♮, D♮, F♮, G♮, D♮, E♮, C♮, B♮, D♮ and B♮, E♮, G♮, D♯/E♭, C♮, B♮, D♮ in English terminology.

27   'Hier ist die RSO Produktion des quasi biographischen Trios, das ausschliesslich aus eigenem Material besteht, einschliesslich des Zitates aus meiner Ballettmusik "Chronika": kein "Walzer" (wie es im "Tagesspiegel" hiess) sondern eher eine "Barcarolle" mit nun auftauchenden Assoziationen einer Puntfahrt auf der Aussenalster, bei der bei einem plötzlich einsetzenden Gewitter Gefahr für Mutter u. Schwester bestand. Auch sonst spiegelt das Stück "en Miniature" das Auf u. Ab der 20er Jahre wieder, mit drohenden Dunkelheiten, dem Anagramm meiner Eltern [...] tragischen Ereignissen u. endlich der Wille zu überleben.'

28   Borchert's play, written in late autumn 1946, was first presented in a radio broadcast. This version was translated into English by David Porter, produced for the 'Third Programme' of the BBC and broadcast three times in November and December 1948. See *The Man Outside: The Prose Works of Wolfgang Borchert*, transl. David Porter (London: Hutchinson, 1952), 73–127, 103. The song has been edited within an article of mine: Peter Petersen, '"Noble little soldier's wife ..." Eine unbekannte Quelle zur frühen Borchert-Rezeption in England', in *Jahreshefte der Internationalen Wolfgang-Borchert-Gesellschaft*, Nr. 14 (2002), Hamburg, 23–30.

FIGURE 7.6 Poster advertising the first showing of *Draußen vor der Tür*
SOURCE: WIKIMEDIA COMMONS

join a cabaret. Yet, what he has experienced in the war never leaves him in peace: he's constantly transformed in his dreams into a sweating, bloody general who plays a xylophone made of human bones, and so his song becomes too serious and is rejected – 'Too direct, you see. You're missing in your youth the carefree casualness of superiority', says the cabaret director to the young soldier. Here, Goldschmidt set the rather idiosyncratic text of the English version alongside the German original:

The world laughs in scorn	*Die Welt hat gelacht*
At the life I must mourn.	*und ich hab gebrüllt.*
And the mists of the night,	*Und der Nebel der Nacht*
Have concealed it from sight.	*hat dann alles verhüllt.*
Only moons grin green	*Nur der Mond grinst noch*
And are seen	*durch ein Loch*
Through the torn curtain!	*in der Gardine!*

Borchert's stage directions require 'soft xylophone music' to accompany the text, and so Goldschmidt's setting as a 'Song for Baritone and Xylophone' is entirely appropriate. And even if the scoring is unusual, this short, racy song deserves both publication and a place in future productions of Borchert's play.

For Goldschmidt, this indirect encounter with the bomb-shattered Hamburg must have been a moving experience. Borchert, another Hamburger, symbolises a further group of victims of the Nazi reign of terror: he was the principal representative of the genre of *Trümmerliteratur* – perhaps best translated as 'writing from the rubble' or 'writing from the ruins'. He died on 20 November 1947, a day before the premiere of his play in the Hamburg Chamber Theatre, succumbing at last to the physical deprivations he had undergone in action at the front. Goldschmidt, despite the safety of his London exile, would have seen the destruction of Hamburg as a reflection of the destruction of his own life. It was all of four decades later before this wound began to heal a little, and Hamburg must be credited with its contributions in making sure that his works emerged from oblivion. One hopes that his music will continue to be performed – perhaps even in the opera house at the Dammtorstraße.

Appendix: The Goldschmidts and the Wiesners

Those relatives of Goldschmidt who were killed by the Nazis are marked with grey shading.

Great-grandparents
Paternal	Israel (Cossel) Goldschmidt
	Sara Goldschmidt *née* Joseph
	Benjamin Lewin
	Sara (called Selly) Lewin *née* Cohn
Maternal	Jacob Wiesner
	Rebecca Wiesner *née* Katzenstein
	Israel Pappenheim
	Betty Pappenheim *née* Cahn

Grandparents
Paternal	Michael Beer Goldschmidt, born Hamburg, 22 January 1831, died Hamburg, 23 August 1869
	Bertha Beer Goldschmidt *née* Lewin, born Hamburg, 6 January 1832, died Hamburg, 4 January 1903
Maternal	Moritz Wiesner, born Kassel, 21 September 1843, died Kassel, 25 January 1905
	Julie Wiesner *née* Pappenheim, born Eschwege, 19 December 1845, died Kassel, 10 September 1888 (during the birth of her daughter Julie)

Great-Uncles and -Aunts
Paternal	–
Maternal	Abraham Wiesner, born 24 July 1837
	Meier Wiesner, born 24 November 1839
	Jettchen Wiesner, born 18 December 1844
	Blümchen Wiesner, born 2 June 1852

Parents

Adolf Michael Goldschmidt, born Hamburg,
27 September 1864, died Hamburg, 6 February 1937,
∞ 30 March 1900 in Kassel to:
Henriette (Henny) Goldschmidt *née* Wiesner,
born Kassel, 25 March 1873, died Brighton-Hove,
Sussex, 6 May 1953; naturalised British citizen from
24 June 1949

Uncles and Aunts

Paternal

Gustav Goldschmidt, born Hamburg, 11 March 1859
Henriette Weiss *née* Goldschmidt, born Hamburg,
28 August 1860, died Theresienstadt (Terezín),
19 October 1942; ∞ Ignatz Weiss, born Prague,
23 July 1857
Daniel Goldschmidt, born Hamburg,
2 September 1861, died Basel; ∞ to Frieda Loewe,
died Basel
Jenny Magnus *née* Goldschmidt, born Hamburg,
24 January 1863; ∞ to Adolf Magnus
John Goldschmidt, born Hamburg, 4 March 1868,
died New York, 1936
Joseph Goldschmidt, born Hamburg, 16 March 1869

Maternal

Bertha Bauer *née* Wiesner, born Kassel,
4 November 1870, died Copenhagen; ∞ Hermann
Bauer (?1899)
Max Wiesner, born Kassel, 4 January 1872, died
Hamburg, after 1918 (suicide)
Leo Wiesner, born Kassel, 25 May 1874, death
unknown; 'he certainly did not manage to leave
Germany',[29] ∞ Bella Wiesner *née* Strauss
Flora Loew *née* Wiesner, born Kassel,
25 January 1876; ∞ to Siegmund Loew in Hamburg,
emigrated before the War to the USA, died after 1945
in California ('they died heartbroken on learning
the news of their son's Fritz and family death by
gassing'[30])

---

29   Goldschmidt, 'My mother's family Wiesner', script.
30   *Ibid.*

Oscar Wiesner, born Kassel, 12 September 1879 or 1877, died 29 July 1911
Gustav Wiesner, born Kassel, 29 March 1882, died Wepener, South Africa, 1964
Albert Wiesner, born Kassel, 12 February 1885 or 1883, emigrated. *c.*1912/1913 to the USA; ∞ unknown
Meta Isaac *née* Wiesner, born Kassel, 7 June 1887; ∞ Hugo Isaac (died young); deported from Holland into a concentration camp, murdered together with daughter Margaret and her husband and two children
Julie Wiesner, born Kassel, 10 September 1888, died 1919

Brothers and Sisters

Ilse Julie Goldschmidt, born Hamburg, 3 May 1901, died Hamburg, 8 June 1901
Manfred Moritz Goldschmidt, born Hamburg, 11 July 1905, died Hamburg, 11 August 1906
NN (girl) Goldschmidt, born Schlangenbad, 20 June 1907, died Schlangenbad, 20 June 1907
Ruth Lotte Abraham *née* Goldschmidt, born Hamburg, 14 August 1908, died Hamburg, 11 June 1935; ∞ 1 December 1932 to George Abraham, Hamburg

Wife

Elisabeth Goldschmidt *née* Bothe, born Oldenburg, 2 March 1910, died London, 13 March 1979; ∞ Berthold Goldschmidt, London, 20 February 1936

Cousins
Paternal
by Gustav Goldschmidt

Amely Heymann *née* Goldschmidt, born Hamburg, killed in a concentration camp (with her husband and two sons)
Paula Sussmann *née* Goldschmidt, emigrated in 1939 to the USA; ∞:
Otto Sussmann, born Hamburg, 14 March 1895, died 10 December 1938 in concentration camp Sachsenhausen

by Henriette Wiesner

Max Weiss, born Ottensen, near Hamburg, 2 February 1884, died Hamburg, 22 May 1954; ∞ Wilhelmine Weiss *née* Schuchardt

by Daniel Goldschmidt	Bernhard Goldschmidt, died 1923
by Jenny Magnus	Max Magnus, died 1920s
	Meno Magnus, fallen during the First World War
	Cilly Levisohn *née* Magnus, born 31 December 1894, deported to Łódź 25 October 1941, further deported on 25 April 1942 and lost; her husband Albert Levisohn, born Hamburg, 17 March 1891, deported to Łódź 25 October 1941, died Łódź 18 February 1942
Maternal	Walter Bauer, born Hamburg, died Zurich, 1966
by Bertha Bauer	Erwin Bauer, born Hamburg 1906, imprisoned in concentration camps Hamburg-Fuhlsbüttel and Dachau, fled to USA, lived in Berkeley, California
	Irma Bauer, born Hamburg, 1908, was hidden in Amsterdam, lived in Berkeley, California
by Leo Wiesner	Lotte Nebel *née* Wiesner, born], 20 October 1909, emigrated to Israel; ∞ Herbert Nebel, born 29 March 1908, died 16 April 1972
	Grete Oppenheimer *née* Wiesner, born Israel, 10 November 1911, died 1959; ∞ Ludwig Oppenheimer, died 1959
by Flora Loew	Fritz Loew, born Hamburg, 1 January 1905, deported to Theresienstadt, murdered in Auschwitz (together with his wife and two children)
	Margot *née* Loew, born 1908, ∞, lived in Seattle
by Gustav Wiesner	Manfred Wiesner, born and ∞ in South Africa, died. *c.*1978 in Pretoria
	Albert Wiesner, born South Africa, died *c.*1973
by Meta Isaac	Gertrud ('Tutti') *née* Isaac, born 1910, lives in Portland, Oregon, USA
	Margaret *née* Isaac 1912, ∞, deported from Holland into a concentration camp, killed (together with her husband and two children)
	Alice Brown *née* Isaac, born 1914, survived Bergen-Belsen and transport to Auschwitz, lives in Hillsborough, California

8
Preisgekrönt und doch kein Glück? Anmerkungen zu Berthold Goldschmidts Belcanto-Oper *Beatrice Cenci*

Barbara Busch

Abstract

‚Forgotten and rediscovered' – such is the framework within which to approach and appreciate the life and work of Berthold Goldschmidt. A key phrase that indicates the influence of socio-political conditions and music-aesthetic currents on Berthold Goldschmidt's biography, and its reflection in the reception of his compositional oeuvre. This is especially exemplified in Goldschmidt's so-called bel canto opera *Beatrice Cenci*, last produced in July 2018 as part of the Bregenz Festival. The difficult, even tragic, situation of the 'British composer of German birth', as he is described in the *Grove Dictionary of Music and Musicians*, is documented in its choice of subject as well as in the history of its reception. In this essay, both the choice of subject and music-dramaturgical conception of *Beatrice Cenci* are addressed, as well as its history of creation and reception.

Berthold Goldschmidt, am 18. Januar 1903 in Hamburg geboren, gehört zu jenen Komponisten, die durch die nationalsozialistischen Machthaber und die damit verbundenen dramatischen politischen Ereignisse gezwungen waren, ins Exil zu gehen. 1935 gelang dem zweiunddreißigjährigen Goldschmidt, der sich als Sozialdemokrat verstand und der gerade angefangen hatte, sich im öffentlichen Musikleben (u.a. mit seiner ersten Oper *Der gewaltige Hahnrei*) zu etablieren, die Flucht aus Deutschland. Er ging nach London, wo er einundsechzig Jahre lang lebte und am 17. Oktober 1996 starb.[1]

---

1 Zur Biographie Goldschmidts vgl. Barbara Busch, *Berthold Goldschmidts Opern im Kontext von Musik- und Zeitgeschichte* (Oldenburg: BIS, 2000), 36–48. Zu den biographischen Stationen in Goldschmidts Londoner Zeit vgl. Jutta Raab Hansen, *NS-verfolgte Musiker in England. Spuren deutscher und österreichischer Flüchtlinge in der britischen Musikkultur*, Bd. 1: *Musik im ‚Dritten Reich' und im Exil*, Schriftenreihe, hrsg. v. Hanns-Werner Heister und Peter Petersen (Hamburg: von Bockel, 1996), 333–60.

Im Exil entstanden zwar bis 1957 noch viele Werke, doch Goldschmidts Versuche, im englischen Musikleben Fuß zu fassen, scheiterten. Seine Tonsprache[2] fand in der Nachkriegszeit, in der sich das Interesse auf serielle Techniken und elektronische Musik konzentrierte, kaum Resonanz: Seiner politischen Verdrängung folgte eine ästhetische. Von dieser Verdrängung betroffen war auch Goldschmidts zweite Oper *Beatrice Cenci*, deren Libretto auf Percy Bysshe Shelleys Tragödie *The Cenci* basiert. Mit ihr wählte Goldschmidt die literarische Verarbeitung einer authentischen Handlung im Italien des späten 16. Jahrhunderts, die bis in die Gegenwart Künstler unterschiedlicher Sparten fasziniert und zu neuen Werken inspiriert hat: Literarisch verarbeiteten den Stoff beispielsweise Alexandre Dumas d. Ä. und Alberto Moravia. Komponisten ließen sich sowohl im Bereich der Vokalmusik als auch in der Instrumentalmusik vom Cenci-Sujet anregen. Opern schrieben nach diesem Stoff u.a. der polnische Komponist Ludomir Różycki und der Argentinier Alberto Ginastera.[3]

Im Folgenden wird – ausgehend von einer Interpretation der Sujetwahl – der musikalische Rückbezug der Vertonung zur Handlungszeit des Sujets exemplarisch illustriert und die musikdramaturgische Konzeption von Goldschmidts Oper *Beatrice Cenci* im Überblick dargestellt. Der Entstehungsprozess und die Rezeptionsgeschichte der preisgekrönten und doch (immer wieder) vergessenen Oper werden vor diesem Hintergrund abschließend nachgezeichnet.

1 Die Sujetwahl als allegorisches Echo

Goldschmidts Sujetwahl verweist auf den von ihm folgenreich erlebten faschistischen Terror in Deutschland: Der römische Edelmann Francesco Cenci tyrannisiert seine Familie, er vergewaltigt seine Tochter Beatrice, sie lässt ihren Vater daraufhin töten und endet deshalb, gemeinsam mit ihrer Stiefmutter Lucrezia, auf dem Schafott. Beatrices vollkommene Abhängigkeit von ihrem tyrannischen Vater sowie ihre psychische Zerstörung durch sein Verhalten bilden eine Parallele zur Machtlosigkeit jener, die wie Goldschmidt Opfer der nationalsozialistischen Herrschaft wurden. Goldschmidts traumatisches Erlebnis der Flucht, des Verlustes vieler Familienangehöriger sowie die abrupte

---

2 Zur Tonsprache Goldschmidts vgl. Busch 2000, 281–99.
3 Vgl. zur Entstehungsgeschichte der Oper *Beatrice Cenci* die Ausführungen in Busch 2000, 190–99 sowie den bereits 1988 von Paul Banks publizierten Artikel ‚The case of *Beatrice Cenci*', in der Zeitschrift *Opera* (XXXIX, 426–432).

Unterbrechung seiner Musikerkarriere führten ihm die Abhängigkeit von den Machthabenden und seine Chancenlosigkeit in einem diktatorischen System brutal vor Augen. Shelleys Tragödie bot Goldschmidt die Gelegenheit, das Erlebte musikalisch zu thematisieren.

Doch die Sujetwahl kann nicht nur als allegorisches Echo auf den Faschismus verstanden werden, sie dürfte auch mit strategischen Überlegungen verbunden gewesen sein: Bereits 1948 hatte Goldschmidt eine Hörspielmusik zu der vom BBC-Redakteur Martin Esslin erstellten Kurzfassung des Dramas von Shelley komponiert. Als er erfuhr, dass der britische Arts Council einen Opernwettbewerb anlässlich des ‚Festival of Britain' 1951 ausgeschrieben und den Gewinnern Aufführungsmöglichkeiten ihrer Opern in Aussicht gestellt hatte, entschloss sich Goldschmidt, seine Hörspielmusik zu einer Oper auszuweiten. Dabei dürfte ihm klar gewesen sein, dass hinter dem Opernwettbewerb das kulturpolitische Anliegen stand, die besonders durch Benjamin Brittens Opern geschaffenen Ansätze einer eigenen englischen Operntradition weiter auszubauen. Goldschmidt, der sich vom Gewinn des Wettbewerbs die Chance erhoffte, als Komponist in England Fuß zu fassen, schien vor diesem Hintergrund gut beraten, den traditionsreichen Stoff eines angesehenen englischen Dichters als Operngrundlage zu wählen.

Mit der ästhetischen Prämisse im Kopf, eine Belcanto-Oper schreiben zu wollen, bat Goldschmidt Martin Esslin, den er als Regisseur in der deutschen Abteilung der BBC kennengelernt hatte, um die Einrichtung des Librettos. Zwar konnte Esslin hierfür gewonnen werden, doch stand er dem Projekt – wie er mir in einem Brief vom 30. Juni 1997 mitteilte – zögernd gegenüber:

> Goldschmidt war sehr darauf erpicht [an dem Wettbewerb] teilzunehmen und bestürmte mich, ich solle meine Cenci-Bearbeitung zur Grundlage einer Oper machen. Ich war recht pessimistisch [...], aber für Goldschmidt war ein Libretto lebensnotwendig, da das Libretto den Zugang zum ganzen Wettbewerb eröffnete. Um mich zu überreden, versprach er mir einen sehr hohen Anteil – ich weiß nicht mehr, ob es 50 oder 33 Prozent waren – von dem Preis und den Tantiemen. So entschloß ich mich, diese Sache, die ich von vornherein für aussichtslos hielt, auf mich zu nehmen.[4]

Goldschmidt nahm umgehend die Arbeit auf, so dass er nach nur einjähriger Arbeit, am 24. April 1950, die fertige Partitur vorlegen konnte.[5] Schließlich ging

---

4 Martin Esslin an Barbara Busch, am 30.6.1997, London, Privatbesitz.
5 Details zur Entstehungsgeschichte der *Beatrice Cenci* finden sich in Busch 2000, 190–94.

er aus dem strengen, mehrstufigen Auswahlverfahren des Opernwettbewerbs, an dem sich eingangs 182 Komponisten beteiligt hatten, als einer der Gewinner hervor: Prämiert wurden Arthur Benjamins Oper *The Tale of Two Cities* (Libretto von Cedric Cliffe nach der gleichnamigen Novelle von Charles Dickens), Alan Bushs *Wat Tyler* (nach einem Libretto seiner Ehefrau Nancy Bush), Karl Rankls *Deirdre of he Sorrows* (Libretto von Karl Rankl nach einem Text von J.M. Synge) sowie Berthold Goldschmidts *Beatrice Cenci*. Ergänzend zu diesen vier Opern zog die Kommission zunächst zwei weitere Kompositionen in Erwägung, deren Namen sie der Öffentlichkeit allerdings nicht preisgab. Um welche beiden Opern es sich handelte, belegen Dokumente, auf die ich bei meinen Recherchen im Archiv des Victoria & Albert Museums stieß. Demnach beriet die Jury lange über Lennox Berkeleys Oper *Nelson*, lehnte schließlich aber die dreiaktige Oper ab. Dies tat sie ebenso mit Wilfried H. Mellers *Tragical History of Christoper Marlowe*.

Der Arts Council erteilte Goldschmidt am 23. Mai 1950 den offiziellen Kompositionsauftrag für (die von Goldschmidt faktisch schon fertig komponierte) *Beatrice Cenci*, womit die Zahlung eines Honorars verbunden war.[6] Mit dem Erhalt der Partitur behielt sich der Arts Council gleichzeitig für zwei Jahre das Recht vor, die erste Produktion der Oper festzulegen. Am 22. Juni 1950 sandte Goldschmidt die Partitur ein und erhielt im Gegenzug das Honorar; zu der in Aussicht gestellten Opernaufführung kam es jedoch nicht.

Im Kontext der Sujetwahl ist abschließend bemerkenswert, dass im Zuge der Entdeckung der *Beatrice Cenci* in den 1990er-Jahren die Frage nach der Aktualität des vertonten Stoffes immer wieder laut wurde. Goldschmidt selbst beantwortet sie mit einem Hinweis auf die Vielschichtigkeit der *Beatrice Cenci* und fasst damit die Bedeutung des Sujets zusammen:

> Es handelt sich um die historische Rechtfertigung dieser Frau, um ein Gleichnis der Opfer des Naziregimes, um die Unterdrückung der Feminität [sic] bis heute und um den Mißbrauch von eigenen Kindern, was man heutzutage täglich in den Zeitungen lesen kann.[7]

Wie Goldschmidt musikalisch auf einen Stoff reagierte, der als Aufschrei gegen Gewalt, politische Korruption und Machtmissbrauch zu verstehen ist, zeigen die nachfolgenden Ausführungen.

---

6 Busch, 193.
7 Goldschmidt zit. n. Ruth Eberhard, ‚Berthold Goldschmidt. Späte Wiedergutmachung', in: Orpheus, 1995, H. 8/9.

2 Musikalischer Rückbezug zur Handlungszeit des Sujets

Beatrice Cenci ist eine dreiaktige Oper mit sinfonisch konzipiertem, durchsichtig angelegtem Orchestersatz, der freitonale Momente aufweist, sich letztlich aber an tonalen Zentren orientiert. Die brutalen Momente von Vergewaltigung, Mord und Hinrichtung entfallen im Libretto; sie ereignen sich quasi hinter der Bühne und schaffen so Raum für eine Fokussierung auf die psychischen Befindlichkeiten der Personen. Die Musik reagiert auf diese Konzeption, indem sie ihrerseits eher zu einer Dämpfung als zu einer Steigerung der Brutalität des Stoffes beiträgt. Die Tragödie verliert dadurch allerdings keinen Funken an Intensität. Ausgehend von Shelleys romantischer Lesart des Renaissance-Stoffs wählte Goldschmidt seinerseits eine historisierende Sichtweise. Bewusst lässt er Klänge der Renaissance und des englischen Barocks in stilisierter Form assoziieren und stellt so musikalisch eine Verbindung zur Handlungszeit des Sujets her. Der Grundklang der Oper ist von dieser Prämisse bestimmt.

Das in einer klassisch-romantischen Tradition stehende symphonische Orchester setzt Goldschmidt im Sinne einer komplexen Mischregistrierung ein, wie sie für das 19. Jahrhundert typisch ist. Gezielt wird dieses vorherrschende Klangprinzip zweitweise durchbrochen: Wenn sich im zweiten Akt Streicher und Bläser gruppenweise gegenüberstehen, so erinnert dies an den Klang englischer Barockkompositionen, wie er sich im ‚broken consort' manifestiert. Darüber hinaus schuf Goldschmidt durch die Art und Weise des Einsatzes des modernen Instrumentariums Momente, die auch Klänge der Renaissance in stilisierter Form assoziieren lassen und so musikalisch eine Verbindung mit der Handlungszeit des Sujets herstellen. Seine Vorstellung eines leicht Patina-artigen Untertons realisierte er durch die bevorzugte Verwendung tief klingender Instrumente bzw. durch den Einsatz tiefer Register wie z.B. gleich zu Beginn der Ouvertüre des ersten Aktes. Zu diesem von Goldschmidt intendierten historisierenden Charakter passt auch das chorartige Auftreten der Blechbläser wie zu Beginn des zweiten Bildes im ersten Akt und gegen Ende des dritten Aktes. Ihr Einsatz lässt sowohl die Venezianische Schule des späten 16. Jahrhunderts als auch Turmmusiken aus Renaissance und Barock anklingen.

Unter den Schlaginstrumenten ist dem Einsatz des Gongs besondere Aufmerksamkeit zu schenken. Zwar gelangt er nur vierzehnmal zum Einsatz, dafür erklingt aber seine dunkle Farbe jedes Mal an exponierter, gut wahrnehmbarer Stelle und ist mit dem Tod in Verbindung zu bringen. Der Einsatz des Gongs ist paradigmatisch für Goldschmidts Umgang mit dem durch Tyrannei, Gewalt und Tod negativ besetzten literarischen Stoff: Goldschmidt verzichtet konsequent darauf, mit einer hektisch, schrill oder brutal klingenden Musik auf das Thema zu reagieren. Stattdessen setzt er gezielt dunkle Klangfarben wie die des Gongs ein, und wählt einen eher ruhigen, Extreme weitgehend aussparenden Grundklang.

3 Die musikdramaturgische Konzeption im Überblick

Das Libretto der *Beatrice Cenci* gibt einen Spannungsbogen vor, den Goldschmidt mit ebenso großem Gespür für zeitliche Proportionen nachzeichnete, wie er auch Arien, Ensemblesätze und Chöre aus musikdramaturgischen Überlegungen geschickt einsetzte. Im Rahmen einer Rundfunksendung aus dem Jahr 1950 formulierte Goldschmidt unmissverständlich sein Anliegen, den Gesangspartien besondere Aufmerksamkeit zu schenken:

> Bei aller konzessionslosen Modernität meiner Musik lag mir daran, in erster Linie eine Oper für Sänger zu schreiben. Ein Bühnenwerk mit dankbaren Partien, die zu erlernen jedem Stimmbegabten Vergnügen und deren Besetzung keinem unserer üblichen Opernensembles Schwierigkeiten machen würde.[8]

Und so verzichtet er einerseits im Rahmen eines vom Tonfall der Sprache angeregten, syllabischen und ihm nachempfundenen Gesangs auf Koloraturen sowie auf größere, abrupte Intervallsprünge und überstrapaziert die Stimmumfänge weder in der Höhe noch in der Tiefe. Andererseits war ihm daran gelegen, dass jeder Protagonist einen solistischen Einsatz erhält.

Faktisch handelt es sich um lyrische Einschübe, die den dramatischen Diskurs durch ihr kontemplatives Moment – ganz im Sinne des klassischen Verständnisses der Arie – unterbrechen und das dramatische Tempo stauen. Zudem sind es die fest im dramatischen Geschehen verankerten *Monologe*, die folglich nur in ihrem jeweiligen inhaltlichen Zusammenhang voll zu erschließen sind und daher nicht von der gleichen musikalischen Geschlossenheit sind wie die Arien. Diese Monologe finden sich im ersten Akt, als Orsino mitteilt, Beatrices Bittschrift nicht weiterzuleiten, und als Beatrice die Gäste um Hilfe bittet. Im zweiten Akt ist Graf Cencis letzter Auftritt vor seiner Ermordung zu nennen und schließlich im dritten Akt Camillos Bestätigung des päpstlichen Hinrichtungsurteils.

Der Wunsch nach *lyrischen Passagen* führte zur Integration von Gedichten Shelleys. So griff Esslin im Rahmen der Librettogestaltung auf einige Strophen

---

8 Goldschmidt zit. n. Busch, 2000, 229.

der Serenade ‚To Sophia' zurück, die getanzt und gesungen den Höhepunkt des festlichen Beisammenseins im Haus Cencis im ersten Akt bilden und das kommende Unheil geradezu heraufbeschwören. Im zweiten Akt fanden zwei Gedichte Shelleys Eingang: Das erste ist ‚A dirge', ein Klagegesang, den Esslin einfügte, um Beatrices Verzweiflung Ausdruck zu verleihen. Das zweite Gedicht ‚Time' wird von Lucrezia vorgetragen, als sie auf die Ankunft der gedungenen Mörder wartet; Goldschmidt hatte es bereits 1943 für tiefe Stimme und Klavier vertont und fügte es nun mit minimalen Veränderungen des Notentextes im Rahmen der Orchestrierung des Klaviersatzes in die Oper ein.[9]

Wenngleich in der Partitur sukzessiv vertonte Textpassagen dominieren, so verfolgt Goldschmidt diesen Ansatz nicht dogmatisch. Im Gegenteil: Bewusst durchbricht er ihn, um musikalisch auf inhaltliche Gegebenheiten zu reagieren. So stehen gegen Ende einer Handlungsphase *Ensemblesätze*, die maßgeblich zu einer musikalischen Spannungssteigerung beitragen: So mündet die erste Handlungsphase des ersten Aktes in einem Terzett, in dem Lucrezia, Beatrice und Bernardo ihr gemeinsames Leiden unter Graf Cenci artikulieren. Ähnlich verhält es sich im zweiten Akt, wo es zu einem kurzen, nur sechs Takte langen Terzett-Einschub kommt. Lucrezia, Orsino und Beatrice sind entschlossen, Graf Cenci zu ermorden; sie bestätigen ihr gemeinsames Vorhaben, sich an dem Grafen zu rächen.

Neben Ensemblepassagen sind es die musikdramaturgisch gezielten Einsätze des gemischten *Chores*, die zur Spannungsintensivierung beitragen: Innerhalb der einzelnen Akte befinden sich die dramatisch spannendsten Momente jeweils im letzten Drittel. Parallel dazu tritt sowohl szenisch als auch musikalisch wirksam der Chor auf. Der gewichtigste Auftritt kommt ihm sicherlich am Ende der Oper zu. Während hier der Chor zunächst die Volksmenge repräsentiert, die für und gegen die Verurteilten Position bezieht, stimmt er wenig später geschlossen eine Totenmesse für die Hingerichteten an. In dieser Passage griff Goldschmidt auf sein bereits 1926 entstandenes (und verschollenes) *Requiem* zurück. Dieser Rückgriff auf ältere Kompositionen steht beispielhaft für die Arbeitsweise Goldschmidts im Londoner Exil. Zugleich stellt es ein weiteres signifikantes Merkmal dieser Oper dar, in deren Sujetwahl bis hin zur Rezeptionsgeschichte sich die schwierige, ja tragische Situation des ‚British composer of German birth' eindringlich widerspiegelt.

---

9 Berthold Goldschmidt: ‚Time'. Song for low voice. Für Tiefe Stimme und Klavier. Nach einem Text von Percy Bysshe Shelley. Satzbezeichnung: Andante maestoso. Jahr der Fertigstellung: November 1943. 1949 Orchesterfassung in *Beatrice Cenci* aufgenommen. UA: 21.4.1985 in Pasadena, Bariton: Sterling Branton, Klavier: Charlotte Zelka. Dauer: 2'30". Verlag: Boosey & Hawkes. Werkautograph: Berthold-Goldschmidt-Archiv der Akademie der Künste Berlin. Klavier- und Orchesterfassung auf Tonträger: Sony S2K 66836 (1995).

4 Jahrzehnte des Vergessens

> Das Werk ist eine richtige ‚Belcanto-Oper' geworden, dem die merkwürdige Mischung des römischen Stoffs und der wundervollen englischen Lyrik gut steht, – es enthält prachtvolle Partien (Sopran, Alt, Bariton und einen weniger wichtigen Tenor), ist spannend und hochdramatisch und leicht aufzuführen.[10]

Mit diesen Worten beschreibt Goldschmidt in einem Brief aus dem Jahr 1951 den gewählten ästhetisch-stilistischen Rahmen seiner *Cenci*-Partitur. Adressat war der Choreograph Kurt Jooss, für dessen Kompanie Goldschmidt bereits 1938 die Ballettmusik *Chronica* mit großem Erfolg komponiert hatte. Nun erhoffte er sich von Jooss Unterstützung hinsichtlich der Uraufführung der *Beatrice Cenci*. Doch dazu kam es vorerst nicht.

Zwar gehörte Goldschmidt mit *Beatrice Cenci* zu den vier Preisgewinnern des Opernwettbewerbs – zur damit in Aussicht gestellten Aufführung kam es aber nicht. Tatsächlich wurde keine der prämierten Opern im Rahmen des ‚Festival of Britain' aufgeführt. Warum? Als die Juroren nach dem Auswahlverfahren erfuhren, welche Komponisten sich hinter den anonym eingereichten Werken verbargen, muss die Fassungslosigkeit der Jury groß gewesen sein – wie Goldschmidt sich erinnerte:

> Alan Bush – ein Kommunist; Karl Rankl – ein reichlich unbeliebter Mann, der mit Lambert (einem Jurymitglied) auf Kriegsfuß stand; Goldschmidt – ich hatte einige erste Auseinandersetzungen mit dem (BBC Redakteur) Stewart Wilson bezüglich meiner Dirigierweise gehabt; und Arthur Benjamin – er kam aus Australien, also wenigstens aus dem Commonwealth. Die Ergebnisse waren aus patriotischer Sicht also nicht gerade erfreulich.[11]

Es ist davon auszugehen, dass Goldschmidt die in Aussicht gestellte Aufführung verweigert wurde, als nach Lüftung seines Inkognitos offensichtlich wurde, dass er kein gebürtiger Engländer war – eine Entwicklung, die in gewisser Hinsicht als typisches Schicksal eines Exilanten bezeichnet werden kann.

---

10 *Ibid.*, 215.
11 Goldschmidt zit. n. Berthold Goldschmidt: *Komponist und Dirigent. Ein Musiker-Leben zwischen Hamburg, Berlin und London*, hg. von P. Petersen und der Arbeitsgruppe Exilmusik am Musikwissenschaftlichen Institut der Universität Hamburg (Hamburg: von Bockel, 2003. 2., erw. Aufl.), 76.

In den folgenden Jahren kämpfte Goldschmidt vergeblich um die Aufführung der *Beatrice Cenci*: Die englischen Opernhäuser zeigten Desinteresse, die Metropolitan Opera nannte wirtschaftliche Schwierigkeiten, und aus Deutschland kam die Kritik, dass bereits das Libretto ungeeignet sei.[12] Goldschmidt verzweifelte und verstummte nach diesen Erlebnissen kompositorisch für fast ein Vierteljahrhundert. Das geringe öffentliche Interesse an seiner musikalischen Stilistik ließ ihn resignieren. Fortan widmete er sich vermehrt und erfolgreich dem Dirigieren. Jörg Rothkamms Interpretation dieser Hinwendung Goldschmidts zum Dirigieren als Kompensationsfunktion für die geringe öffentliche Wahrnehmung als Komponist ist zuzustimmen.[13] Geradezu euphorische Kritiken erhielt er, als er im Januar 1952 an der Niederländischen Oper Amsterdam *Cavalleria rusticana* von Pietro Mascagni und *I Pagliacci* von Ruggiero Leoncavallo dirigierte.[14] 1959 dirigierte Goldschmidt für die BBC die erste vollständige Wiedergabe der 3. Sinfonie Gustav Mahlers in England. In der Folge setzte er sich erfolgreich für die Rezeption der Musik Mahlers in Großbritannien ein. Dennoch dauerte es weitere Jahre bzw. Jahrzehnte bis Musiker, Musikwissenschaftler und Produzenten den Komponisten Berthold Goldschmidt Anfang der 1980er Jahre wiederentdeckten. Ausgelöst wurde dies durch die bruchstückhafte, konzertante Aufführung von Goldschmidts erster Oper *Der gewaltige Hahnrei* am 26. März 1982 in der Londoner St. Peter's Church durch Instrumentalisten und Gesangssolisten vom Trinity College.

5 Wiederentdeckung als bewegende Hommage

Mit dem Zeitpunkt der Fertigstellung der *Beatrice Cenci* im Jahr 1950 geriet das Werk in Vergessenheit. Es vergingen achtunddreißig Jahre bis zur konzertanten Uraufführung Goldschmidts zweiter Oper am 16. April 1988 in der Londoner Queen Elizabeth Hall. Die London Chamber Symphony und der Pro Musica Chorus of London musizierten unter der Leitung von Odaline de la Martinez. Weitere sechs Jahre verstrichen, bis am 30. August 1994 im Rahmen der Berliner Festwochen *Beatrice Cenci* zum ersten Mal in Deutschland konzertant in der Berliner Philharmonie aufgeführt wurde. Lothar Zagrosek leitete das Deutsche Symphonie-Orchester Berlin (RSO) und den Rundfunkchor Berlin; für

---

12   Busch, 256–67.
13   Vgl. Jörg Rothkamm, *Berthold Goldschmidt und Mahlers x. Symphonie. Zur Entstehung der Konzertfassung von Deryck Cooke*, Bd. 6: *Musik im ‚Dritten Reich' und im Exil*, Schriftenreihe, hrsg. v. Hanns-Werner Heister und Peter Petersen (Hamburg: von Bockel, 2000).
14   Zitate aus den damals erschienenen Kritiken finden sich in Busch 2000, 47f.

das Plattenlabel SONY spielten sie die Oper zudem auf CD ein. Wenige Wochen später kam es dann am 10. September 1994 zur szenischen Uraufführung der *Beatrice Cenci* in Magdeburg. Sowohl die Berliner als auch die Magdeburger Aufführung wurden mit anhaltenden Ovationen zu einer bewegenden Hommage an Berthold Goldschmidt, der im Alter von einundneunzig Jahren nicht nur die Wiederentdeckung seiner Oper *Beatrice Cenci* erlebte, sondern auch die seines Gesamtschaffens.

Eine Rezeption seiner Werke im Konzertleben setzte 1984 allmählich ein. In diesem Jahr erlebte Goldschmidt als Gast der in Österreich stattfindenden Mürztaler Werkstatt die Uraufführung seiner Werke *Marche Militaire* für Militärkapelle aus dem Jahr 1937/38 und – mit über fünfzigjähriger Verspätung – *Letzte Kapitel* auf zwei Gedichte von Erich Kästner für Kammerchor, Sprecher, Klavier und Schlagzeug – komponiert 1930/31. Am nordamerikanischen Pasadena Conservatory of Music California fand 1985 ein Konzert statt, das erstmals ausschließlich Goldschmidts Werken gewidmet war. Im gleichen Jahr kam es, wiederum im Rahmen der Mürztaler Werkstatt, zu einer weiteren Uraufführung. Zu hören war eine Auftragskomposition der Walter-Buchebner-Gesellschaft: Goldschmidt hatte das Gedicht ‚Belsatzar' von Heinrich Heine für Chor a cappella vertont.

Neben dem bereits 1982/83 komponierten *Klarinettenquartett* zählt dieser Chorsatz zu den ersten Werken, mit denen Goldschmidt sein langjähriges kompositorisches Verstummen brach. Goldschmidts erneutes Komponieren ab Anfang der 1980er Jahre war eng verbunden mit seiner gleichzeitig einsetzenden Wiederentdeckung: Zum einen erkannte die sich zu dieser Zeit langsam entwickelnde Exilmusikforschung Goldschmidt nicht nur als einen sich lebhaft erinnernden Zeitzeugen, sondern auch die Bedeutung seiner Kompositionen. Zum anderen begannen Interpreten wie Simon Rattle, das Mandelring Quartett und Kolja Lessing Goldschmidts Werke aufzuführen. Die Tonträgerindustrie zog nach, so dass Goldschmidt Mitte der 1990er Jahre zum Medienstar der Klassikszene avancierte.

In diesem Kontext erfolgte im September 1994 die oben bereits erwähnte szenische Uraufführung der *Beatrice Cenci* am Theater der Landeshauptstadt Magdeburg. Überzeugt von der künstlerischen Qualität des Werks stellte Mathias Husmann, der Dirigent der Uraufführung, fest:

> Die Oper *Beatrice Cenci* von Berthold Goldschmidt ist jung wie am Tag ihrer Entstehung. [...] Musikalische Substanz, geistige Disziplin, handwerkliche Qualität und ein natürliches Bekenntnis zur Tradition setzen Maßstäbe jenseits aller Moden und zwingen zur kritischen Betrachtung

der Gegenwart. [...] Als Werk eines Musikers, der die Oper von innen heraus – als Kunstgattung wie als Kunstbetrieb kannte, bevor er selber eine Oper schrieb [...], hat *Beatrice Cenci* alle Voraussetzungen, Eingang in den Repertoirekanon zu finden.[15]

Mit der konzertanten deutschen Erstaufführung der *Beatrice Cenci* in Berlin und ihrer Magdeburger Inszenierung sowie mit Harry Kupfers Inszenierung des *Gewaltigen Hahnrei* an der Komischen Oper in der Spielzeit 1994/95 erreichte die ‚Goldschmidt-Renaissance' 1994 einen eindrücklichen Höhepunkt. Die Fähigkeit des Zeitzeugen Goldschmidt, sich sehr lebhaft zu erinnern und brillant zu erzählen, war ein entscheidender Bestandteil dieser bewegenden Hommage. Umso mehr überrascht die drastisch formulierte Aussage des Südwestfunk-Redakteurs Paul Fiebig, der wenige Wochen nach Berthold Goldschmidts Tod von einem Feature über Goldschmidt als Opernkomponist im Rahmen des sog. Musikliterarischen Studios Abstand nahm und mir mitteilte: ‚Über Goldschmidt haben wir, denke ich, in letzter Zeit das Nötige produziert; vom Thema Literaturoper erwarte ich mir nicht viel Neues; Schreker und seine Schüler waren ausreichend vertreten.'[16] Wenngleich diese kategorische Ablehnung nicht als exemplarisch zu bezeichnen ist, so verweist sie doch auf den Umstand, dass die durchweg positive Resonanz des Publikums (nicht nur) auf Goldschmidts abendfüllende Bühnenwerke in einem gewissen Widerspruch steht zur immer wieder eingeschränkten Akzeptanz beider Opern durch Rezensenten und Entscheidungsträger des Kulturbetriebs.

6 Sukzessiver Eingang ins Opernrepertoire?

Im Nachklang der konzertanten und szenischen Aufführungen der frühen 1990er-Jahre erfolgte am 26. November 1995 am Stadttheater Bern die Schweizer Erstaufführung des *Gewaltigen Hahnrei* in Anwesenheit des Komponisten. Drei Jahre später, am 10. Januar 1998, folgte eine Inszenierung am Staatstheater Darmstadt – Goldschmidts einstiger Wirkungsstätte der Jahre 1927–29. In dieser Zeit kehrte *Beatrice Cenci* an den Ort ihrer Entstehung zurück: Die szenische Erstaufführung in Großbritannien feierte ihre Premiere am 9. Juli 1998 mit der Trinity College Opera. Unter der musikalischen Leitung

---

15   Mathias Husmann zit. n. Programmheft zur szenischen Uraufführung von *Beatrice Cenci* am 10. September 1994 am Theater der Landeshauptstadt Magdeburg.
16   Paul Fiebig an Barbara Busch, Baden-Baden, 31. Oktober 1996; Privatbesitz.

von Gregory Rose führte Stephen Langridge Regie. Nach insgesamt drei Aufführungen verschwand *Beatrice Cenci* für rund fünfzehn Jahre ebenso aus den Spielplänen wie auch der *Gewaltige Hahnrei*. Während der *Gewaltige Hahnrei* als die Entdeckung der Spielzeit 2013/14 in Bremerhaven gefeiert wurde, war es bereits am 26. Mai 2012 zur Neuinszenierung der *Beatrice Cenci* am Theater Dortmund gekommen. Hier übernahm Johannes Schmid kurzfristig die Regie für die erkrankte Regula Gerber. Die Renaissancekostüme von Andrea Schmidt-Futterer standen im Kontrast zum schlichten, archaischen Bühnenbild von Roland Aeschlimann. Auf diese Inszenierung, deren Premiere ‚bloß etwa einhundert Besucherinnen und Besucher'[17] begeistert feierten, reagierte die (hinsichtlich des Werkes positiv gestimmte) Kritik gespalten: Während beispielsweise Udo Pacolt der Ansicht war, Johannes Schmid habe *Beatrice Cenci* als einen ‚packenden Krimi' inszeniert, ‚zu dem die historischen Kostüme [...], die den muffigen Staub der damaligen Zeit zu atmen schienen, und das düster gehaltene Bühnenbild [...] – besonders in der Kerkerszene – prächtig passten,'[18] kam Christoph Zimmermann zu der Überzeugung: ‚Aus diesem Werk wäre optisch mehr herauszuholen gewesen – hoffentlich geschieht dies schon bald einmal anderswo.'[19]

Tatsächlich geschah dies sechs Jahre später, als die Oper am 18., 22. und 30. Juli 2018 im Rahmen der Bregenzer Festspiele im dortigen Festspielhaus als ein Fest für die Sinne zu erleben war – hier mit der Besonderheit, dass erstmalig in deutscher Sprache gesungen wurde. Als Grundlage diente die provisorische Version eines deutschsprachigen Librettos, das Goldschmidt selbst um 1951 angefertigt haben dürfte.[20] Alle drei Vorstellungen dieser mittlerweile auch auf DVD[21] erhältlichen Inszenierung waren ausverkauft.[22]

Der Einbindung der *Beatrice Cenci* in die renommierten österreichischen Festspiele ist das enorme Presseecho zu verdanken, das sich (bei aller Wertschätzung und ungeachtet der hervorragenden Publikumsresonanz bei

---

17 Udo Pacolt, 'Dortmund: Beatrice Cenci von Bertold Goldschmidt', *Online Merker* (2012), https://onlinemerker.com/dortmund-beatrice-cenci-von-bertold-goldschmidt/ [letzter Aufruf: 29.01.2020].

18 *Ibid.*

19 Christoph Zimmermann, ‚Dortmund: Beatrice Cenci von Berthold Goldschmidt. Premiere', *Online Merker* (2012), https://onlinemerker.com/dortmund-beatrice-cenci-von-berthold -goldschmidt [letzter Aufruf: 29.01.2020].

20 Vgl. Busch 2000, 218. Auf dieser Basis richteten Johannes Erath, Olaf A. Schmitt und Johannes Debus den Text für die Bregenzer Inszenierung ein.

21 United DVD 751408 oder Blue-Ray 751504.

22 Mündliche Information erhalten vom Dramaturgen Olaf A. Schmitt in einem persönlichen Gespräch am 30. Juli 2018.

der von mir miterlebten Abschlussvorstellung) jedoch nicht als Plädoyer für dieses einst preisgekrönte Werk entpuppt. So bleibt es eine optimistische Spekulation, ob die skizzierten Inszenierungen der 2010er-Jahre darauf verweisen, dass Goldschmidts Opern, respektive *Beatrice Cenci*, sukzessive Eingang in den Repertoirekanon der Opernhäuser finden werden – kulturgeschichtlich wünschenswert wäre dies ohne Zweifel!

9
'A Place of Refuge in Your Arms': Reizenstein's *Anna Kraus* as Holocaust Opera

Malcolm Miller

Abstract

One major work stands out from the large compositional output of émigré composer and pianist Franz Reizenstein (1911–1968), in respect of its close relationship to his personal experience as a refugee, the one-act radio opera *Anna Kraus* (1952). It was the BBC's first 'radio opera' and the British entry for the 1952 Italia Prize. Remarkably, however, since its first broadcasts, it has never been revived. It is my contention that *Anna Kraus* represents a stimulating commentary on the experience and trauma of the Holocaust. I trace the opera's genesis and reception within the context of the composer's life and contemporary social-political events of the time, and propose that its artistic achievement resides in three main aspects: its contemporary musical language; its innovative form belonging to the emerging genre of 'radio opera'; and how it is one of the earliest operas to grapple with the theme of the Holocaust and its psychological impact. Its continued relevance in our own time suggests that the opera deserves a long-overdue revival.

1 Introduction

Within the substantial oeuvre of largely abstract instrumental and vocal works by the émigré composer and pianist Franz Reizenstein (1911–1968), there is one which relates closely to his own experience as a refugee, the one-act radio opera *Anna Kraus* (1952). Commissioned by the BBC, it was the BBC's first 'radio opera' and Britain's entry for the Italia Prize in 1952. A very public, large-scale drama of love, jealousy and vengeance, concerning a German refugee and concentration camp survivor in an English village, the BBC's first 'radio opera', *Anna Kraus*, explores issues of 'exile' in a musically innovative way. Remarkably, however, since its first broadcasts in 1952 and 1953, it has never been revived. Similar to the fate suffered by operas by other émigré composers, such as Berthold Goldschmidt (1903–1996) and Hans Gál (1890–1987), the neglect may result from many reasons, ranging across stylistic issues, the changing nature of audiences, and attitudes to émigré composers. Yet whilst both Goldschmidt and Gál have enjoyed long-delayed revivals, Reizenstein still awaits one. My purpose here is to counter the critical silence surrounding an operatic work of high quality that deserves to be revisited through a scholarly re-evaluation, enhanced by the benefit of hindsight over a seventy-year period. I hope thereby also to make a case for a modern revival, either on-air or staged.

It is my contention that *Anna Kraus* represents a profoundly stimulating commentary on the experience and trauma of the Holocaust and exile, conceived by a refugee composer who could empathise with his subject. In my essay, I trace the opera's genesis and reception within the context of the composer's life and contemporary social-political events of the time. I propose that its artistic achievement resides in three main aspects. Firstly, its musical language was fully contemporary, whilst dramatic and accessible. Secondly, the work represents technical and formal innovation within the new genre of radio opera. As one contemporary critic observed, it was 'not only musically interesting but historically important as one of the first attempts to use pure broadcasting technique'.[1] Finally, it is one of the earliest operas about the Holocaust and perhaps the earliest to engage deeply with the topic of refugees.[2] Rather than an abstracted critique of totalitarian regimes as developed in some operas of that time, *Anna Kraus* explores the psychological issues surrounding the trauma of the refugee and survivor experiences, set in a postwar British setting. Reizenstein's profound and intense treatment of this subject, of topical relevance in 1952, acquires a more universal significance in our own time.

To support these contentions, my account draws on archival material not previously brought to light. Firstly, I examine Reizenstein's correspondence with his librettist, Christopher Hassall (1912–1960), in the Christopher Hassall Collection at Cambridge University Library, and in the private collection of the composer's son.[3] Secondly, I draw on internal BBC correspondence and panel reports concerning Reizenstein's music and the opera from the BBC

---

1 Scott Goddard, 'Asking too much', *News Chronicle*, 7 March 1953.
2 A radio opera in Hebrew entitled *Hagader* ('The Fence') was composed as early as 1947 by Yehuda Wohl (Berlin 1904–Tel-Aviv 1988). Its drama focuses on inmates in a concentration camp. Wohl emigrated to British Mandate Palestine in 1933. A recording is available online from the National Library of Israel at: https://www.nli.org.il/en/items/NNL_MUSIC_AL0038 04244/NLI. I am most grateful to the musicologist Irit Youngerman for drawing my attention to the work.
3 Christopher Hassall collection, Add. 8905, Cambridge University Library. All letters cited from Reizenstein to Hassall are to be found in Folder 10, at GBR/0012/MS Add.8905/10/R 20–24. Documents, synopses and scripts are in Folder 8. I am very grateful to the librarians at CUL for making the material accessible for my research. I am also grateful to John Reizenstein, the composer's son, for sharing correspondence, including letters from Hindemith and Hassall.

Written Archives in Caversham.[4] Finally, I discuss for the first time contemporary reviews and articles, some held in the Reizenstein holding at the Royal Academy of Music.[5] My analysis of the music draws on surviving recordings of radio broadcasts from 1952 and 1953.[6]

The article unfolds as follows. Part One considers Reizenstein's path as a refugee composer. Part Two describes the genesis of the opera through his close collaboration and friendship with his librettist, Christopher Hassall, and his BBC producer, Douglas Cleverdon. Part Three explores the genre of radio opera, its aesthetics, challenges, and critical reception. Part Four explores how the music dramatises the refugee/survivor experience, while Part Five explores the opera's personal and social-political contexts. I conclude with a plea for a revival of a work neglected for some seventy years.

2   Reizenstein's Path as a Refugee Composer

To fully appreciate the significance of the opera in all its facets, it is first necessary to understand the composer's biography and the way in which his refugee experience exerted a formative influence on his artistic development. Particularly important is how he overcame many hurdles during his career, especially within his dealings with the BBC.

Franz Reizenstein grew up in an artistic and musical Jewish family in Nuremberg, the youngest child of Dr Albert Reizenstein (1871–1925), a medical doctor, and Lina Kohn (1880–1963). The young Franz showed musical talent already by the age of five. From 1930, he studied composition with Paul Hindemith and piano with Leonid Kreutzer at the Berlin State Academy.[7]

---

4   I am grateful to the BBC Written Archives for making the files concerning Reizenstein accessible for my research. All cited letters, internal memos, advisory panel reader reports, relating to Reizenstein's music and the opera, unless specified, are drawn from the BBC Written Archive, Caversham, as specified in footnotes.
5   I am grateful to the Librarians of the RAM for making the Reizenstein material accessible for my research.
6   A recording from 1952 of *Anna Kraus* is available in the National Sound Archive, part of the Douglas Cleverdon Collection. I am grateful to Jonathan Del Mar and John Reizenstein for making available their copies of off-air recordings of the 1952 and 1953 BBC productions. I am grateful to Radio Bremen for a private study copy of their July 1953 production.
7   For more biographical information, see firstly, the article 'Franz Reizenstein' by Simon Wynberg on the website of the Orel Foundation and, secondly, Hugo Cole and Malcolm Miller, 'Reizenstein, Franz', Grove Music Online, Oxford Music Online [Online], Oxford, Oxford University Press. Available at: https://doi-org.libezproxy.open.ac.uk/10.1093/gmo/9781561592630.article.23169.

Concert programmes from that period attest to Reizenstein's Modernist predilections, both as composer and pianist.[8]

With the Nazi rise to power in 1933, Hindemith urged his Jewish students to leave as soon as possible; he himself fled to Switzerland in 1938.[9] Reizenstein left for London in 1934, armed with his teacher's letter of recommendation[10] and sponsored by a maternal uncle, Bruno Kohn, who had emigrated earlier with his wife. Reizenstein gained a place at the Royal College of Music, studying composition with Vaughan Williams and conducting with Constant Lambert. He also took private piano lessons with the legendary Solomon.[11] Being younger than many other émigré composers, such as Goldschmidt, Gál or Wellesz, meant that Reizenstein's style was still in a formative stage.[12]

As a result, Reizenstein evolved a distinctive hybridity that combined influences of both the Modernist Hindemith and the English school of his new teachers, as well as, especially in the vocal music, early Britten, which is particularly evident in *Anna Kraus*. As scholars such as Florian Scheding have noted, the aesthetic climate in Britain in the 1930s and 1940s was largely anti-modernist and, to an extent, xenophobic.[13] The result was that many émigré composers turned away from their earlier progressive styles, either ceasing creative work or shifting to more acceptable conservative approaches. Reizenstein was an exception, eventually recognised as one of the foremost composers his generation. Yet even he exemplified the trend by turning, in the 1950s, to more popular genres such as film music, whilst expressing his innate sense of musical humour as shown by his still popular contributions to the witty 'Hoffnung Music Festivals' conceived by Gerard Hoffnung (1925–59), a fellow émigré.

As a composer in a Modernist style, Reizenstein had his works performed from early on at new music concerts such as at the London Contemporary Music Club (LCMC). He was included in the British entry to the 1939

---

8   A Hindemith student concert on 5 March 1932 featured Reizenstein's Movement for Clarinet and String Quartet, and on 7 July 1932, his Sonata for Solo Cello. In a concert on 16 July 1932 of Kreutzer's students, four performed Romantics (Schubert, Chopin, Brahms), whilst Reizenstein played Hindemiths's *Klaviermusick* Op.37 II teil: Reihe kleiner Stucke. I am grateful to John Reizenstein for sharing the programmes with me.
9   Reizenstein remained in touch with Hindemith; he received letters during a London visit in 1955, and later in 1959, mentioning *Voices of Night*. His widow Gertrud Hindemith wrote to him in 1965–66. I am grateful to John Reizenstein for sharing the material.
10 Hindemith's letter is in the personal collection of John Reizenstein.
11 The British pianist Solomon Cutner CBE (1902–88) was known simply as 'Solomon'.
12 The same point is made by R.L. Henderson, 'English by Adoption', *The Listener*, vol. 65:1661, 26 January 1961, 201.
13 See for instance, Florian Scheding, 'Problematic Tendencies', in Erik Levi (ed.), *The Impact of Nazism on Twentieth Century Music* (Vienna: Böhlau, 2014), 247–71.

International Society for Contemporary Music (ISCM) meeting in Poland. In 1940, Reizenstein spent some months in internment in Douglas on the Isle of Man, where, alongside fellow émigrés like Hans Gál, he kept active as a pianist and conductor; he also completed composition of his *Ballet Suite*, which he then conducted with the orchestra of internees.[14]

Soon after an early release in January 1941, thanks to the advocacy of Vaughan Williams,[15] he applied to the BBC as a pianist and was encouraged by Leonard Isaacs, then controller of the BBC European Service, who eventually secured Reizenstein's first recital in January 1942. However, internal disagreements about Reizenstein's abilities threatened to scupper the offer. Fortunately, Arthur Bliss, appointed the BBC's Director of Music shortly after, decided the matter, noting that Reizenstein was a 'more than competent' pianist and should broadcast a programme of 'Mendelssohn, Chopin, Bartók and other forbidden composers'.[16]

Reizenstein's experience with the BBC as a composer comprised a pattern of rejections, resubmissions, and eventual acceptances of his works for broadcast on the Home Service. During the war years, several works, which were warmly received by publishers and performers, critics and recording companies, were rejected after being submitted to the BBC for the Home Service. The BBC's Advisory panels, consisting mainly of British composers and conductors, expressed admiration for his 'craftsmanship', yet often expressed coolness towards his Hindemithian style, in general resisting anything too modern for audiences. Leonard Isaacs remained a stalwart supporter, thus Reizenstein's works, until the end of the Second World War, were often performed and broadcast by the European Service, whilst refused by the Home Service.[17] In that regard, Reizenstein's experience followed the pattern of the émigré composers in which, as Florian Scheding has written, the BBC's role was 'ambiguous'. It provided a haven for the émigrés in all aspects of music-making and education, yet at the same time banned their compositions from the Home

---

14 Susan Snizek, '"Spiritual Vitamins": Music in Huyton and Central Internment Camps May 1940 to January 1941', in *Cultural Heritage and Prisoners of War: Creativity Behind Barbed Wire*, edited by Gilly Carr, and Harold Mytum (Taylor & Francis Group, 2012), ProQuest Ebook Central, https://ebookcentral.proquest.com/lib/open/detail.action?doc ID=957600. 34–50.

15 Denied army service on account of his poor eyesight, Reizenstein worked until the end of the war as a railway clerk, also performing at many wartime concerts.

16 Arthur Bliss, Internal Circulating Memo, to OMD, 25 November 1941, BBC WAC BBC/R/RCONT/RCONT1/31015.

17 Of several works submitted to the BBC's advisory panel during the Second World War, all were rejected, then accepted postwar.

Service during the war years due to its political and economic consequences and contexts.[18]

Two examples provide illustration. The Cello Concerto, composed in 1936, submitted first in 1937 and promised a broadcast, was rejected in 1940. After the war, in January 1948, it was accepted for performance by William Pleeth and the London Philharmonic Orchestra under Sir Adrian Boult at the Royal Albert Hall, at an 'Experimental Rehearsal' followed by a discussion chaired by Alan Bush.[19] Reizenstein's sense of humour prevailed when he wrote to the BBC's Deputy Director of Music Kenneth Wright: 'it is the same work which I played to you before the War and I am glad to say it has survived the bombs! Whether it is going to survive the criticism of those present at the discussion, is another matter, however'.[20]

Another example of a work sidelined due to Reizenstein's refugee status is the *Piano Concerto no.1* (1941). He played it several times during the war years, conducted by Sir Henry Wood, Adrian Boult and Walter Goehr, and with several live broadcasts on the European Service. In 1943 BBC Panel Advisors recommended it,[21] yet the Director of Music Arthur Bliss dismissed it since 'there are many British works that have been waiting for performance that we must include first'. Bliss's comment reflects the view expressed by public personalities and bodies at the time, namely that the BBC needed to devote more time to British music. Indeed, during the Second World War the BBC produced a list of German and Austrian composers, including émigrés, whose works were effectively banned from the Home Service during wartime; the main reason was to avoid contracts with Nazi-German and Austrian publishing firms. Since Reizenstein's publishers, Boosey & Hawkes, and Lengnick, were British, he was not on the list. However, his music appears to have been still treated in a similar way, implying he was still considered not 'sufficiently' British.[22] The Piano Concerto was finally approved in December 1945, and, in the following June, Eric Warr wrote, 'in my opinion it is a good work, well designed and sensibly scored. We ought to include it in an autumn programme with the composer again playing the piano'.

---

18   Scheding, 'Problematic Tendencies'.
19   It took place on 24 January 1948 presented by the Committee for the Promotion of New Music (CPNM).
20   Reizenstein letter to Kenneth Wright; BBC Written Archives Centre, BBC WAC BBC/R/RCONT/RCONT1/31015, 15 January 1948.
21   John Ireland report; BBC WAC BBC/R/OM/R27/616, 23 April 1943.
22   See chapter 6.4, Jutta Raab Hansen, 'Ban on Alien Composers', in *NS-verfolgte Musiker in England: Spuren deutscher und österreichischer Flüchtlinge in der britischen Musikkultur*, Vol.1, *Musik im ,Dritten Reich' und im Exil* (Hamburg: von Bockel, 1996), 181–99.

By 1953, Reizenstein was, fortunately, declared 'panel-free', yet that did not in itself guarantee numerous broadcasts. Rather, it signalled a new attitude towards Reizenstein's abilities as also a new stylistic phrase, in which contrapuntal complexity was tempered with a simpler, more accessible lyricism. This was especially notable in the large-scale choral cantata *Voices of Night* (*1950–1*), settings of great English poetry arranged by the poet and writer Christopher Hassall, broadcast in June 1952. Even here, however, widespread critical acclaim was peppered by nationalist prejudice as shown in comments by the BBC's Panel Advisor William Alwyn, a noted composer: 'apart from the personal wish that the text had been set by Vaughan Williams or Walton, I feel I must recommend this work – it is a clever achievement of a composer of foreign extraction and it should prove very effective'.[23]

3 Genesis of *Anna Kraus*, Collaboration with Christopher Hassall and Douglas Cleverdon

It was the success of *Voices of Night* which led directly to the commission for *Anna Kraus* (1951–52), as also, later in 1958, to the oratorio *Genesis*, composed for the Three Choirs Festival (and broadcast). All three works were composed in collaboration with Christopher Hassall with whom Reizenstein became close, lifelong friends. They shared numerous projects, including a planned (never-realised) TV opera (see Figure 9.1).[24]

Christopher Hassall (1912–1963) was a multi-talented actor, poet, librettist and translator, famous for having been Ivor Novello's lyricist between 1935 and 1949 for individual songs and several hit musicals, and the author of poetry, plays and three biographies of the actor Stephen Haggard (1948), the poet Edward Marsh (1959), and Rupert Brooke (1964).[25] As well as *Anna Kraus*, he wrote other opera libretti including Anthony Hopkins's *A Man from Tuscany*

---

23   William Alwyn Panel Report, BBC WAC BBC/R/OM/R27/61620.12.50. VW refers to Vaughan Williams.
24   Hassall and Reizenstein had further operatic projects which did not come to fruition, including Edmond Rostaud's *Cyrano de Bergerac*, the rights already assigned to Alvano, who composed his opera in 1939. Nonetheless, Reizenstein's *Overture to Cyrano de Bergerac* is one of his most striking orchestral works. One of their last projects was an unrealised TV Opera, entitled *Postman's Knock*, with a completed synopsis and script.
25   Christopher Hassall, *The Timeless Quest: Stephen Haggard* (London: Arthur Baker Ltd, 1948); Christopher Hassall, *Edward Marsh, patron of the arts, a biography* (London: Longmans, 1959); Christopher Hassall, *Rupert Brooke: a biography* (London: Faber, 1964).

FIGURE 9.1 Newspaper photo cutting of a 1954 recital in Bath by Franz Reizenstein and Christopher Hassall, highlighting their lifelong professional relationship and friendship subsequent to *Voices of Night* (1951) and *Anna Kraus* (1952)
REPRODUCED BY KIND PERMISSION OF JOHN REIZENSTEIN

(1951), William Walton's *Troilus and Cressida* (1954), and Arthur Bliss's TV Opera *Tobias and the Angel* (1961).

Hassall was introduced to Reizenstein by a friend as, 'a connoisseur of English literature' who 'has also made a close study of the relationship between words and music'.[26] Hassall was well known to BBC Features producer Douglas Cleverdon (1903–1987), who was interested in developing new ways of 'interweaving words and music'.[27] In late 1951, Hassall supplied Cleverdon with a synopsis for *Anna Kraus* that he and Reizenstein had been working on, and which resulted in an official commission on 7 February 1952, in the following

---

26 Franz Reizenstein, 'Composer's Forum – Voices of Night', *London Musical Events*, March 1957.
27 The Cleverdon papers are available at: Cleverdon II mss., Lilly Library, Indiana University, Bloomington, Indiana, USA. Reizenstein had previous experience composing for 'Features', for Leonard Cottrell's 1949 documentary *Men Against the Sea*.

words: 'Third[28] would like you to undertake the radio opera "Anna Kraus", with libretto by Christopher Hassall, at an approximate length of 60 minutes.'[29] All were keen to enter the work for the Italia Prize,[30] which meant broadcasting it by 25 July, then sending a recording to the jury, to allow time for the decision by September. Thankfully, only half the score was required by 1 May for the advisory panel comprising Benjamin Frankel, Gordon Jacob and Clarence Raybould. They were asked to select a work of sufficient quality to have 'a real chance of competing on the international plane'.[31] From the two submitted, *Anna Kraus* was chosen with glowing reports.[32]

Cleverdon's deep concern for the new medium was expressed in numerous explanations to convince the BBC Music Department that the project was neither conventional opera nor pure drama, but fell between the departments of Features, Drama and Music. When it became clear that operatic voices would be needed, the project was taken over by Music's opera section, with Cleverdon as producer. The title role of Anna was sung by Victoria Sladen, who had trained in the 1930s in Berlin, and who spoke and sang throughout with a discernible 'German' accent.[33] Initially, Cleverdon had suggested the émigré Peter Gellhorn as conductor, yet the role was assigned to Norman del Mar, with the Camden Theatre as studio.[34]

---

28   'Third' was the familiar nickname of the BBC's 'Third Programme', 1946–67, devoted to the arts including classical music. The Home Service, set up in 1939, also featured classical music; the 'Light Programme' was set up in 1945 for light music.

29   The fee division suggests the project was deemed primarily musical. A letter from R.G. Walford, BBC WAC, R19/37/1, 27 March 1952 states 80 guineas for Hassall and 200 guineas to Reizenstein 'to cover composition, orchestration', in addition to the usual recording rights and right of first performance. A repeat broadcast was 26 shillings per minute, divided Reizenstein 2: Hassall 1.

30   The Italia Prize is an annual international radio award, held in September, organised by the RAI, the Italian equivalent of the BBC.

31   Douglas Cleverdon, letter to Benjamin Frankel, BBC WAC, R19/37/1, 4 May 1952.

32   The Opera Orchestra, due to have been disbanded, was retained at sixty-one players, though Reizenstein requested only forty-five. See, Cleverdon letter of 5 March 1952 and the reply from Frank Wade, 24 March 52, BBC WAC, R19/37/1.

33   Victoria Sladen (1910–1999), originally Victoria May Schlageter, a well-known British opera singer, studied in Berlin in the 1930s, sang with Sadlers Wells, Convent Garden (from 1947) and Doyle Carte (from 1954). Well known in Puccini roles, she sang in the BBC premiere of Gerhard's *La Duenna* (1949). The full cast for *Anna Kraus* was: Pavel Black: Lloyd Strauss Smith, tenor; Rev. Mark Naylor: William Parsons, bass; Eleanor Leveridge: Joan Cross, mezzo sop; Myra Leveridge: Monica Warner, contralto; Bertram Callow: Norman Lumsden, baritone; Station Officer Mitchell: Enrys Lloyd, baritone; Anna's Parents and sister: Gladys Parr, Frank Sale, Elsa Stock.

34   Cleverdon had observed 'I believe Peter Gellhorn is not experienced on radio; but against this, I believe that he is particularly interested in Reizenstein's music.' Letter from Cleverdon, 2 May 1952 BBC WAC, R19/37/1.

The opera aired on 25 July as planned, and two weeks later Francesco Formosa, of RAI Radio Italiana, wrote to reassure Cleverdon that the 1952 Italia Prize jury had received and listened to the recording.[35] In the event, the winning work was the radio ballet *Le Joueur de Flute* by Marius Constant, a French avant-gardist, whose use of electro-acoustics perhaps motivated the choice.[36] However, *Anna Kraus* elicited enthusiastic press responses. Denby Richards in *Music and Musicians* referred to it as 'the operatic and musical event of the radio world'. He added that 'this opera-for-broadcasting, the BBC's entry for the 1952 Italia Prize, is one of the most effective and moving works I have heard on the air'; ascribing its success to the creative team, he singles Reizenstein out for praise: 'I doubt whether any present-day composer could more effectively have realised the blend of words and music.'[37]

The exposure the opera received due to the Italia Prize led, importantly, to *Anna Kraus* being taken up by various European radio stations, particularly in Germany, Austria and Switzerland.[38] Two days after the broadcast, Cleverdon received a letter from one Klaus Blum, musicologist and advisor to Radio Bremen, expressing his idea that a German production 'would and should find in this country an interested set of listeners'. Blum had written a thesis about 'radio opera' and was keen to discover more about *Anna Kraus*.[39] Congratulating the producer, he added 'this music was very much to my liking [...] It was new, but at the same time neither incomprehensible nor "unmusical" – it was a pleasure to listen to it.'

Correspondence with Radio Bremen continued in December 1952, when Cleverdon confirmed that the BBC would be preparing a new production to broadcast, with the same cast, on 5 and 6 March 1953.[40] Radio Bremen's

---

35   Letter of 7 August 1952, from Francesco Formosa, RAI Radio Italiana, Rome, to Douglas Cleverdon; BBC written Archives Centre, BBC WAC, R19/37/1.
36   Cleverdon won the Italia Prize in 1951 with *The Face of Violence* by Jacob Bronowksy and music by Anthony Hopkins (which had aired in 1950), and famously, won in 1954 with Dylan Thomas's *Under Milk Wood*.
37   Denby Richards, 'On the air ...', *Music and Musicians*, September 1952.
38   Hassall collection, CUL. Letters from Reizenstein to Hassall mention royalties from broadcasts in Bremen (Germany) and Linz (Austria), and possible relays in Basel (Switzerland) and Klagenfurt (Austria).
39   Letter from Klaus Blum to Cleverdon. BBC WAC, R19/37/1, 25 July 1952. Blum's thesis is 'Die Funkoper. Phänomenologie und Geschichte einer neuen Junstgattung.' Blum wrote to Cleverdon: 'In the first place I should like to congratulate you on this enterprise ... the pronunciation as well as the separation from the musical background was marvellous.'
40   Letter to Cleverdon from Dr Goslich [Radio Bremen], BBC WAC, R19/37/1, 19 Dec 1952. Goslich requested vocal scores and Cleverdon asked him to send a formal request to BBC. He mentioned that there were only three vocal scores, and one was in New York, but 'I shall be very glad to give you any assistance in my power in the preparation of your German production.'

production took place shortly after on 2 July 1953, conducted by Siegfried Goslich, using Klaus Blum's translation.[41] Blum had made one small yet significant alteration: the concentration camp's true name 'Flossenburg' was changed to the fictional 'Flaxenburg'. The alteration both generalises the notion of 'camp' and may have been significant for German audiences at the time.

4   'Radio Opera' and Its Challenges: Aesthetic Aims and Critical Reception

The success of *Anna Kraus* was as much due to its innovative use of the radio medium as to its radical choice of subject. In order to appreciate the way Reizenstein rose to the challenge of the new genre, it is necessary to trace its history, the BBC's particular approach to it, and the way it was received by contemporary critics.

'Radio opera' has a particularly intriguing history, dating back to the earliest beginnings of radio. Apart from the technical challenges of broadcasting from opera houses, several European composers, including Werner Egk, Martinů, and even Walter Goehr, had, already by the 1930s, formulated essays designed solely for the sound medium.[42] That the genre was still experimental in 1952 is shown by Douglas Cleverdon's *The Radio Times* preview, describing *Anna Kraus* as 'an attempt to establish a new radio convention for the interweaving of words and music'.[43] Cleverdon mentions other works he had produced at around the same time, including *The Dark Tower* by Louis MacNeice, and *The Rescue* by Edward Sackville-West, both to music by Benjamin Britten. *Anna Kraus* was the only work he called a 'radio opera', and, reflecting on it later, he found the term problematic as 'critics tended to judge it by the standards of the opera house rather than as a piece of radio.'[44]

Yet critics were keenly aware of the challenges of 'radio opera' and judged *Anna Kraus* on how successfully it surmounted them. For the reviewer in *The Times*, a successful radio opera was one in which 'librettist and composer

---

41   I am grateful to Andreas Kisters and Gabriela Bertoldi of Radio Bremen for providing me with a recording and the translated libretto.
42   See Lionel Salter, 'Radio Opera', in *New Grove Online, Oxford Music Online* [*Online*], Oxford, Oxford University Press.
43   Douglas Cleverdon, 'An Opera for Broadcasting', *The Radio Times*, 20 July 1952, 29.
44   Douglas Cleverdon, 'The Dilemma of Radio Opera', letter in *The Listener*, 3 May 1956. He refers to Bronowski and Fricker's *My Brother Died* and *The Death of Vivien* by Rene Hague and Fricker as 'melodramas'.

succeed in creating an aural picture so complete, unequivocal and self-evident as to make the listener forget the absence of the stage and of a visible action'. *Anna Kraus* came 'pretty near a complete realization of that ideal.'[45]

The realisation of the ideal was the result of much effort and even daring from the creative team. In the run-up to the 25 July broadcast, Cleverdon had arranged an extra rehearsal on 8 July, with full cast and orchestra, purely to test out various radiophonic effects, to avoid wasting time during the broadcast proper. Since the story unfolded in seven distinct scenes, the lack of visible staging necessitated radio techniques such as cross-fading, varied microphone placements, experimental sounds (of natural surroundings, footsteps, phone rings, church bells, water, birds). Judging acoustics and balance was also necessary, for instance thinning orchestral textures to enable separation of words and accompaniment, and to enable dovetailing between orchestral underscore and the diegetic music[46] in scenes featuring church organ or piano playing.[47]

On 9 July, Cleverdon emphasised the underlying aim: 'Our intention in Features Department is to develop a new form of radio opera, conceived, written, orchestrated and performed with the microphone as an essential ingredient of the production.' It required 'a new method of production in which the criterion of judgement should be, not merely the quality of the music and the singing, but the total effect as a piece of radio.'[48]

It was that aspect which divided the BBC advisory panellists. For Benjamin Frankel, himself a distinguished composer for concert and film, *Anna Kraus*, whilst 'excellent, often beautiful and dramatic, [...] has not made up its mind whether to be melodrama with music, realistic radio drama, or opera'.[49] Gordon Jacob disagreed: 'As a work specifically written for broadcasting [...] it does not seem to me to have the defects mentioned by Mr Frankel. The libretto is well conceived for the medium of Radio and the realistic sound effects are

---

45 'Opera written for Broadcasting', *The Times*, 29 July 1952.
46 'Diegetic' refers to music which forms part of the dramatic action and is heard by the characters.
47 Cleverdon, internal memo (6 May 1952) requests the experimental session 'to try out certain technical matters of balance, cross-fading, acoustics and so on, in order that we may have plenty of time to make alterations before the score is finally completed'. He requests four attendants to shift things around; large screens; one piano and one Hammond organ, one timp., ten yard lengths of felt or matting; three lazy arms and two stand mikes; props to make sounds like bells, telephone, etc. The 'abnormal' layout is sketched in a diagram. BBC WAC, R19/37/1, 6 May 1952 and 8 July 1952.
48 Cleverdon, internal memo, 9 July 1952, BBC WAC, R19/37/1.
49 See Frankel's full report, 10 May 1952. BBC WAC BBC/R/OM/R27/616.

necessary in the absence of visual effects. The music is direct and surprisingly simple from its composer. It is all the more apt and telling for that.'[50]

Most critics concurred with Jacob. Felix Apprahamian, for instance, admired Reizenstein's contrapuntal style and how it was flexible enough for the demands of the drama,[51] adding that Reizenstein 'should be able to take film music in his stride'.[52] Similarly, Martin Cooper, writing in the *Daily Telegraph*, defined the problems of radio opera as comprehensibility of text and ease in following scene changes, and opined that Reizenstein 'was often strikingly successful in solving these problems.' Cooper traced a debt to Britten in the 'colloquial recitative', and whilst expressing a wish for Britten's 'spareness of orchestral texture' as found in *The Rape of Lucretia*, believed that 'the big moments of Reizenstein's opera could be most effective in the theatre'. He concluded that the opera was 'a remarkable achievement not only for its absolute quality as music but as an essay in a form which will almost certainly grow in importance in the near future'.[53]

That prediction proved correct; even with the advent of TV opera in the 1960s, radio operas continued to evolve, with notable examples in the 1970s and 1980s and beyond.[54] Mosco Carner, best known as a Puccini expert, saw radio opera as still in a 'fledgling' state and, like Cooper, noted how *Anna Kraus* was an improvement on works by Martinů and Nino Rota that used a narrator. He praised the clarity of Reizenstein's text setting which 'follows the inflexion of ordinary speech', and suggested that, as it was 'a very ingenious piece for radio,' he 'would back it at least for a place' in the Italia Prize.[55]

Of course, there were a few sceptics such as Edward Sackville-West, who, writing in the *New Statesman*, found the opera 'too short for its subject and for the complicated idiom'. However, for all its 'faults', it was also 'an interesting and courageous experiment, which I hope to have a chance of hearing again.'[56]

---

50   Gordon Jacob's report adds: 'The work seems to me to be quite up to the Italia Prize standard and is certainly to be recommended for broadcasting in the ordinary way.' The third panellist, Clarence Raybould, concurs. See BBC WAC BBC/R/OM/R27/616, 14 May 1952.

51   Felix Apprahamian, 'Music for Today', *London Musical Events*, September 1952. The review praises Reizenstein's 'contrapuntal facility' which is 'never at a loss when it comes to developing his material'.

52   Reizenstein's film scores include the Hammer horror film *The Mummy* (1959). Immediately after *Anna Kraus* he was eager, as the correspondence shows, to compose more for BBC Features.

53   Martin Cooper, 'A Challenge to Composers', *Daily Telegraph and Morning Post*, 2 August 1952.

54   Radio operas by Henze and Thea Musgrave, for instance.

55   Mosco Carner, 'An Opera for broadcasting', *Time and Tide*, 16 August 1952.

56   Edward Sackville-West, 'An Opera for Broadcasting', *New Statesman*, 2 August 1952.

Fortunately, such a chance was to appear in the BBC's second production on 5 and 6 March 1953. Previewing it for *The Listener*, Colin Mason reminded the public that *Anna Kraus* was the 'only work of its kind written in this country', which had 'made something of a sensation'. Mason, underlining how both libretto and music made full use of radio possibilities, highlighted the music's effective portrayals of each character. His commentary was one of the few to delve into Reizenstein's musical language, admiring its 'deep sense of melodic unity based on principles of intervals and phrase', vocal lines that are 'flexible, singable and beautifully shaped', concluding that it was a 'genuine operatic work in which both the parts and the whole have a convincing and unified musical form'.[57] It was those qualities which made the dramatic action, with its moving backcloth of the Holocaust, come alive with urgency and conviction.

5   Musical Dramatisation of the Refugee and Survivor Experience

To appreciate just how Reizenstein's music characterises the themes relating to the refugee experience, Holocaust trauma, and antimodernism, it is necessary to understand the plot in some detail. The synopsis provided in Cleverdon's *Radio Times* preview for the premiere is usefully concise, so I quote it here in full. The opera,

> tells the story of a German refugee, Anna, employed as a housekeeper in an English village. The house is occupied by two maiden ladies, Eleanor and Myra Leveridge. Eleanor, the elder, is an invalid with harmless but inconvenient delusions; her sister Myra, on the other hand, is one of the most active members of local society. At the Rector's suggestion, she has taken as a lodger a young Polish music student named Pavel Black, once an inmate of a prison camp. Anna and Pavel, exiles in a strange land, are in love; but Bertram Callow, the village shopkeeper and organist, is also in love with Anna, and bitterly jealous of Pavel. He poisons her mind against him by insinuating that, while a prisoner, Pavel had collaborated with the Nazis. Anna's suspicions are confirmed when she overhears Pavel boasting of his exploits in the camp at Flossenburg, where her own parents had been done to death. She does not realise that Pavel, deluded by Callow and not entirely sober, has fabricated the story with the naïve intention of impressing Miss Myra. In her imagination Anna hears the

---

57   Colin Mason, 'An Opera for Broadcasting', *The Listener*, 26 February 1953. Mason also observed 'even the minor parts are well defined'.

voices of her murdered parents and sister calling for vengeance; and she kills Pavel, only to learn from the Rector that although Pavel was indeed at Flossenburg, he was as much an innocent victim as any of his helpless companions. In a final aria Anna laments the tragic destiny of herself and her family, and drowns herself in the river.[58]

Describing the music, Cleverdon added that it was 'continuous, though punctuated here and there by a few lines of spoken dialogue', with 'a kind of recitative'. Overall, 'the orchestral sound is accepted as the natural accompaniment to or expression of the thoughts and utterances of the characters of the drama'.[59]

Instead of the term 'libretto', Cleverdon preferred 'words' or 'script', since they belong more to drama than conventional opera.[60] Yet Hassall's text is indeed often libretto-like. As well as everyday speech, there are beautiful moments of poetry, memorable rhyming verses for the main arias, and lines in quasi-Shakespearian or elevated biblical style to convey the emotional intensity. This is especially so in the set pieces, including Anna's three main arias, one at the start 'I am happy', and two at the very end, which rise to heights of inspiration; the duets for Anna with the Rector, with Callow, and a more impassioned love duet with Pavel; the climactic trio and 'wordless chorus'; and the Rector's final 'tale of liberation of Flossenburg'.

A brooding mood at the very start of the opera is set with only a few orchestral chords, followed by the first radio sound effect of fire truck bells and door knocks, which announce Sergeant Mitchell of the local fire brigade. Anna answers the door with a German accent, eliciting from Mitchell the comment 'Foreigner, eh?'[61] Her reply, 'yes, born in Munich ... the Rector will explain',[62] affirms her sense of insecurity, heightening the social critique of postwar xenophobia. As the Rector recounts the situation of the elderly sisters, and how the delusional Miss Eleanor may need to be kept under lock and key, Anna exclaims 'No, never' – a dramatic interjection affirming her devotion as a carer.

Indeed, the tension between Anna's outward goodness and her inner emotional turmoil are intentionally foregrounded in this scene, through a richly flowing dialogue between the Rector and Anna. Yet the bright triadic motif (developed later) gives way to more disjointed, dissonant turbulent texture when the Rector alludes to the war. As he sings 'Ah yes, when your native land was ruled by a bestial tyranny you escaped, so they have told me', the orchestra

---

58 Cleverdon, 'An Opera for Broadcasting', 29.
59 *Ibid.*
60 Cleverdon, BBC memo, 1 July 1952; BBC WAC, R19/37/1.
61 In the German translation by Klaus Blum, both officer Mitchell and Anna speak with a German accent, yet he still remarks 'Ausländerin!'.
62 All libretto quotations are from the BBC Script, in the RAM Reizenstein Archive.

wells up. Anna's inner trauma is conveyed in her line, which soars over the cataclysmic orchestra: 'I escaped but my mother, my father, my sister, they all were barbarously done to death like cattle.' The tension subdues for the Rector's calming plea to Anna to find healing in the 'remote and peaceful valley', conveyed by soothing woodwind and strings.

The calm mood links seamlessly to Anna's first aria, where Reizenstein adapts the traditional ternary ABA' opera aria form to highlight her hidden trauma. The opening and closing sections show an expansive lyricism redolent of Berg, with solos for violin, horn and cellos over gently pulsating strings.

> At last I am happy,
> Here where the old stone bridge
> Shadows the tranquil uneventful stream;
> Here where your roofs of thatch
> Lazily smoulder, and stars keep watch
> Stars quiet as in a dream
> The dream of a child.

Suddenly, the music intensifies to an expressionist, dissonant climax, with brusque brass, sliding string, and syncopated scales, to evoke Anna's 'wild dreams':

> But not my dream. My dreams are wild!
> They ring with echoes of calling voices,
> Voices I knew, faces I loved.

A climactic sustained high note on 'But' conveys her inner pain, links back from this central interlude to the return of the earlier mood for the final lines:

> But at last I am happy
> at last I can lie down to sleep,
> And wake at daybreak undismayed,
> Refresh'd and unafraid,
> Only at night those voices wake and weep.

The aria concludes with a touching major triad in high strings and rising harp arpeggio. The image of the stream as metaphor for 'happiness' is all the more poignant, as it later becomes the site of Callow's evil machinations and her final suicide.

The scene continues with an arioso-like dialogue about guilt and forgiveness, with Anna unable to forgive. The scene splits into two parts as Anna goes to care for Miss Eleanor and the Rector watches. He sings in a low tessitura over a poignant march-like figure with sweetly flowing woodwind, cross-fading over to Anna's fragmentary exchanges with Miss Eleanor, characterised by a distinctively shrill, trill motif that evokes her mental illness. The Rector reflects: 'Anna Kraus, I see her up there at the window, An angel of mercy ... If only I could heal her bitterness. Ah God, that there should ever be a canker in the rose!' The Rector's voice of 'healing' arouses sympathy for Anna as a victim of her trauma, even if her 'unstable' mind leads to the tragic outcome.

The scene change to the village church and Bertram Callow is effected through a cross-fade from a cadential close in the minor to the bright sound of a church organ. Since both Callow and Pavel Black are musicians, the use of diegetic music, namely the sounds of organ and piano, highlights music itself as a topic. The Rector sees it as a 'healing balm' for Anna, whilst for Callow it symbolises conflict with Pavel. At the church, Anna exclaims 'your music gives me such happiness', yet the orchestra's nervous energy evokes Callow's jealousy, as he mocks Pavel's 'high-brow improvisations', with stage directions requesting 'unconventional chords'. There certainly seems here to be a deliberate, even witty, autobiographical allusion in Callow's xenophobic resistance to musical Modernism; a friendly jibe at the sort of attitudes Reizenstein had already suffered in his career.

Anna and Callow's walk to the nearby bridge is evoked in radio sound effects of footsteps inside and outside, 'outdoor' sounds of birds and flowing water, yet the accompanying music is full of foreboding, as Callow poisons Anna's love for Pavel. When the love duet for Anna and Pavel begins, it is already imbued with her anxiety. The scene is introduced by a cross-fade to Pavel's piano-playing, diegetic music that dovetails into non-diegetic orchestral underscore, stark, sinewy woodwind counterpoints contrasted by strident strings.

The love duet portrays their shared feelings as refugee and survivor with an impassioned intensity, with racing, modal-tonal harmonies. The anguished climax highlights both their isolation and mutual support:

> The rivers of life run red and deep, the rivers are full of rocks. Is there nowhere any peace, nowhere a place of refuge?
> [...]
> a place of refuge in your arms; [...] we both are strangers in a strange land, but while we cling together we are safe.

The sidestep from passion to perfidy is swift; the lighter mood when Anna brings flowers for Miss Eleanor's birthday shifting to angst as Anna sees Pavel's knife with the initials P.S.. Since it stands for the German version of Pavel Black

('Paul Schwarz'), Anna's suspicions, planted by Callow, intensify. A comedic interlude follows in Callow's village shop scene, where Miss Myra, and later Pavel, buy elderberry wine. 'Buffo-esque' parody, where Callow persuades Pavel to boast about his role in the war to impress the Miss Myra, is sardonic, caricatured. Walking home, unison string pizzicati suggest Pavel's increasing tipsiness, brass and side drum adding Shostakovich-like piquancy to his drunken swagger.

The climactic trio where Anna overhears Pavel boast of being an overseer at Flossenburg recalls the turbulence of the opening scene. The sudden interruption to an eerily modal, archaic wordless humming over string tremolos of Anna's hallucination is striking, as her murdered father, mother and sister rouse her to vengeance. The unusual effects elicited special mention in several of the reviews.

From here on, events move rapidly: Anna strikes Pavel with his dagger, the orchestra's climactic outburst is followed by silence, broken by Anna's speaking voice ('Dead – I must call the police'). Mournful strings lead to the final phase, driving forward with renewed excitement. Anna's vengeance aria grows from broad phrases to an opulent orchestral texture, *Wozzeck*-like in power yet ending on a major triad, which suits Hassall's impressively Shakespearian couplets:

> Unquiet spirits take your rest./Sleep well, sleep sound, among the bless'd.
> The score is paid, the beats is slain./Justice, long buried, is born again.
> Another tyrant bows his head;/Another Judith strikes him dead.
> The tyrannies of men are ever past/My loved ones, here I stand wash'd clean at last.

The intensity and hysteria of Anna's high vocal line portrays with conviction the ferocity of her repressed guilt. The Rector's discovery of Pavel's death elicits for the first time, in contrast to his usually subdued lyricism, an impassioned outcry. Their dialogue, symmetrically echoing the opening scene, is accompanied by increasingly intense orchestration. The Rector's aria about saving Pavel at the liberation of Flossenburg, where Anna's family perished, is accompanied by militaristic galloping energy, pitch percussion, pizzicatos, and brittle brass:

> Then we broke the gates of hell at Flossenburg. The tanks rolled on but Pity made me linger; for here were souls in bondage in direct need of mercy. There in the throng that gathered round like ghosts, all pale and wasted, I saw a young man standing. He gazed at me with sunken eyes that pleaded for compassion. His name was Schwarz ... why did you let him die like this?

Anna's gasp at the name 'Schwarz' is accompanied by a funereal, limping timpani beat, a touching, poignant effect. The Rector's voice drops to its lowest register as he urges Anna to seek fresh air during his prayers. Anna makes her way to the bridge for her final aria, a tripartite meditation on suffering and redemption, Hassall's quasi-biblical language, echoing Psalm 130, set to hymn-like vocal phrases interspersed with clarinet melody over gently pulsating strings and an undulating legato bass line. The watery sound effects recall the earlier scene at the bridge with Callow that set the whole tragedy into motion. Here, by contrast, the broad, eloquent lines and haunting harmony effect a purifying process and moving resolution.

> Out of the deep, O Lord, I cry, /Out of the Deep.
> On these unpitying stones, chill water whispering by
> Here let me die. [skip 16 lines]
> Out of the deep I cry out of the deep./Unloose these chains of life. Grant me Thy sleep.
> O Pavel, look my arms are open wide./Be waiting on the shadowy river side
> If there is life beyond this wilderness of pain/Forgive, forgive me, bring me comfort once again.
> If nothing lies beyond and all our hopes must end,/Farewell, farewell for ever, my beloved friend.

In this aria, Reizenstein's inspiration rises to the heights, whilst the final drowning is accompanied by music which sinks deeper and deeper, merging with watery sounds, from where the epilogue, the orchestra's welling cadence overlaid with 'realistic' sounds of footsteps and distant cries of 'Anna, Anna', sum up Anna's soulful tragedy.[63]

From the perspective of operatic tradition, *Anna Kraus* has all the ingredients of what Apprahamian calls 'acceptable contemporary verismo'.[64] Indeed, we find operatic tropes such as the jealous Iago-like machinations of Callow, the mad scenes for Anna, with hallucinations of her murdered family, with echoes of Donizetti's *Lucia di Lammermoor* and Verdi's *Macbeth*; the final suicidal drowning echoes that of twentieth century operas, not least Britten's *Peter*

---

63 In the Radio Bremen version (broadcast July 1953), the epilogue ends the opera powerfully, omitting the cries of 'Anna Anna' from the BBC version.
64 Apprahamian, 'Music for Today', *London Musical Events*, September 1952.

Grimes, and Berg's *Wozzeck*, with its double murder and suicide by drowning in Act III.[65]

As cited in reviews of the time, the most similar precursor in mood and topic was Gian Carlo Menotti's Pulitzer-winning *The Consul*. Premiered in the USA in 1949, the BBC broadcast it in 1950. Like Reizenstein, Menotti, an Italian immigrant to the USA, was considered an 'enemy alien' during the Second World War. He explores aspects of his experience in a plot which, rather abstractly, deals with the dangers of totalitarian bureaucracy in obtaining (or preventing) visas for refugees, and the story ends with a murder and suicide of the two protagonists, a magician and his wife. *Anna Kraus* is more specific, both geographically and historically, about its political context.

6 Operatic Meanings: *Anna Kraus* in Personal and Social-Political Contexts

If, on one level, the opera might be considered as part of a long operatic tradition, at the same time its subject matter gains in significance in connection with the composer's personal experience, in the context of the social-political events and attitudes of the time.

Anna Kraus is a tale about a refugee. Yet, whilst Reizenstein was a refugee himself, it would be simplistic to simply equate him with either Anna or indeed Pavel, the Modernist musician. Reizenstein's close family, unlike the fictional Anna's, survived the war. His mother and elder sister Lotte (1904–1982), an artist, joined him in London in 1937, following much effort to secure visas. His brother Max (1902–1970), after a brief imprisonment in a German camp, escaped to New Zealand with his non-Jewish wife and young son, eventually returning to Europe after the war. Nonetheless, Reizenstein would have known, as did many refugees, of more distant family having perished in the camps.

Reizenstein's refugee experiences would have made him more aware of the protagonists' nexus of conflicting attitudes, feelings and ideas. The opera provided an opportunity to explore certain issues of great relevance, enhanced by the insights derived from autobiographical resonances. Misreading Reizenstein's close connection to the subject as a disadvantage, the 1952 edition of *The Annual Register* claimed that the 'composer's emotions were too closely engaged in the sufferings of the heroine, a refugee from political oppression'. Such an evaluation both ignored the warm critical reception accorded to the opera, whilst

---

65   See the reviews and previews by Sackville-West, Colin Mason, and Mosco Carner, cited earlier, which mention Britten and Berg.

also implying the questionable notion that a composer's empathy with their operatic characters represents a weakness when it could be interpreted as a strength. Above all, the comment seemed to ignore the successful ways that composer and librettist artfully deployed their skills to highlight and develop important Holocaust-related themes which had received scant attention in opera before.[66]

Moreover, the *Annual Register*'s assumption that Anna was a political refugee is both mistaken and misleading. The opera's opening scene relates how Anna's whole family were imprisoned and murdered, which clearly implies that she was Jewish. Had Anna been a political refugee, her family would not have been murdered. A remarkable document in the Hassall collection offers confirmation. It is a detailed synopsis which contains a description of Anna omitted from the script: 'The violence of her underlying hatred for the oppressors of her people has brought about a dangerous duality in her nature.'[67] The phrase 'the oppressors of her people' highlights how Anna, like Reizenstein, was Jewish. Similarly, Pavel's surname 'Schwarz' is German, rather than Polish, implying he may have been Jewish. The choice of Flossenburg as the camp is also significant. Set up in 1938 originally for political and criminal prisoners, there were Jewish prisoners there from the start, yet after August 1944, a large influx of some 22,000 Polish and Hungarian Jewish prisoners arrived.[68] This would accord with the Rector's description of finding Pavel.

Within the operatic action, the question of Anna's Jewish identity is far from central; the focus is on universal issues, including the psychological consequences of unresolved wartime trauma. Nonetheless, it is striking that all the published previews and reviews, and the BBC scripts, avoid describing Anna as Jewish, preferring the more neutral 'German refugee'.[69] One explanation might be that it reflected a sensitivity to an over-emphasis of Jewish identity, avoiding potential antisemitism; another might be that it is a form of repression.[70] In the early postwar period, many Jewish families did not speak much about

---

66 Ivison S. Macadam (ed.), *The Annual Register – A Review of Public Events at Home and Abroad for the year 1952* (London: Longmans, Green and Co., 1953), 385.
67 See Hassall collection, GBR/0012/MS Add 8905 8/3 (1), opera synopses and originals.
68 Todd Huebner, 'Flossenbürg Main Camp', in Geoffrey P. Megargee (ed.), *The United States Holocaust Memorial Museum Encyclopaedia of Camps and Ghettos, 1933–1945*, Vol. 1 (Bloomington: Indiana University Press, 2009), 559–66. Available at https://doi.org/10.2307/j.ctt16gzb17.21 [accessed: 17.08.2022].
69 Cleverdon, 'An Opera for Broadcasting', 29.
70 A similar tendency colours Hassall's adaptation of the libretto to *La Duenna*, an operetta by the émigré Roberto Gerhard, also for the BBC. Hassall was asked to delete any reference to the Jewish identity of the character of Don Isaac. See Hassall collection, document signed by (R.G.), dated 5 March 1951.

their wartime or camp experiences, even though there was substantial public discussion.[71]

Certainly, the topic was relevant to wider international debate. Whilst Cleverdon, upon initially receiving the synopsis from Hassall and Reizenstein, had noted, curiously, that 'the subject, with its recollections of prison camps, seems to me rather dated', he added 'it has enough dramatic power I think to provide a basis for radio opera.'[72] Emphasising its relevance, the critic Mosco Carner, himself an Austrian refugee, wrote that 'The subject has been drawn from contemporary life, from events that could be imagined as having happened only in our time and no other. This very fact lends the libretto, irrespective of its treatment, a dramatic colour engaging our interest.'[73]

The operatic tale about a German-Jewish refugee and a Polish-Jewish camp survivor, vividly conveyed through musical characterisation, would have been especially topical in 1952 on many levels. Britain had opened its doors to some 70,000 refugees, mainly Jewish, from Nazi Europe during the 1930s, and subsequently helped survivors after the war. The social issues and problems arising from the hosting of refugees would have been current in the immediate postwar period, including coping with trauma such as loss of family, and adapting to a new life as a 'foreigner' in Britain.

Indeed, the serious issues relating to the Holocaust which the opera addresses had a wide socio-political significance in several ways. First of all, the question of guilt and forgiveness, as displayed in the Rector's moral stance, and Anna's refusal to forgive relates both to religious attitudes as also to then recent war trials. The year 1951 represented the end of Germany's denazification process and the start of negotiations with the newly formed 'Claims Conference' for reparations for Israel and the Jewish community. These were ratified in the Luxembourg Agreements of 1952 under the leadership of the German Chancellor Konrad Adenauer. Consequently, there was much international public debate surrounding moral issues of guilt and forgiveness about which the composer may well have been aware. The impact of the Claims Conference affected Reizenstein when, in 1957, he was commissioned to contribute musical transcriptions from oral sources for a publication entitled *Liturgie Sephardie*, an anthology of traditional Sephardi melodies. The volume

---

[71] See for instance, Naama Sheffi, *The Ring of Myths* (Brighton: Sussex Academic Press, 2001), 61.

[72] A less dramatic early version in the Hassall collection has the protagonists as Anna Kramer and Fred Smith. Smith is revealed to be Schmidt, a German soldier, who pretends he was an SS officer, which impels Anna to take revenge. See Hassall collection, GBR/0012/MS Add 8905 8/3 (1), opera synopses and originals.

[73] Carner, 'An Opera for broadcasting'.

was published by the World Sephardi Federation with financial support from the Claims Conference, which required all those receiving fees to have been victims of Nazism, and it appears to have been Reizenstein's only foray into the world of traditional Jewish music.[74]

Second, the idea of refugee community and support organisations is symbolised by the mutual support expressed in the love duet of Anna and Pavel. Remarkably alongside Reizenstein's high professional profile, he continued to contribute to many refugee cultural activities.[75]

Third, the diagnosis of what later would be termed 'post-traumatic stress disorder', or PTSD, is exemplified in Anna's hallucinations and inner voices, compelling her to take vengeance. It is as if the composer and librettist were exploring, sympathetically, the dangers of 'survivor's guilt'. Whilst, on the surface, Anna appears to enjoy the benefits of acculturation to her adopted home, the 'quiet English village', in reality she suffers from powerful inner guilt that impels the tragic outcome. The opera thus acts as a warning as well as being a psychological thriller.

7 Conclusion

The evident topicality of *Anna Kraus* raises the question as to why there was so little emphasis on the story in published reviews at the time. It also suggests that the opera and the issues it raises deserve our current attention.

In addition, the initial success of *Anna Kraus* makes it all the more remarkable that, following the initial BBC broadcasts, the opera was never revived. One might speculate on possible reasons. Whilst the antimodernism of the 1930s and 1940s had dissipated by the following decade, by the 1960s, the so-called Glock-period, the avant-garde was in vogue, and even Second Viennese School serialism was seen as conservative. In a sense, then, Reizenstein was doubly disadvantaged; early on he was considered too Modernist, and later too conservative.[76]

---

74   *Liturgie Sephardie* was published in 1959 by Valentine Mitchell, for the World Sephardi Federation, edited by O. Camhy, and supported by funds from the 'Conference on Jewish Material Claims against Germany'. A series of letters inviting Reizenstein to participate are in the collection of John Reizenstein, to whom I am grateful for the information.

75   *AJR Journal*, November 1964, on the occasion of Reizenstein's award of the Nuremberg Kulturpreis, adds 'We extend our sincerest congratulations to Mr. Reizenstein who, throughout the years, has taken an interest in the efforts of the AJR and repeatedly rendered his voluntary services for the benefit of the older ones in our midst.'

76   Reizenstein received only nine hours of air-time during a five-year period. See Reizenstein correspondence with Gerald Abraham and Hans Keller, 1967–8; BBC WAC BBC/R/RCONT/RCONT12/21250.

Yet whilst his struggle for performances and broadcasts in Britain continued, fortunately his music was appreciated abroad. In 1964, he was awarded the Kulturpreis of his native city of Nuremberg, having earlier performed his Piano Concerto no.2 Op.37 to inaugurate their new Meistersinger Hall. Similarly, in 1966, he was appointed a visiting Professor of Composition at Boston University. Perhaps a similar tendency was evident in the repeat broadcasts of *Anna Kraus* for European audiences.

With the benefit of twenty-first century hindsight, one might speculate that it was the friendship between Reizenstein, the German-Jewish émigré composer, and Hassall, the English man of letters, that enabled them to jointly address, in operatic form, a potentially highly emotive topic of the Holocaust with the necessary detachment and insight. Whilst they both experienced the war years, and its harrowing impact first hand, at the heart of their collaboration was a shared love for the sheer craftsmanship of their respective arts.

As I hope to have shown, their joint achievement, *Anna Kraus*, offers a powerful symbol of the cultural transfer which enriched British society in the postwar period. The combination of a musical language drawn from German and British influences, and the dramaturgical themes of refugee experience, treated in an experimental medium, was unique and special. The vision and daring shown in the first British radio opera stands as a challenge, seventy years on, for a revival, to bring its dramatic power to vivid life again either in studio or on operatic stage.

10
Von großen Erfolgen in der Zwischenkriegszeit zu relativer Vergessenheit: Die Komponisten Bruno Granichstaedten und Robert Katscher im Exil

Hanja Dämon

Abstract

Bruno Granichstaedten (1879–1944) and Robert Katscher (1894–1942) were two Vienna-born operetta composers who fled from National Socialism in 1938. Both died in exile before the end of the Second World War, Katscher in 1942 in Hollywood, and Granichstaedten in 1944 in New York. Internationally successful, they had gained a reputation in the USA before they became refugees. Similar to many other artists, however, life in exile derailed their previously impressive careers. I discuss here how the US press reported on both composers before and after their flights from Nazi-occupied Europe. This article also sheds light on their activities in the USA, for example on the adaptation of Katscher's German-language stage hit *Bei Kerzenlicht* (By Candlelight, subtitled *12 Chansons around a small comedy in three acts*, text: Karl Farkas) for Broadway in 1938 as the musical *You Never Know*, with new contributions by Cole Porter. Granichstaedten, in turn, remained active until his death and devised new works, including operettas and screenplays, although most of his compositions in exile did not make it to stage or screen.

1   Einleitung

Der Aufsatz beschäftigt sich mit den Biografien von zwei in Wien geborenen jüdischen Komponisten, die beide vor dem Zweiten Weltkrieg im Bereich der Operette und des musikalischen Unterhaltungstheaters international sehr erfolgreich waren, deren Namen allerdings heute weniger geläufig sind: Bruno Granichstaedten (1879–1944) und Robert Katscher (1894–1942). Sie schufen Musik zu Bühnenwerken, die im In- und Ausland erfolgreich gespielt wurden, und betätigten sich als Librettisten und Textautoren. Wie etliche andere mussten sie nach der Machtergreifung der Nationalsozialisten aus Europa fliehen. Beide versuchten in den USA in ihrem Metier Fuß zu fassen, wo sie bereits Erfolge gefeiert hatten, und daher nun berechtigte Hoffnungen hegten, daran anknüpfen zu können. Beide Komponisten starben jedoch noch vor Ende des Zweiten Weltkrieges. Außer ihrem Beruf, ihrem Geburtsort und Sterbeland verbindet die beiden also, dass sie in den USA schon ein gewisses Ansehen genossen, bevor sie den Weg ins Exil antraten. Ihr Bestreben, mit ihren Operetten und deren Adaptionen das amerikanische Publikum für sich einzunehmen und Regisseure, Bühnenbildner, Dirigenten und Sänger für Aufführungen zu gewinnen sowie ihre Versuche, sich im Filmgeschäft zu etablieren, sollen hier aufgezeigt werden. Die Fragen, denen dieser Beitrag nachgeht, sind folgende: Konnten sie nach geglückter Übersiedlung Ende der 1930er Jahre aus ihren früheren Erfolgen Nutzen ziehen? Wie gestaltete sich der Prozess der Flucht aus Wien in die USA im Einzelnen? Wie wurden sie von der US-amerikanischen Presse und branchenrelevanten Publikationen wahrgenommen und welche Möglichkeiten ergaben sich, auch in der erzwungenen Emigration in ihrem Beruf weiterzuwirken? Granichstaedten und Katscher sind natürlich keine Einzelfälle, dennoch habe ich ihre Biografien gewählt, um den jeweiligen Kontrast zwischen ihrer einstigen Popularität und ihrer relativen gegenwärtigen Vergessenheit herauszuarbeiten. Auch die Darbietungen im Exil von Granichstaedtens Lebensgefährtin Rosalie Kaufmann (1910–1979), die gemeinsam mit ihm geflüchtet war, sollen hier Erwähnung finden. Sie trug mit ihren Auftritten in Clubs und Cafés während der gemeinsamen Exilzeit erheblich zum Unterhalt des Paares bei.

Das Schaffen von etlichen in der Zwischenkriegszeit erfolgreichen und vielversprechenden Künstlerinnen und Künstlern ist nach Absetzung ihrer Werke im Nationalsozialismus oft bis weit in die Nachkriegszeit verdrängt worden. Dies gilt insbesondere für den Bereich der Unterhaltungsmusik.[1] Erst in den letzten beiden Jahrzehnten begann sich dahingehend etwas zu verändern, indem Werke ehemals populärer, aber heute mehrheitlich unbekannter Musikschaffender, wiederentdeckt werden. Das in Amsterdam ansässige Operetta Research Center etwa widmet sich seit 2006 allen Aspekten der Operettenforschung und trägt dazu bei, verdrängte Personen und Stücke der Vergessenheit zu entreißen. Noch wenige Jahre zuvor hatte Marion Linhardt 1999 im Rahmen ihrer Forschungen zur Operettengeschichte hinsichtlich des heute gespielten und bisher untersuchten Operettenrepertoires festgestellt: ‚Das Repertoire ist nur deshalb *überschaubar*, weil niemand darüber *hinausschaut*.'[2] Um bei Granichstaedten zu bleiben: Seine erfolgreichste

---

[1] Vgl. Christoph Dompke, *Unterhaltungsmusik und NS-Verfolgung, Musik im ‚Dritten Reich' und im Exil* (Neumünster: Von Bockel, 2011).

[2] Marion Linhardt, ‚Ausgangspunkt Wien. Operette als Gegenstand theaterwissenschaftlicher Auseinandersetzung', in Hans-Peter Bayerdörfer (Hrsg.), *Musiktheater als Herausforderung.*

Operette der Zwischenkriegszeit *Der Orlow* erlebte zwar die eine oder andere Wiederaufführung, zum Beispiel 1958 in Wiener Raimund-Theater, und es gibt auch Einspielungen von ihr, sie ist aber dennoch heute weitgehend unbekannt, wenn man es mit der Popularität zur Zeit seiner Uraufführung vergleicht.[3] Selbiges gilt für die Werke von Robert Katscher.

Wesentlich bekannter und populärer sind heute die Operetten nichtjüdischer Komponisten wie zum Beispiel Franz Lehár oder auch Ralph Benatzkys Erfolgsstück *Im weißen Rössl*, zu dem Granichstaedten wie auch Robert Gilbert und Robert Stolz als musikalische Einlagen gedachte Schlager beisteuerte.[4] Auf die bis Jahrzehnte nach dem Krieg andauernde fehlende Aufarbeitung der Biografien jener ins Exil vertriebenen oder ermordeten Komponisten, Librettisten und Bühnenstars weist Eva Philippoff 2005 in ihrem Artikel ‚Die ermordete Operette' hin: Sie nimmt einen Ausstellungskatalog zur 91. Sonderausstellung des Historischen Museums der Stadt Wien 1984/1985 über die Operette als Beispiel, da in diesem Hinweise auf etliche aus Österreich vertriebene Operettenkomponisten und Librettisten sowie zahlreicher Interpretinnen und Interpreten der Zwischenkriegszeit fehlen.[5] Erst ab den 1990er Jahren wurden Biografien von Operettenkünstlerinnen und – künstlern in Hinblick auf Exil und Verfolgung genauer untersucht.[6] Es steht aber außer Zweifel, dass immer noch viele Namen wiederzuentdecken sind, um weitere Einblicke in das Thema Musikschaffende im Exil zu bekommen. Dazu gehören die beiden hier vorgestellten Komponisten.

2 Werdegänge der beiden Komponisten

Bruno Granichstaedten wurde am 1. September 1879 in Wien geboren und erhielt seine musikalische Ausbildung am Leipziger Konservatorium. Einer seiner Lehrer dort war der Komponist, Dirigent und Pädagoge Salomon Jadassohn (1831–1902).[7] Granichstaedten kehrte anschließend nach Wien

---

    Interdisziplinäre Facetten von Theater- und Musikwissenschaft (Tübingen: Niemayer, 1999), 167–76 (167).

3 Vgl. Thomas Aigner, *Der musikalische Nachlass Bruno Granichstaedtens* (Wien, 2004) 6 und Martin Trageser, *Millionen Herzen im Dreiviertel Takt. Die Komponisten des Zeitalters der ‚Silbernen Operette'* (Würzburg: Königshausen & Neumann), 121–29.

4 Granichstaedten steuerte die Einlage ‚Zuschau'n kann i net' bei.

5 Eva Philippoff, ‚Die ermordete Operette', *Germanica* 36/2005, http://germanica.revues.org /1533 [letzter Aufruf: 27 April 2020].

6 *Ibid.*

7 Heinz Wagner, *Das große Operettenbuch. 120 Komponisten und 430 Werke* (Berlin: Parthas, 1997), 87.

zurück, fand eine Anstellung an der Wiener Hofoper und erarbeitete sich vor allem als Operettenkomponist einen internationalen Ruf. So informierte im Oktober des Jahres 1912 die US-amerikanische Tageszeitung *The Washington Post* ihre Leserinnen und Leser über einen Besuch des Komponisten in den USA und nannte ihn im Zuge dessen ‚one of the spectacular musical personages to arrive in America last winter'.[8] Daher brachte diesem Artikel zufolge jede New Yorker Zeitung einen Beitrag über den Gast aus Europa. Anlass der Reise war die Aufführung seines Operettendebüts *Bub oder Mädel* unter dem Titel *The Rose Maid* in den Vereinigten Staaten, wo das Werk sehr erfolgreich lief und sich in New York ganze fünf Monate auf dem Spielplan hielt.[9] Die *Washington Post* berichtete, dass Granichstaedten während seinem Aufenthalt jede Cabaret-Vorstellung in diversen New Yorker Cafés besuchte, die sich ihm bot, um die dort gebotene Musik zu studieren.[10] Tatsächlich hielten amerikanische Rhythmen Einzug in seine Musik, die nicht nur beeinflusst von seinem eigenen USA-Aufenthalt, sondern auch durch Erzählungen des Direktors des Theaters an der Wien Hubert Marischka (1882–1959) über dessen eigenen Reisen angeregt worden sein dürften.[11] Insbesondere mit seiner modernen, mit Jazz-Elementen versetzten Operette *Der Orlow* feierte er Mitte der Zwanzigerjahre in Wien einen fulminanten Erfolg (Erstaufführung: 3. April 1925 im Theater an der Wien), auf den hier noch eingegangen wird. Eine weitere Operette Granichstaedtens mit dem Titel *Reklame*, die im Februar 1930 im Theater an der Wien Premiere hatte, setzte ebenfalls auf Musikstile, die aus den USA importiert wurden, und eine New Yorker Kulisse. Dennoch verstand er es aber auch, ‚urwienerische Musik' zu komponieren.[12] Für seine Operetten verfasste Granichstaedten die Libretti oft selbst oder in Zusammenarbeit mit anderen Autoren. Außerdem schrieb er Drehbücher zu musikalischen Unterhaltungsfilmen und steuerte dann meist die Musik zu diesen bei.[13]

Der am 20. Mai 1894 in Wien geborene Robert Katscher beteiligte sich ebenfalls häufig an Libretti, zu denen er die Musik beisteuerte. Nach einem Studium der Rechtswissenschaften, welches ihm den Doktortitel einbrachte,

---

8   ‚Odd Herr Granichstaedten', *The Washington Post*, 6 Oktober 1912, SM2.
9   Vgl. Dan Dietz, *The Complete Book of 1910s Broadway Musicals* (Lanham: Rowman & Littlefield, 2021), 156.
10 *Ibid.*
11 Ulrike Petersen, *Operetta after the Habsburg Empire* (Berkeley: unveröffentlichte Dissertation, 2013), 61.
12 Günter Tolar, *So ein Theater. Die Geschichte des Theaters an der Wien* (Wien: Ueberreuter, 1991), 210.
13 Zum Film *Zwei in einem Auto* (R: Joe May, 1932) etwa komponierte Granichstaedten nicht nur die Filmmusik sondern war zudem als Co-Autor am Drehbuch beteiligt.

studierte er Musik unter anderem bei dem bekannten Komponisten Hans Gál (1890–1987). Einer von Katschers großen internationalen Erfolgen wurde *Die Wunderbar* von 1930. Über die sehr erfolgreiche Aufführung von *Die Wunderbar* in Berlin – die Uraufführung hatte in den Wiener Kammerspielen stattgefunden – resümiert etwa der Journalist und Autor Paul Marcus, der unter dem Kürzel PEM zahlreiche Kritiken verfasste, in seinen Erinnerungen: Die Librettisten ‚hatten die Idee ausgeheckt, das ganze Theater in ein Nachtlokal zu verwandeln; die Zuschauer sollten das Gefühl haben, in das Bühnengeschehen der Wunderbar mit einbezogen zu sein.'[14] Das Libretto dieses musikalischen Zweiakters entstand in Zusammenarbeit mit Karl Farkas und Géza Herzceg, und brachte Katscher einen sehr guten Ruf als Komponist ein.[15] ‚Wenn die Elisabeth nicht so schöne Beine hätt' stammt daraus – vermutlich der ‚meistgesungene Schlager der zwanziger Jahre überhaupt', ein Erfolg, der selbst die Verfasser verblüffte.[16] Katschers zusammen mit Siegfried Geyer und Paul Frank verfasstes Stück ‚Essig und Öl' mit dem Beinamen ‚Ein Märchen aus Wien', das 1932 in den Wiener Kammerspielen uraufgeführt wurde, erreichte im deutschsprachigen Raum ebenfalls große Popularität. Insbesondere das daraus stammende Lied ‚Der Dr. Lueger hat mir einmal die Hand gereicht' wurde in Österreich sehr bekannt, und kann heute in einer Interpretation Hans Mosers im Internet angehört werden.[17] Zu Katschers nachhaltigsten Erfolgen im englischsprachigen Raum wiederum zählt ‚When Day is Done' (engl. Text: Buddy DeSylva), eine Adaption des Schlagers ‚Madonna, du bist schöner als der Sonnenschein', der aus einer Revue stammt. Dieser ‚song of romantic reverie when the day's labors are over' war im Juni 1927 erstmals von Paul Whiteman eingespielt worden.[18] Whitemans Interpretation dieses Musikstücks hatte den sogenannten ‚sweet jazz' populär gemacht, während dem Musikstück auch Elemente der Wiener Operettentradition im Stil von Franz Lehár und Emmerich Kálmán zugeschrieben werden, die auf den europäischen Ursprung des Songs verweisen.[19] Auch nach Katschers Tod

---

14 PEM (Paul Marcus), *Und der Himmel hängt voller Geigen. Glanz und Zauber der Operette* (Berlin: Blanvalet, 1955), 181.

15 Monika Kornberger, *‚Einmal sang die Liebe uns ein Lied'. Deutscher Schlager der Zwischenkriegszeit und seine Protagonisten in Wien* (Dissertation: Graz, 2018), 317.

16 Markus Georg, *Karl Farkas. ‚Schau'n Sie sich das an'. Ein Leben für die Heiterkeit* (Wien: Amalthea, 1983), 101.

17 ‚Hans Moser: Der Dr. Lueger hat mir die Hand gereicht – Wien 1932', *YouTube*, https://www.youtube.com/watch?v=x8rH-DCLgIo [letzter Aufruf: 15 August 2021].

18 Joshua Berrett, Louis *Armstrong and Paul Whiteman: Two Kings of Jazz* (Yale: Yale University Press: 2004), 104.

19 Marvin E. Paymer, *Sentimental Journey. Intimate Portraits of America's Great Popular Songs 1920–1945* (Darien: Two Bytes Publishing, 1999), 100.

wurde die deutschsprachige Vorlage nicht unter den Teppich gekehrt, sondern darauf hingewiesen, dass es sich um den Song ‚Madonna' handle, auf den Whiteman bei einer Europa-Tour gestoßen war und mit einem englischen, auf US-amerikanisches Publikum zugeschnittenen Text versehen wurde.[20] Trotz Katschers großer Publikumserfolge zu seinen Lebzeiten ist sein Name heute fast vergessen. Bisher wurden bis auf die 2021 in Buchform veröffentlichte Dissertation von Monika Kornberger über deutsche Schlager der Zwischenkriegszeit, die auch eine ausführlich recherchierte Biografie des Komponisten beinhaltet, noch keine weiteren wissenschaftlichen Recherchen zu Robert Katscher und seinem Schaffen publiziert.[21]

Wie Granichstaedten hatte Katscher ebenfalls schon vor seiner Flucht die Gelegenheit, die Vereinigten Staaten unter wesentlich anderen Umständen zu bereisen. Die amerikanische Filmzeitschrift *Hollywood Reporter* kündigte im August 1933 seine erste USA-Reise an.[22] Ein weiterer Aufenthalt in den Vereinigten Staaten folgte 1935, diesmal mit dem direkten Ziel, für Hollywood-Filme Musik zu komponieren. *Motion Picture Daily* hatte im Februar dieses Jahres vermeldet, dass er von der Produktionsfirma MGM angestellt worden sei.[23] Die Einladung und die Anstellung hatte er sowohl seinen Bühnenerfolgen zu verdanken als auch dem Erfolg von ‚When Day is Done' in den USA.[24] Ende März 1935 kam Katscher dann in Hollywood an, wie *Variety* und *New York Times* mitteilten.[25] Im Juni schließlich kündigte die *Los Angeles Times* an, dass ‚Katscher, Vienna Composer of Musicals' zum Film käme. Dieser Artikel erwähnte, dass Katschers Werke wie *Wonderbar* und der Song ‚When Day is Done' in Hollywood wohl bekannter seien als der Name des Komponisten, der im Übrigen auch Autor und Produzent sei – ‚a truly one-man show' –, und dieser mitsamt seiner Ehefrau in Beverly Hills wohne.[26] Katscher hoffe, so die *Los Angeles Times*, bald einen Auftrag zu erhalten und an die Arbeit gehen zu können.[27] *The Washington Post* verlautbarte, dass Katscher, immerhin schon einige Monate zu diesem Zeitpunkt in Hollywood, noch nicht einmal ein Büro oder ein Klavier zur Verfügung gestellt bekommen hatte, wo er

---

20 'Paul Whiteman, Dinah Shore ...', *Variety*, 9 Juni 1943, 31.
21 Monika Kornberger, *‚Einmal sang die Liebe uns ein Lied'. Deutscher Schlager der Zwischenkriegszeit und seine Protagonisten in Wien* (Wien: Hollitzer, 2021), 364–92. In der gleichnamigen in Graz entstandenen Dissertation von 2018 siehe 302–30.
22 'Composer Coming', *Hollywood Reporter*, 23 August 1933, 2.
23 'M-G-M Signs Ruben for Single Picture', *Motion Picture Daily*, 12 Februar 1935, 8.
24 Rudolf Ulrich, *Österreicher in Hollywood* (Wien: Verl. Filmarchiv Austria, 2004), 228.
25 'Broadway', *Variety*, 27 März 1935, S. 60; 'Screen Notes', *New York Times*, 23 März 1935, 11.
26 'Katscher, Vienna Composer of Musicals, Comes to Film', *Los Angeles Times*, 2 Juni 1935, A10.
27 Ibid.

Songs ausprobieren könne.²⁸ ‚Katscher Starts', vermeldete *Variety* dann am 10. Juli 1935, und gab an, dass der Komponist von der Filmproduktionsfirma Metro endlich eine Aufgabe erhalten und gemeinsam mit dem Texter Ned Washington ‚When Morning Comes' verfasst hatte.²⁹

Während dieses Aufenthalts dürften allerdings keine Kompositionen für den amerikanischen Film entstanden sein, die dann auch verwendet wurden oder ihn als Verfasser auswiesen. Die Internet Movie Database (IMDb) listet nur für 1941 eine Tätigkeit Katschers als Komponist in Hollywood auf, und zwar für den Film *Gambling Daughters* (R: Max Nosseck), die ihm allerdings keine Nennung in den Credits einbrachte.³⁰ Außerdem nennt IMDb Katscher als einen von zahlreichen Autoren die an dem Film *Tales of Manhattan* (1942, R: Julien Duvivier) beteiligt gewesen sein sollen, aber ebenfalls ‚uncredited' blieben. Dass Katscher zu letzterem Film die Musik beisteuern würde (was dann aber augenscheinlich nicht geschah), vermeldete Hans Kafka (ebenfalls in Wien geboren und nun im Exil in den USA) gegen Ende November 1941 in seiner im *Aufbau* erscheinenden Kolumne über Hollywood.³¹ Bereits 1937, also vor seiner Exilzeit, hätte sich Katscher an dem Hollywood Remake des deutschsprachigen Erfolgsfilms *Episode* (1935, R: Walter Reisch) beteiligen sollen, wie die *New York Times* im Mai dieses Jahres mitteilte.³² Dieser Film wurde allerdings nie gedreht.

3   Granichstaedtens und Katschers große Bühnenerfolge

Granichstaedtens ‚Der Orlow ... hat für die Operette Neuland erschlossen', schrieb die *Wiener Zeitung* am Tag nach der Uraufführung der Operette am Theater an der Wien.³³ Die in New York angesiedelte Handlung dreht sich um den in einer Autofabrik als Maschinist angestellten Alex Doroschinsky, eigentlich Alexandrowitsch, ein nach der russischen Revolution geflüchteter Großfürst. Er ist verliebt in die Tänzerin Nadja, auf die auch der Besitzer der Autofabrik, Joe Walsh, ein Auge geworfen hat. Zu Schlagern auch abseits von der Bühne wurden aus dieser Operette ‚Für dich, mein Schatz, hab' ich mich schön gemacht' und ‚Da nehm' ich meine kleine Zigarette'. Die Stars der Erstaufführung waren Hubert Marischka, Betty Fischer (1887–1969) und

---

28   Sidney Skolski, 'Hollywood: The Gossipel Truth', *The Washington Post*, 25 Juni 1935, 16.
29   'Katscher Starts', *Variety*, 10 Juli 1935, 53.
30   'Robert Katscher', https://www.imdb.com/name/nm0441499/ [letzter Aufruf: 10 Mai 2020].
31   'Hollywood Calling – Hans Kafka Speaking', *Aufbau*, 28 November 1941.
32   'News from Hollywood', *New York Times*, 13 Mai 1937, 31.
33   *Wiener Zeitung*, 4 Mai 1925, 6.

Elsie Altmann (1899–1984). Der bekannte österreichische Schauspieler Hans Moser (1880–1964) hatte einen Auftritt im letzten Akt. Durch den stürmischen Publikumsapplaus bei der Premiere war der Erfolg, den Granichstaedten dann mit dieser Operette erzielte, bereits abzusehen.[34]

Der Orlow gehörte zu den ersten Operetten, die mit Jazz und Blues versetzt waren, und Granichstaedten war mit diesem musikalischen Einfall ‚vielleicht der modernste' Wiener Operettenkomponist jener Jahre geworden.[35] Dem Zeitgeist der 1920er entsprechend, integrierte Granichstaedten eine Jazz-Kapelle in das sonst übliche Orchester.[36] Mit amerikanischem Setting und amerikanischen Rhythmen, die man bis dahin generell weniger mit Operette assoziierte, – speziell von in Wien verfassten und uraufgeführten Operetten – traf *Der Orlow* einen Nerv.[37] Allein im Theater an der Wien brachte es das Stück 1925 und 1930 auf über 400 Aufführungen.[38] Zwischen 1926 und 1991 erschienene Publikationen zur Geschichte des Theaters an der Wien erwähnen Granichstaedtens Erfolge am Haus (insbesondere mit dem *Orlow*).[39] In zwei nach der Jahrtausendwende veröffentlichten Darstellungen zum Haus bleiben Granichstaedtens Operettenerfolge unerwähnt.[40] Natürlich ging und geht die Geschichte des Theaters weiter, aber dass dieser große Erfolg der Zwischenkriegszeit nun im 21. Jahrhunderts unberücksichtigt bleibt, mag schon einen Grund darin haben, dass sich das Werk auch aufgrund des nationalsozialistischen Verbots nicht auf den Spielplänen halten konnte und dadurch weitgehend in der Versenkung verschwand.

Der Orlow wurde nach dem phänomenalen Erfolg im Theater an der Wien sogar zweimal verfilmt, zunächst 1927 als Stummfilm (Regie: Jakob Fleck und Louise Kolm-Fleck). Seit Beginn des Filmemachens griffen Filmemacherinnen und Filmemacher Operettenstoffe auf. Vor Einführung des Tonfilms kam den Kinozuschauern bei Operettenverfilmungen dennoch eine Auswahl der Operettenmelodien bei einer Vorführung zu Ohren, da die Vorstellungen in der Regel von Motiven aus der jeweiligen Operette begleitet

---

34 *Ibid.*
35 Tolar, 210.
36 Siehe zu diesem Thema Konrad Nowakowski, '"30 Negroes (Ladies and Gentlemen)": The Syncopated Orchestra in Vienna', *Black Music Research Journal* (Fall 2009), 229–82 (270).
37 Vgl. zu diesem Thema Melanie Eunike Goerth, *Amerikanismen in der Wiener Operette der Zwischenkriegszeit*, (unveröffentlichte Dipl. Arbeit: Wien, 2013).
38 Anton Bauer, *150 Jahre Theater an der Wien* (Wien: Amalthea-Verl., 1952), 246.
39 Vgl. Raoul Biberhofer, *Das Theater an der Wien. 1801–1926* (Wien: Karczag, 1926), 79; Tolar, *op. cit.*
40 Attila E. Láng, *200 Jahre im Theater an der Wien. ‚Spectacles müssen seyn.'* (Wien: Holzhausen, 2001); Tadeusz Krzeszowiak, *Theater an der Wien. Seine Technik und Geschichte 1801–2001* (Wien: Böhlau, 2002).

wurden. Die als Filmpioniere geltenden Flecks, die Regisseure des ersten *Orlow*-Films, versuchten zudem ihre Filme mit Grammophon-Einspielungen zu synchronisieren.[41]

Eine weitere Verfilmung kam im Herbst 1932 als *Der Orlow. Der Diamant des Zaren* (D 1932, Regie Max Neufeld) in die Kinos. Die Handlung wich wenig von der Vorlage ab, wurde allerdings von New York nach Berlin verlegt.[42] Die Besetzung weist zahlreiche Schauspieler auf, die bald nach Abschluss des Films Verfolgungen durch die Nationalsozialisten ausgesetzt waren. Kurt Lilien, 1882 als Kurth Lilienthal in Berlin geboren, wurde 1943 im KZ Sobibor in Polen ermordet.[43] Kurt Fuß, geboren 1892 in Leipzig, überlebte mehrere Konzentrationslager, unter ihnen Dachau und Buchenwald.[44] Eugen Neufeld, Bruder von Regisseur Max Neufeld und zwischen 1927 und 1933 hauptsächlich in Berlin tätig, bekam Schwierigkeiten wegen seiner antinationalsozialistischen Einstellung.[45] Auch der Regisseur Max Neufeld erhielt Arbeitsverbot im sogenannten ‚Dritten Reich' wegen fehlendem ‚Ariernachweis'.[46]

Die Existenz zweier Verfilmungen von *Der Orlow* zeigt die unmittelbare Vernetzung zwischen damals aktuellen Bühnenerfolgen und Filmemachern, die sich diese Erfolge rasch zu Nutze machen wussten. Verfilmungen popularisierten den jeweiligen Operettenstoff weiter, oft auch über Europa hinaus. Dennoch wurden Film und Operette in zeitgenössischen Berichten manchmal auch als in Konkurrenz stehende Unterhaltungsformen gesehen: ‚Kampf Operette gegen Tonfilm' titelte zum Beispiel die Wochenzeitschrift *Die Fledermaus* 1934 in einer Besprechung einer aktuellen Operette.[47] Dies betraf vor allem die zu Beginn der 1930er Jahre entstandene Tonfilmoperette, die nicht mehr zwangsläufig auf bereits vorhandenen Bühnenerfolgen basierte, sondern oft auf extra für den Film verfassten Drehbüchern.[48] Der Aufschwung dieses

---

41   Richard Traubner, 'Operette als Stoff und Anregung. Entwicklungen im Musikfilm 1907–1973', in Katja Uhlenbrok (Hrsg.), *MusikSpektakelFilm. Musiktheater und Tanzkultur im deutschen Film 1922–1932* (München: Ed. Text + Kritik, 1998), 9.

42   *Paimann's Filmlisten* (Wien) 17. Jg., Nr. 865/4.22.1932.

43   Weniger, 226.

44   *Ibid.*, 126.

45   Weniger, 265.

46   Armin Loacker, 'Max Neufeld: Schauspieler, Regisseur, Produzent. Ein biographischer Abriss' in Ders. (Hrsg.), *Kunst der Routine. Der Schauspieler und Regisseur Max Neufeld* (Wien: Verl. Filmarchiv Austria, 2008), 10–87 (64f).

47   *Die Fledermaus. Wochenblatt für Theater, Film, Musik, Radio, Sport, Mode und Gesellschaft*, 22 Dezember 1934, 8.

48   Vgl. Kevin Clarke, ‚Walzerträume: Wien als Setting in Bühnen- und Tonfilmoperetten vor und nach 1933' in Rainer Rother (Hrsg.) ‚*Wenn ich sonntags in mein Kino geh'. Ton – Film – Musik 1929–1933* (Bönen: Kettler, 2007), 106–33.

Genres bot gute Möglichkeiten für Operettenkomponisten, die Granichstaedten zu nutzen wusste. Er blieb nicht auf die Bühne fixiert, sondern konnte sich vor seiner Exilzeit auch im deutschsprachigen Film als Autor und Komponist etablieren und rief auch Kollegen, die bisher nur für die Bühne komponiert hatten, zum ‚mittun [...] mitschaffen' an dem damals relativ neuen Medium Tonfilm auf.[49]

Auch Katscher lieferte Filmmusiken, im deutschsprachigen Raum etwa zu den populären Filmen des Regisseurs Walter Reisch, und seine *Wunderbar* wurde sogar in Hollywood verfilmt. Auf zahlreiche Aufführungen des Stücks im In- und Ausland – wie damals üblich mit Bearbeitungen[50] – folgte 1934 mit *Wonderbar* (R: Lloyd Bacon) eine Verfilmung mit dem Sänger, Schauspieler und Entertainer Al Jolson in der Hauptrolle. In der Filmliteratur wird *Wonderbar* als einer jener sogenannten ‚pre-code' Filme erwähnt, in welchen noch deutliche homosexuelle Anspielungen die Zensur passieren konnten, als es nach der Einführung einer strikteren Regelung im selben Jahr des Erscheinens möglich gewesen wäre.[51]

Ein weiterer großer Erfolg Katschers wurde *Bei Kerzenlicht* nach einem Bühnenwerk von Siegried Geyer (das Stück wurde übrigens ebenfalls in Hollywood verfilmt). Katscher zog für seine Version Karl Farkas für die Bearbeitung heran. Wie die *Badener Zeitung* im August 1937 berichtete, feierte das Stück, dem Katscher den Untertitel *12 Chansons um eine kleine Komödie* gab, nach seiner beifallsbegleitenden Uraufführung am Deutschen Volkstheater in Wien im In- und Ausland weitere Erfolge.[52] Bei einer Jahrzehnte später erfolgten Wiederaufnahme von *Bei Kerzenlicht* in den Kammerspielen des Theaters in der Josefstadt in der Spielzeit 2003/2004 trat Katschers Autorenschaft in den Hintergrund, denn er wird auf dem Programm nicht als Verfasser genannt. Dort stehen nur Katschers Co-Autoren Karl Farkas und Siegfried Geyer. Die ‚musikalische Komödie in drei Akten' wurde zwar mit Musik von Robert Katscher aufgeführt, dennoch fehlen im Programm Anmerkungen zum Komponisten.[53] Auch Katschers Hit *Die Wunderbar*, dessen Handlung in einem Nachtlokal angesiedelt ist, wird in diesem Programmheft als eine Farkas-Revue bezeichnet, obwohl in zeitgenössischen Quellen bei beiden Werken fast immer der Komponist ebenso an prominenter Stelle

---

49   Bruno Granichstaedten, ‚Kritik der Kritik', *Neues Wiener Journal*, 4 März 1930, 5.
50   Siehe Ethan Mordden, *Sing for your Supper: The Broadway Musical in the 1930s* (New York: Palgrave, 2005), 40.
51   Richard Barrios, *A Song in the Dark. The Birth of the Musical Film* (New York 1995) 413–16.
52   '12 Chansons um eine kleine Komödie', *Badener Zeitung*, 18 August 1937, 3.
53   Programmheft *Bei Kerzenlicht*: Kammerspiele Spielzeit 2003/2004.

oder sogar als Hauptautor genannt wurde.⁵⁴ Katschers *Wunderbar* wurde sowohl als Operette als auch als musikalisches Spiel bezeichnet. Während Granichstaedtens Bühnenwerke trotz seiner musikalischen Experimente und Neuerungen als Operetten definiert werden, so verschwimmen – wie das Beispiel der *Wunderbar* zeigt – die Bezeichnungen, wenn es um Katschers kompositorisches Schaffen geht. Katscher zeichnete sich zudem auch für die Musik einer auf einem Libretto von Farkas und Fritz Grünbaum basierenden, wohl augenzwinkernd sogenannten ‚unbeabsichtigten Operette' verantwortlich: *Der Traumexpress* von 1931, ein weiteres Beispiel dafür, wie Genregrenzen in der Aufbruchsstimmung der Zwischenkriegszeit aufgebrochen und nicht mehr so starr gehandhabt wurden.⁵⁵

Die genannten Operetten und musikalischen Schauspiele wurden von den Nazis wegen der jüdischen Herkunft des Komponisten als ‚entartet' angesehen. Die sogenannte ‚Reinigung des deutschen Kulturlebens' nach 1933 in Deutschland und ab 1938 in Österreich, die die Auslöschung des gesamten jüdischen beziehungsweise als jüdisch angesehenen Kultur- und somit auch Musikschaffens bezweckte, war ein zentrales Anliegen der Nationalsozialisten. Herbert Gerigk, der ‚Leiter der Hauptstelle Musik [...] für die Überwachung der gesamten geistigen und weltanschaulichen Schulung und Erziehung der NSDAP' schrieb im Vorwort des von der Reichsleitung der NSDAP in Auftrag gegebenen und 1940 publizierten ‚Lexikon der Juden in der Musik':

> Die Namen der ‚Größten' aus der Zeit vom Weltkriegsende bis zur Neuordnung des Reiches sind versunken. Sie sind sogar so gründlich vergessen, dass beim zufälligen Wiederauftauchen eines solchen Namens mancher sich kaum entsinnen wird, dass es sich um einen berüchtigten früher viel genannten Juden handelt.⁵⁶

Das ‚Lexikon' liefert neben den Namen von jüdischen Musikern und Musikerinnen auch ein Titelverzeichnis ihrer bekanntesten Werke. Es zeigt sich deutlich die antisemitische Mission und Motivation dieser Nazipublikation; Komponisten und Interpreten und Interpretinnen von Unterhaltungsmusik rassistisch zu entwerten. Neben Bruno Granichstaedten und seinem *Orlow* befinden sich in dieser Auflistung weitere sehr erfolgreiche Wiener

---

54 '12 Chansons um eine kleine Komödie', *Badener Zeitung*, 18 August 1937, 3.
55 Birgit Peter, 'Der Revuefilm in Österreich, 1945–1955', *Maske und Kothurn*, Vol. 46, 2000, 51–59 (52).
56 Theo Stengel und Herbert Gerigk, 'Das Lexikon der Juden in der Musik, Berlin 1940. Faksimile', in Eva Weissweiler (Hrsg.), *Ausgemerzt! Das Lexikon der Juden in der Musik und seine mörderischen Folgen* (Köln: Dittrich, 1999), 182.

Operetten-Komponisten, die während der Nazi-Herrschaft vertrieben und verfolgt wurden. Unter ihnen Leo Ascher (geb. 1880 in Wien, gest. 1942 in New York), Oscar Straus (geb. 1880 in Wien, gestorben 1954 in Bad Ischl), Edmund Eysler (geb. 1874 in Wien, gest. 1949 in Wien, wo er in einem Versteck in Wien die Nazizeit überlebt hatte). Zum Zweck und zur Handhabung dieses Lexikon heißt es dort noch, es solle keine ‚Verewigung der jüdischen Erzeugnisse geliefert werden, sondern eine Handhabe zur schnellsten Ausmerzung aller irrtümlich verbliebenen Reste aus unserem Kultur- und Geistesleben'.[57] Der Großteil der Komponisten und auch der Librettisten populärer Unterhaltungsmusik der Zwischenkriegszeit galten als ‚nichtarisch', worauf ein antisemischer Zeitungsartikel im nationalsozialistischen Blatt *Arbeitersturm* im April 1938 hinwies.[58] In einem Tagebucheintrag weist der Komponist Ralph Benatzky (1884–1957), ein Nazi-Gegner und später ebenfalls in den USA im Exil, ebenfalls darauf hin, dass alle wesentlichen Protagonisten im Bereich der Operette (bis auf ihn selbst und Lehár) jüdischer Herkunft waren – von den Wiener Komponisten zählte er übrigens unter anderem Granichstaedten und Katscher zu den wichtigsten Vertretern dieser Kunst.[59] Auch viele Librettisten und Sängerinnen und Sänger waren jüdisch. Einige konnten ihre Heimatländer nach Machtübernahme der Nationalsozialisten rechtzeitig verlassen, viele wurden jedoch von den Nazis ermordet.[60]

Für Granichstaedten waren die Lebensumstände bereits vor seinem erzwungenen Exil nicht mehr ideal. Trotz seiner vorangegangenen Erfolge blieben im Lauf der 1930er Jahre zunehmend Aufträge aus. Daher hatte Granichstaedten Anfang 1938 offensichtlich finanzielle Probleme und musste sich Geld von einem Freund borgen, welcher ihn dann wegen nicht erfolgter Rückzahlung verklagte, wobei es jedoch nicht zu einer Verurteilung des Komponisten kam.[61] Der Historiker Oliver Rathkolb wies darauf hin, dass die Schwierigkeiten für etliche Vertreter moderner und ‚avantgardistische[r]' Musik in Österreich nicht erst im Nationalsozialismus, sondern bereits in dem katholisch-konservativen Klima des Austrofaschismus nach 1933 begonnen hatten. Er nennt Granichstaedten in einer Reihe von Komponisten, deren

---

57 *Ibid.*
58 Theo Stengel, 'Verjudete Wiener Musik', *Arbeitersturm*, 16 April 1938, 11.
59 Klaus Hödl, '"Widerstreitende Gedächtnisse" Das Bemühen um ein jüdisch-deutsches Selbstverständnis', in Elke-Vera Kotowski (Hrsg.), *Das Kulturerbe deutschsprachiger Juden* (Berlin: DeGruyter, 2015), 56–69 (59).
60 Vgl. Matthias Kauffmann, 'Operetta during the Nazi Regime', in Anastasia Belina und Derek B. Scott (Hrsg.), *The Cambridge Companion to Operetta* (Cambridge: Cambridge University Press, 2019), 261–71 (263).
61 Siehe 'Bruno Granichstaedten freigesprochen', *Kleine Volks-Zeitung*, 22 Januar 1938, 10.

Lage sich schließlich durch die Zäsur der Nazi-Machtergreifung abermals verschärfte und endgültig zur Auswanderung zwang.[62]

4   Granichstaedtens Fluchtweg über Europa in die USA

Nach dem sogenannten Anschluss im Jahr 1938 flüchtete Bruno Granichstaedten zuerst nach Luxemburg. An seiner Seite hatte er die Sängerin Rosalie Kaufmann (geb. 1910 in Wien, gest. 1979 in Florida), die nach einer ersten geschiedenen Ehe Granichstaedtens, aus der zwei Kinder hervorgegangen waren, zur Lebensgefährtin des Komponisten wurde. Angeblich führte ihr sehr abenteuerlicher Fluchtweg zu Fuß über die Sauer, nachdem Granichstaedten in Trier noch einmal seinen *Orlow* dirigieren konnte. Zuvor war Granichstaedten von den Nazis interniert und in ein Auffanglager an der tschechischen Grenze gebracht worden, nach gelungener Intervention aber wieder freigelassen worden war.[63] Am 3. Oktober 1938 wurden sie jedenfalls bei einer Fremdenpolizeikontrolle in einem Luxemburger Hotel entdeckt.[64] Die mit Granichstaedten befreundeten Sängerin Betty Fischer war dort ebenfalls im Exil. Sie ließ ihre persönlichen Beziehungen spielen, damit das Paar Aufnahme fand.[65] Granichstaedten und Kaufmann hatten zwar bei ihrer Flucht nur das allernotwendigste dabei, doch fanden sie bald Auftrittsmöglichkeiten beim Luxemburger Radio, das in den Worten Granichstaedtens ‚emigrierte[r] Wiener Kunst, die in der Fremde eine Heimat sucht' gegenüber aufgeschlossen war.[66] Das nach der Ankunft gänzlich mittellose Paar war im Luxemburger Exil zunächst auf Unterstützung des jüdischen Hilfskomitees ‚Esra' angewiesen, trotzdem landete der Komponist im Dezember 1939 einen großen Erfolg mit der

---

62   Oliver Rathkolb, 'Exodus von Wissenschaft und Kultur aus Österreich in den Jahren des Faschismus', in École Française de Rome (Hrsg.), *L'émigration politique en Europe aux XIXe et XXe siècles. Actes du colloque de Rome (3–5 mars 1988)* (Rome: École Française de Rome, 1991), 443–61 (457).

63   Stefan Frey, 'Bruno Granichstaedten', in Claudia Maurer Zenck, Peter Petersen (Hrsg.), *Lexikon verfolgter Musiker und Musikerinnen der NS-Zeit*, (Hamburg: Universität Hamburg, 2008), https://www.lexm.uni-hamburg.de/object/lexm_lexmperson_00002831 [letzter Aufruf: 16 August 2021].

64   Guy Wagner, 'Ein Fall unter vielen – Bruno Granichstaedten', abrufbar unter: http://guywagner.netfirms.com/pdf/Granichstaedten.pdf [letzter Aufruf: 16 Aug 2021].

65   Stefan Frey, 'Betty Fischer', in Claudia Maurer Zenck, Peter Petersen, Sophie Fetthauer (Hrsg.), *Lexikon verfolgter Musiker und Musikerinnen der NS-Zeit* (Hamburg: Universität Hamburg, 2017), https://www.lexm.uni-hamburg.de/object/lexm_lexmperson_00004918 [letzter Aufruf: 16 August 2021].

66   Teilnachlass Bruno Granichstaedten, Mappe 3.

im Exil komponierten und uraufgeführten Operette *Sonili*.⁶⁷ Er verfasste *Sonili* für den damaligen Kinderstar Sonja Haagen, die die Hauptrolle übernahm und mit dem titelgebenden Spitznamen gerufen wurde. Mit diesem Werk versuchte der Komponist sich in Luxemburg zu etablieren, einem Land, das zu dieser Zeit durch die Ankunft von Exilanten einen ‚unerwarteten musikalischen Aufschwung erlebte'.⁶⁸ Einem US-amerikanischen Zeitungsbericht zufolge wurde *Sonili* auch in Brüssel gespielt.⁶⁹ Die Operette gilt heute als verschollen, trotz Versuchen des Künstlers und Verwalters des Luxemburgischem Lied-Archivs Jean Kandel, *Sonili*, oder zumindest Teile davon, wiederzuentdecken.⁷⁰ In einem Blogbeitrag von 2010 bittet er um Hinweise nach Spuren zu dem Werk.⁷¹ Auch 2020 wiederholte er den Aufruf.⁷² Ebenso interessierte sich Germaine Goetzinger vom Centre National de littérature in Mersch, die zum Exil in Luxemburg forscht, für den Verbleib der Operette und machte durch ihre Anfrage bei der Wienbibliothek den Archivar Thomas Aigner überhaupt erst auf deren Existenz aufmerksam.⁷³ Aigner wiederum, der den musikalischen Nachlass Granichstaedtens aufgearbeitet hat, weist darauf hin, dass viel auf der Flucht vor den Nazis und in den Kriegswirren verloren gegangen sei. Manches wiederum sei über Granichstaedtens Witwe Rosalie Kaufmann zurück nach Wien gelangt und im Dezember 2003 ‚in völlig ungeordnetem Zustand' vom Auktionshaus Dorotheum versteigert und von der Wienbibliothek angekauft worden.⁷⁴

Luxemburg blieb nur eine Zwischenstation für Granichstaedten und Kaufmann. Rechtzeitig gelang dem Paar die schon seit der Flucht nach Luxemburg geplante Weiterreise in die USA, drei Monate bevor die Nazis im Mai 1940 Luxemburg besetzten.⁷⁵ Das Schiff ‚Westernland' der *Holland-American Line* brachte die beiden im Februar 1940 nach New York.⁷⁶ An Bord dieses Schiffs waren mehrheitlich Flüchtlinge, 406 an der Zahl von insgesamt

---

67   Wagner.
68   Germaine Goetzinger, Gast Mannes, Pierre Marson, *Exilland Luxemburg 1933–1947. Schreiben – Darstellen – Musizieren – Agitieren – Überleben*, Centre National de Littérature 15. Mai–15. Dezember 2007, (Mersch: Centre national de littérature, 2007), 144.
69   Anon., 'Big BMI Exploitation Drive Planned', *Broadcasting*, 1 Juni 1940, 93.
70   Desislava Schengen, 'Wer kennt "Sonili"?', *Tageblatt*, 12 Oktober 2010.
71   Jean Kandel, '"Sonili": Lëtzebuerger Lidder däerfen net verluer goen', 10 November 2010, https://www.rtl.lu/meenung/lieserbreiwer/84997.html [letzter Aufruf: 28 März 2020].
72   Shari Pleimelding, 'Lëtzebuerger Lidder – nach ëmmer op der Sich nom Sonili!', 21 April 2020, https://moien.lu/jean-kandel-sonili/ [letzter Aufruf: 18 Mai 2020].
73   Aigner, 6.
74   *Ibid.*, 22.
75   Goetzinger, Mannes, Marson, 250.
76   'Ocean Travelers', *New York Times*, 3 Februar 1940, S. 17.

517 Passagieren. Aus diesem Grund wurde es für diese Überfahrt in ein Dritte-Klasse-Schiff umgewandelt.⁷⁷ In den USA änderte Granichstaedten seinen Nachnamen in Grant und fand 1940 unter diesem Namen Aufnahme bei der Verwertungsgesellschaft BMI (Broadcast Music, Inc), um für deren Lizenzträger Musik zu komponieren.⁷⁸ ‚A new name which has been added to the BMI list of composers represents a great reputation and is as new to the man who bears it as it is to the BMI', schrieb das branchenspezifische Wochenblatt *NAB Reports* und sang ein Loblied auf das Renommee des Komponisten.⁷⁹ Ein anderer Bericht über BMI zählt ihn zu der ersten Riege europäischer Komponisten der vergangenen dreißig Jahre.⁸⁰ Auch andere Exilanten wie Ralph Benatzky und Hermann Leopoldi wurden im darauffolgenden Jahr von der Gesellschaft beschäftigt.⁸¹ Die Zusammenarbeit mit BMI schien Granichstaedten im Herbst 1941 mit Hoffnung zu erfüllen, gleichzeitig ließ er anklingen, dass er nicht so einfach an frühere Erfolge anknüpfen werde können:

> Die neue Verlagsanstalt B.M.I. wird mir sicher einen Jahresvertrag geben. Es sind zwar erst 4 Nummern erschienen, aber ich höre die schmeichelhaftesten Dinge. Wegen *Musik um Mozart* verhandle ich schon mit der Sam Goldwyn United Artists. Es muss also klappen. Ich muss mir halt alles was ich in Wien schon besessen hatte, wieder erarbeiten.⁸²

Granichstaedtens Optimismus hinsichtlich seiner Möglichkeiten als Filmkomponist beruhte darauf, dass er, wie er schreibt, bereits in Hollywood engagiert gewesen war.⁸³ Laut einem Bericht in *Variety* war der Komponist 1930 für einen Viermonatsvertrag für MGM in die USA geholt worden.⁸⁴ Granichstaedten hatte nach seiner Rückkehr nach Wien Journalisten sehr begeistert über den Aufenthalt in Hollywood erzählt.⁸⁵ Dennoch blieb er im späteren Exil in Verhandlungen mit der Produktionsfirma MGM erfolglos. Das von Granichstaedten erwähnte Stück *Musik um Mozart* hatte er in Wien fertiggestellt, aber es war dort nicht mehr zur Aufführung gelangt, wobei ursprünglich

---

77 '406 Refugees Arrive from Reich on Liner', *New York Times*, 4 Februar 1940, 36.
78 'BMI buys Rights to 2000 Songs', *Motion Picture Herald*, 1 Juni 1940, 49.
79 *NAB Reports*, Vol. 8, No. 21, 24. Mai 1940, 4273.
80 Anon., 'Big BMI Exploitation Drive Planned', *Broadcasting*, 1 Juni 1940, 93.
81 'Refugee Tunesmiths Composing for BMI', *Variety*, 23 Juli 1941.
82 Ernst Kaufmann, *Bruno Granichstaedten. Ein Dokumentarfilm über das Schicksal des Wiener Komponisten. Recherchen und Treatment*, o. S.
83 Teilnachlass Bruno Granichstaedten, Mappe 3.
84 'Recognition in Hollywood', *Variety*, 10 September 1930, 7.
85 'Wien in Hollywood', *Freiheit!*, 9 September 1930, 6.

eine Premiere am Burgtheater vorgesehen war.[86] Eine englische Bearbeitung für die Bühne namens *Music and Love, Mozart* vollendete Granichstaedten 1941.[87] Granichstaedtens Teil-Nachlass in der Wienbibliothek beinhaltet zwar keine Fassung des Mozart-Stücks, aber andere im Exil entstandene Arbeiten. Es gibt einen 24-seitigen Drehbuchentwurf von 1941 mit dem Arbeitstitel *Der Mann, der das Pulver erfand* (*Berthold Schwarz*) und eine sogenannte ‚Filmnovelle' mit dem Titel *Patient No. 345/Second Front*, die 1942 in Washington entstand, und mit der der Autor vermutlich auch Hoffnungen verknüpfte. Es handelt sich um dicht mit Maschinenschrift getippte zweiunddreißig Seiten, gezeichnet Bruno Granichstaedten-Grant. Die Handlung spielt in einem Irrenhaus, enthält einiges an Musik (am Anfang hört man Puccini und am Ende Händel, dazwischen Grieg), und unter den Protagonisten taucht unter anderem ein Nazi-Spion auf.[88] Beide Bücher sind in deutscher Sprache verfasst.

Granichstaedten entwarf außerdem 1943 die Operette *Die Nackte Wahrheit*, deren Handlung im Jahr 1943 in den USA angesiedelt ist. Sie beginnt mit der fünfzigsten Geburtstagsfeier eines Emigranten aus Budapest, einem erfolgreichen Schirmfabrikanten, der mit einer gebürtigen Wienerin verheiratet ist und eine in Amerika geborene Tochter hat.[89] Neben jeder Menge operettentypischer Verwechslungen gibt es Zeitbezüge: Die Schirmfabrik stellt jetzt Fallschirme für die Armee her.[90] Ein weiterer Protagonist der Handlung musste als Gegner Mussolinis Italien verlassen.[91] Der zweite Akt der Handlung spielt teilweise im ‚Café Vienna' in New York, das auf der Bühne dargestellt wird ‚wie es ist, nur in der Dekoration und Beleuchtung stark idealisiert'.[92] Auch in diesem Café traten Bruno und Rosalie Granichstaedten regelmäßig gemeinsam als Duo auf, welches 1944 mit dem Slogan ‚Beliebter denn je ... Vienna Café' warb.[93] 1942 wurden sie als ‚Hors D'oeuvres' einer ‚musikalischen Speisekarte', serviert von Maria Collm, angekündigt.[94] Granichstaedten verfasste im Exil außerdem den

---

86 Wienbibliothek im Rathaus: Ernst Kaufmann, *Bruno Granichstaedten Biografie. Ein Buchprojekt von Ernst Kaufmann* [unpublished Exposé], 1–22 (21).
87 Siehe Library of Congress, *Catalog of Copyright Entries. Part 3 Musical Compositions*, Vol. 36 1941, 1597. Als Datum des Copyright-Eintrags wird dort der 6. September 1941 angegeben, welcher lautet ‚singspiel, buch und gesangsstexte u.m mit freier, teilweiser benützung von Mozart motiven. Klavierauszug'.
88 Teilnachlass Bruno Granichstaedten, Mappe 3.
89 Teilnachlass Bruno Granichstaedten, Mappe 2. *Die nackte Wahrheit*, 1.
90 *Ibid.*
91 Teilnachlass Bruno Granichstaedten, Mappe 2. *Die nackte Wahrheit*, 2.
92 Teilnachlass Bruno Granichstaedten, Mappe 2. *Die nackte Wahrheit*, 15.
93 'Beliebter denn je ... Vienna Café. Veranstaltungsanzeige', *Aufbau*, 19 Mai 1944, 14.
94 'Maria Collm serviert im Café Vienna, 50 West 77th Street, N.Y.C.', *Aufbau*, 13 November 1942, 17.

Text zu einer ‚musikalischen Komödie' namens *Russian Serenade*. Die Mappe mit diesem Werk im Teilnachlass trägt einen Stempel vom April 1944. Der deutsche Titel wird als *Russische Märchen 1944* angegeben. Zu beiden dieser Werke, *Die Nackte Wahrheit* und *Russian Serenade*, dürfte sich keine Musik erhalten haben.

5   Musikalisches Wirken Granichstaedtens in Emigrantenkreisen

Granichstaedtens Hoffnungen, Anschluss im Filmgeschäft zu finden oder ein neues breitenwirksames Stück in den USA für ein größeres Publikum auf die Bühne bringen zu können, blieben unerfüllt. Allerdings konnte er zumindest in Emigrantenkreisen in verschiedenen Cafés und Bars an der Seite anderer prominenter Musikschaffender wirken. Einige Etablissements in New York galten als populäre Versammlungsorte der exilierten Operetten- und Kabarettszene, in denen Unterhaltungsprogramme auf die Beine gestellt wurden. Auch das nun unter dem Namen Grant auftretende Paar trat dort in Erscheinung. Die ‚bildschöne Rosalie Grant' trug zum Beispiel im *Broadway Fiaker* in der 223 West 80. Straße Wiener und ungarische Lieder, sowie ‚alte und neue' Kompositionen Granichstaedtens vor, womit sie bereits mit ihrem ersten Auftritt am 25. Oktober 1940 das Publikum ‚restlos erobert' hatte.[95] Außerdem kam in diesem beliebten Treffpunkt für Emigranten auch eine von Granichstaedten arrangierte ‚Kurzoperette' mit dem Titel *Love in the Fiaker* zur Aufführung, bei der Rosalie eine Rolle an der Seite des ebenfalls ins Exil getriebenen Sängers Igo Guttmann (geb. 1892 in Wien, gest. 1966 in New York) übernahm.[96] Der *Aufbau* beschrieb diese Darbietung als einen ‚musikalischen Genuss'.[97] Gleichfalls 1940 fand der Sing-Sketch *Die musikalische Speisekarte* von Granichstaedten lobende Anerkennung im *Aufbau*.[98]

Im darauffolgenden Jahr dirigierte Granichstadten im Oktober eine von ihm komponierte und geschriebene Operette in einem Vorspiel und drei Akten namens *Wenn die Musik spielt* im Theresa L. Kaufman Auditorium.[99] Die Erstaufführung fand am 25. Oktober 1941 statt, als Regisseur wird Robert Riemer

---

95   'Broadway Fiaker', *Aufbau*, 1 November 1940, 7.
96   John M. Spalek, Sandra M. Hawrylchak, *Deutschsprachige Exilliteratur seit 1933: USA* (Boston: K.G. Saur, 2000), 408.
97   'Broadway Fiaker', *Aufbau*, 22 November 1940, 9.
98   'Broadway Fiaker', *Aufbau*, 6 Dezember 1940, 12.
99   Eugen Semrau, *Robert Stolz: sein Leben, seine Musik* (Salzburg: Residenz, 2002), 72.

verzeichnet.[100] Neben Rosalie Grant traten wiederum Igo Gutmann und eine Reihe weiterer emigrierter Künstlerinnen auf.[101] Eine Anzeige im *Aufbau* kündigt es als ‚die große Granichstaedten-Premiere' und als das ‚musikalische Großereignis von New York' an, bei dem insgesamt zehn Sängerinnen und Sängern auf der Bühne standen, während das Management der Produktion Gustave Kotanyi oblag.[102] Die dieser Ankündigung folgende Kritik im *Aufbau* fiel mäßiger aus. Zu sehr wäre die Produktion ‚in den ausgefahrensten Gleisen einer längst verstorbenen Operettentradition' verhaftet. Das Libretto wurde gescholten, da die Handlung zwar in New Jersey spielte aber mehr zu St.Pölten passen würde, allerdings wurde die Musik als ‚reizend, charmant und einfallsreich' empfunden. Sie zeige ‚das Können eines Altmeisters der Wiener Operette, dessen *Auf Befehl der Kaiserin* und *Orlow* einst den Weltruhm dieser Kunstgattung begründen half.'[103]

Im Mai 1942 stand Bruno Granichstaedten zusammen mit Emmerich Kálmán, Ralph Benatzky, Paul Abraham und anderen am Dirigentenpult, um im Rahmen eines Konzerts, das vom ‚Committee for the Preservation of Austrian Art and Culture' organisiert wurde, ‚Meister der Wiener Musik' zu dirigieren. Auch Kálmán, Benatzky und Abraham versuchten, sich in den USA zu etablieren und Arbeit zu verschaffen, doch auch ihnen gelang kein wirklicher Durchbruch. Im Gegensatz zu den beiden hier vorgestellten Komponisten überlebten sie den Zweiten Weltkrieg und konnten bis auf Abraham, der psychisch erkrankte, weiter musikalisch wirken. Die Forschung hat sich bisher schon weit mehr mit ihnen befasst als mit den beiden hier vorgestellten Komponisten. Zu den drei oben genannten gibt es bereits wissenschaftliche Literatur.[104]

Darbietungen der Granichstaedtens fanden in den USA auch im kleineren Rahmen statt.[105] 1941 verzeichnet die *Austrian-American League* einen Auftritt

100   Frithjof Trapp, Bärbel Schrader u. A. (Hrsg.), *Biographisches Lexikon der Theaterkünstler, Band 2. Handbuch des deutschsprachigen Exiltheaters* (München: K.G. Saur), 543.
101   Regina Thumser, 'Operette im Exil', in Christian Klösch, Regina Thumser, *'From Vienna'. Exilkabarett in New York 1938–1950* (Wien: Picus Verlag, 2002), 116–19 (117).
102   'Wiener Operetten-Uraufführung in New York', *Aufbau*, 24 Oktober 1941, 9.
103   'Wenn die Musik nur gespielt hätte ...', *Aufbau*, 31 Oktober 1941, 10.
104   Klaus Waller, *Paul Abraham: Der tragische König der Operette. Eine Biographie* (Norderstedt: Books on Demand, 2017); Fritz Hennenberg, *Ralph Benatzky: Operette auf dem Weg zum Musical; Lebensbericht und Werkverzeichnis* (Wien: Steinbauer, 2009); Stefan Frey, ‚Unter Tränen lachen'. *Emmerich Kálmán. Eine Operettenbiographie* (Berlin: Henschel Verlag, 2003). Freys Buch ist auch in einer englischen Übersetzung erschienen: *'Laughter Under Tears': Emmerich Kálmán: an Operetta Biography* (Culver City: Operetta Foundation, 2014).
105   Thumser, 117.

des Paares am 27. November bei einem Open House Evening der Junior Division der Gesellschaft, welcher dazu dienen sollte, Jugendgruppen unterschiedlicher Länder zu vernetzen.[106] Laut Kurznotiz zu dieser Veranstaltung begleitete Granichstaedten dabei Gesangsvorträge Rosalie Kaufmanns. Letztere hatte unter ihrem in den USA angenommen Namen Rosalie Grant zusätzlich mehrere Auftritte in verschiedenen Nachtclubs und Hotels, zum Beispiel im Essex House in New York, wo sie Songs und Arien in Französisch, Russisch, Spanisch und Englisch darbot.[107] Im Café Old Europe war sie ebenfalls zu hören und zu sehen.[108] Zudem war sie im Diamond Horseshoe (Hotel Paramount) in einer Revue namens *Post-War Preview* (*The Musical Shape of Things To come*) engagiert.[109]

Während Granichstaedten in Luxemburg noch einen großen Erfolg mit einer neuen Operette verzeichnete, die heute allerdings als verschollen gilt, konnte er in den USA nur noch in Emigrantenkreisen auftreten und musste in seinem letzten Lebensjahr in den USA als Barpianist ein Auskommen finden. Zeitungsmeldungen von 1944 deuten allerdings darauf hin, dass durchaus noch Neues von ihm zur Aufführung vorgesehen war, wenn er nicht plötzlich mit vierundsechzig Jahren in New York einer Herzkrankheit erlegen wäre. Ihnen ist zu entnehmen, dass gleich zwei von Granichstaedten verfasste und komponierte Operetten in diesem Jahr in den USA für eine Aufführung geplant waren. So wurde das bereits erwähnte Mozart-Stück unter dem Titel *The Life of Mozart* als ‚mid-season production' der bekannten Theaterimpresarios Shuberts angekündigt.[110] Daneben wurde ein weiteres Werk von Granichstaedten namens *The Singing Caesar* im März 1944 als sein Broadwaydebüt annonciert.[111] Dieses Stück bezeichnet Rudolf Ulrich in seinem Buch über Österreicher in Hollywood in einem Eintrag zu Granichstaedten als Satire auf Mussolini.[112] Auch die *New York Times* kündigte das Stück mit diesen Worten an.[113] Laut dem in der New Yorker Exilzeitung *Aufbau* erschienenen Nachruf zu Granichstaedten von Juni 1944 handelt es sich um eine Neuadaptierung seiner Operette *Die Bacchusnacht* von 1923, die

---

106 Anon., 'Mitteilungen der Austrian-American League', *Austria* (New York), 1 Jahrgang, Heft Nr. 7, Dezember 1941, 5.
107 'General: Possibilities', *The Billboard*, 11 April 1942, 4.
108 *Aufbau*, 3 Oktober 1941, 10.
109 'Diamond Horseshoe', *Variety*, 2 Juni 1943, 46.
110 'The Musical Parade', *The Music Magazine/Musical Courier*, Vol. 130, 1944, 22; 'The Final Curtain', *The Billboard*, 10 Juni 1944, 32.
111 Phineas J. Biron, 'Strictly Confidential', *The Sentinel. The American Jewish Weekly Chicago*, 2 März 1944.
112 Ulrich, 165.
113 Sam Zolotow, 'Revised "Sheppey" Due in the Spring', *New York Times*, 14 Januar 1944, 15.

er ‚mit neuer Musik ausgestattet' hatte.[114] In dieser Operette, in der im Finale sexuelle Libertinage gefeiert wird, tritt Kaiser Nero als Charakter auf, der als Anspielung auf den italienischen Diktator gesehen werden kann.[115] Beide dieser geplanten und bereits angekündigten Werke scheinen aufgrund des Todes des Komponisten im Mai 1944 nie zur Aufführung gekommen zu sein, denn es ließen sich keine Belege finden.

Rosalie Grant absolvierte nach dem Tod Granichstaedtens weitere Auftritte, zum Beispiel im *Vienna Café* in der 77. Straße.[116] ‚Unwahrscheinlich schön, unwahrscheinlich charmant' und als ‚sichtlich die wandelnde Erfüllung dessen [...], was sich jeder amerikanische Revue-Direktor in seinen kühnsten Träumen unter einer Wiener Sängerin vorstellt', beschreibt *Der Aufbau* Grants dortiges Auftreten. Sie betrieb später selbst ein Lokal in der Tradition bereits hier genannter Emigranten-Treffs. Es hieß *Rosalie's Gloriette*, war ‚charmingly decorated' und servierte wienerisches Essen, nebenbei trug die Inhaberin dort auch Lieder vor.[117]

Im 13. Wiener Gemeindebezirk ist eine Gasse nach Bruno Granichstaedten benannt und im Bezirksmuseum Landstraße (1030 Wien) ist ihm ein Gedenkraum gewidmet, der Exponate des Komponisten ausstellt. Außerdem veröffentlichte der Autor und Regisseur Ernst Kaufmann, ein Neffe Rosalie Kaufmanns, 2014 eine Granichstaedten-Biografie in Romanform.[118] In der Wienbibliothek, die auch einen Teil-Nachlass des Komponisten in der Handschriften- sowie der Musiksammlung besitzt, befindet sich ein Treatment (Vorstufe zum Drehbuch) von Kaufmann für einen von ihm geplanten Dokumentarfilm über Granichstaedten. Granichstaedtens Name ist heute einem breiteren Publikum weitgehend unbekannt, trotz der Popularität seiner Werke vor dem Zweiten Weltkrieg wie etwa *Bub oder Mädel* (1908), *Auf Befehl der Kaiserin* (1915), und *Der Orlow* (1925), und trotz der oben angeführten Bemühungen, an ihn in Österreich zu erinnern.

6 Katschers Schaffen im Exil

Robert Katscher und seine Ehefrau Agnes, eine gebürtige Budapesterin, lebten ab dem Sommer 1938 in den Vereinigten Staaten. Die Einreise erfolgte unter

---

114 'Wie wir hören. Bruno Granichstaedten', *Aufbau*, 2 Juni 1944, 5.
115 Albert Gier, *Wär' es auch nichts als ein Augenblick: Poetik und Dramaturgie der komischen Operette* (Bamberg: University of Bamberg Press, 2014), 352.
116 *Austro American Tribune*, Februar 1945, 6.
117 *Cue: The Weekly Magazine of New York Life*, 1956, 39; 55; 103.
118 Ernst Kaufmann, *Wiener Herz am Sternenbanner: Bruno Granichstaedten* (Lich: Edition AV, 2014).

einer Österreich-Quote, wie die *New York Times* nach ihrer Ankunft schrieb. Dem Beitrag zufolge hatte das Paar nach seiner Ankunft in Paris rasch die Zusage erhalten, in die USA immigrieren zu dürfen, wo sie um die US-amerikanische Staatsbürgerschaft ansuchen wollten.[119] Dasselbe plante auch der Komponist Heinz Reichert, der ebenfalls mit seiner Frau auf demselben Schiff wie die Katschers eingereist war.[120] Auch dem *Hollywood Reporter* war es im Herbst 1938 eine Meldung wert, dass Katscher die US-Staatsbürgerschaft beantragte.[121] Gemäß einem von Katscher ausgefüllten Zensus-Formular von 1940 betrug Katschers Arbeitsausmaß im Jahr 1939 zweiundfünfzig Wochen. Er gab also an, über das ganze Jahr beschäftigt gewesen zu sein, und dass er fünfzig Stunden pro Woche arbeitete. Zu diesem Zeitpunkt war das Paar in New York gemeldet. Was seine kompositorische Tätigkeit anbelangt, so findet sich sein Name am Programm des im Februar 1939 in Maryland aufgeführten und vom Emigranten Kurt Robitschek (geb. 1890 in Prag, gest. 1950 in New York) inszenierten ‚Vaudeville' – Stücks *Laughter over Broadway*, und zwar als Mitverfasser gemeinsam mit Abe Burrows und Frank Galen des Eröffnungssongs ‚Vaudeville Marches On'.[122]

Als Anerkennung von Katschers Schaffen in den USA zählt sicherlich, dass er als erster Flüchtling aus Österreich und Deutschland in die American Society of Composers, Authors and Publishers (ASCAP) aufgenommen wurde, nachdem er aus der österreichischen Gesellschaft der Autoren, Komponisten, Musikverleger (AKM) ausgetreten war.[123] Wie andere geflüchtete Komponisten kämpfte Katscher um die Tantiemen seiner Kompositionen aus Österreich. Er war sogar der erste, der einen Anwalt einschaltete, und *Variety* erwartete, dass andere geflüchtete Musikschaffende seinem Beispiel folgen würden.[124] Er erzielte als erster Erfolge in dieser Hinsicht, indem sein Anwalt ihm half, auf einem von AKM auf einem New Yorker Bankkonto deponierten Betrag von 1.700 Dollar zuzugreifen.[125] Für andere Komponisten wiederum stellte sich diese Frage gar nicht: ‚no play, no pay', vermerkte *Variety* betreffend Komponisten wie Emmerich Kálmán (1882–1953), Oscar Straus (1870–1954), Edmund Eysler (1874–1949) und Granchichstaedten in einem Bericht vom Mai 1938, der außerdem darauf hinwies, dass ‚nicht-arische' Künstlerinnen

---

119 'Viennese Musicians here', *New York Times*, 26 Juni 1938, 37.
120 *Ibid.*
121 'Rambling Reporter', *The Hollywood Reporter*, 28 September 1938, 2.
122 'Unit Review. Laughter over Broadway', *Variety*, 1 März 1939, 42.
123 'Robt. Katscher 1st Refugee to make ASCAP', *Variety*, 15 März 1939, 39.
124 'Shut out of Performance Fees by Nazis, Refugee Attaches German Funds in United States', *Variety*, 4 Januar 1939.
125 *Ibid.*

und Künstler nicht das Recht besaßen, vor einem Ablauf von zehn Jahren ihre Mitgliedschaft in der AKM zu kündigen, obwohl ihre Werke wohl kaum gespielt werden würden.[126] Die AKM wurde schließlich noch im selben Jahr in die deutsche Gesellschaft STAGMA eingegliedert, der Großteil österreichischer ‚nicht-arischer' Musikschaffenden wurden in Folge dieses Transfers nicht übernommen, andere konnten nun doch austreten.[127]

Ein Werk, das in den USA in den späten 1930ern unter Beteiligung Katschers in den USA auf die Bühne kam, war eine Adaptation von *Bei Kerzenlicht*. Die Zeitung *Der Wiener Tag* hatte bereits 1937 vermeldet, dass der amerikanischen Produzent J.J. Shubert Katschers *Bei Kerzenlicht* erworben hatte.[128] Diese Produktion kam unter dem Titel *You Never Know* in einer Bearbeitung des bekannten US-amerikanischen Komponisten Cole Porter (1893–1964) in New York auf die Bühne. Die *New York Times* berichtete am 18. September 1938 über die bevorstehende Premiere dieser Zusammenarbeit.[129] Auch *Variety* beleuchtete im selben Monat das anstehende Projekt der beiden, bei dem Porter zusätzlich die Produzentenrolle übernahm, weshalb das Stück als Cole Porter's *You never Know* annonciert werden sollte.[130] Katscher verlangte laut diesem Artikel jedoch einen Hinweis auf seine eigene Autorenschaft. Auch wurden zu diesem Zeitpunkt noch fünf neue Songs von Porter angekündigt, während fünf Originalsongs vom österreichischen Komponisten behalten werden sollten. Die englischsprachige Übersetzung des deutschen Librettos hatte Roland Leigh vorgenommen. Für die Bearbeitung und Adaptierung für das US-Publikum wurde zusätzlich George Abbot herangezogen.[131]

Obwohl *You Never Know* Katschers *Bei Kerzenlicht* als Vorbild diente und darauf basierte, wird Katschers Anteil an *You Never Know* in der Rezeption als ‚peripher' bezeichnet.[132] Dennoch wird in zeitgenössischen Ankündigungen und Kritiken Katscher als Komponist gleichwertig neben Cole Porter erwähnt,

---

126 'Non-"Aryans" Must Give 10 Years' Notice to Quit Austrian Perf. Society', *Variety*, 11 Mai 1938, 38.
127 Siehe Hartmut Krones, 'Das Ende der "alten" A.K.M. (März 1938), die Gründung der "neuen" AKM (Juni 1945) und die Folgen', https://www.akm.at/wp-content/uploads/2016/02/Kurzfassung-Studie-von-H.-Krones-ueber-AKM-und-NS-Zeit.pdf [letzter Aufruf: 10 Januar 2021].
128 'Wiener Musiklustspiele für Amerika', *Der Wiener Tag*, 14 Mai 1937, 11.
129 'This Weeks Openings', *New York Times*, 18 September 1938, 157.
130 'Inside Stuff-Legit', *Variety*, 7 September 1938.
131 *Ibid.*
132 Cliff Eisen und Dominic McHugh (Hrsg.), *The Letters of Cole Porter* (New Haven: Yale University Press, 2019), 323.

Katschers Anliegen also berücksichtigt.¹³³ Der Erfolg scheint jedoch mäßig gewesen zu sein. Der Rezensent im *Wall Street Journal* etwa empfand die Liedtexte interessanter als die Musik der beiden Komponisten, und die Aufführung und das Stück insgesamt als okay.¹³⁴ Auch die Bühnenzeitschrift *The Stage* urteilte, dass Porter und Katscher es verabsäumt hätten, ‚catchy tunes' einzuflechten.¹³⁵ Über den letztlichen Misserfolg des Werks, schrieb der Musikwissenschaftler Cliff Eisen, dass dieser darauf zurückzuführen sein könnte, weil die intime Atmosphäre des Originals nicht beibehalten wurde.¹³⁶ Nach den ersten Aufführungen waren außerdem nicht viele von Katschers Original-Songs übriggeblieben. Er wurde aber weiterhin als Co-Komponist in Anzeigen und Rezensionen genannt und das Werk brachte es zu Katschers Lebzeiten auf insgesamt achtundsiebzig Aufführungen.

Im Herbst 1942 kam es dann in New York zu einer Wiederaufführung (in deutscher Sprache und von Karl Farkas inszeniert) von *Die Wunderbar*. Der *Aufbau* bezeichnete ‚dieses Stück [als] wohl eines der interessantesten und originellsten – teils Operette, teils Kabarett und teils Show'.¹³⁷ Der *Aufbau* berichtete, dass selbst in Deutschland *Die Wunderbar* unter den Nationalsozialisten zur Aufführung gelangte, wenn auch andere Autoren angegeben waren. In einer Notiz von Juni 1941 heißt es dazu, dass die Nazis trotz achtjähriger Herrschaft immer noch keine eigenen Operetten imstande zu schaffen wären und daher auf Werke zurückgriffen ‚von denen jedes Kind weiß, dass ihre Autoren Juden sind'.¹³⁸

Laut Nachrufen zu Robert Katscher in US-amerikanischen Zeitungen verstarb der Komponist im Februar 1942 im Cedars of Lebanon Krankenhaus an Spätfolgen einer (nicht belegten) KZ-Internierung.¹³⁹ Er war erst achtundvierzig Jahre alt. Hans Kafka eröffnete in seiner Hollywood-Kolumne im *Aufbau* den Nachruf zu Katscher mit folgenden Worten:

---

133 Nelson B. Bell, 'Musical Farce at National Is a Lively Item', *The Washington Post*, 22 März 1938, X6; 'News of the Stage', *New York Times*, 21 September 1938, 31; 'You Never Know', *Boxoffice*, 1 Oktober 1938, 35.
134 C.H.S., 'The Theatre: The First 1938 Musical', *Wall Street Journal*, 23 September 1938, 9.
135 J. Fletcher Smith, 'New York Stage', *The Stage*, 10 November 1938, 13.
136 Cliff Eisen, 'You Never Know. Anatomy of a Flop', in Don M. Randel, Matthew Shaftel and Susan Forscher Weiss (Hrsg.), *A Cole Porter Companion* (Urbana, Il.: University of Illinois Press, 2016), 242–60.
137 '*Die Wunderbar* wird aufgeführt', *Aufbau*, 30 Oktober 1942, 13.
138 'Wie wir hören', *Aufbau*, 13 Juni 1941, 12.
139 'Robert Katscher', *New York Times*, 25 Februar 1942, 20; 'The Final Curtain', *The Billboard*, 7 März 1942, 27.

> You may never notice the presence of a next-door neighbor (if he is a good one); but one day you are struck by his absence, even if it is such sudden and pathetic as Robert Katscher's. He died last week, while working on his musical score to *Tales of Manhattan*.[140]

Auch Kafka führt das Ableben des Komponisten auf ein Leberleiden zurück, welches dieser sich in Folge eines ‚Zusammentreffens' mit den Nazis in Wien zugezogen hatte. Über seine Position in Hollywood heißt es wiederum, dass die Filmproduzenten seine Anwesenheit und Fähigkeiten nicht genügend geschätzt haben, und Katscher, ein eher zurückhaltender Mensch, sich leider selbst nicht ausreichend und mit genügend Ausdauer in Hollywood verkauft habe. Erst bei seinem Begräbnis schienen sich die Hollywood-Leute auf ihn zu besinnen. So etwa erschien dort ein einflussreicher Vertreter von Paramount, nämlich der Executive Head des Studios, bei dem sich, so Kafka, Katscher jahrelang vergeblich um einen Auftrag bemüht hatte.[141] Auch der *Hollywood Reporter* gab den Tod des Komponisten bekannt, dieser sei ‚nach längerer Krankheit' verstorben und ASCAP arrangiere das Begräbnis.[142] Der Musiker Paul Whiteman, der ‚When Day is Done' zu seinen Lieblingssongs zählte, spielte das Lied bei der am 25. Februar 1942 stattfindenden Trauerfeier an der Orgel.[143]

7 Schlussfolgerung

Beide der hier vorgestellten Komponisten komponierten genreübergreifend zwischen Operette, musikalischem Unterhaltungstheater und Musical. Bei Katscher treten diese Überschneidungen vielleicht noch deutlicher hervor, aber auch Granichstaedtens *Orlow* ‚kündigte [...] eine durchaus zukunftsversprechende Symbiose der Operette mit dem damals noch blutjungen Musical an'.[144] Katscher und Granichstaedten waren außerdem dem Film gegenüber aufgeschlossen. Sie waren zudem nicht ausschließlich Komponisten, sondern ebenso Textautoren. Ihre jeweils prompten Aufnahmen in die konkurrierenden US-amerikanischen Unternehmen ASCAP (Katscher) und BMI (Granichstaedten) zeugen davon, dass ihre Erfolge nicht nur in Europa,

---

140   'Hollywood Calling – Hans Kafka Speaking. Obituary', *Aufbau*, 6 März 1942, 18.
141   *Ibid.*
142   'Robert Katscher Funeral Services', *Hollywood Reporter*, 25 February 1942, 4.
143   'Musical Figure Taken by Death. Robert Katscher, Who Wrote "When Day is Done", Passes at 45', *Los Angeles Times*, 25 Februar 1942, A10.
144   Josef Stolz, 'Bruno Granichstaedten – "Da nehm ich meine kleine Zigarette"', *Illustrierte Neue Welt*, Nr. 3, März 1994, o.S.

sondern auch in den USA Anerkennung fanden und beide dort nach ihrer geglückten Flucht als ‚große Namen' angesehen wurden. Die im Exil vorherrschenden wirtschaftlichen, sozialen und kulturellen Verhältnisse und die Tatsache, dass auch weitere prestigeträchtige Kollegen in den USA Zuflucht gefunden hatten, machten es ihnen jedoch schwer, sich durchzusetzen und an frühere Erfolge anzuknüpfen.[145] Die Flucht vor dem NS-Regime ins US-amerikanische Exil stellte für beide in Wien geborenen Komponisten einen immensen Einschnitt in ihrem überwiegend erfolgreichen Schaffen dar. Ihr künstlerisches Wirken erfuhr durch die veränderten Lebens- und Arbeitsbedingungen im Exil eine starke Wendung, wenngleich beide versuchten sich anzupassen und, solange es die Gesundheit erlaubte, produktiv blieben. Pläne, die diese beiden Komponisten noch hegen mochten, wurden in Folge von Krankheiten mit Todesfolge jedoch zunichte gemacht. Sie hätten womöglich noch Potential gehabt das Musikleben in New York beziehungsweise in Hollywood zu bereichern, vorausgesetzt sie hätten es mit ihren Werken geschafft sich amerikanischen Vorlieben anzupassen.

---

145 Zum Musikexil in den USA siehe etwa Werner Grünzweig, 'Bargain and Charity. Aspekte der Aufnahme exilierter Musiker an der Ostküste der Vereinigten Staaten', 297–310; und Albrecht Dümling, 'Zwischen Außenseiterstatus und Integration. Musiker-Exil an der amerikanischen Westküste', 311–37. Beide erschienen in: Hans Werner Heister, Claudia Maurer Zenck, Peter Petersen (Hrsg.), *Musik im Exil. Folgen des Nazismus für die internationale Musikkultur* (Frankfurt am Main: Fischer Taschenbuch Verlag, 1993).

11
Encounters with the Émigré Experience: Discovering the Chamber Music and Songs of Peter Gellhorn

Norbert Meyn

Abstract

This chapter retraces the author's journey of discovery during the Arts and Humanities Research Council (AHRC)-funded research project 'Exile Estates and Music Restitution – The Legacy of Conductor/Composer Peter Gellhorn' at the Royal College of Music in 2016. Born in Breslau, Peter Gellhorn (1912–2004) studied at the Staatliche Hochschule für Musik in Berlin (1929–34). His father was Jewish, and in 1935 he emigrated to the UK. From 1935 to 1939 he worked at Toynbee Hall, an arts centre dedicated to social reform in East London. Following his internment on the Isle of Man in 1940/41 he worked for the Vic-Wells opera company in London. After the war, he embarked on a successful career as a conductor and chorus master, with tenures at the Royal Opera House, Glyndebourne Opera and the BBC. Around the time of his emigration, at Toynbee Hall, during internment and occasionally after the Second World War, Gellhorn wrote a substantial amount of chamber music, piano music and songs, the manuscripts of which are now in the British Library. In 2016, a team of musicians and researchers at the Royal College of Music (RCM) prepared editions from these manuscripts and performed many of the pieces in workshops, concerts and recordings. This article explores these musical works in the context of Gellhorn's story as a resourceful and influential musician in Britain.

In this article I would like to give an overview of the compositions of Peter Gellhorn, most of which were edited for publication and performed during the AHRC-funded research project 'Exile Estates and Music Restitution – The Legacy of Conductor/Composer Peter Gellhorn' at the Royal College of Music in 2016. Gellhorn's main contribution to musical life in Britain was as a conductor and repertoire coach at the Royal Opera House, Glyndebourne, the BBC and other institutions. He was also an excellent pianist and accompanist. His output as a composer, while certainly not lacking in quality or originality, cannot rival that of colleagues with larger, better-known oeuvres. His compositions are significant today because they give an insight into his personal and artistic journey as a highly gifted musician who was forced to emigrate and, despite the many difficulties that this entailed, made a significant contribution to the cultural life of his adopted country. These works reflect his musical training in Berlin, his migration to Britain after being excluded from musical life because of his Jewish family background,[1] his work at Toynbee Hall – a visionary educational institution in London's East End –, his internment as an 'enemy alien' on the Isle of Man and, to some extent, his subsequent career as a conductor and coach at the centre of British opera and choral music.[2]

In a filmed interview in preparation for a concert featuring some of his music at London's Wigmore Hall in 2002, entitled 'Continental Britons', Peter Gellhorn, then aged eighty-nine, related the following story:

> A fairy once bestowed three virtues on the German people: Being honest, being intelligent and being a Nazi. However, there was a catch. One could only ever possess two of those at a time. If one was honest and a Nazi, one could not be intelligent. If one was intelligent and a Nazi, one could not be honest. And if one was honest and intelligent, one could not possibly be a Nazi.

This witty tale showed his characteristic response to the Nazi ideology that had impacted his life so much – humour, defiance and a passion for overcoming human idiocy through the arts and education.[3] In the same interview, Gellhorn described the atmosphere of fear and denunciation he experienced as a young musician in Berlin after the Nazis came to power. Fortunately for him, in 1935 he received an invitation for a 'holiday' in England from two friends of Lotte Reiniger, a pioneering animation film maker for whom he had written a number of scores. This facilitated his escape to Britain, where he would spend the rest of his life.

The Wigmore Hall concert, organised by the Forum for Suppressed Music at the Jewish Music Institute in association with the exhibition 'Continental

---

1 Gellhorn was listed among Jewish musicians excluded from the Reichsmusikkammer, the musician's guild under the Nazis, on 14 September 1938. Source: Bundesarchiv Sign.: R 55/21302, see https://www.lexm.uni-hamburg.de/object/lexm_lexmperson_00003455# [accessed: 04.02.2021].
2 See Terence Curran and Norbert Meyn, 'Peter Gellhorn (1912–2004): Biography', RCM Editions, 2017, available as a free PDF download from RCM Research Online, https://researchonline.rcm.ac.uk/id/eprint/2091/ [accessed: 29.07.2022].
3 Peter Gellhorn, Video 1, Interview with Geraldine Auerbach and Martin Anderson on 9 January 2002, time code 0.21.00 (video available on request from the author through the RCM Library).

Britons' at the Jewish Museum London, featured Gellhorn's 1935 *Intermezzo for Violin and Piano*, alongside works by fellow émigré composers Hans Gál, Berthold Goldschmidt, Karl Rankl, Franz Reizenstein, Mátyás Seiber, Leopold Spinner, Vilém Tauský and Egon Wellesz. While most of these composers had published significant oeuvres and found public recognition, Gellhorn's legacy as a composer was hardly known at all and, barring a single song ('I want to sing a Song', Boosey & Hawkes, 1949), none of his works had ever been published. The inclusion of Gellhorn's work in this concert, and in the subsequent recording 'The Émigré Composers' on Nimbus Records, highlighted for the first time Gellhorn's contribution as a composer.[4]

I met Peter Gellhorn in 1999, a year after completing my postgraduate singing-degree at the Guildhall School of Music & Drama. I auditioned for the opera- and concert agent Helen Sykes and had been asked to present myself at the private residence of one Peter Gellhorn in East Sheen in London, where I would be thoroughly vetted. Gellhorn, already in his late eighties, was extremely welcoming and animated. He seemed to know the accompaniments to all my arias from memory, and his musical ear was infallible. His advice regarding repertoire and vocal matters served me well, even years later.

The interview with Martin Anderson and Betty Sagon Collick was filmed in the same house, full of musical memorabilia, which I had visited less than two years before. It was through this interview that I found out about Peter's compositions. One by one he went through the scores and told the stories of the works he had written in Berlin, during his first years in London, as an internee on the Isle of Man and after the war. Astonishingly, at the age of eighty-nine, he was able to play long excerpts from these works from memory, more than half a century after he had written them. When Martin suggested that they should be performed, he responded with a question: 'What's the next step?'

After his death in 2004, his family deposited his manuscripts in the British Library. In early 2016, I applied for a grant from the Arts and Humanities Research Council (AHRC) that would enable me to explore Gellhorn's legacy through this mostly unknown body of unpublished compositions that had not been performed in the UK or elsewhere for many years. Many of my colleagues at the Royal College of Music had worked with Gellhorn at one time or another and praised his extraordinary musicianship, but not one of them knew that he had also been a composer. I was fascinated by Gellhorn's life story and curious what his music might sound like, and I was spurred on by the discovery of pieces written shortly before and after his emigration as well as during his

---

4 CD, *The Émigré Composers*, Nimbus Records, NI 5730/1, 2004.

internment as an 'enemy alien' on the Isle of Man, a little known but important episode in British history during the Second World War.

With the AHRC grant we were able to engage Terence Curran as Cultural Engagement Fellow as well as Bruno Bower and a group of RCM student assistants as editors, and we set out to undertake archival research, oral history interviews with Gellhorn's children and colleagues, as well as performance editions of many of these works. This resulted in a substantial biographical essay about Gellhorn, which is now freely available alongside the edition. Importantly, we were also able to engage advanced RCM students and some professional musicians to play many of the pieces in workshops and concerts, and we recorded most of them in the RCM studios. The Gellhorn Edition (RCM Editions) can be downloaded from the 'RCM research online' depository, and the recordings are available on YouTube and through a dedicated website.[5]

Peter Gellhorn was born in Breslau in 1912. By the time he was eleven, his father, a Jewish architect and former officer in the German army, had left the family and, in 1923, Gellhorn moved to Berlin with his mother and younger sister. His talent was spotted and supported early on, and he was able to earn money for himself and his family by coaching singers while he was still a teenager. Gellhorn entered the 'Staatliche Akademische Hochschule für Musik' at the age of sixteen while he was still a pupil at the Schiller Realgymnasium.[6] He studied conducting, piano and composition, and for his final concert he was invited to conduct the Berlin Philharmonic Orchestra.[7] His conducting-teacher was Julius Prüwer, Furtwängler's assistant in Berlin. Gellhorn's son Sangeet recalls a story that Prüwer made his father read the stock exchange reports aloud while playing Beethoven's Piano Sonata Op 110, and then transpose it up a semitone,[8] something he is reported to have managed admirably. We know he studied composition with Leo Schrattenholz (1872–1955),[9] and he attended lectures by Paul Hindemith too.[10] Hindemith is perhaps the main influence in his early compositions, which are among his most ambitious. It is

---

5   'Peter Gellhorn: The Musical Legacy', www.petergellhorn.com [accessed: 27.04.2020].
6   Marian Malet and Anthony Grenville (eds.), *Changing Countries* (London: Libris, 2002), 10f.
7   YouTube, 'Interview with Mary Gellhorn about her father, the conductor and composer Peter Gellhorn (1912–2004)', RCM, 14 April 2016, time code 0.48.30, https://www.youtube.com/watch?v=3ClH_T5q7kM [accessed: 05.09.2021].
8   YouTube, 'Interview with Sangeet Gellhorn about his life and his father Peter Gellhorn (1912–2004)', RCM, 21 April 2016, time code 0.32.00, https://www.youtube.com/watch?v=474THKtTAJU [accessed: 27.04.2020].
9   Peter Gellhorn, *Video 1*, time code 0.14.00.
10 YouTube, 'Interview with Sangeet Gellhorn', time code 0.07.00.

likely that some of Gellhorn's scores from the time were lost, but at least some have survived.

Written in the year when Gellhorn was awarded the Gold Medal of the Preussische Akademie der Künste, Berlin, for his outstanding achievements as a student,[11] the *Kleine Suite for oboe and piano* (1932) has a stark and Modernist feel, meandering through the fringes of tonality within accessible rhythms and melodic shapes, comparable in style to neoclassical works by Hindemith and Stravinsky. The faster movements, especially the Präludium (prelude), offer a firework of harmonic surprises in an energetic flow of unpredictable melodic turns and dense piano chords, while the slower movements give space for lyricism and poetic reflection.[12] Sadly, we have no information about any performances of the piece or for whom it may have been written. However, our recording with Rebecca Watt, oboe, and Lucy Colquhoun, piano, clearly shows that the fourteen-minute suite in five movements offers great contrast and character and is a perfect vehicle for an experienced oboist. The characteristic use of quick harmonic progressions with frequent unpredictable turns can also be found to various degrees in Gellhorn's two string quartets.

FIGURE 11.1 Gellhorn's Gold Medal from the Prussian Academy of the Arts for outstanding achievements as a student
PHOTO COURTESY OF CATHERINE CHEUNG

11 Curran and Meyn, 3.
12 The movements of the *Kleine Suite for oboe and piano* are: Präludium (Allegretto vivace), Lied (Andante non troppo, lento), Harlequin (Allegretto non troppo, Capitano (Allegretto alla marcia) and Finale (Allegretto vivace).

While still a student at the Akademie, Gellhorn was commissioned by Lotte Reiniger (1899–1981), a pioneer of silhouette animation films, to write a number of short film scores, namely *Carmen* (1933), *Puss in Boots* and *The Stolen Heart* (1934), and *The Little Chimney Sweep* (1935).[13] Reiniger had grown up in Berlin before the First World War and developed a technique of painstakingly cutting out her figures and scenery from card and animating it by hand. In 1926 she had produced one of the world's first feature length animation films, *Prince Achmet*. Reiniger and her husband Carl Koch left Germany in the mid-1930s and settled in London after the war.[14] Gellhorn and Reiniger stayed in touch and collaborated again in 1956 with *The Star of Bethlehem*.

The *String Quartet No.1*[15] has a harmonic language similar to the *Kleine Suite*, but feels much more unsettled and troubled. Written in 1933/34, just after Hitler came to power, the piece conveys a sense of agony, protest, defiance and pride. The first movement starts with long passages of interweaving melodic lines without any recognisable tonal relationship. The second movement is a slow theme with variations, culminating in a sarcastic dance. A frantically searching Scherzo is followed by a haunting duet of the first and second violins with a solemn pizzicato accompaniment in the fourth movement. The fifth movement alternates between resolute and desperately yearning passages, punctuated by a recurring motif of four consecutive chords. The piece has many special moments, but it is the almost hypnotic fourth movement that stands out. Overall, the piece, recorded for our project by the Alke Quartet, seems designed to shake up the listener and could certainly not be classified as easy listening. Soh-Yon Kim, the first violinist of the quartet, recalled that Gellhorn's music sounded 'so different from anything we had worked on before, because of the movement of Gellhorn's melodies, his harmonic language and the length of phrases. There were many things that were unpredictable, things you would not normally expect.'[16] Sometimes a similarity with Hindemith, Bartók or Shostakovich was pointed out, but without clear

---

13   Curran and Meyn, 'Peter Gellhorn', 15.

14   Pamela Hutchinson, 'Lotte Reiniger: animated film pioneer and standard-bearer for women', *The Guardian*, 2 June 2016, https://www.theguardian.com/film/2016/jun/02/lotte-reiniger-the-pioneer-of-silhouette-animation-google-doodle [accessed online: 22 November 2021].

15   The movements of the String Quartet Nr. 1 are: I: Allegro Moderato, II: Thema mit Variationen, Andante, III: Scherzo, Allegro vivace, IV: Intermezzo, Andante Lento, V: Rondo, Allegro.

16   Soh-Yon Kim speaking in YouTube video: YouTube, 'Peter Gellhorn – The Musical Legacy', RCM, 22 November 2016, time code 0.11.35, https://www.youtube.com/watch?v=MjyzieuGqoI [accessed: 27.04.2020].

evidence it is hard to pinpoint specific influences. Soh-Yon also remarked that 'listening to one work is not enough, you have to listen to several of his pieces, and then you start to get his style, his sense of humour and his sense of irony. He put so much of his personality into his music, you get used to the kind of man he probably was.'[17]

The much lighter *String Quartet No.2* was not professionally recorded but performed in one of our project's workshops. It is dated November 1935, two months after Gellhorn's escape from Germany, where a professional future had become impossible for him. The twenty-two-year-old managed to flee with the help of Lotte Reiniger and some of her British friends. He crossed the border to France on a train, pretending to go on holiday. At the beginning of his time in Britain he stayed with a friend of Reiniger in Ascot. The mood of the *String Quartet No. 2* is a lot less troubled than the first, and the displays of virtuosic energy and mind-bending harmonic shifts seem lighter and more playful. A weight seems to have fallen from the composer's shoulders between those two pieces. The Andante lento in the first movement displays melancholic and surging melodic lines, alternating with more dynamic passages with frequently morphing harmonies. The second movement, marked Andante, creates a sense of melancholy as the drawn-out melodic lines seem to meander. The Scherzo, with elements of folk dancing and bass drones, is another example of Gellhorn's ability to combine traditional pastoral elements and rhythmic frameworks with unexpected harmonic progressions and turns, and the final fourth movement launches into a virtuosic and playful final Allegro molto with a witty and celebratory feel.[18] The quartet is an attractive work that somehow reflects the more positive outlook Gellhorn felt in Britain, and it certainly deserves further exploration. Sadly, there is no evidence of any performances of either string quartet during Gellhorn's lifetime. It is possible that the manuscripts stayed behind in Germany with his mother (who was not Jewish) and only found their way back into his possession after the war. This may also be the case with the cantata *Baida der Kosak* (1935) for soloists, choir and chamber orchestra. It is clear from the 2002 video interview that Gellhorn was particularly fond of this substantial piece, which sadly has never been performed to date.

---

17   *Ibid.*, time code 0.11.55.
18   A workshop recording of the String Quartet Nr. 2 can be made available to researchers on request through the Royal College of Music Library.

FIGURE 11.2
Portrait of the young Peter Gellhorn
(year unknown)
COURTESY OF THE GELLHORN
FAMILY ARCHIVE

1 Toynbee Hall, 1935–39

Toynbee Hall, founded in 1884 in London's East End by the philanthropists Samuel and Henrietta Barnett, was Gellhorn's first place of employment in Britain from 1935 to 1939. It was set up as a place for future leaders to live and study there as resident volunteers, and to come face to face with the poverty in the surrounding area. It gave them the opportunity to develop practical solutions through education in the arts. Activities included music lessons, classes, various ensembles, public theatrical performances and even opera. Many of the institution's alumni kept a lifelong connection with Toynbee Hall and worked to bring about radical social change all over Britain.[19]

This must have been a stimulating environment for the young Gellhorn who taught piano and harmony, directed ensembles and wrote music, including incidental music for several plays.[20] He also conducted his first opera performance at Toynbee Hall, Gluck's *Orpheus and Euridice*, with designs by Lotte Reiniger. Gellhorn eventually became Director of Music at the hall, and a

19 See 'Our History', website of Toynbee Hall, https://www.toynbeehall.org.uk/about-us/our-history/ [accessed: 22.11.2021].
20 Curran and Meyn, 4.

number of compositions have survived from this productive time. Gellhorn was part of a community and wrote for specific performers and occasions in an accessible style that was clearly aimed at pleasing audiences rather than developing the Modernist style of his earlier pieces.

Among these compositions from the Toynbee Hall years are two beautiful pieces for violin and piano, *Capriccio* (1936) and *Intermezzo* (1937). They were written for two fellow-German émigrés whom Gellhorn had already known during his time in Berlin, the virtuoso performer and teacher Max Rostal (1905–1991) and his pupil Maria Lidka (1914–2013), who remained a lifelong friend. Rostal taught in London during and after the war and famously took the young Norbert Brainin, Siegmund Nissel and Peter Schidlof under his wing during the war. They would later form the Amadeus Quartet with the cellist Martin Lovett. Lidka was a highly influential performer and became a Professor at the Royal College of Music in the 1970s. The *Capriccio* (two and a half minutes), dedicated to Rostal, is a real virtuoso showpiece. It starts with joyous and surging semiquaver triplet runs in both the violin and piano parts. This is intersected with a more reflective and almost melancholic waltz before the fireworks begin anew. In contrast, the Intermezzo (five minutes) is a stunning, more expansive piece with a slow and gorgeous feel. The D minor Andante theme is followed by a humorous più mosso with march-like, dotted rhythms. Both pieces are completely tonal, there are no traces of the relentless and challenging shifts of harmony that can be found in the earlier pieces. They were clearly written to appeal to a more conventional audience, and they remain ideal as a crowd-pleasing gems in any violin recital programme.

The *Trio Suite for two violins and viola* (also 1937) is just under fifteen minutes long and looks back to 18th- and early 19th-century works by Bach, Haydn or Mozart. One might speculate that the work was composed for a particular ensemble at the hall, perhaps comprising Gellhorn's students. Unlike the two violin pieces it does have the 'Gellhorn-twist' with the familiar interweaving lines and surprising harmonic turns, and could therefore be described as neoclassical, deriving inspiration from Stravinsky and Hindemith, rather than a pastiche of baroque music. The Overture has a Baroque feel, complete with trills, and is followed by a solemn Allemande. The Courante contains many unpredictable turns that take us to the very edge of tonality while ending, surprisingly, with a perfectly tonal resolution. The Sarabande consists of a beautiful melody for the first violin, accompanied by the second violin and viola in calm pizzicato quavers. The Bourrée is a lively dance reminiscent of the first movement of Bach's Brandenburg Concerto no.3. The piece finishes with a Gigue, with the three instruments going off in more and more unexpected directions in long semiquaver runs, coming together after each section in surprising cadences. The *Trio Suite* is a brilliant demonstration of Gellhorn's ability to adopt historical musical forms to his individual style of composition, and I find it both fascinating and entertaining. It would form an effective foil to the contrasting quartets within a concert programme.

Gellhorn also wrote a couple of pieces for the piano duo John Tobin and Tilly Connely. Tobin was Director of Music at Toynbee Hall before Gellhorn took over. The fifteen-minute *Sonata for Two Pianos* was written in 1936. For our project, the piece was recorded by Eleanor Hodgkinson and Jakob Fichert. The first movement with its celebratory, stately feel is followed by a warm and yearning Andante lento, with increasingly expansive chords in the middle section. The third and final movement, Tarantella, is an exhilarating virtuosic tour de force.

The second piece for two pianos, *Totentanz* (Dance of the Dead, 1937), was played in one of our workshops but sadly not recorded. It is dark and almost prophetic in nature. It is reminiscent of Liszt's *Mephisto Valse No. 1*. A cynical dance with a cold, mechanical character is interrupted by recurring devilish off-beat bass chords, evoking disturbing images of an increasingly bizarre demonic bacchanal. This is followed, as an after-thought, by a short, sombre *quiet* section. Both works are highly effective and idiomatic contributions to the two-piano medium, which was popular at that time, less so in more recent years.

Two vocal compositions have survived from the Toynbee Hall years, and both were recorded for our project. The stunningly beautiful and haunting 'Autumn' is a setting of a poem by Walter de la Mare (1873–1956). The poem speaks of the emptiness after a beloved person is gone. The song unfolds seamlessly over just two pages. It builds towards a climax on the words 'Your ghost, where your face was', and the texture is reduced to an unaccompanied vocal line in *piano* on the final words 'silence, where hope was'. The immediacy and power of expression in this song makes one wish that Gellhorn had written more for voice and piano, but sadly there are only two more songs, one dedicated to his young wife in the year of their wedding (1943), and the other written for his daughter Barbara. Notably, neither of them is in German. The second vocal composition from the late 1930s is a setting of a short lament by Racine (1639–1699), *Ah! Par quel*, a duet for soprano and mezzo-soprano.

The manuscripts in the British Library collection also include incidental music to Shakespeare's *Romeo and Juliet* and *Le malade imaginaire* by Molière from Gellhorn's time at Toynbee Hall. Overall, this was a productive time for Gellhorn as a composer.

2   Music Written during Internment on the Isle of Man

The Blitz invasion of Holland and Belgium in 1940 sent shock waves through British society and stoked fears of invasion aided by a 'fifth column' of foreign nationals. When Churchill decided to 'collar the lot' and intern all German and Italian nationals as 'enemy aliens' in 1940, Jewish refugees and German and Austrian citizens loyal to the Nazis were thrown together in makeshift camps before being shipped to the Isle of Man, which had already been used for internment in the First World War. Fellow émigré composer Hans Gál described this experience in his diary *Music behind Barbed Wire*.[21] It is a moving account of the many hardships – such as being cut off from relatives, random deportations to Canada and Australia, cramped conditions and monotonous food – but Gál also recounts positive aspects of the story such as the camaraderie and the many educational and artistic activities, including the creation of the bilingual comic revue *What a Life!* in Central Camp in the capital Douglas.[22]

Gellhorn spent eight months in internment, first in Warth Mills in Bury near Manchester, and then in Mooragh Camp in the north of the Isle of Man in the excellent company of fellow émigré musicians including Paul Hamburger and Hans Keller. The (slightly older) pianist Ferdinand Rauter describes their joint musical activities in his diary of 1940.[23] Especially for young musicians like Gellhorn, Hamburger or Keller, this was a stimulating environment. Without access to sheet music, Gellhorn was forced to reconstruct and perform entire programmes of piano music from his extraordinary musical memory.[24] There were a number of excellent string players at hand, and there was a choir (male only because of the gender segregation) which Gellhorn directed.

The most substantial and original of the compositions from the Isle of Man is *Mooragh* for a four-part male choir (or four soloists) and strings, dated August 1940. It is a setting of a poem by F.F. Bieber that had been published in the camp newspaper, the *Mooragh Times*.[25]

> Beyond barbed wire
> The sea,
> And the sun's last fire

---

21 Hans Gál, *Music Behind Barbed Wire*, English translation by Eva Fox-Gál (London: Toccata Press, 2014).
22 Hans Gál, *What a Life!*, RCM Editions 2021, sheet music edition by Norbert Meyn and Louis Stanhope, with full score, parts and introductory materials, available for free download from RCM Research Online.
23 Peter Gellhorn, *Video 1*, time code 0.36.00.
24 Ferdinand Rauter's 1940 diary, written in Gabelsberger shorthand, can be found in the Music and Migration collection at the University of Salzburg. It has been partially transcribed and then translated into English by Ferdinand Rauter's daughter Andrea Rauter, who kindly shared this information with the author.
25 Sadly, it has not been possible to find further information about the author of the poem. Images of the newspaper are available online: Edward Victor, 'Isle of Man', http://www.edwardvictor.com/Holocaust/2005/isle_of_man_main.htm [accessed: 02.01.2020].

Burning up a tree
And a cottage on the green hill.
Gulls idle on the beach,
Then rise into the air and cry.
The field across the bay we cannot reach,
We can but pace our cage and let our hungry eye
Take in far loveliness which will remain.
Beyond our sadness and beyond despair,
Beyond our stubborn hope, beyond our fair
And puzzled sense of justice.
They will stand,
This bay, this pier, this beach, this sea,
This distant friendliness of wooded land –
To bid farewell to us when we are free.

This moving and powerful piece starts with a slowly rising bass line and gently syncopated string chords. It builds towards the moment when the gulls 'rise up in the air and fly', followed by a violin solo full of longing and melancholy. The piece, which is generally tonal but makes use of subtle and interesting harmonic shifts, continues in a subdued atmosphere with wistful harmony and occasional outbursts of despair. Eventually a calmer, more consoling feeling prevails in the certainty that the internees will be freed eventually. There is no evidence that the piece was performed during Gellhorn's internment or indeed his lifetime. However, since the creation of an edition at the RCM in 2016, the musical group Ensemble Émigré has performed this powerful and engaging work on several occasions in London, Manchester and on the Isle of Man, and a live recording from Mooragh Town Hall in 2017 can be found online.

Gellhorn also wrote two pieces 'for strings without double bass' for players in the camp. With the absence of other sheet-music they were probably written on the spur of the moment so people had something to play. *Andante* (four and a half minutes) is constructed as a fugue and has a lyrical, quasi-religious atmosphere. *The Cats* (November 1940, approximately two and a half minutes) is a caricature with quirky rhythms and slurs, evoking images of bendy felines. There must have been cats roaming around the camp, presumably unimpeded by the barbed wire, unlike the unfortunate internees. Manx cats are known to have very short or no tails, which makes them particularly interesting. One of the violinists in the first performance of *The Cats* was Hans Keller, who later became an influential writer and broadcaster.[26]

---

26 Peter Gellhorn, *Video 1*, time code 0.12.00.

FIGURE 11.3   Peter and Olive Gellhorn on their wedding day in 1943
COURTESY OF THE GELLHORN FAMILY ARCHIVE

After his release from internment in 1941, Gellhorn eventually found employment as an assistant conductor and musical coach for the Vic-Wells opera company, where he met his future wife, the singer Olive Layton, a member of the chorus. On the evening of their wedding, he conducted a performance of *La Traviata* with a cast including Joan Cross and Peter Pears.[27] In the same year he wrote both the words and the music of a beautiful love song, 'I Want to Sing a Song', in popular style. It is dedicated to Olive and was published in 1949 by Boosey & Hawkes. It is the only composition by Gellhorn that was published during his lifetime.

Towards the end of the war, Gellhorn was assigned war work in an electrical factory in London. Then, from December 1945, he was engaged by the Carl Rosa Opera company, where he conducted a total of 115 performances in the following year. This brought him to the attention of David Webster, the manager of the newly formed company at the Royal Opera House, Covent Garden and a fellow émigré, the experienced Austrian opera conductor and composer Karl Rankl (1898–1968), who had been chosen as music director in 1946. In her biography of Rankl, Nicole Ristow places their first meeting in Leeds, where Webster and

---

27   Curran and Meyn, 6.

FIGURE 11.4   Peter Gellhorn on a London street in 1951
COURTESY OF THE GELLHORN FAMILY ARCHIVE

Rankl were auditioning singers for the chorus.[28] It is likely that Gellhorn was at least aware of the older colleague from his student days in Berlin, where Rankl had worked as chorus master and conductor with Klemperer and Zemlinsky at the Kroll Oper (1928–31) and also conducted performances at the Städtische Oper in 1932. In 1947 Gellhorn joined the Covent Garden company as Head of Music Staff. There he helped to develop the company into the first full time opera company in Britain and conducted a total of 260 performances over seven years (at Covent Garden and on tour).

In 1954, Gellhorn left Covent Garden and started to work at Glyndebourne, the company in Southern England which had been revolutionising and internationalising opera in Britain with a team including many émigré musicians from Germany and Austria, led by the conductor Fritz Busch and the director Carl Ebert. Gellhorn worked there, first as a coach and then as chorus master. Between 1956 and 1961 he also conducted thirty performances at Glyndebourne, mostly of operas by Mozart, the company's core repertoire. Mezzo-Soprano Janet Baker, who sang in the chorus at Glyndebourne, admired his 'relentless search for excellence' and the way he made the singers work to

---

28   Nicole Ristow, Karl Rankl: *Leben, Werk und Exil eines österreichischen Komponisten und Dirigenten* (Neumünster: von Bockel Verlag, 2017), 292.

achieve it.[29] Another member of the chorus, Laura Sarti, remembers that he played the piano like an orchestra: 'He knew all the Mozart operas by heart, including the instruments!'[30] Then, in 1961, Gellhorn became the Director of the BBC Chorus, later known as the BBC singers. With them he prepared countless performances for broadcast and for the BBC Proms, and he collaborated with leading conductors of the time. He also championed the music of contemporary composers such as Messiaen and Berio. After his retirement from the BBC in 1972 he continued to work as a guest conductor, for instance at the opera school of the Royal College of Music from 1981–88, in addition to giving masterclasses and teaching privately. One of his many pupils was the young British composer George Benjamin.[31]

Gellhorn did return to composition on a few occasions, writing a few smaller chamber music pieces and some piano music for children. In 1956 he wrote another score for a film by Lotte Reiniger, *The Star of Bethlehem*.[32] This was then performed as a separate piece for small string orchestra and chorus by the Barnes Choir and again by the BBC Singers. It is a 'global' Christmas cantata and features Christmas carols from many nations, including the English carol *The First Noel*. The use of songs from many nations as a way of affirming a universal rather than a national perspective is significant in the context of Gellhorn's experience as a refugee and migrant who moved from one cultural context to another. We can find similar approaches amongst the work of other émigré composers. For instance, émigré pianist Ferdinand Rauter and the singer Engel Lund made a feature of this in their polyglot programmes of 'Songs from many Lands' in the 1930s and 1940s, which they toured all over Europe, Scandinavia and the United States and presented in the National Gallery Concerts in London during the war.[33] Mátyás Seiber (1905–1960), who had developed an interest in Hungarian folk music during his studies with Zoltán *Kodály* in the 1920s and became an influential teacher of composition in Britain, also arranged folk songs from many nations.

In 1972 Gellhorn was commissioned by the Richmond Festival to write a cantata for solo voices and wind instruments, *Aucassin & Nicolette*. The piece is based on a 12th- or 13th-century French love story about the relationship

---

29   YouTube, 'Interview with Dame Janet Baker', RCM, 21 September 2014, time code 0.30.32, https://www.youtube.com/watch?v=lvAKsMtCHhQ [accessed: 28.04.2020].
30   YouTube, 'Interview with Laura Sarti', RCM, 13 July 2014, time code 0.56.00, https://www.youtube.com/watch?v=HKmzINq-iQM [accessed: 15.04.2021].
31   Gellhorn eventually introduced George Benjamin to Messiaen in Paris, where he continued his studies. See YouTube, 'Interview with Sangeet Gellhorn', time code 1.18.00.
32   Peter Gellhorn, *Video 1*, time code 0.48.50.
33   See CD, *Engel Lund's Book of Folk Songs*, Nimbus Records 5813/14, 2010.

of a nobleman with a socially inferior woman.[34] Finally, in 1992 he wrote a stunningly beautiful song for his daughter Barbara, 'Aedh wishes for the Cloths of Heaven', a setting of Yeats's famous love poem that finishes on the words 'tread softly, because you tread on my dreams'. It is a completely tonal, exquisitely crafted miniature in F Major, written in a gently pulsating three-quarter rhythm, perhaps stylistically reminiscent of early 20th-century Viennese songs. It was performed a few times by Barbara, who was a semi-professional singer, and recorded for our project by soprano Louise Fuller and pianist Lucy Colquhoun. This seems to have been his final composition.

3   Conclusion

In a Covent Garden Programme from 1948, Gellhorn's biographical note reveals that he considered composition to be an important element of his career and mentions that in the last few years of his studies in Berlin (1932–34), he 'concentrated on composing and, among other things, wrote music for the Silhouette films of Lotte Reiniger'.[35] Later programmes, for example one from the Inverness Choral Society in 1958, also identified him as a composer: 'Gellhorn (...) is known, not only as a conductor and pianist, but as a composer.'[36] However, Gellhorn's musician-son Sangeet believes his father did not ultimately have the inner drive to express himself through composition, although he could do it beautifully and immaculately when he chose to.[37] Sangeet also felt that his father remained emotionally rooted in 18th- and 19th-century music, in the music of Bach and Mozart in particular.[38] In his roles as a conductor, pianist-performer, and musical coach, he could live this passion and pass it on to others, and he found fulfilment in working towards the highest possible standards of performance. Mezzo-Soprano Janet Baker made the point that the sheer commitment to musical performance she learned from Gellhorn and other émigrés helped her and her generation of

---

34   See Hermann Suchier, *Aucassin und Nicolette: Kritischer Text mit Paradigmen und Glossar*, 10 edn., (Paderborn,1932), X–XVI.
35   Covent Garden programme for *The Magic Flute*, 1948 season, www.petergellhorn.com [accessed: 20.04.2020].
36   Gellhorn's artist biography in a concert programme of the Inverness Musical Society (26 November 1958). The programme is available on www.petergellhorn.com [accessed: 20.04.2020].
37   YouTube, 'Interview with Sangeet Gellhorn', time code 0.42.00.
38   *Ibid.*, time code 1.15.00.

FIGURE 11.5
Peter Gellhorn at
St. James's Palace, 1984
COURTESY OF THE
GELLHORN FAMILY
ARCHIVE

British musicians to move 'from a national to an international world'.[39] His lifelong friend, the émigré violinist Maria Lidka, with whom he gave many recitals, once called him 'Der beste Musiker Englands' (England's best musician).[40]

Gellhorn's compositions allow us to engage emotionally with the reality of forced migration, demonstrating a fragmented journey across multiple environments with different priorities. These led him from the dynamic creative environment of 1930s Berlin, the thriving crucible for musical Modernism, to the social and educational ambitions in a radically different context at London's Toynbee Hall, the experience of internment as a so-called 'enemy alien', and the increasingly international music scene in Britain after the Second World War. Debates about migration and its impact on culture are at an all-time high

---

39 YouTube, 'Interview with Dame Janet Baker', time code 0.54.20.
40 Jutta Raab Hansen, *NS-verfolgte Musiker in England: Spuren deutscher und österreichischer Flüchtlinge in der britischen Musikkultur*, Bd. 1: *Musik im ‚Dritten Reich' und im Exil, Schriftenreihe*, hrsg. v. Hanns-Werner Heister und Peter Petersen (Hamburg: von Bockel, 1996), 299, footnote 635.

today, but our intellectual and emotional understanding of the cultural and personal implications of migration are still limited. Gellhorn's compositions spanning nearly seventy years, whilst smaller in scope than the oeuvres of better-known composers, are significant in the context of his story. Gellhorn's music and story are evidence of the dynamism and inspiration that refugees and immigrants can bring to their adopted society, as well as the challenges and opportunities that migration creates for the individual.[41] They lead us into a realm where music and politics overlap. The joke at the beginning of this article shows that Gellhorn himself maintained a keen interest in politics and human rights throughout his life. His daughter Mary called him 'quite a humanitarian' and remembered that after his death she found his bank account full of standing orders to charities like Practical Action and Amnesty International.[42] It is my hope that the performance editions and recordings produced through our project at the Royal College of Music, set into the context of Gellhorn's life story, will both inspire more performances and a greater understanding of Gellhorn the composer. For, alongside his contribution to music in Britain as conductor, teacher, coach and all-round musician, as I hope I have shown, his compositions shed a unique light on his individual émigré experience and the broader relationship between migration, music and culture.

Appendix 1: Complete List of Works (Prepared by Terence Curran in 2016 for RCM Editions)

Pieces in bold are available as free PDF Downloads (RCM Editions) through the RCM's Research Online depository: https://researchonline.rcm.ac.uk/id/eprint/69/

BERLIN

1928:	*3 kleine Klavierstücke*
1932:	**Kleine Suite for oboe and piano**
1933:	*Carmen* [film score for Lotte Reiniger]
	String Quartet No. 1
1934:	*Puss-in-Boots* [film score for Lotte Reiniger]
	The Stolen Heart [film score for Lotte Reiniger]
1935:	*The Little Chimney Sweep* [film score for Lotte Reiniger]

---

41 For a philosophical exploration of this theme, see Vilem Flusser, *The Freedom of the Migrant* (Chicago: University of Illinois Press, 2003).

42 YouTube, 'Interview with Mary Gellhorn', time code 0.49.40.

LONDON, TOYNBEE HALL

	Baida der Kosak, cantata
	String Quartet No. 2
	Stück für Violoncello und Klavier vierhändig
1936:	*Minuet für zwei Blockflöten*
	Polonaise für Flöte, Horn und vier Geigen
	Skizze zur Klaviersonate [*unfinished/lost*]
	Capriccio für Violine und Klavier
	Trauermarsch für vier Blockflöten
	Sonata for two pianos
1937:	*Intermezzo für Violine und Klavier*
	Trio-Suite for two violins and viola
	Dance of the Dead for piano duet
	Novelette for piano [copy of published edition held in BL main collection]
1938:	**Autumn for voice and piano**
1939:	*Romeo and Juliet*, incidental music to the play by Shakespeare
	Le malade imaginaire, incidental music to the play by Molière
	Ah! Parquel for vocal duet and piano

INTERNMENT ON ISLE OF MAN

1940:	**Mooragh for male choir and strings**
	Andante **for string orchestra without double bass (or string quartet)**
	Two studies for unaccompanied violin
	***The Cats* for string orchestra without double bass**
	Serenade for string orchestra without double bass [*unfinished/lost*]

LATER WORKS

1943:	*I Want To Sing A Song*, for voice and piano [published edition, 1949]
1948:	String Quartet [*unfinished/lost*]
1952:	Miscellaneous pieces.
1953:	Ten short pieces for children, for piano
1954:	***The Linnet* for mixed choir**
1956:	*The Star of Bethlehem*, music for the film by Lotte Reiniger
1958–1960s:	Occasional arrangements for various ensembles, including *Il Seraglio* (1958), music by Mozart arranged for chamber ensemble for the film ballet by Lotte Reiniger

1972:	*Aucassin and Nicolette*, a tale for solo voices and wind instruments
1976:	**Thoughts on a Chinese Tune for 2 clarinets and piano duet**
1977:	*Dialogue* for violin and viola with string orchestra
1982:	*Trio Suite for Children* for pianoforte, violin and violoncello
1995:	*Aedh wishes for the Cloths of Heaven* for voice and piano

Appendix 2: Timeline

1912	Born in Breslau as the first child of architect Alfred Gellhorn and his wife Else
1923	Moves to Berlin with his mother and sisters
1933	Completes his studies in Berlin
1935	Emigrates to Britain
1935–39	Works at Toynbee Hall, eventually as Director of Music
1940–41	Interned at Warth Mills in Bury and on the Isle of Man
1941	Becomes assistant conductor with Sadler's Wells Opera (then based in Burnley, Lancashire)
1945	Becomes conductor of the Carl Rosa Opera Company
1947–53	Head of Music Staff and assistant to Karl Rankl at Royal Opera House. (Rankl resigned in 1951 and was followed by a series of guest conductors.) Gellhorn conducted at ROH and on tour.
1954–61	Working at Glyndebourne as conductor and chorus master
1961–72	Becomes conductor of the BBC Singers (renamed BBC Chorus under Gellhorn but reverted to BBC Singers in 1972). Retires when sixty years old.
1967	Co-founder and conductor of Opera Barga in Italy
1970	During the 1970s and 1980s, Gellhorn works variously as a coach, teacher and conductor at the National Opera Studio, Dartington, Guildhall School of Music & Drama and Trinity College of Music.
1973–2000	Conductor of the Barnes Choir
1981–88	Coach and conductor at Royal College of Music's Opera School
2004	Dies in London aged ninety-two

12
Visits in Four Cities: Stations in the Musical and Familial Life of the Song Composer Max Kowalski (1882–1956)

Nils Neubert

Abstract

This essay examines the four documented encounters between the song composer Max Kowalski (1882–1956) and his nephew Michael Kowal in Berlin (1936), New York (1950), London, and Geneva (the latter two visits in 1955), biographically and musically. Michael Kowal's recollections provide both inspiration and a framework for a discussion of three song collections that together illustrate the broad poetic and thematic range across Kowalski's output of more than 250 songs: the fourteen *Kinderlieder* (1936), the *Acht Lieder auf Gedichte von Hafis* (1948), and the *Sieben Lieder auf Gedichte von Rainer Maria Rilke* (1951).[1] These songs and visits find Kowalski in three significant stages of his life and career: (1) his years as a member of the Frankfurt Kulturbund in Nazi Germany, (2) his final period of compositional productivity after the war in London, following his second marriage, and (3) the year before his death, by which point he had stopped composing.

In recent years, the composer Max Kowalski (1882–1956) and his songs have become far better known to scholars, performers, and the music-loving public than they had been in previous decades – a remarkable trend which is indubitably a result of the continued devotion and care of several generations of musical colleagues, researchers and, perhaps most importantly, family members. Following Kowalski's death in 1956, Oscar Kowal (1894–1984), who admired his oldest brother and his compositions greatly, remained engaged in promoting his legacy with publishers, scholars, and performers both in the United States and in Europe.[2] His efforts are continued to this day by his son

---

1 Michael Kowal, 'Erinnerungen an Max Kowalski', in Joachim Brügge (ed.), *Facetten I: Symposien zur Kammermusik von Jean Sibelius, zum Liedkomponisten Max Kowalski und zur Liszt Rezeption* (Tutzing: Hans Schneider, 2014), 191–93.
2 Wolfgang Holzmair, 'Max Kowalski: Daten, Fakten, Stationen, Umfeld – ein erweiterter Lebenslauf', in *Facetten I*, 137. Oskar Kowalski (1894–1984) emigrated to New York City in May 1938 and changed the spelling of his first name to Oscar, and the family name to Kowal

Michael Kowal. Associate Professor Emeritus of English at New York City's Queens College, and a scholar of both English and German literature, Michael Kowal has contributed to the field as an author and poetic translator, and as a dedicated and forthcoming facilitator and resource to many.[3] His accounts of the four only meetings between him and his uncle Max Kowalski (see note 1) provide the pillars for the forthcoming discussion.

Born on 10 August 1882, in Kowal, Poland (then Russia), Kowalski grew up in Ballenstedt, Frankfurt (where he attended school), and Bingen am Rhein, where his father Abraham Michael Kowalski held a position as cantor and religious education teacher until his early death in 1907.[4] Little is known about Max Kowalski's earliest musical training, aside from the fact that it must have involved vocal and piano studies, and was likely guided by his father.[5] In 1903 and 1904, concurrently with his law studies (1900–1906),[6] Kowalski studied singing in Berlin with the renowned baritone Alexander Heinemann (1873–1919). Presumably instructed in the cantorial tradition by his father,[7] he also worked as a part-time cantor in Bingen from 1903 to 1905, as well as in 1907,

---

during the United States naturalisation process. According to an interview with Michael Kowal on 23 June 2021, his father – a businessman in the metal industry – had a lifelong interest in the political and legal sciences, and might have pursued studies, even a career, in these fields, had he not left school prior to completing his A-Levels to pursue an apprenticeship in industrial business economics, following the death of his father in 1907. His wife, Trude Kowal, had trained as a pianist under Moritz Mayer-Mahr (1869–1947) in Berlin.

3   Kowal, 'Erinnerungen', in *Facetten 1*, 191–93; Kowal, 'Max Kowalski by Michael Kowal', in (album) *Lieder by Max Kowalski*, Wolfgang Holzmair and Thérèse Lindquist, Bridge Records, 9431 (2015), 9–15. Michael Kowal (b. 1932 in Berlin) majored in English at New York City's Queens College, began his graduate studies at Princeton University, and earned a PhD in comparative literature from Yale University. He spent two years as a Fulbright scholar in in Florence, Italy (1955–56), and Augsburg, Germany (1977–78). In addition to the recording notes/translations cited just above, his poetic translations appear in the editions by Recital Publications (Huntsville, TX) cited in note 22 below.

4   Holzmair, 'Max Kowalski: Daten', 137f; Jutta Raab Hansen, 'Max Kowalski (2008, updated in 2013 and 2019)', Personendaten, in Claudia Maurer Zenck, Peter Petersen, and Sophie Fetthauer (eds.), *Lexikon verfolgter Musiker und Musikerinnen der NS-Zeit*, hosted at the University of Hamburg since 2005, last modified on 19 June 2019, https://www.lexm.uni -hamburg.de/object/lexm_lexmperson_00003097.

5   Theresa Lechthaler, 'Max Kowalski: Leben und Werk des Komponisten' (Term paper, Landesschulamt Frankfurt, 2015); Raab Hansen, 'Max Kowalski', Personendaten.

6   Luitgard Schader, 'Neben meinem Hauptberuf bin ich Lieder-Komponist', in *Max Kowalski: Songs*, Melinda Paulsen and Lars Jönsson, Zuk Records, 335 (2014), 3. Kowalski studied law in Heidelberg (spring 1900), Berlin (fall 1900), and (as of fall 1902) Marburg, where he earned his doctorate in 1906.

7   Holzmair, 'Max Kowalski: Daten', 138f.

following his father's death.[8] Starting in 1909, he took private composition lessons with Bernhard Sekles (1872–1934) in Frankfurt, and subsequently enrolled at the city's Dr. Hoch'sches Konservatorium for five semesters from 1911 until 1913, where he studied composition (again under Sekles, and as a senior classmate to the precocious Paul Hindemith [1895–1963]), as well as score reading, counterpoint, musical form, and conducting.[9]

Kowalski's compositional career began in Frankfurt during the years just prior to the Weimar Republic, and continued under the auspices of the Jüdischer Kulturbund (Jewish Cultural Alliance) during his years in the Third Reich, as well as in London after 1939.[10] He produced an oeuvre of more than 250 songs, about one third of which were published by reputable companies until 1933/34.[11] His songs, which reflect the tonal and formal aesthetics of the late 19th century, were performed, recorded, and in some cases premiered by notable singers of the day. After spending several decades in relative obscurity,

---

8   Kowal, 'Max Kowalski by Michael Kowal', 9.
9   'Vierunddreißigster Jahresbericht / Dr. Hoch'schen Conservatoriums für alle Zweige der Tonkunst zu Frankfurt a. M.: ausgegeben am Schlusse des Schuljahres 1911/1912', http://publikationen.ub.uni-frankfurt.de/frontdoor/index/index/docId/37456; 'Fünfunddreißigster Jahresbericht / Dr. Hoch'schen Conservatoriums für alle Zweige der Tonkunst zu Frankfurt a. M.: ausgegeben am Schlusse des Schuljahres 1912/1913', http://publikationen.ub.uni-frankfurt.de/frontdoor/index/index/docId/37457; 'Sechsuddreißigster Jahresbericht / Dr. Hoch'schen Conservatoriums für alle Zweige der Tonkunst zu Frankfurt a. M.: ausgegeben am Schlusse des Schuljahres 1913/1914', http://publikationen.ub.uni-frankfurt.de/frontdoor/index/index/docId/37458. Listed in these annual reports as 'Kowalski, Max', 'Kowalski, Dr., Max,' and 'Kowalsky [sic] Max,' respectively, he studied score reading with Karl Breidenstein (1871–1966), musical form and counterpoint with Berhard Sekles, and conducting with Fritz Bassermann (1850–1926).
10 Holzmair, 'Max Kowalski und der jüdische Kulturbund 1933 bis 1941', in *Facetten I*, 155f. Established on 16 June 1933 as the Kulturbund Deutscher Juden (Cultural Alliance of German Jews), and forced to change its name to Jüdischer Kulturbund (thus omitting the term 'German') as of 1935, the organisation employed circa 2,000 professionals (around 1300 men and 700 women) in the fields of music, theatre, and the visual arts, who had been laid-off by German institutions. Prior to the 1938 *Kristallnacht* pogroms that would initiate a decline in the organisation's activities until its closure and dissolution by the Gestapo in 1941, the Kulturbund had grown to a network of nearly fifty institutions across Germany, with a membership of more than 70,000; see also, Nils Neubert, 'Max Kowalski's *Japanischer Frühling*: A Song Collection from the Period of the Jewish Cultural Alliance in Nazi Germany' (Dissertation, CUNY Graduate Center, 2017), 70, https://academicworks.cuny.edu/gc_etds/1893 [accessed: 21.07.2020].
11 Schader, 'Neben meinem Hauptberuf', 3; Holzmair, 'Anhang: Max Kowalski – Werkkatalog', in *Facetten I*, 252–65, lists 235 songs, not accounting for the early, pre-Op. 1 songs. Kowalski's publishers included Raabe & Plotho (Berlin), Simrock (Berlin & Leipzig), Eos (Berlin-Schöneberg), Leuckart (Leipzig), Zimmermann (Leipzig), Associated Music Publishers (later Boosey & Hawkes, New York), and the Universal Edition (Vienna).

these songs have experienced a return to stages, recording studios, sheet music publications, and scholarly literature on both sides of the Atlantic.[12]

While the lyrics Kowalski drew upon are predominantly in German, they encompass a considerable range of literary styles, themes, time periods, cultural origins, and spirituality, including major German-speaking writers, as well as non-German and non-Western text sources and inspirations, in both translation and adaptation. The noted Austrian baritone Wolfgang Holzmair, who researched and performed Kowalski's works over several years, remarks:

> [Kowalski] finds a unique musical and emotional language for each one of his poets. Rilke does not sound like Giraud, Hölderlin not like [Hafez], Verlaine not like Heine, Hesse not like the Japanese poetry in Bethge's adaptations, Goethe not like George. Kowalski knows and loves literature.[13]

The composer's abilities as a singer, pianist, singing teacher, and répétiteur are abundantly evident in his works, and have found acknowledgement in a spectrum of voices that bridges his day and ours.[14] His own position on his

---

[12] Recordings were made by Paul Bender (1875–1947), Willy Berling (1909–1994), Hans Hotter (1909–2003), Otto von Rohr (1914–1982), and Ernst Victor Wolf (1889–1960). Premieres were given by Alexander Kipnis (1891–1978) and Heinrich Schlusnus (1888–1952). More recently, Kowalski's songs have been performed and recorded by baritone Wolfgang Holzmair (b. 1952), mezzo-soprano Melinda Paulsen (b. 1964), and soprano Ingrid Schmithüsen (b. 1960). For a more extensive (if still partial) list of performers and further information on published and unissued recordings, see also, Nils Neubert, 'Max Kowalski's *Japanischer Frühling*', 43–45, 220–21, https://academicworks.cuny.edu/gc_etds/1893 [accessed: 21.07.2021]; see also, Joachim Brügge, 'Max Kowalski und seine Sänger', in *Facetten I*, 205–12.

[13] Holzmair, 'Max Kowalski: Ein Anwalt seiner Lieder' (Graduate thesis, Universität Mozarteum Salzburg, 2013), 79–80: '[Kowalski findet] für jeden seiner Dichter eine eigene musikalische und emotionale Sprache [...]. Rilke klingt nicht wie Giraud, Hölderlin nicht wie Hafis, Verlaine nicht wie Heine, Hesse nicht wie japanische Lyrik in Bethges Nachdichtung, Goethe nicht wie George. Kowalski kennt die Literatur, und er liebt die Literatur.'

[14] Artur Holde, 'Zeitgenössische jüdische Komponisten III. Der Frankfurter Kreis', *Frankfurter Israelitisches Gemeindeblatt*, 13/1 (1934): 9, cited in in Joachim Martini, *Musik als Form geistigen Widerstandes. Jüdische Musikerinnen und Musiker 1933–1945. Das Beispiel Frankfurt am Main*, Vol. 2 of 2 (Frankfurt: Brandes & Apsel, 2010), 115, 254; Nathan Ehrenreich, cited in Judith Freise and Joachim Martini (eds.), *Jüdische Musikerinnen und Musiker in Frankfurt 1933–1942. Musik als Form geistigen Widerstandes: Ausstellungsbegleitheft* (Frankfurt: Lembeck, 1990); Hans F. Schaub, 'Wir erinnern an: Max Kowalski', *Zeitschrift für Musik*, 113/7 (1952): 407f; 'Obituaries', Leo Baeck Institute Center for Jewish History, 'Guide to the Papers of Max Kowalski (1882–1956), 1909–1978, AR 7049 / MF 724', processed

compositions unites jocund modesty with humanist assuredness: 'Whether my songs are good I cannot say; the texts certainly are.'[15]

Kowalski's output has often been considered in the context of his primary occupation in Germany as a lawyer, and for about the first two decades of his compositional career – incidentally, the period during which his music enjoyed its most significant public success in Germany – he was practicing law full time.[16] Even so, his classification as an 'avocational composer,' if projected onto the oeuvre as a whole, would be a misjudgment, in part at least, given that a considerable portion of Kowalski's mature works (even if lacking publication after 1934) emerged from his full-time musical career in London, as well as from an active period prior to exile in association with the Kulturbund, which overlapped with increasing legislative restrictions on his legal practice. Michael Kowal adds: '[H]e was a musician through and through, and music was his primary concern.'[17]

Though representative segments of Kowalski's biography and career have been drawn into sharper focus in recent years, the English language literature

---

by Viola Voss, Series I: Personal, 1909–1978, Box 1, Folder 5; Hans Ferdinand Redlich, 'Max Kowalski († 4.6. 1956)', *Musica* XI (1957): 584; Philip Lieson Miller, 'Kowalski, Max', in Friedrich Blume (ed.), *Die Musik in Geschichte und Gegenwart*, Vol. 16 supplement (Kassel: Bärenreiter, 1979), 1049–50, later in ed. Ludwig Finscher (ed.), *Die Musik in Geschichte und Gegenwart*, Personenteil, Vol. 10, rev. ed. (Kassel Bärenreiter, 2003), 583f; Miller, 'Kowalski, Max', typewritten translation located at 'Biographical Articles', Leo Baeck Institute Center for Jewish History, 'Guide to the Papers of Max Kowalski (1882–1956), 1909–1978, AR 7049 / MF 724', processed by Viola Voss, Series I: Personal, 1909–1978, Box 1, Folder 2; Miller, 'Kowalski, Max', in Stanley Sadie (ed.), *The New Grove Dictionary of Music and Musicians*, Vol. 10 (London: Macmillan, 1980), 223f, later in Stanley Sadie (ed.), *The New Grove*, 2nd edition, Vol. 13(London: Macmillan, 2001/2002), 849f, Italian version: Alberto Bassi (ed.), *Dizionario enciclopedico universale della musica e dei musicisti*, Vol. 4 (Turin: UTET, 1986), 18; Peter Gradenwitz, 'Max Kowalski (1882–1956), Rechtsanwalt und feinsinniger Musiker', in *Bulletin des Leo Baeck Instituts* 58 (Jerusalem: Jüdischer Verlag, 1981), 41–51; Gottfried Eberle, 'Ein zweiter Pierrot lunaire. Der Komponist Max Kowalski (1882–1956)', *musica reanimata-Mitteilungen*, 30 (1998), 1–5; Eberle, 'Der andere Pierrot lunaire, Neues über Max Kowalski', *musica eanimate-Mitteilungen*, 58 (2006), 1; Susan Morehead, 'Max Kowalski: His Music and Life', unpublished, n.d., 35 pages (kindly provided by the author); Holzmair, 'Ein Max Kowalski Liederabend aus Sicht des Interpreten', in *Facetten I*, 241, 244; Holzmair, 'A Concert of Lieder by Max Kowalski from the Perspective of the Interpreter', in *Lieder by Max Kowalski*, Wolfgang Holzmair and Thérèse Lindquist, Bridge Records, 9431 (2015), 5; Theresa Lechthaler, 'Max Kowalski: Leben und Werk des Komponisten' (Termpaper, Landesschulamt Frankfurt, 2015); Schader, 'Neben meinem Hauptberuf', 2.

15   Kowal, 'Max Kowalski', 14.
16   Kowalski himself stated in a 1930 Festschrift: 'Aside from my main profession, I am a song composer', cited in Schader, "Neben meinem Hauptberuf", 3.
17   Kowal, 'Erinnerungen', 191: '[E]r war durch und durch Musiker, sein Hauptanliegen war die Musik [...]'.

on the composer and his works is still relatively compact, particularly with respect to discussions of the songs themselves and their place in Kowalski's nature, and the environments in which he lived.[18] In what follows, we will explore these aspects through the lens of four encounters between Michael Kowal and his uncle Max Kowalski in Berlin, New York, London, and Geneva, respectively – four cities that partially frame the exile journeys and lives of the Kowalski and Kowal families.

1   1936: Berlin

When Kowalski visited his youngest brother Oskar and family in Berlin in early April of 1936, he had been a member of the Frankfurt Kulturbund for about two years.[19] His law practice had been affected by an early wave of antisemitic legislation following Hitler's appointment as Chancellor on 30 January 1933, and with the passing of the *Schriftleitergesetz* on 4 October 1933, he could no longer publish his compositions in Germany.[20] Through the asynchronous support of his composer colleagues Arnold Schoenberg (1874–1951) and Paul Graener (1872–1944), both of whom provided Kowalski with reference letters, he managed to publish his *Sechs Lieder aus dem Westöstlichen Divan von Goethe*, Op. 17 (1933) with the Universal Edition in Vienna in 1934, which would be the last publication during his lifetime.[21] With the exception of his song

---

18 In addition to recent literature listed in notes 13 and 14, Brügge (ed.), 'Künstler und Emigration – Max Kowalski', in *Facetten I*, 107–265, includes articles by Joachim Brügge, Josef Berghold, Jutta Raab Hansen, Wolfgang Holzmair, Michael Kowal, Hildemar Holl, Julia Hinterberger, and Dorothea Hofmann.

19 Holzmair, 'Max Kowalski und der jüdische Kulturbund 1933 bis 1941', in *Facetten I*, 157. The Frankfurt chapter was formed on 17 April 1934, and Kowalski was one of the 24 members of its commission for music.

20 These included the 'Judenboykott' (1 April 1933), and the 'Gesetz zur Wiederherstellung des Berufsbeamtentums' (7 April 1933). Kowalski continued his practice as an *Altanwalt* (licensed before 1914) until 1938, though under considerable restrictions. See Martin Hirsch, Dietmut Majer, and Jürgen Menck (eds.), *Recht, Verwaltung und Justiz im Nationalsozialismus: Ausgewählte Schriften, Gesetze und Gerichtsentscheidungen von 1933 bis 1945 mit ausführlichen Erläuterungen und Kommentierungen*, 2nd unabridged edition (Baden-Baden: Nomos, 1997), 229–30.

21 The *Sieben Gedichte von Hafis* (1933), and the *Rokoko Lieder* (1933, originally *Vier Schäferlieder*, extended by three songs and reordered), completed around the same time, were labeled as opp. 18 and 19, respectively, but remain unpublished. Graener's letter (in the private collection of Michael Kowal) is dated 25 September 1930 and Holzmair, 'Max Kowalski: Daten', 143f, notes that Graener (who would serve as vice-president of the Reichsmusikkammer from 1935–1941) would surely not have endorsed Kowalski at a

cycle *Zwölf Lieder aus Pierrot Lunaire*, Op. 4 (1913) for medium voice and piano, all of his works fell out of print in Germany after 1933, and in Austria following the *Anschluss* (12 March 1938).[22] The Kulturbund became Kowalski's primary forum after 1933 and, though sometimes regarded as complex and controversial, the organisation played a crucial role in his reception and productivity during his remaining years in Nazi Germany.[23] Joachim Martini notes: 'As of 1933, Max Kowalski devotes all his energy to the cause of the Kulturbund, participates in the organisation of concerts, and occasionally accompanies his songs.'[24] Kowalski continued working with a number of fine singers during these years, was able to have new works premiered, and was also active as a reviewer for journals such as the *Israelitisches Familienblatt*.[25]

---

later point. Schoenberg's letter, dated 9 October 1933, is stored at 'Schönberg, Arnold', Leo Baeck Institute Center for Jewish History, 'Guide to the Papers of Max Kowalski (1882–1956), 1909–1978, AR 7049 / MF 724', processed by Viola Voss, Series II: Correspondence, 1910–1957, Box 1, Folder 42.

22 Like Schoenberg (whose settings date from 1912), Kowalski set poems from Hartleben's translations of Giraud's *Pierrot Lunaire*. Kowalski's cycle of twelve songs for medium voice and piano, published by Simrock in two volumes in 1913, remained in print after the war owing to its 1928 publication with Associated Music Publishers (now Boosey & Hawkes) in New York. The work inspired a partial orchestration by Max Rudolf (March 1946, English translation by John Bernhoff, unpublished and in the private collection of Michael Kowal), and an arrangement for voice and five instruments by Johannes Schöllhorn (1992, published by Editions Henry Lemoine). Opp. 1–11, and 17, as well the first editions of the *Acht Lieder auf Gedichte von Hafis* (1948), and the *Sieben Lieder auf Gedichte von Rainer Maria Rilke* (1951), both edited by Walter Foster, were originally reprinted/issued by Recital Publications (Huntsville, TX), and are now available through Classical Vocal Reprints (Fayetteville, AR). Opp. 12, 13 and 16 are now available through the Thomi-Berg Musikverlag (Planegg, Germany), and the Zimmermann editions of opp. 14 and 15 are distributed by Schott (Mainz, Germany). Two further volumes of first editions (edited by Luitgard Schader and Melinda Paulsen) were published by Schott in 2017: Volume 1 contains the *Jüdische Lieder* (1935–37), *Heine-Lieder* (1937) and *Lieder auf Englische Texte* (1941–46); Volume 2 contains the *Sechs Lieder auf Gedichte von Friedrich Hölderlin* (1950–51) and the *Sieben Geisha-Lieder* (1951). A critical edition of the *Japanischer Frühling* (1934–1938) is contained in Neubert, 'Max Kowalski's *Japanischer Frühling*,' 108–19, 193–207 (see note 10).
23 Holzmair, 'Kulturbund', in *Facetten I*, 159.
24 Martini, *Musik als Form geistigen Widerstandes*, Vol. 1 of 2, 231: 'Von 1933 setzt Max Kowalski seine ganze Energie für die Sache des Kultubundes ein, beteiligt sich an der Organisation der Konzerte und begleitet gelegentlich auch seine Lieder.'
25 Holzmair, 'Kulturbund', 161f; 'Concert Programs', Leo Baeck Institute Center for Jewish History, 'Guide to the Papers of Max Kowalski (1882–1956), 1909–1978, AR 7049 / MF 724', processed by Viola Voss, Series III: Musical Career, 1922–1956, Box 1, Folder 51. Surviving concert programs document additional performances with the Gesellschaft für Jüdische Volksbildung, Die Jüdischen Tonkünstler Frankfurts, and the Jüdische Winterhilfe. Other

While he composed a few individual songs in 1934 and 1935 (these would later become part of larger collections), it would take Kowalski until 1936 to complete another collection, his fourteen *Kinderlieder*, which he brought with him on his Berlin visit and dedicated to his then four-year-old nephew Michael.[26] This period also brought forth the eight *Jüdische Lieder* (1935–37), translated from Yiddish by Ludwig Strauss (1892–1953), the altogether fourteen songs of the *Japanischer Frühling* (1934–38, adaptations by Hans Bethge [1876–1946]), the *Sechs* (actually seven) *Heine-Lieder* (1937), and the *Zwölf Lieder auf Gedichte von Li-tai-pe* (1938/39, adaptations by Klabund [= Alfred Henschke, 1890–1928]).[27] We now see an extended period of the predominance of non-German and non-Western poets and themes in Kowalski's works, which – at least initially – was likely prompted in large part by increasing sanctions by the Nazis on the use and presentation of 'Aryan' materials by the Kulturbund, which took full effect around the time of the 1936 Berlin Summer Olympics, and also fell upon Austrian works and composers after the *Anschluss* in 1938.[28] Following the conference known as the 'Reichsverband der jüdischen Kulturbünde' (5–7 September 1936), the Kulturbund promoted originally Jewish work with an increased commitment.[29] Notably, therefore, Jewish texts constitute nearly the smallest portion of Kowalski's settings, barring his four *Lieder auf Englische Texte* (1941–46), and a single translation from Danish called 'Im Garten des Serails,' Op. 3, No. 5 (1913).[30]

With all that said, determining to which exact 'brand' of 'exoticism' Kowalski ultimately subscribed is complicated, given that he had set non-German and non-Western poetry prior to 1933. Moreover, he had studied with Bernhard Sekles, who – consistent with a larger aesthetic trend in German culture dating back to at least the late 18th century – had himself set poems inspired by

---

performances, yet, likely occurred at private house concerts. The foregoing is noted also in Neubert, 'Max Kowalski's *Japanischer Frühling*', 70.

26 Kowal, 'Erinnerungen', 191; The heading of the manuscript's typewritten table of contents reads: 'Dem lieben Mitata | zum Geburtstag | ein kleines Liederheft | vom | Onkel Max | 2. April 1936'.

27 Holzmair, 'Werkkatalog', in *Facetten I*, 249, 259 lists seven Heine songs (a group of six plus one individual setting).

28 Holzmair, 'Kulturbund', 157; 'Concert Programs,' Leo Baeck Institute Center for Jewish History, 'Guide to the Papers of Max Kowalski (1882–1956), 1909–1978, AR7049/ MF 724', processed by Viola Voss, Series III: Musical Career, 1922–1956, Box 1, Folder 51. From 1935 onward, concert programs show a decline in the presentation of Kowalski's pre-1934 works, barring songs that set texts originating in other languages, such as the *Goethe-*, *Verlaine-* and *Pierrot-Lieder*.

29 Holzmair, 'Kulturbund', 155.

30 The foregoing is noted also in Neubert, 'Max Kowalski's *Japanischer Frühling*', 41.

(and adapted from) poets in other languages and cultures, for instance those of Friedrich Rückert (1788–1866) and Georg Friedrich Daumer (1800–1875).[31] And then, of course, there was also a kind of 'escapism' prevalent throughout the early 20th century that turned away from the grim realities at home to engage with beauty (and peace) farther afield.[32] Considering Kowalski's oeuvre in its entirety, it would seem that his inspirations were ultimately just as much aesthetic in nature as they were at times pragmatic, for he continued to set Eastern texts in exile, and why would he have done so if not out of personal affinity?[33]

The lyrics to the fourteen *Kinderlieder*, which were composed between 24 March and 12 April 1936 and are set for medium voice and piano, fit into this context insofar as their authors are, as yet, anonymous. The songs take the seeming simplicity of their surface from that of the rhymes themselves, all of which are set in major keys: A – G – G – E♭ – D – G – F – B♭ – E♭ – G – F – G – B♭ – B♭.[34] As for their musical meters, half of the songs are in 2/4, four in 4/4, two in 3/4, and one in 6/8 – in an assortment of tempi and characters that range from standard German and Italian markings to instructions such as 'Langsam und innig,' or 'Polkatempo.' Most of the melodies remain largely diatonic, though not entirely without some light chromatic inflection, or the kind of subtle text/word-painting that is emblematic of Kowalski's more serious compositions, particularly in those songs that feature animals like the rooster and finch (Song 2, 'Unser Hans hat Hosen an' [Our Hans is wearing pants]), the wolves (Song 3, 'Eins, zwei – Polizei' [One, two – police]), the snail (Song 5, 'Ei, wie langsam' [Ah, how slowly]), the goat (Song 6, 'Es ging ein' Zieg' [There went a goat]), and the cat and mouse (Song 9, 'Grau, grau Mäuschen' [Grey, grey little mouse]). Since the melodies also tend to favour the mediant and dominant scale degrees (rather than the tonic), they are certainly less 'on the nose' than one might otherwise expect in the context of children's songs; moreover, occasional musical and expressive markings seem to nod beyond the conventional characteristics of the genre. While all songs but Song 4, 'Hans, mein Sohn, was machst du da?' (Hans, my son, what are you doing [there]?), begin without any pianistic introduction, seven of the fourteen songs (Nos. 4, 5, 8, 9, 11, 12, and 13) contain brief, whimsical postludes, all but that of Song 12, 'Meine Mu' (My

---

31   Dorothea Hofmann, 'Das "Eigene" und das "Andere"', in *Facetten 1*, 231.
32   *Ibid.*, 229.
33   A slightly more detailed discussion of the foregoing appears in Neubert, 'Max Kowalski's *Japanischer Frühling*', 39–42.
34   Twelve songs (composed between 24 March and 2 April and dedicated on the latter date) are listed and numbered on the typewritten table of contents of the manuscript, later extended by two songs (7 and 9, listed as 6a and 7a, respectively, in handwriting) that were composed on 10 and 12 April, most likely in Frankfurt.

Mo[ther]), marked as *Tänzchen* (little dance),[35] in which the piano 'allows the child to listen in recurrent delight.'[36] Kowalski's inclusion of such a dance in Song 11, 'Hänschen, willst du tanzen' (Little Hans, would you like to dance) – in which the child in the text actually refuses to dance – is among the numerous musical and textual 'winks' that can be enjoyed across this collection.

One should note the relative breadth of atmosphere in these 'children's songs', which feature humour ranging from innocently playful to gently biting, and even lighthearted (yet wistful) hints of romance. Song 4, 'Hans, mein Sohn,' and Song 14, 'Wiegenlied' (Cradle song) have slightly more chromatic middle sections in the minor mode and thus a somewhat more 'grown-up' dimension to them. The overall range of the collection (A3 in Song 5, 'Ei, wie langsam,' to F5 in Song 8, 'Denkt ihr denn' [So you think]) is comparatively wide – be it in the treble voice(s) for which it is scored, or down an octave – and Kowalski's jocular leaps of sevenths and tritones, too, seem unconventional.[37] The opening song, 'Ich hab mir mein Kindel' (I have [laid] my little child [gently to sleep]), has a hymn-like character, while many others (Nos. 2, 4, 5, 6, 8, 9, 11, and 12) are expectedly merry and childlike. Song 7, 'Grete Müller heiß' ich' (My name is Grete Müller), nestles one of the more unexpected text passages of the collection, ('Wenn ich sterb, dann bin ich tot, begräbt man mich unter Rosen rot' [When I die, then I am dead, and they'll bury me beneath red roses]), in an almost 'Schlager'-like cantabile with a rising melismatic conclusion that appears to represent the girl's ascent to heaven, accompanied by singing angels. Song 10, 'Rote Kirschen ess' ich gern' (I like to eat red cherries), and Song 13, 'Guten Abend, Ännele' (Good evening, Ännele [Annie]), appear to be musicopoetic hybrids of children's song and popular love song, and in Song 3, 'Eins, zwei – Polizei,' Kowalski sets one of many traceable versions of a traditional German nursery rhyme of unknown authorship. The concluding, waltz-like 'Wiegenlied' – the cover of which includes a separate, handwritten dedication to Michael Kowal on his birthday – stands out in the collection as a bonafide *Lied* tastefully infused with popular flair (a flavour that Kowalski always employed judiciously, but excelled at, even in his serious works), with a more expansive, chromatically inflected cantilena, fuller range and texture in the piano, a more serious – even philosophic – turn of text and music in its

---

35   Sectional division is implied in the manuscript of Song 12, thus the marking may have been omitted inadvertently.
36   Kowal, 'Erinnerungen', 191.
37   Pitches are given here in Scientific Pitch Notation (SPN, also known as American Standard Pitch Notation [ASPN], or International Pitch Notation [IPN]).

middle section, and a real sense of 'finale.'[38] In sum, this collection of delightful and elegant miniatures is imbued with many of the compositional and stylistic hallmarks typical of Kowalski's *Lieder*, if – appropriately – not with the same expressive density. Michael Kowal adds:

> [The *Kinderlieder* contain] some of his happiest inspirations. [...] Here, as perhaps only in his jazz-influenced piano pieces, Kowalski speaks with a directness unhedged by irony, full of sweetness and humorous sympathy. It is, in my opinion, genuine popular music in the sense of appealing to people at every level of musical intelligence, and had these miniatures been able to be published when written, they might have found their audience and enjoyed the [widespread] appreciation they deserve.[39]

2 1950: New York

The next reunion between uncle and nephew would not occur until fourteen years later in Kew Gardens, a central neighbourhood in the New York City borough of Queens, where Oscar Kowal had come with his family in May of 1938 to find refuge from the exceeding threats in his homeland, and had managed to rebuild a gainful career within New York's recovering post-depression business market.[40] This time, Kowalski was visiting from London, and the middle brother, Bernhard (1884–?), was visiting from São Paulo (Brazil), where he – the first of the three brothers to leave Germany – had emigrated in 1936, following incarceration at the Dachau concentration camp in 1935.[41] Kowalski, who had 'endured a great deal' by the time of this reunion, had himself been arrested following *Kristallnacht*, incarcerated at the Buchenwald concentration camp from 11–27 November 1938, and had been released under the condition that he relinquish his estate and leave Germany.[42] With the permitted amount of ten Reichsmark to his name, he left for London in late March 1939, where his daughter Vera (1922–2007) had been staying with relatives since February of

---

38 The handwritten cover sheet reads: 'Wiegenlied | dem lieben Mitata gewidmet | zum 2. April 1936 | vom | Onkel Max'.
39 Kowal, 'Max Kowalski', 12.
40 Raab Hansen, 'Max Kowalski', Personendaten.
41 *Ibid.*
42 *Ibid.*; Kowal, 'Erinnerungen', 192; Kowal, 'Max Kowalski', 13. Kowal considers the possibility that Kowalski remained in Germany as late as he did to protect his mother, who was still living in Berlin, and/or that his Polish birth may have restricted the opportunities for an exit visa.

the previous year.[43] While London had initially been intended as a stopover on the longer journey to the United States, Kowalski resolved to remain there after missing a transfer ship.[44]

Despite the relative safety that England provided, Kowalski's new life there was not without considerable professional and personal hardships. Disbarred in Germany in 1938[45] (he would further be stripped of his German doctorate in 1940),[46] he had entered England as a musician, that is, in the third of four ranked categories of professional significance.[47] At least initially, his adjustment to his new home country, its language and its customs, was somewhat complicated by the fact that he had attended a humanistic grammar school in Germany that focused on Latin and Greek, rather than on English.[48] Already in his late fifties when he reached London, he appears to have faced greater challenges establishing himself than some of his junior colleagues.[49] Britain's declaration of war on 3 September 1939 rendered all refugee visas invalid, and also brought with it rising xenophobia and antisemitism.[50] Austro-German musicians who settled in England during this period were at times subject to a kind of double standard in that they were respected as performers and educators, but kept at arm's length, professionally speaking, and being a composer primarily of German Lieder would have played a part in Kowalski's predicaments.[51] Like many, he was affected by the BBC's 1940 Ban on Alien Composers, the resulting professional fallout of which is difficult to determine.[52] Above all

---

43 Raab Hansen, 'Max Kowalski', Personendaten; Holzmair, 'Max Kowalski: Daten', 150; Schader, "Neben meinem Hauptberuf", 5.
44 Holzmair, 'Max Kowalski: Daten', 153.
45 Raab Hansen, 'Max Kowalski', Personendaten.
46 *Ibid.*, Verfolgung/Exil; Schader, abstract to 'Max Kowalski', in *Komponisten der Gegenwart* (Munich: edition text + kritik, forthcoming – my thanks to Dr Schader for sharing the abstract with me prior to publication of the article), 1. See also, Michael Hepp, (ed.), *Die Ausbürgerung deutscher Staatsangehöriger 1933–45 nach den im Reichsanzeiger veröffentlichten Listen*, 3 Volumes (Munich: Saur, 1985, 1988). Kowalski became a British citizen after the end of the war in 1945.
47 Holzmair, 'Max Kowalski: Daten', 150; Gradenwitz, 49 (see note 14).
48 Gradenwitz, 49.
49 Raab Hansen, 'NS-verfolgte Musiker in England von 1933 bis 1946: "What the politicians spoil, the artists repair!"', in *Facetten 1*, 123–135.
50 *Ibid.*, 130f.
51 *Ibid.*, 126; Holzmair, 'Max Kowalski: Daten', 150; Raab Hansen, *NS-verfolgte Musiker in England: Spuren deutscher und österreichischer Flüchtlinge in der britischen Musikkultur* (Hamburg: Von Bockel, 1996), 436. Kowalski's music was presented by the Freier Deutscher Kulturbund, one of several holding centers for refugee musicians founded in London shortly before the war.
52 Raab Hansen, 'NS-verfolgte Musiker', 133.

though, a total of seventeen family members would ultimately fall victim to the horrors of Nazi Germany, including Kowalski's first wife, Anna (by suicide in October of 1938, following multiple incarcerations beginning in January of 1937), and his mother, who had stayed behind in Germany following the emigration of her three sons and perished in the Theresienstadt ghetto sometime after January 1943.[53]

Kowalski now earned his livelihood as a freelance musician, teaching, singing in the choir of a synagogue, and tuning pianos[54] – a newly learned craft 'in which he was soon in demand as an expert.'[55] He was also active as a copyist, pianist, cabaret performer, opera chorister, composer of incidental music, and conductor.[56] Over time, he built a reputation as a respected singing teacher and répétiteur, and his clients – some on the roster at the Royal Opera House at Covent Garden[57] – included the German bass-baritone Hans Hotter (1909–2003), who reportedly worked with Kowalski during engagements in London after the war, and performed and recorded his songs.[58] Outside the singing profession, Kowalski's social circle in postwar London included, among others, the pianist Artur Schnabel (1881–1951), and the conductors Bruno Walter (1876–1962), Otto Klemperer (1885–1973), and Erich Kleiber (1890–1956).[59]

As he struggled to stay afloat and gradually established himself professionally during the months and years following his arrival in England, Kowalski's compositional activities remained on hiatus until after the war.[60] They resumed in what can be characterised as a final, extended outpouring following his marriage to his second wife Gertrud Remak in 1946, even without the prospect of new publications, which would not occur again until the early 21st century, despite the sometimes repeated efforts by musical colleagues in and outside of

---

53 Gradenwitz, 49; Raab Hansen, 'Max Kowalski', Personendaten; Holzmair, 'Max Kowalski: Daten', 141, 150. Kowalski and his wife had been living in separation since the late 1920s.
54 Raab Hansen, 'NS-verfolgte Musiker', 126.
55 Kowal, 'Max Kowalski', 13.
56 Holzmair, 'Max Kowalski: Daten', 152; Kowal, 'Max Kowalski', 13; Schader, abstract to 'Max Kowalski', 1.
57 Gradenwitz, 50.
58 Schader, abstract to 'Max Kowalski', 1.
59 Holzmair, 'Max Kowalski: Daten', 153.
60 His earlier London-based compositions are *Ein Liederzyklus auf Vierzeiler der Omar Chajjam* (1941), *Sieben Lieder auf chinesische Gedichte* (1947, first song composed in 1939), *Lieder auf englische Texte* (1941–1946), the *Kleine Suite für Klarinette* (1947), and a single setting of Bethge's titled 'Ihre Locken' (1947), a recent edition of which by Tobias Bröker can be viewed at https://www.tobias-broeker.de/rare-manuscripts/g-l/kowalski-max/, [accessed: 21.07.2021].

the United Kingdom.[61] Nevertheless, selections from his *Pierrot Lunaire* were orchestrated in 1946 by Max Rudolf (1902–1995) in the United States, and there were sporadic radio broadcasts of his music in Germany following the war.[62]

During his visit to New York in 1950 – which would also be the last time that all three brothers would come together – Kowalski brought with him the *Acht Lieder auf Gedichte von Hafis* of 1948 (adaptations by Klabund set from 3 October to 11 November of that year), which is his second collection setting the Persian bard and mystic Hafez (Xāwje Shams-od-Dīn Moḥammad Ḥāfeẓ-e Shīrāzī [1315–1390]).[63] They are predominantly love poems, both sacred and secular in tone, in which the first and last song form a kind of philosophical (and, if subtly, musicopoetic) frame around the inner six,[64] which traverse romantic love (Songs 2–5), love that transcends life and death (Song 6), and the solace of song in life and death (Song 7). The cycle ultimately describes the letting go of love in the physical form of other and self, resulting in the acceptance of one's own ephemerality. Michael Kowal notes that in this work, which effectively ushers in Kowalski's late period, we see for the first time a kind of farewell to life.[65]

Most of the songs contain introductions and/or postludes of varying length and elaboration, the very first introduction marked 'Wie in wehmütiger Erinnerung an ferne Zeiten' (As in wistful memory of distant times). In many places, the piano gently doubles the voice. Tonally, the collection hovers

---

61   Kowal, 'Max Kowalski', 13, recalls her as 'a strong-minded, practical, and efficient woman from a solid middle-class Berlin background, who supplied [Kowalski's] restless temperament with a foundation of well-regulated domesticity.' She is also listed under her name from her first (widowed) marriage, 'Gertrude Blumenfeld-Remak,' in Martini, *Musik als Form geistigen Widerstandes*, 231; 'Holde, Artur', Leo Baeck Institute Center for Jewish History, 'Guide to the Papers of Max Kowalski (1882–1956), 1909–1978, AR 7049 / MF 724', processed by Viola Voss, Series II: Correspondence, 1910–1957, Box 1, Folder 20.

62   See reference to *Pierrot* and Max Rudolf's orchestration in note 22; two sources point to a broadcast on a Munich radio station in April 1949: 'Reviews – Loose', Leo Baeck Institute Center for Jewish History, 'Guide to the Papers of Max Kowalski (1882–1956), 1909–1978, AR 7049 / MF 724', processed by Viola Voss, Series III: Musical Career, 1922–1956, Box 1, Folder 53; 'Rostal, Max', Leo Baeck Institute Center for Jewish History, 'Guide to the Papers of Max Kowalski (1882–1956), 1909–1978, AR 7049 / MF 724', processed by Viola Voss, Series II: Correspondence, 1910–1957, Box 1, Folder 38.

63   The earlier *Sieben Gedichte von Hafis* (adaptations by Daumer) of 1933 are labeled as Op. 18 and were thus clearly intended to follow the publication of the *Sechs Lieder aus dem Westöstlichen Divan von Goethe*, Op. 17, which was to be his last. Another collection that met with the same fate is the *Vier Schäferlieder*, Op. 19, extended by three songs that same year, reordered, and titled *Rokoko-Lieder*. Both collections are also referred to in note 21.

64   Kowal, 'Erinnerungen', 192.

65   *Ibid.*

around F♯ minor and its relative major and chromatic mediant (f♯ – f♯ – A – A – a – f♯ – f♯ – f♯), and while Kowalski does use the same tonic and related textures in several adjacent songs, his range of moods, tempi, meters, and emotional atmospheres reflect the poetry's own sense of simultaneous variety and unification. In Holzmair's words:

> [Kowalski] lends his creative talents [to the wise sayings of the greatest lyric poet in the Persian tongue, Hafez (ca. 1320–1389)], and brings forth a West-Eastern Divan in eight short songs with often exquisitely spare means, the majority of which are in minor keys. A heading for the whole could be taken from the lyrics of the seventh song: 'All that comes to pass is but suffering and song.' Man can be joyful and without grievance only when he leaves behind his flawed actions and overcomes (self)love. Then Allah will smile upon him 'so mellifluously.'[66]

Besides their key, Song 1 ('So lange wir im Licht sind' [So long as we are in the light]) and Song 2 ('Bülbül singt im Rosengarten' [Bulbul sings in the rose garden]) also share the meter of 3/4. However, whereas the lyrical Song 1 (Poco lento) ruminates on the alternation of light and darkness in life giving way to eternal sunlight in death, Song 2 (Allegretto) moves from daytime to nighttime as it anthropomorphises the longing – and perhaps the impending rendezvous – of the Persian nightingale *Bülbül*. A musicalised call with a lilting hint of hemiola at the end of each but its final iteration alternates with waltz-like textures throughout this 'scene' of two pages, where it first serves as the song's pianistic introduction, then underpins a couple of text passages in which the poet alludes to the bird's plea and/or verbalises its own supplication to the yearned-for beloved ('Liebes Kind, lass mich nicht länger warten' [Dear child, don't make me wait any longer]), and is finally fragmented in a brief postlude. Song 3, 'In meinen Schläfen jagt das Blut' (Blood is coursing in my temples; Allegro assai e con brio in 4/4 with a recurring pattern of 4/4+2/4), has gushing, continuous chordal triplets in the right hand, supported by walking (largely chromatic) lines in the left, which are interrupted at the climactic

---

66   Holzmair, 'Ein Max Kowalski Liederabend aus Sicht des Interpreten', in *Facetten I*, 243: '[Kowalski] leiht [den Lebensweisheiten des größten Lyrikers persischer Zunge, Hafis (ca. 1320–1389)] sein schöpferisches Talent und fördert so mit oft äußerst sparsamen Mitteln einen West-Östlichen Divan in acht kurzen Liedern zutage, von denen die meisten in Moll stehen. Über dem Ganzen könnten die Worte aus dem siebenten Lied stehen: *Alles, was geschieht, ist nur Leid und Lied*. Glücklich und ohne Beschwerde wird der Mensch erst sein, wenn er sein fehlerhaftes Tun abstreift und die (Selbst)Liebe überwindet. Dann wird Allah ihm lächeln "so lieblich"'.

'Suleikas (Lippe)' (Suleika's [lip]), and before the postlude. This basic texture is retained (though now in 9/8 and 'Langsam') to support the romantic cantabile of Song 4, 'Mein Auge ist nur dazu da' (My eyes exist for one purpose alone). Song 5, the both ecstatic and dulcet 'Allah lächelt mir' (Allah smiles upon me), returns to *Allegretto* in a somewhat provocatively mellow play on compound meters (primarily 9/8 with several measures and shorter phrases in 6/8, and a measure each in 12/8 and 3/8), its inner section turning to the parallel major, and presenting several quasi-exotic effects such as a Phrygian supertonic and subtle flourishes in the piano. The song concludes with an extended postlude. Song 6, 'Mein Wille ist so schwach' (My will is so feeble), a form of recitative in 6/8 marked 'Molto moderato et [sic] espressivo,' initiates the final three-song arc in F♯ minor with lyrical fragments (several of which are uttered a cappella) that turn into more connected phrases. Further momentum is gained in the waltz-like Song 7, 'Alles was geschieht' (All that comes to pass; Andante sostenuto), the first nine bars of which are underlaid melodically by the left hand alone, and the postlude of which is preceded by another unaccompanied line, 'Dann lächle du' (Then you shall smile) – a device which, as noted above, is also employed in Song 6, as well as earlier on in Songs 2–4. The cycle's concluding song, 'Nun bin ich ohn' Beschwerde' (Now I am without burden), echoes Song 1 on several levels, most literally through its identical tonality and, less audibly so, in its poetic meter (iambic trimeter).[67] The songs are further connected by a shared theme of death and transcendence, a broad, nostalgic cantilena – which in both songs begins with an outlined descent from dominant to tonic – and even a subtle figurative and colouristic reference to the piano introduction of Song 1 in its fourteenth measure, amid a turn to D minor on the words 'Und was ich je gelitten um dich und deinen Tod, ist von mir abgeglitten wie Rauch im Abendrot' (And all that I ever suffered over you and your death has slipped from me like smoke in sunset). A rousing turn back to F♯ minor ushers in what Michael Kowal considers one of the most poignant passages across Kowalski's works, on the words 'Gesühnt ist meine Fehle. Gott will mir Gutes tun.' (My sins have been atoned for. God wishes to be good to me.), and which in his estimation might even be indicative of Kowalski's own religious attitudes:

> His lineage was Jewish, which shaped him profoundly, but he didn't want to be altogether confined by this. He remained a seeker spiritually, at

---

[67] Kowalski rarely emphasises poetic meter over syntax in his songs (neither does Klabund in his poems). As such, Song 1 is set in 3/4, whereas Song 8 is in 6/8 with three momentary turns to 9/8.

least to the extent that within the artistic realm his scope included songs of the Virgin Mary, as well as Jewish and far-Eastern spirituality.[68]

In addition to these songs, Kowalski also presented his nephew, at that time a burgeoning clarinetist, with yet another musical gift dedicated to him, the cheerful *Kleine Suite für Klarinette und Pianoforte* (composed in 1947), which, as Kowal notes, stands in contrast to Kowalski's more serious works, and thus may have been an enjoyable diversion for the composer, who was known for his sense of humour.[69] A reference in the journal *Aufbau*, a publication of the German-Jewish Club in New York City from 15 September 1950, reads:

> One of the best representatives of contemporary lyricism, Max Kowalski, who relocated from Frankfurt to London after Hitler's takeover, and is currently staying in New York, has the great gratification that his songs and song cycles are once again frequently performed in European – especially German – concert halls and radio stations with great success. The 'Pierrot Lunaire-Lieder,' which had been among his most often-sung works, are back at the top. Also frequently performed are his Chinese and Japanese songs.[70]

That this reference was clearly the outcome of an interview or correspondence with the paper in 1950 attests to the fact that, in addition to the meaningful and long-awaited family reunion, this visit also ended up having some professional significance for Kowalski.[71]

---

68 Kowal, 'Erinnerungen', 192f: 'Er entstammte dem Judentum und war davon tief geprägt, wollte sich jedoch nicht völlig davon begrenzen lassen. Er blieb spirituell ein Suchender, in dem Maße, dass wenigstens auf künstlerischem Gebiet sein Spektrum sowohl Marienlieder als auch jüdische und fernöstliche Geistigkeit umschloss.'
69 *Ibid.*
70 Anon., 'Max Kowalski', *Aufbau* 16/37 (1950), 14. The Leo Baeck Institute stores digital copies of *Aufbau* at 'Aufbau (New York, 1934–2004)', https://archive.org/details/aufbau. The clipping is located at 'Reviews – Loose', Leo Baeck Institute Center for Jewish History, 'Guide to the Papers of Max Kowalski (1882–1956), 1909–1978, AR 7049 / MF 724', processed by Viola Voss, Series III: Musical Career, 1922–1956, Box 1, Folder 53: 'Einer der besten Vertreter zeitgenössischer musikalischer Lyrik, Max Kowalski, der nach Hitlers Machtergreifung seinen Wohnsitz von Frankfurt am Main nach London verlegte und augenblicklich in New York weilt, hat die grosse Genugtuung, dass seine Lieder und Gesangszyklen in den europäischen und speziell in den deutschen Konzertsälen und Sendestationen wieder häufig mit starkem Erfolg zur Aufführung gelangen. Die "Pierrot Lunaire"-Lieder, die zu den meistgesugenen Werken Kowalskis zählten, stehen wieder an erster Stelle. Viel aufgeführt werden ausserdem seine Chinesischen und Japanischen Lieder.'
71 See also, Neubert, 'Max Kowalski's *Japanischer Frühling*', 78f.

3   1955: London and Geneva

In the summer of 1955 – prior to spending a year in Florence, Italy, as a Fulbright scholar – Michael Kowal visited Max Kowalski and his wife in London. During this stay of several weeks, he witnessed his uncle's active career, success, and popularity as a singing teacher and vocal coach, who was also enjoying a certain recognition for his compositions.[72] Radio broadcasts and concerts had occurred in Germany on the occasion of Kowalski's seventieth birthday in 1952.[73] Nevertheless, Kowal also became aware of Kowalski's more melancholy side during this visit, which had usually been concealed by a jovial aura.[74] According to the works catalogue (see note 11), Kowalski had not composed any new works since 1954. The *Arabische Nächte* (1953/1954) would remain his final completed composition, prior to which – in addition to setting poetry originating in Japanese, Indian, and Arabic – he had drawn renewed inspiration from German-speaking poets including Conrad Ferdinand Meyer (1825–1898), Friedrich Hölderlin (1770–1843), Stefan George (1868–1933), and Rainer Maria Rilke (1875–1926).[75] Michael Kowal contrasts these latter four collections with the lighter and more lyrical Eastern-themed works:

> These cycles display again the integrity of tone and text, of emotional and musical construction [...], but now reinforced with a certain austerity, even harshness, the melodic line stripped to its essence, yet rich in expressive force and technical skill.[76]

Kowalski composed the *Sieben Lieder auf Gedichte von Rainer Maria Rilke* between 17 January and 3 July 1951, following his visit to the Kowals in New York.[77] Holzmair contextualises this important late achievement:

---

72   Kowal, 'Erinnerungen', 192.
73   Kowal, e-mail message to author, 24 May 2016.
74   Kowal, 'Erinnerungen', 192.
75   Kowal, 'Max Kowalski', 14, offers the notion that the end of the war and renewed contacts with Germany, 'now freed from the Nazi curse', may have inspired Kowalski's eventual return to setting German poetry.
76   Kowal, 'Max Kowalski', 14f.
77   The *Rilke-Lieder* were published with Recital Publications, and the individual dates of composition, which Kowalski customarily entered on the cover of each manuscript/fair copy, are provided at the end of each song in the edition. The other works from this final period are: *Sechs Lieder auf Gedichte von Friedrich Hölderlin* (1950/51), *Sieben Geisha-Lieder* (1951), *Sechs Lieder auf indische Gedichte* (1951–52), *Fünf Lieder auf Gedichte von Stefan George* (1952), and *Arabische Nächte: Sieben Lieder auf arabische Gedichte* (1953/54), of which the *Hölderlin-* and *Geisha-Lieder* were published by Schott in 2017 (see note 22).

Rilke's poems are music in and of themselves, rich with the melodies and images of language. The poet himself was opposed to their being set to music. When one reads the poems or recites them aloud, one understands why it is so difficult to construe them musically: the music of their language! Few composers have succeeded in setting Rilke. Kowalski belongs to this elect circle. In the best of altogether seven musical settings of Rilke poems, he achieves a depth of feeling and therefore an expansion of expression that constitute a real summit in his already impressive oeuvre.[78]

While Kowalski remains true to his previous compositional maxims, the 'Rilke-Lieder' do display some subtle points of evolution. For one thing, the piano part contains notably fewer doublings of the vocal line, and the collection also has a more varied tonal plan in which no two adjacent songs share the same tonic, many songs involve mixture of mode, and three songs begin and end in different tonalities: e/E(→C♯) – A♭ – c – f(F) – a(~>E) – A♭ – c♯ (→B). Beyond the realm of explicit text/word-painting and musical scene-setting that Kowalski surely also inhabits, it is perhaps through his less than usual use of tonality and modality here that he both allows and dares the listener, on a musical level, to grapple with the meanings of Rilke's poems, almost as a reader would when reading them. Correspondingly, passages that are more expressive or narrative than they are reflective or seeking – as well as each song to its own degree – tend to be held together tonally in such a way as suffices to remain unmistakably clear in statement and aspect. This layer (and polarity) of expression allows Kowalski to change 'tone' in ways that, as needed, can give the impression of being closer to recitation (albeit sung) than to lyrical singing.

As in previous works, the melodies tend to eschew the tonic scale degree, favouring the mediant, dominant, and submediant instead, and, like the Hafez settings, most of these songs feature varied types of introductions and postludes. Kowalski also continues to employ common meters: five of the seven Rilke songs are in 4/4 (though occasionally inflected with individual measures in 2/4 or 5/4 [Song 6]), and again we see the mixture of compound meters in

---

78   Holzmair, 'Ein Max Kowalski Liederabend', 242f: 'Rilkes Gedichte für sich genommen sind schon Musik, reich an Sprachmelodie und -bildern. Der Dichter selbst stand ihrer Vertonung ablehnend gegenüber. Liest man die Gedichte oder rezitiert sie laut, versteht man, warum es so schwierig ist, sie musikalisch zu deuten: ihre eigene Sprachmusik! Wenigen Komponisten glückten Rilke-Lieder. Kowalski gehört zu diesem Kreis der auserwählten. In den besten der insgesamt Sieben in Musik gesetzten Gedichten Rilkes erreicht er eine Tiefe der Empfindung und damit eine Erweiterung des Ausdrucks, die in seinem an sich schon beeindruckenden Werk einen echten Höhepunkt darstellt.'

Songs 2 and 4, both of which are in 9/8 with individual bars or shorter passages in 12/8 and 6/8.

Song 1, the solitary and reflective 'Vigilie' (Vigil) a syllabic setting ('Langsam') in E (mixture of mode is likely employed here to bring out the poetic contrast of [moon]light and darkness), excurses to the mediant G♯, which, after momentary stations on B and A, prepares the conclusion on the submediant C♯. Luitgard Schader's description – of a decorated recitation in a late-romantic tonal language and through-composed form, in which rhythm, meter, and tessitura emerge from the text – comes to mind.[79] The renascent cantabile of Song 2, 'Aus einem April' (From an April [Once in April]), is ushered in by an introduction that utilises the enharmonic exchange from G♯ to A♭ (again in both modes), and the call of a lark receives pianistic allusion in bar 9. A more chromatic and briefly dramatic middle section finds repose in the retransition to A♭ via its secondary dominant B♭, and the song concludes with a brief postlude. We are torn from this first atmospheric arc by the brooding pianistic introduction ('Ziemlich bewegt' in 4/4, marked '*pp* (geisterhaft)' [ghostly]), of 'Ernste Stunde' (Solemn hour). This material functions as a kind of structural (and tonal) marker between the strophes that gives way to a stentorian declamation in which each strophe reaches a sobering, self-reflective realisation – a sort of uncanny 'punch-line,' if you will – in a new tonality (c~>g~>f♯~>c), and whose final utterance is followed by a defiant postlude marked *fff*.

We return to Kowalski's (and Rilke's) more introspective side in 'Immer wieder' (Time and again), a recitational musing on familiar and devoted togetherness (Molto moderato) that blends compound meters in F minor and concludes in F major, from which we are once again torn by the wild, proud, and martial pianistic texture of 'Der Panther' (The panther, 'Bewegt, aber nicht zu schnell' in 4/4), which like the caged animal makes attempts to leave its 'home' of A minor towards F♯ minor and G♯ minor, but transitions into a slower, more somber and resigned second part in A minor that settles towards E unstably and unresolved. In a floating melodic descent, we reach what to this author ranks among Kowalski's most tender, warmhearted, and touching creations, the 'Liebeslied' (love song) in A♭ major ('Langsam und mit tiefer Empfindung' [slow and with deep feeling]), which blends parlando and cantabile in its pensively intimate poem. In the concluding passage 'Auf welches Instrument sind wir gespannt? Und welcher Spieler hat uns in der Hand?' (Upon which instrument are we strung? And what player has us in his hand?), Kowalski paints the text with a lowered submediant (♭6) and an arrival on iii – elements that seem

---

79   Schader, abstract to 'Max Kowalski', 2.

to function here as the musical equivalents for the literary question marks in Rilke's existential contemplation.[80] The cycle concludes with the mystical and dramatic 'Der Ast vom Baume Gott' (The branch from the tree [of] God), which like 'Der Panther' comprises contrasting sections, the first a fateful declamation in C♯ minor, the second turning inward at first in C♯ major to reach a first climax on F♯ major, followed by a plaintive turn to B minor, and a triumphant processional in B major that – instead of giving in to the conspicuous temptation of a grand conclusion – fades in a gradated *diminuendo* from *forte* to *pianissimo* over seven bars.

The 1955 summer visit also included get-togethers with Kowalski's daughter Vera, and his sister-in-law from his first marriage, Tilly, who with her husband, Dr Georg Neumann (George Newman in England), had looked after a fifteen-year-old Vera during the early London days (1938/39).[81] Reportedly, Kowalski, who had taken a liking to English ways, was at this time in contact with the BBC and continued to engage in lively correspondence with old musical comrades in Germany, many of whom enjoyed visiting him in his comfortable home at 22 Adamson Road NW3, Swiss Cottage.[82] Indeed, Kowal notes that the early 1950s were evidently the first and only time in Kowalski's life that he was able to devote himself completely to music, and under agreeable circumstances:[83]

> The composer's last years appear to have been spent in an atmosphere of domestic calm and professional contentment. He had become a sought-after singing teacher and vocal coach, his works could once again be heard in concerts and on the radio in Germany and in England, and his house, thanks to the social talents of his wife, became a center of hospitality for many visitors.[84]

Michael Kowal would meet his uncle for the final time later that summer in Geneva, Switzerland, where the children of Kowalski's second wife were living with their respective spouses. One recollected piece of characteristically avuncular advice shared during this get-together was to 'refrain from making any

---

80 Rilke's original has the word *Geiger* (violinist), which Kowalski has as *Spieler* (player).
81 Raab Hansen, 'Max Kowalski', Personendaten.
82 Kowal, 'Erinnerungen', 193; Anon., 'KOWALSKI', *Jewish Chronicle*, 22 June 1956, 2. My thanks to Jutta Raab Hansen and Malcolm Miller for this reference.
83 Kowal, 'Erinnerungen', 192.
84 Kowal, 'Max Kowalski', 15.

uncalled-for comparisons between Geneva and London.'[85] Kowalski died the following year, on 4 June 1956, in London.[86]

In brief conclusion, it is encouraging to note that, owing to a sometimes delicate yet unbroken thread of engagement and support over nearly seven decades, Kowalski's music has begun to reclaim a place in the artistic, scholarly, and transnational cultural consciousness of our time that was ultimately (if not entirely) denied to him in his. It is my hope that this essay will serve as yet another stimulus, resource, and point of departure for scholars and performers to delve into the compelling and moving life story and repertoire left behind by Max Kowalski, as there are numerous works and projects still awaiting and deserving a closer (and, in some cases, first) look. Greater clarity of Kowalski's London period, for instance, will undoubtedly emerge from a comprehensive study of his diaries (1939–1956), which have been digitised. Along with the manuscripts of hitherto unpublished songs and song collections, sketchbooks, and other documents and materials, they are in the private collection of Michael Kowal, to whom I would like to extend a final word of gratitude for his continued help at any and every turn of my research, and for his personal recollections that paved the way for this work.

---

85 Kowal, 'Erinnerungen', 193.
86 Anon., 'Kowalski', *Jewish Chronicle* (see note 82): 'On June 4th at the Westminster Hospital peacefully, the composer Dr. Max Kowalski of 22 Adamson Road NW3, Dearly beloved husband of Gertrud and loved by his brothers, brother-in-law, daughter and son-in-law.'

13

Der österreichische Musiker Ferdinand Rauter als Musiktherapeut in Camphill bei Aberdeen in Schottland (1945 bis 1947)

Jutta Raab Hansen

Abstract

After their first concert 'Folksongs of many lands' in Hamburg 1929, the Icelandic singer Engel Lund and her Austrian pianist Ferdinand Rauter went to London in 1935, making it their headquarters for concerts in and outside of Great Britain. After the Austrian *Anschluss*, the Munich Treaty in 1938 and start of the Second World War in 1939, Rauter, well connected in émigré circles and in London musical life, successfully approached British colleagues and political officials to lighten the plight of the Austrian musicians, who were forbidden to work and even interned after May 1940. After staying in London during the war, in the fall of 1945 Rauter left for Camphill near Aberdeen. There he joined a project led by Dr Karl König from Vienna, involving Austrian refugees who, based on their experiences in Austria and Switzerland, lived and worked in a community for children with special needs from 1940, providing care for body and soul based on the anthroposophical precepts of Rudolf Steiner. Convinced that music could play a special role in treating these patients, Rauter became one of the earliest music therapists in Britain. The paper describes Rauter's relationship to anthroposophy and its representatives in Britain, and his varied experiences during his time in Camphill, the birthplace of the successful global movement characterised by its extraordinary ethos.

Der österreichische Pianist Ferdinand Rauter gehört im Zusammenhang mit dem Exil von deutschen und österreichischen Musikern zu den herausragenden Persönlichkeiten. Durch seine vielfältigen Kontakte als Mediator zwischen exilierten und einheimischen Musikern agierte er als deren Vertreter. Bei Verhandlungen mit Repräsentanten der britischen Regierung gehörte er ebenfalls zu den Initiatoren des Refugee Musicians Committee (1941) und der Austrian Musicians' Group (1942), aus der sich dann später die bis heute existierende Anglo-Austrian Music Society (1943) entwickeln sollte.[1] In verschiedenen Quellen wird zudem erwähnt,[2] dass Ferdinand Rauter nach dem Ende des Zweiten Weltkrieges einige Zeit als Musiktherapeut tätig war.[3] Er selbst schreibt dazu: ‚Im Dezember 1945 verließ ich London mit der Absicht, mich in Schottland in einem Heim für zurückgebliebene Kinder ganz der Musiktherapie zu widmen'.[4] Nichtsdestotrotz wird Rauter in verschiedenen Camphill-Publikationen als Mitarbeiter kaum erwähnt. Zum achtzigjährigen Jubiläum von Camphill Bewegung 2020 wird Rauter zwar als Musiker, nicht aber als Musiktherapeut gewürdigt.[5] Diese wertvolle Seite an Ferdinand Rauters Persönlichkeit, körperlich und seelisch eingeschränkte Kinder auf eine besondere Weise wahrzunehmen und sich ihnen zu ganz widmen, soll in diesem Aufsatz ihre Wertschätzung erfahren.

In überlieferten Camphill-Quellen fanden sich bisher kaum Belege zu Ferdinand Rauters Tätigkeit.[6] Genauere Einblicke konnten nur seine Tagebücher im Archiv der Paris-Lodron Universität Salzburg geben (Music und Migration Collections: ‚Ferdinand Rauter').[7] Glücklicherweise sind sie, die er von seinem zwölften bis zu seinem fünfundachtzigsten Lebensjahr führte,[8] fast vollzählig erhalten geblieben. In einen Taschenkalender protokollierte er nahezu kontinuierlich seinen Tagesablauf in Gabelsberger Kurzschrift. Diese Eintragungen wiederum mussten erst transkribiert werden, um sie auswerten zu können. Prof. Nils Grosch als Direktor des Archivs und seine Mitarbeiterin

---

1 Carolin Stahrenberg, ‚Ferdinand Rauter', in Claudia Maurer Zenck, Peter Petersen, Sophie Fetthauer (Hg.), *Lexikon verfolgter Musiker und Musikerinnen der NS-Zeit* (Hamburg: Universität Hamburg, 2017), https://www.lexm.uni-hamburg.de/object/lexm_lexmperson_00006054 [Zugang: 25.01.2021].
2 *Ibid.*
3 *Ibid.*; Richard Steel, 'Art in Community – Community as Art: Karl König's Therapeutic Impulse for the Illness of His – and Our – Time', 2020, https://www.karlkoeniginstitute.org/images/archive_documents/Art_in_Community.pdf [accessed: 27.09.22], 5; The Warth Mills Project online; www.warthmillsproject.com; Ferdinand Rauter, 80. Aus: Bericht von Ferdinand Rauter über dessen Internierung sowie die Entwicklung der Austrian Musicians' Group und Anglo-Austrian Music Society 1940–1973, o.D. (1973), 451f. MMCS Ferdinand Rauter, Box 3, 56 (3) ‚Die Presse', Artikel zum Tod Ferdinand Rauters mit Würdigung seiner Tätigkeiten.
4 Ferdinand Rauter, Aus: Bericht von Ferdinand Rauter, 451.
5 Vgl. Steel, Art in Community – Community as Art, 3.
6 Vgl. Karl König-Archiv in Kleinmachnow bei Berlin. An dieser Stelle möchte ich mich für die großzügige Unterstützung von Richard Steel, Autor und Direktor des Karl König Instituts für Kunst, Wissenschaft und Soziales Leben e.V. bedanken.
7 Die Sammlung in Salzburg umfasst die Jahre 1933 bis 1985. Die Jahrgänge 1936 und 1948 fehlen. E-Mail von Ulrike Dorothee Rapp vom 21.09.2022.
8 Andrea Rauter: Gedanken über meinen Vater ‚Rau' – Unveröffentl. Manuskript 2016.

Ulrike Dorothee Rapp ermöglichten dies mit großem persönlichem Einsatz. Finanzielle Zuwendungen des Harpner-Fund der Anglo-Austrian Society und des Österreichischen Zukunftsfonds unterstützten die Transkriptionen. Ihnen beiden und den genannten Stiftungen bin ich zu Dank verpflichtet. Andrea Rauter, Ferdinand Rauters Tochter, schulde ich außerdem großen Dank für die Erlaubnis, diese Tagebücher nutzen zu dürfen, soweit deren persönlicher Inhalt von der Familie freigegeben war. Sie stand mir außerdem für ein Interview im März 2020 in London zur Verfügung und beantwortete meine Fragen via E-Mail.

1 Lebensweg von Ferdinand Rauter bis 1945

Ferdinand Rauter wurde am 4. Juni 1902 in Klagenfurt in Österreich geboren. Eine frühe Prägung erfuhr der musikalische Knabe durch die Tätigkeit seines Vaters, Karl Leonhard Rauter, der an einer Blindenschule arbeitete. Als Ferdinand elf Jahre alt war, übernahm der Vater die Leitung der Blindenschule in Aussig an der Elbe, heute Ustí nad Labem in Tschechien: Seine Frau Katharina, geborene Lepuschitz, unterstützte ihn dabei. Ferdinand, der sich als begabter Klavierschüler erwies, wurde dort in das elterliche Berufsleben einbezogen: Er begleitete mitunter den Unterricht an seinem Instrument und trug bei Veranstaltungen der Schule Klavierstücke vor. Es folgte in Dresden ein Chemiestudium an der Technischen Hochschule und parallel dazu ein Musikstudium an der Orchesterschule der Sächsischen Staatskapelle. Daneben korrepetierte er der Tänzerin Mali Stürenburg bei ihren Auftritten. Von 1926 bis 1928 arbeitete er sowohl als Chor-Repetitor am Theater Münster als auch mit dem Choreographen Kurt Jooss, dem späteren England-Exilanten.[9] (Siehe hierzu auch in diesem Yearbook den Aufsatz von Barbara Busch.)

Ein Zufall gab dem Leben Rauters eine neue Richtung: Am 7. Dezember 1929 sprang der Pianist in Hamburg aus Anlass eines Liederabends der isländischen Sängerin Engel Lund mit der Groupo Franco Allemande ein (MMCS, Rauter Box 1, Index 1929–1948). Fortan blieb Rauter ihr Begleiter. Jahre später erinnerte er sich:

> I would never have thought when I walked through a wood in 1929 where the mushrooms grew in order to get something for the pot, that half an hour later I would meet a lady who was called Engel Lund and became actually decisive for my whole life. She came up with Ravel's Jewish Songs

---

9 Stahrenberg, ‚Ferdinand Rauter', in online *Lexikon verfolgter Musiker*, 2017.

and I had never heard them. When she stood there and sang, something happened, which was quite new to me. She transformed herself, she became a rabbi. I heard God's voice through her. It was so strong and so intense, that I said to her: 'I think, we should stay together all our lives.'[10]

Und wirklich, von diesem Tag an traten beide bis 1960 gemeinsam auf. Lund war eine der ersten, die Volkslieder aus aller Welt in (insgesamt 21 Sprachen), vom Klavier begleitet, in Konzertsälen aufführte.[11] Rauter schildert ihren gemeinsamen Beginn:

The songs were such, that her reputation grew and after a rather short time she became known all over Germany. Then came the first tour to England, France and Switzerland, then the whole Europe actually. In Hamburg, where we had started, the demand was so great, that in one week we had ten concerts.[12]

Neben Auftritten in Deutschland gab es Gastspiele in Skandinavien und England.[13] Nach der Ablehnung einer Konzertanfrage der Reichsmusikkammer 1933 für einen Auftritt in Dresden[14] wandten sich Lund und Rauter nach Dänemark und übersiedelten 1935 nach London. Dort lebten sie, trotz Arbeitsverbots für ausländische Musiker,[15] weiter von ihren Auftritten und Tourneen: So reisten sie am Neujahrstag 1938 via Halifax nach New York, besuchten auch die National Broadcasting Company (NBC), und kehrten nach einem Abstecher in Pittsburgh Ende März nach England zurück.

Noch in den USA hatte Rauter am 12. März 1938 die Nachricht erreicht, dass deutsche Truppen in Österreich einmarschiert und eine Rückkehr ausgeschlossen war. Ein abschlägiges Gespräch am 29. dieses Monats wegen seines in Aussig lebenden Vaters auf der tschechoslowakischen

---

10   Engel Lund and Ferdinand Rauter, Interview with contemporary witnesses and herself, RCM Project Music, Migration and Mobility, Youtube, https://www.youtube.com/watch?v=VuMNhNStlSM [accessed: 22.09.22].
11   *Ibid.*
12   *Ibid.*
13   Rauter besuchte London zum ersten Mal im Juni 1930; am 26. Juni erlebte er ein Konzert in der Grotrian Hall (heute Wigmore Hall). Vgl. MMCS, Ferdinand Rauter, Box 1, Index Tagebücher 1929–1948.
14   ‚Sorry, Herr Goebbels, we are too busy', siehe MMCS Rauter, Box 3, Mappe 6 (4), Zeitungsausschnitt ‚Express & Neues' 1972, in dem Rauter davon berichtet.
15   Die Londoner Konzertagentur Ibbs and Tillett benachrichtigt am 9.1.1936 Miss MacLeod darüber, dass Engel Lund problemlos nach GB einreisen könne. MMCS, Ferdinand Rauter, Box 6, Nr. 89 (4).

FIGURE 13.1　Engel Lund and Ferdinand Rauter
© NATIONAL PORTRAIT GALLERY, LONDON (PHOTO BY HOWARD COSTER)

Gesandtschaft – nach dem Einmarsch der Wehrmacht in die ČSSR – und sein Vorsprechen am 7. April 1938 auf dem deutschen Konsulat verliefen ergebnislos.[16] Im November 1938 erfolgte die Eingliederung Aussigs ins Deutsche Reich und Rauter sollte seinen Vater nie wiedersehen. Auf sein Ersuchen um ein gültiges Papier genehmigte ihm das Home Office nach erster Ablehnung, Polizeibefragung und weiterer Vorladung am 7. Juli 1938 eine

---

16　MMCS, Rauter, Box 1, Index Tagebücher 1929–1948, siehe die Einträge an den genannten Daten.

einjährige Aufenthaltsgenehmigung, die offenbar im weiteren Verlauf verlängert wurde.[17]

Rauter wohnte zu dieser Zeit bereits gemeinsam mit Engel Lund bei Eileen MacLeod, genannt Mac, in 50 Clarendon Road, Bezirk Notting Hill in Nordwest-London.[18] Mac, eine weithin geschätzte Sprachtherapeutin, unterrichtete Mitarbeiter der BBC im Bush House, Foreign Service.[19] Ihre Mutter, Mrs MacLeod, aus einer begüterten Familie von der Isle of Sky stammend, lebte wie auch mitunter ihr Sohn und Macs Bruder Cyril in diesem Haus. Ein Glücksfall für den Flüchtling Rauter, bei diesen großzügigen Frauen[20] ein sicheres Zuhause gefunden zu haben. Auf der anderen Seite kümmerte sich Rauter um viele häusliche Belange. Lund und die MacLeod-Familie waren Teil seines stetig wachsenden Freundeskreises, der sich dort regelmäßig traf. In London kannte Rauter schon bald ‚Gott und die Welt', darunter Leute aus unterschiedlichen Berufsgruppen;[21] befreundete Flüchtlinge vom Kontinent und Briten, aber insbesondere Musiker aus Österreich und Deutschland und deren Ehepartner: Egon Wellesz, Georg Knepler (Austrian Centre), Hans Gál, Robert Müller-Hartmann, Helene und Sebastian Isepp, Emmy Heim, Dea Gombrich und ihren Ehemann Sir John Forsdyke (Direktor des British Museum), Ilse Wolf, Norbert Brainin, Siegmund Nissel, Hans (Peter) Schidlof, Paul Hamburger, Peter Stadlen, Erwin Stein und Tochter Marion, den Schriftsteller Elias Canetti[22] und den österreichischen Kulturpolitiker, Juristen, Schriftsteller und Musikwissenschaftler Hermann Ullrich (Mitarbeiter am Austrian Centre und des Free Austrian Movement),[23] um nur einige zu nennen. Kammermusikpartner, Gesprächspartner und Freund bis zu seinem Weggang nach Camphill Ende 1945 war der Flüchtling Arnold Rosé, ehemaliger Konzertmeister der Wiener Philharmoniker, den Rauter zum Musizieren und Gespräch oft besuchte und

---

17 Vgl. MMCS, Ferdinand Rauter, Box 1, Index 1929–1948, siehe Einträge unter den genannten Daten.
18 Tagebuch-Eintrag vom 28.03.1938, Vgl. MMCS, Sammlung Ferdinand Rauter Box 1.
19 Interview Andrea Rauter, Februar 2020. Eileen MacLeod übersetzte in Engel Lund's ‚Book of Folk-Songs' von 1936 Lieder aus acht Originalsprachen ins Englische. Vgl. Ausgabe Nimbus 2014, Translator's Note.
20 ‚Geld spielte keine Rolle.' Interview JRH mit Andrea Rauter, London, Februar 2020.
21 *Ibid.*
22 Mit Dr Wolf und Canetti in der National Gallery. Vgl. MMCS, Ferdinand Rauter, Box1, Index 1929–1948, Eintrag vom 01.07.1943.
23 Vgl. Österreicher im Exil, Großbritannien 1938–1945, Eine Dokumentation, DÖW 1992, 362. Rauter pflegte weiteren Kontakt mit Ullrich, nachdem dieser nach Österreich zurückgekehrt und Senatspräsident geworden war. Vgl. Postkarte von Ullrich an Rauter vom 27.12.1979, in MMCS, Ferdinand Rauter, Box 3, 47(5).

dies mit Pilze-Suchen und Kochen für Freunde verband.[24] Unter den Briten finden sich Namen wie die Pianistin Myra Hess, wie Ralph Vaughan Williams, Maud Karpeles und Imogen Holst, der Schriftsteller Holroyd-Reece oder selbst der Beamte Ernest N. Cooper,[25] die sich bei den Behörden für die Flüchtlinge verwendeten. Hinzu kamen all diejenigen, die zum Kreis der Anthroposophischen Gesellschaft bzw. ‚Christian Community' in London gehörten.

Nachdem Rauter im Dezember 1940 aus der Internierung auf der Isle of Man entlassen worden war,[26] setzte er sich zusammen mit Maud Karpeles und Ralph Vaughan Williams im neugegründeten Musicians' Refugee Committee für die Freilassung von Musikern aus der Internierung ein. Er arbeitete danach erfolgreich mit Hans (Peter) Schidlof und Norbert Brainin über Monate,[27] um sie auf den Unterricht mit hohen Ansprüchen bei dem Berliner Geigenprofessor Max Rostal vorzubereiten. Rauter beteiligte sich an der Gründung der Anglo Austrian Musicians' Society. Er verkehrte im Bloomsbury House, in dem die Flüchtlingsorganisationen untergebracht waren, um dort Erleichterungen für Musiker zu erwirken.

Noch etwas anderes zeichnet den Klagenfurter in Großbritannien aus: Neben seinen Verpflichtungen als Musiker und Klavierlehrer, als Mitglied und ‚Motor' verschiedener Komitees ist er als Botaniker und Pilzkenner, als Kinderbetreuer, Klavierstimmer, Konzertagent, Elektriker, Chauffeur,[28] Heizer, Koch, Hauswirtschaftler und später herausragender Fotograf tätig. Rauter ist sich für keine Tätigkeit zu schade, er packt dort an, wo er gebraucht wird. Er knüpft Kontakte, denkt auch an andere, wenn er zum Beispiel Freunden in London Hühner und Gänse zu Weihnachten aus Aberdeen besorgt, verpackt und verschickt.[29] Sein Tagesablauf ist perfekt durchorganisiert. Abends ist er oft Gastgeber und spielt für seine Gäste Klavier solo oder begleitet befreundete Musiker oder Sänger. Wie seine Tagebücher zeigen, lässt er sich trotz kriegsbedingter Einschränkungen und Bombenangriffen nicht davon abhalten,

---

24   Vgl. MMCS, Ferdinand Rauter, Box 1, Index 1929–1948, Tagebücher Dezember 1940, 1941 und 1942. Rauter fuhr eigens von Clent, Sunfield Children's Home, West Midlands, wo er sich gerade aufhielt, zur Beerdigung von Arnold Rosé nach London, um dort am 28.8.1946 eine Rede zu halten. Vgl. MMCS, Ferdinand Rauter, Box 1, Index 1929–1948.
25   Ernest N. Cooper, Alien Departement im Home Office, setze sich für die Belange ausländischer Musiker ein. Vgl. Raab Hansen, NS-Verfolgte Musiker in England, Hamburg 1996, Kapitel 5.3., 122f, 126f.
26   Stahrenberg, ‚Ferdinand Rauter', in online *Lexikon verfolgter Musiker*, 2017.
27   Vgl. MMCS, Rauter, Box 1, vgl. Tagebücher 1940, 1941 und 1942.
28   Am 23.04.1946 macht er einen Ausflug ‚mit den großen Kindern im neuen Terraplane nach Aboyne'.
29   16.12.1946; Gänse in Aberdeen ansehen, 17.12.1946: für £10 Gänse und Enten nach London geschickt. Vgl. MMCS, Ferdinand Rauter, Box 1, Tagebuch 1946.

Konzertverpflichtungen und persönliche Verabredungen auch außerhalb Londons einzuhalten. Es scheint, als setzten die Schwierigkeiten des täglichen Lebens ungeahnte Kräfte in dem Exilanten frei.

2 Die Begegnung mit Claire (Clarisse) Kösten

1940, während seiner Internierung auf der Isle of Man, lernte Rauter den Wiener Flüchtling Josef Kösten kennen.[30] Kösten bat den relativ früh entlassenen Rauter, seiner Familie in London einen Besuch abzustatten. Wenige Tage darauf erfüllte Rauter seine Zusage und lernte bei dieser Gelegenheit[31] neben ihrem jüngeren Bruder Manfred (Freddy)[32] die sechzehnjährige Clarisse Kösten kennen: Ein intelligentes Mädchen, das zudem hervorragend Klavier spielte. Daraus entwickelte sich allmählich Zuneigung und eine scheue Liebe über mehrere Jahre, die von den Eltern nicht gutgeheißen wurde: Clarisse, von Rauter in seinen Tagebüchern Klairle genannt, war zweiundzwanzig Jahre jünger[33] als Rauter[34] und wuchs in einer liberalen jüdischen Familie auf.[35] Rauter wiederum, in Österreich römisch-katholisch getauft, hatte sich in den zwanziger Jahren in Dresden der von Steiner begründeten Anthroposophie und damit verbundenen Christengemeinschaft, einer religiösen Erneuerungsbewegung außerhalb der Staatskirchen, die in Stuttgart ihren Ausgang nahm, zugewandt.[36] Daran hielt er ein Leben lang fest. Wie seine Tochter ausführt, gehörte Rauter auch zu den Gründungsmitgliedern der Christengemeinschaft in 1001 Finchley Road in Golders Green.[37] Um nach dem

---

30 Josef Kösten, geboren 29.6.1889 in Kolomea, damals Galizien, gestorben 22.11.1974 in London, siehe Carolin Stahrenberg, ‚Claire Rauter', in Claudia Maurer Zenck, Peter Petersen, Sophie Fetthauer (Hg.), *Lexikon verfolgter Musiker und Musikerinnen der NS-Zeit* (Hamburg: Universität Hamburg, 2017), https://www.lexm.uni-hamburg.de/object/lexm_lexmperson_00007088 [Zugang: 26.09.2022].

31 MMCS, Box 1, Tagebuch von 1940, Eintrag vom 20.12.1940.

32 Manfred Kosten, geboren 24.11.1928, siehe Stahrenberg, ‚Claire Rauter', in online *Lexikon verfolgter Musiker*, 2017.

33 Geboren am 8.9.1924 in Wien, gestorben am 21.12.2011 in London.

34 Geboren am 4.6.1902 in Klagenfurt, gestorben am 6.12.1987 in London.

35 Gerald Davidson, Claire Rauter and Freddy Kosten, 'Between two Worlds', in Marion Trestler (ed.), in *Vienna – London: Passage to Safety. Emigré portraits in photographs and words* (Vienna: Synema, 2017), 46–63 (53).

36 Dies geschah mit Hilfe der Chrambach-Familie, den Großeltern von Dieter Hornemann. Vgl. Andrea Rauter, E-Mail an John vom 4. Mai 2013 und mir überlassen. Rauter-Archiv JRH, Siehe auch Ritchie, Seite 15.

37 E-Mail von Andrea Rauter an John vom 4. Mai 2013.

Willen der Eltern Abstand zu Rauter zu bekommen, verpflichtete sich die noch nicht volljährige Clarisse Kösten für eine Tätigkeit in Camphill. Dort hatte sie pflegebedürftige Kinder zu versorgen, und es war ihr Ziel, an einer integrativen Camphill-Schule als Pädagogin zu arbeiten.[38] Hielt die Beziehung zu Rauter weiterhin, könne sie dann – wie ihre Eltern meinten – selbst entscheiden.[39]

3 Das Projekt von Karl König

Flüchtlinge aus Österreich um den Wiener Arzt Dr. Karl König[40] und Dr. Ita Wegman, Mitarbeiterin Rudolf Steiners, anthroposophische Ärztin und Klinikgründerin in Arlesheim (Schweiz),[41] hatten auf der Grundlage der Lehre Steiners in den zwanziger Jahren ein Konzept entwickelt, praktiziert und in Kursen für Ärzte und Therapeuten in Europa gelehrt, um behinderte Kinder durch Förderung in gemeinschaftlichem Zusammenleben mit speziell ausgebildeten Ärzten, Heilpädagogen und Betreuern ein erfülltes Leben zu ermöglichen.[42] Zu der ersten Gruppe gehörten Hans Schauder,[43] Rudi Lissau, Alex Baum, Barbara Lipsker, Trude Blau bzw. Amman, Edy Weisberg, Liesel Schwab bzw. Schauder und Bronja Hüttner. Nach dem Anschluss Österreichs am 11. März 1938 und der Nazi-Politik mittels Euthanasie ‚unwertes Leben' auszumerzen, entschlossen sich neben dieser auch eine zweite, jüngere, Gruppe von 1936 mit Peter Roth, Thomas Weihs, Alix Roth, Carlo Pietzner und mehrere (nichtgenannte) Frauen zum Exil nach Großbritannien. Karl König, der wie

---

38   Stahrenberg, ‚Claire Rauter', in online *Lexikon verfolgter Musiker*, 2017.
39   Davidson, Rauter and Kosten, 56.
40   König, A Biographic Synopsis, http://www.karlkoeniginstitute.org/images/downloads/Koenig_Biographic_Synopsis.pdf. [Zugang: 08.09.2021].
41   Diese Klinik ‚wurde von Rudolf Steiner als „Musteranstalt der anthroposophischen Medizin"' bezeichnet. Ita Wegman starb 1943 in Arlesheim; vgl. Michaele Glöckler, Ita Wegman, www.biographien.kulturimpuls.org/detail [Zugang: 22.09.2022].
42   Zu Beginn der sechziger Jahre wurde das ‚bisherige Schullandheim für Seelenpflegebedürftige Jugendliche ... jetzt in ein zweites großes Dorf für Erwachsene umgewandelt'. Vgl. Friedwart Bock, ‚Die Geschichte und Entwicklung Camphills', in Pietzner (Hg.), *Camphill: Fünfzig Jahre Leben und Arbeiten mit Seelenpflege-bedürftigen Menschen* (Stuttgart: Freies Geistesleben, 1991), 33–52 (43).
43   Der Arzt Hans Schauder, legte als einer der ersten überhaupt eine Promotion ‚Zur Frage der therapeutischen Möglichkeiten der Musik bei Geisteskranken' vor, angenommen an der Med. Fakultät der Universität Basel am 11.07.1939. Rauter erwähnte weder Schauder noch genannte Arbeit in seinem Tagebuch 1945 bis 1947.

Peter Roth und seine Schwester Alix[44] zur Flucht gezwungen war,[45] erreichte am 8. Dezember 1938 die britische Hauptstadt. Hier setzten er und seine Gruppe in die Tat um, was sie 1927 in Österreich begonnen hatten: Ein Kind ist nach Steiner mehr als seine leibliche Erscheinung, wie auch immer sein geistiger Zustand sein mag.[46] Das Kind war bereits ‚eine geistige Wesenheit, bevor es geboren wurde' und eine Behinderung ‚von besonderer Bedeutung für den Menschen und bestimmt, sein Leben zu verwandeln'.[47] Und so versucht der Betreuer, die geistige Wesenheit des Kindes, ‚sein Ich', zu erreichen. Das Kind mit Behinderung sei allen anderen gegenüber ebenbürtig und es lohnte, mit ihm zu arbeiten und es individuell zu fördern.

In Schottland, unweit von Aberdeen, kamen Anke Weihs (bzw. Weihs-Roth-Nederhoed), Alix Roth und Tilla König, Königs Ehefrau, im März 1939 vorläufig in Kirkton House[48] unter, einem ehemaligen Pfarrhaus genannt Whitsun, nahe Insch in Aberdeenshire. Im Mai 1939[49] begann hier unter spartanischen Bedingungen das heilpädagogische Projekt. Wenige Monate später bescherte der Kriegsbeginn erst einmal einen Rückschritt, denn sämtliche männliche Flüchtlinge wurden zu ‚enemy aliens' erklärt. Die verheirateten Männer der Gruppe einschließlich Karl König wurden im Mai 1940[50] auf der Isle of Man interniert, die unverheirateten unter ihnen nach Kanada in Internierungslager verschifft. Im Juni zogen Trude Amman, Anke Roth (bzw. Weihs-Roth-Nederhoed), Tilla König, Trude Blau, Marie Korath geborene Blitz, Alix Roth und Barbara Lipsker mit Kindern weiter nach Camphill, einem Landstrich mit mehreren Gebäuden nahe der Küste am Nordufer des Flusses Dee unweit von Aberdeen[51] gelegen. Die Gebäude, zwischen denen die Mitarbeiter und Kinder oft täglich wechselten, hießen von Westen in Richtung Nordosten Camphill House, Murtle House, Newton House und Carnlee House. Unterhalb des

---

44   Hans Dackweiler, Peter Roth, Forschungsstelle Kulturimpuls – Biographien Dokumentation, www://biographien.kulturimpuls.org [Zugang: 01.01.2021].

45   Ritchie, J.M., 'Dr Karl König and the Camphill Movement', in Anthony Grenville and Andrea Reiter (eds.), 'I didn't want to float; I wanted to belong to something', Yearbook of the Research Centre for German and Austrian Exile Studies, Vol. 10 (2008), 173f.

46   Karl König, 'Drei Grundpfeiler von Camphill', in Pietzner, 26–32 (27).

47   *Ibid.*, 28.

48   Kirkton House wurde dann 1940 aufgegeben, es lag zu abseits, hatte keinen Wasseranschluss und zu Beginn auch keinen Stromanschluss, Richard Steel, Karl König-Institut, E-Mail vom 18.6.2020 an JRH.

49   Bock, ‚Die Geschichte und Entwicklung Camphills', in Pietzner (ed.), 33; Steel, Art in Community – Community as Art, 3.

50   Wie aus seinen Tagebüchern hervorgeht, war Rauter in der Internierung Karl König nicht begegnet.

51   Friedwart Bock, ‚Der ausgebreitete Kreis. Ein Porträt Camphills', in Pietzner, 97.

Flusses lag das baufällige Heathcoat House, das bald aufgegeben worden war. Über den Fluss gab es damals nur eine Brücke und eine verlassene Fähre.[52] Der nächste Zuganschluss lag in Aberdeen. Sechs Monate später, mit der Freilassung der Männer um Dr. König aus der Internierung und dem *spiritus rector* nun vor Ort, konnte die Arbeit in der Community in Camphill beginnen.[53]

> From the beginning Karl König and his wife Tilla trained the young helpers to create a family-based healing haven of culture, art, education and therapies around and with needy children – and adults, who were themselves traumatised.[54]

Selbst entwurzelt wie zahlreiche ihrer Schutzbefohlenen, von denen einige auch mit dem Kindertransport gerettet worden waren, legten sie unter großer Kraftanstrengung, zu der Verzicht und berufliche Umorientierung gehörten, die Grundlagen für das heute weltweit berühmte Projekt. Darunter neben Priestern, Ärzten, Pädagogen, Tänzern, Bildhauern, Malern, Schriftstellern und Amateurmusikern auch Ferdinand Rauter.[55]

Im Juli/August 1945 fand an diesem Ort die erste offene medizinische Konferenz mit über achtzig Teilnehmern statt.[56] Damit wurde Camphill Ausgangspunkt und Namensgeber der heute auf mehreren Kontinenten in zwanzig Ländern bestehenden heilpädagogischen Einrichtungen für Kinder, einhundert sozialtherapeutischen Dorfgemeinschaften mit Erwachsenen, dazu Projekten wie Flüchtlingsarbeit, Traumatherapie und Lebensberatung im Alter.[57]

4 Christengemeinschaft: Vorgeschichte zu Rauters Aufbruch nach Camphill

Rauter hatte vor seinem Exil bereits Kontakt zur sogenannten ‚Christian Community' in England, die im Advent 1929 auf dem Dachboden eines Hauses

---

52 E-Mail von Richard Steel an JRH vom 18.06.2020; Übersicht über Camphill: Wasserfarben-Zeichnung von Günter Lehr 1952.
53 Siehe ‚Karl König – A Biographic Synopsis', pdf.datei online.
54 Steel, Art in Community – Community as Art, 3.
55 *Ibid.*, 3ff.
56 *Ibid.*
57 Wikipedia, https://de.wikipedia.org/wiki/Camphill [Zugang: 31.12.2020]. Die hier zu lesende Behauptung, dass es sich bei den Gründern um sämtlich jüdische Flüchtlinge handelte, entspricht nach meinen Recherchen nicht den Tatsachen.

in Highgate mit einem öffentlichen Gottesdienst ihren Anfang nahm, aufgenommen. Die Initiative für deren Etablierung in England und Schottland ging von dem deutschen ‚Priester' und ‚Oberlenker' Alfred Heidenreich aus,[58] den Rauter bereits am 12. Mai 1931 in London getroffen hatte.[59] Heidenreich und seine Frau Marta Heimeran gehörten zu der ersten Gruppe, die von Rudolf Steiner in Dornach 1922 zu Priestern geweiht worden waren.[60] Da Heidenreich eine besondere Beziehung zur Musik hatte, lud er auch Musiker zu Konzerten in die neue Gemeinde in London ein. Wie der Kontakt beider zustande kam, bleibt offen. Fest steht, dass Heidenreich mit regelmäßigen Begegnungen 1941 und 1942 auch zu Rauters Freundeskreis gehörte.[61] Den erkrankten Heidenreich besuchte Rauter eigens am 7. Juli 1941 in London und hörte einen seiner Vorträge (20. September 1941) in Friends House. Rauter besuchte die Gottesdienste und begleitete auch einige, die Heidenreich abhielt (7. Dezember 1941 und 29. November 1942): ‚Weihehandlung sehr schön'.[62] Heidenreich nahm auch die Einladung zum Gulasch-Essen bei Rauter im April 1942 an.[63] Wenig später besuchte Heidenreich das von der Austrian Musicians' Group veranstaltete zweite Festkonzert zu Ehren des einhundertjährigen Bestehens der Wiener Philharmoniker am 11. Juni 1942 in der Wigmore Hall,[64] oder beide trafen sich zu Gesprächen (8. Dezember 1942).[65] Auf jeden Fall hatte Rauter mit Heidenreich den wichtigsten Repräsentanten der ‚Christian Community' in Großbritannien kennengelernt, mit dem er zudem das Für und Wider seines Camphill-Vorhabens erörtern konnte.

Am 15. September 1942 findet sich die erste Erwähnung von Dr. Karl König im Rauter-Tagebuch: ‚Ing. Roth überbringt Grüße von Dr. König, dem Leiter

---

58   Von 1931 an gab es ein bescheidenes Gemeindehaus in 1001 Finchley Road, Golders Green. Die Sonntagsgottesdienste wurden schon bald bis zum Kriegsende in ‚The Studio' in Chalk Farm abgehalten. Dann begründete Evelyn Frances (verheiratete Capel) die Christian Community in Glenilla Road, die nach Fertigstellung der Kirche 1949 deren Hauptsitz in London wurde. E-Mail von Richard Steel, Karl König Institut vom 14.12.2020 an JRH.

59   Vgl. MMCS, Ferdinand Rauter, Box 1, Tagebücher Index 1929–1948; Taco Bay, Alfred Heidenreich, Forschungsstelle Kulturimpuls – Biographen, Dokumentation, http://www.biographen.kulturimpuls.org/detail [Zugang: 20.12.2020].

60   Helmut Zander, *Rudolf Steiner: Die Biographie* (München: Piper, 2011), 443.

61   Weitere Tagebücher von 1943 bis zur Abreise Rauters nach Aberdeen Ende 1945 waren mir nicht zugänglich.

62   Vgl. MMCS, Ferdinand Rauter, Box 1, Tagebücher 1941 und 1942; Heidenreich und seine Frau.

63   Vgl. MMCS, Ferdinand Rauter, Box 1, Tagebücher 1941 und 1942.

64   Rauter trat darin mit dem Rosé-Quartett auf. Vgl. 96. Verzeichnis von Ferdinand Rauter betreffend die österreichischen Konzerte in London 1941–1945, o.D. (1973), DÖW 8462, in *Österreicher im Exil: Großbritannien 1938–1945*, 1992, 467.

65   Vgl. MMCS, Ferdinand Rauter, Box 1, Tagebücher 1941 und 1942.

der anthroposophischen Anstalt, in der auch Heidenreich jetzt ist.'[66] Aus dem Tagebuch von Karl König geht hervor, dass sich König und Rauter am 10. Juli und am 11. Dezember 1943 in 1001 Finchley Road trafen und miteinander sprachen. Drei Tage später wurden Kinder medizinisch untersucht und tags darauf spielte Rauter abends Schumann, Schubert, Chopin und Beethoven. Nach der nächsten Visite am 26. August 1943 tauschten sich König und Rauter über Zeit und Bach als ‚Rätsel der Musik' aus.[67] Am 12. April 1944 kommt es nach der Aufnahme des autistischen Kindes von Mrs Coke zur Begegnung von König, Rauter und Engel Lund in 1001 Finchley Road.[68]

Am 2. September 1945 gaben Rauter und Engel Lund ihr letztes gemeinsames Konzert im Austrian Centre vor Lunds Abreise nach Dänemark.[69] Rauter konzentrierte sich nun bis zu seiner Abreise nach Camphill auf Veranstaltungen der ‚Christian Community', Kontakte mit Anthroposophen und Camphill-Mitarbeitern. Am 19. September 1945 bot Rauter Dr. König seine Mitarbeit in Camphill an. Im Haus der Christengemeinschaft in 34 Glenilla Road, London Belsize Park, besprechen beide Rauters Pläne dazu. König zeigt sich offen, zumal sich Claire Kösten dort schon seit einigen Monaten bestens bewährte. Rauter notiert: ‚Er ist mit allem einverstanden' und ‚sagt, dass er sich auf mich freut.'[70] Am 13. November sehen sich die beiden bei einem Vortrag Königs ‚über das Goetheanum', ‚die Dreigliederung des Menschen und die Notwendigkeit, die Kinder in diesem Sinne zu erziehen'. Dann noch einmal am 2. Dezember bei einer Weihehandlung und sechs Tage später[71] bei einem Auftritt Rauters mit den Diabelli-Variationen in der Anthroposophischen Gesellschaft im Steiner House in Marylebone.[72] Camphill war offenbar ein wichtiger Schritt für ihn, sich mit seinem Glauben auch praktisch in der gemeinsamen Tat mit anderen auseinanderzusetzen.

---

66 Vgl. MMCS, Ferdinand Rauter, Box 1, Tagebücher 1942; Ing. Roth, als FAM Aberdeen bezeichnet. Es scheint sich hier um eine Verwechslung zu handeln, mit großer Wahrscheinlichkeit ist Peter Roth, Camphill, gemeint.
67 Tagebuch König, Einträge vom 10.07., 11.07, 14.07. und 26.08.1943, Karl König Institut Kleinmachnow.
68 König, Tagebuch, Eintrag vom 12.05.1944, Karl König Institut, 14532 Kleinmachnow.
69 Vgl. MMCS, Ferdinand Rauter, Box 1, Tagebuch 1945, Eintrag vom 02. und 09.09.1945.
70 Vgl. MMCS, Ferdinand Rauter, Box 1, Tagebuch 1945, Eintrag vom 19.09.1945.
71 Vgl. MMCS Rauter Box 1, Tagebuch 1945, Einträge vom 19.09., 13.11., 02.12. und 08.12.1945.
72 Steiner House, 35 Park Road in Marylebone, London NW1, von 1926 bis 1937 im Auftrag der Rudolf-Steiner-Gesellschaft erbaut, vgl. https://www.rsh.anth.org.uk [Zugang: 04.04.2021]. Bei dieser Gelegenheit begegnete Rauter Georg Adams (1894–1963), Mitarbeiter Steiners in Dornach, Chemiker, Mathematiker, Übersetzer, Simultanübersetzer von Steiner-Vorträgen in England, Vortragender, Seminarleiter der Anthroposophischen Gesellschaft in England, http://biographien.kulturimpuls.org [Zugang: 04.04.2021].

5 Claire Kösten auf Camphill

Claire bzw. Clarisse Kösten ging etwa ein Jahr vor Rauter, also um den Jahreswechsel 1944/1945, nach Camphill. Dort arbeitete sie gemeinsam mit ihrer Freundin Marianne Gorge,[73] Flüchtling aus Wien wie sie selbst, als Kinder-Betreuerin nahezu rund um die Uhr.[74] Nach Steiner offenbarte sich die Idee von einer anthroposophischen Gemeinschaftsstruktur insbesondere im nahen Zusammenleben von Kindern und Erwachsenen.[75] Den Mitarbeitern wurde kein Gehalt bezahlt.[76] Das hatte für den Gründer der Anthroposophie durchaus einen Sinn, denn damit ‚würde der entscheidende Schritt zur dreigestaltigen sozialen Ordnung' getan. Dazu gehörten erstens ‚die Welt der Wirtschaft und Arbeit', zweitens ‚die Welt der Ideen und Gedanken' und drittens ‚die rein menschliche soziale Welt'. Nur so könnten ‚zwischenmenschliche Beziehungen und Freundschaften jenseits von Sympathie und Antipathie (entstehen)'. Anders ausgedrückt, eine sinnvolle Arbeit der Mitarbeiter bedeutete, anderen Nutzen zu bringen. Camphill und weitere Gründungen sind nach Karl König keine ‚Behinderten-Einrichtungen' und ‚wollen auch keine sein'. König begriff sie als ‚Wohnplätze ... für Angehörige einer „neuen menschlichen Gesellschaft"'.[77]

6 Rauters Zeit in Camphill

Nach einer privaten Abschiedsparty Mitte Dezember 1945 verabschiedet sich Rauter wenig später in Blackheath bei London von Arnold Rosé. Trotz zurückliegender Ankündigung des Geigers, ‚dass er nie mehr spielen würde', widmeten sie sich gemeinsam der 16. und 15. Sonate von Mozart, die auch eine Bedeutung im Leben von Rauters Vater hat.[78]

---

73 Marianne Gorge arbeitete bereits seit Oktober 1942 in Camphill und berichtet, dass Hans Schauder einmal wöchentlich mit allen Mitarbeitern gemeinsam sang: Johannes M. Surkamp, *The lives of Camphill: An Anthology of the Pioneers* (Floris Books, 2007), 37; vgl. auch Marianne Gorge, 'My Life Story', in Trestler (ed.), *Vienna – London: Passage to Safety*, 122–31.
74 Interview JRH mit Andrea Rauter, Februar 2020.
75 Peter Roth, ‚Miteinander leben – füreinander wirtschaften', in Pietzner (ed.), 63f (64).
76 Interview JRH mit Andrea Rauter, Februar 2020.
77 Wilhelm Ernst Barkhoff, ‚Camphill – Aufgang im Untergang', in Pietzner (ed.), 7.
78 Vgl. MMCS, Ferdinand Rauter, Box 1, Tagebuch 1945, Eintrag 16.12.1945.

Am 18. Dezember 1945 um 12:25 Uhr geht Rauters Zug vom Bahnhof King's Cross via Edinburgh (Ankunft 8:55 Uhr am nächsten Tag) nach Aberdeen ab. Er schildert seine Gefühle:

> die letzten Tage und vor allem die Wärme und Freundschaft der Dodwells[79] lassen mich etwas schwer von London weggehen, und nun, wo ich im Zug nach Edinburgh sitze, habe ich recht gemischte Gefühle. Ich fühle plötzlich, dass ich doch stark nach London gehöre und die Arbeit oben in C.H. scheint mir plötzlich ungeeignet für mich – dies war aber zu erwarten, und wenn ich erst angefangen habe, wird es sich ja zeigen – nun will ich Klärle sehen – ich kann alles noch nicht fassen.[80]

Nach verspäteter Ankunft in Edinburgh und Übernachtung bei Kitty Trevelyan[81] besucht er bis zur Abfahrt des Zuges nach Aberdeen am nächsten Tag um 14:10 Uhr noch den Komponisten Hans Gál[82] in der Universität, der ihm sein neues sinfonisches Gedicht über eine alte irische Melodie vorspielt.[83] Im Zug dann schreibt Rauter Liedtexte für ‚Klärles Weihnachtsgeschenk', denkt zurück an das schwere vergangene Jahr der Trennung und ist in Erwartung von Claire vollkommen aufgeregt.[84] Zudem hatte sich die Situation mit ihren Eltern verschlechtert, wie er aus einem Telefonat am 2. Dezember 1945 von ihr erfahren hatte.[85] In seinen Tagebüchern von 1945 bis 1947 beschreibt Rauter

---

79 Janet D. ist seine Klavierschülerin und ihr Bruder Peter D. fährt mit einem Taxi sein Gepäck nach Kings Cross während Rauter radelt und noch bei Jennings und dem Reisebüro Station macht.
80 Vgl. MMCS, Ferdinand Rauter, Box 1, Tagebuch 1945, Eintrag 17.12.1945.
81 Kitty Trevelyan hatte Rauter auf der Konferenz der Christengemeinde in Yeaton Peverly bei Shrewsbury, die vom 08.09. bis 10.09.1945 mit etwa fünfzig Teilnehmern einschließlich Priestern aus London stattfand, kennengelernt. Rauter gab dort Klavier-Vorträge und spielte auch zur Weihehandlung. Vgl. MMCS, Ferdinand Rauter, Box 1, Tagebuch 1945, Eintrag 08.09.-10.09.1945.
82 Rauter war dem Komponisten Hans Gál lt. Tagebuch im Mai 1938 in London begegnet. Beide waren auf der Isle of Man 1940 interniert und Rauter hatte u.a. 1941 einen Gál-Klavierabend im Austrian Centre besucht. Vgl. MMCS, Ferdinand Rauter, Box 1, Tagebücher-Index genannter Jahre.
83 ‚Das Thema wurde immer vor dem Forces Programme gespielt.' MMCS, Ferdinand Rauter Box 1, 1945, Eintrag 19.12.1945. Es handelte sich dabei um *Liliburlero. Improvisations on a Martial Melody for Orchestra* op. 48 (1945), Novello (1950), now Music Sales; www.hansgal.org/works; siehe auch E-Mail Eva Fox-Gál an JRH, 12.04.2021.
84 Vgl. MMCS, Ferdinand Rauter, Box 1, Tagebuch 1945, Eintrag 19.12.1945.
85 ‚Eben hat Klärle aus Murtle angerufen – um ¾ 1 h/ und ich habe ihre Stimme gehört! – die Eltern haben sie verstoßen – sie fragt, ob sie an Levy schreiben soll, / und sie sagt,

den Alltag in Camphill – ein Kontrast zu seinem vorherigen Leben, der größer nicht hätte sein können.

Die ersten vierzehn Tage in Camphill sind darin für den Leser mit einem Index belegt. Beginnend mit dem 30. Dezember 1945 bis zur endgültigen Abreise nach London am 25. Juni 1947 sind die Tagebücher jedoch weitgehend einsehbar. Am 6. Januar 1946 heirateten Rauter und Claire Kösten in Camphill. Alfred Heidenreich traute sie, Peter Roth war ihr Trauzeuge. Am Tag darauf brachen sie zu ihrer Hochzeitsreise auf, die sie über den Lake District und London führte und am 24. Januar 1946 wieder zurückkehren ließ.[86]

Die Gründe für seine Abwesenheiten sind Tagungen, Auftritte, Unterrichtsstunden und Kurse im Rahmen der Christengemeinschaft in England, aber auch Konzerte und BBC-Aufnahmen mit Engel Lund, die offenbar noch vor Rauters Abreise nach Camphill vertraglich vereinbart worden waren. 1947, nach einem geplanten dreiwöchigen Aufenthalt in London Ende April verzögerte eine schwere Krankheit Rauters Rückkehr um weitere vier Wochen bis zu seiner Rückkehr Anfang Juni. Zwei Wochen später, am 25. Juni 1947, verließ er mit Claire Rauter und Baby Andrea, geboren an Heiligabend 1946,[87] Camphill für immer.

7 Musiktherapie in Camphill

In den vorhandenen Quellen zeigt sich, dass die Bezeichnung ‚Musiktherapeut' in den Jahren 1945 bis 1947 nicht auftaucht. Auch nicht in der Vorbesprechung Königs mit Rauter in London. Diese Berufsbezeichnung wählte Rauter offenbar erst im Jahr 1973, im Rückblick seine Tätigkeit in Camphill[88] beschreibend. Rauters Tätigkeit als Musiktherapeut, so wie er sich selbst begriff, war in erster Linie fest an die Rituale der Christengemeinschaft und an das Leben der Camphill-Gemeinschaft gekoppelt und mit der Betreuung von

---

      ich soll mit Dr. König sprechen – dies streifen wir aber nur – sonst stammeln wir beide recht / unzusammenhängendes Zeug und lachen …' Vgl. MMCS, Ferdinand Rauter, Box 1, Tagebuch 1945, Eintrag 02.12.1945.

86 Vgl. MMCS, Ferdinand Rauter, Box 1, Tagebuch 1946, Einträge 06.01.1946 bis 24.02.1946. Rauter unterbrach seinen Camphill-Aufenthalt dreizehn Mal. Er hielt sich somit 1945 elf Tage, 1946 insgesamt 262 und bis Juni 1947 noch einmal 94 Tage in Camphill auf. Bei vier dieser Reisen begleitete ihn auch seine junge Frau Claire. Vgl. Tagebücher Ferdinand Rauter 1945, 1946 u. 1947.

87 Vgl. MMCS, Ferdinand Rauter, Box 1, Eintrag Tagebuch vom 24.12.1946.

88 80. Aus: Bericht von Ferdinand Rauter über dessen Internierung sowie die Entwicklung der Austrian Musicians' Group und Anglo-Austrian Music Society 1940–1973, o.D. (1973), 451f.

‚seelenpflege-bedürftigen' Kindern[89] verbunden. Dort zu arbeiten bedeutete, sich ganz in die Community einzubringen, wie Marianne Gorge skizziert:

> All the work that had to be done every day was carried out in a joyful mood, with dedication and loving care. ... In those early days of Camphill the children with special needs were not 'cared for' in the traditional sense. Rather, we shared our lives with them, and they accompanied us in the various tasks that had to be done. ... Special therapies were only developed much later. The structure and rhythm of daily life was both harmonizing and healing forever.[90]

Die Kinder, auch die der Mitarbeiter, gehörten immer dazu; der Tag hatte für die Freiwilligen 24 Stunden. Als Rauter begann, befanden sich mindestens zwölf pflegebedürftige Kinder in Camphill.[91] Karl König wurde zudem in London von Eltern aufgesucht, die ihm ihre Kinder zur Beobachtung in seiner kleinen Klinik in der Harley-Street anvertrauten. Rauter hatte dort auch für diese Kinder Klavier gespielt.[92] Es sprach sich auch vor Ort herum, dass behinderte Kinder hier aufgenommen wurden:

‚Die Erziehungsbehörde erfuhr von unserem Versuch und sandte einige Kinder nach Camphill. Es kamen immer neue Anfragen, und bald reichte der Platz nicht mehr aus, um allen Anforderungen gerecht zu werden', wie König zwanzig Jahre später bemerkt.[93] Außerdem wurden Ende 1945 in dem neu erworbenen ‚düsteren' Haus Newton Dee, an das Murtle-Grundstück grenzend, zwölf ‚verwahrloste' Jugendliche aufgenommen, mit denen Thomas Weihs[94] ‚einen kleinen Bauernhof' bewirtschaftete.[95]

> Also – and this is something that is not well known, even in Camphill – right from the beginning there were young adults. Amongst the first 'children' in Kirkton House was Rudi Samoje, who was 29 already! Karl König

---

89 Diesen Terminus prägte zum ersten Mal Rudolf Steiner. Karl König, ‚Zur Musiktherapie in der Heilpädagogik', in Hildebrand R. Teirich (Hg.), *Musik in der Medizin. Beiträge zur Musiktherapie* (Stuttgart: G. Fischer, 1959), 77–87 (87).
90 Surkamp, 37.
91 Christof-Andreas Lichtenberg, ‚Karl-König. Ein Lebensbild', in Pietzner (Hg.), 15–23 (22).
92 Tagebücher Karl König, 25., 26.08.1943 und 11., 12.05.1944; Karl König Institut Kleinmachnow.
93 Karl König, ‚Drei Grundpfeiler von Camphill', in Pietzner (Hg.), 26–32 (27).
94 Der Arzt und Heilpädagoge Thomas Weihs (1914–1983) begegnete bereits in Wien Karl König und Peter Roth und gehörte zu den Pionieren der Camphill-Bewegung. Vgl. www.biographien.kulturimpuls.org [Zugang: 11.04.2021].
95 Friedwart Bock, ‚Die schottische Region', in Pietzner (Hg.), 97–108 (98f.).

had wanted to start the 'Village Community' already in 1945 in Newton Dee and take on more adults (he called it then a 'pastoral-medizinische Siedlung'), but due to strange circumstances it didn't work out and so the proper start was with Botton Village that was officially opened in 1956.[96]

Um zu verstehen, wie sich das Leben für die Erwachsenen in der Community überhaupt gestaltete, hier einige wichtige Details: Es gab nahezu wöchentlich Bibelabende, zu denen auch Referenten von außerhalb eingeladen wurden. Doch Rauter nahm daran erst nach einigen Monaten teil. Seine häufige Abwesenheit erregte oft Argwohn und Kritik, vor allem bei Tilla König.[97] ‚Morgenländische Mysterien' wurden von Trude Blau[98] und von Rauter im Mai 1946 vorgelesen.[99] Rauter spielte bei den feierlichen Weihehandlungen an Sonntagen in Camphill oder Murtle Klavier.[100] Etwa zweimal monatlich traf man sich in Camphill, um über Organisatorisches zu sprechen. Aber auch referiert wurde dabei zum Beispiel über anthroposophische Aspekte der Theosophie als Geheimwissenschaft.[101] Im September 1946 beschäftigte sich die Runde mit Eurythmie und dem Thema Geheimwissenschaft.[102] Dieses Thema wird dann im Januar 1947 wiederum in members' meeting mit Steiners drittem Vortrag aus der Serie ‚Das Geheimnis des Menschen' beendet. Vieles deutet darauf hin, dass bei dem hohen gemeinsamen Arbeitspensum kaum eine tiefergehende Auseinandersetzung mit den Erkenntnissen Steiners stattfand. Aufschlussreich war ein Ereignis im Februar 1947, als nach einem Vortrag über Julian de Crespigny Rauter gegen elf Uhr nachts Uhr ‚mehr tot als lebendig'[103] in sein Bett komplimentiert wurde.

Ende Juni 1947 erläuterte Rauter diesem Kreis die Gründe für ihren beider Weggang. Auch dazu gibt sein Tagebuch detailliert Auskunft, denn es wird deutlich, dass jeder Tag für die Mitarbeiter vollkommen ausgefüllt war. Sitzungen

---

96   E-Mail vom 28.11.2020 an JRH von Richard Steel, Karl König Institut Kleinmachnow.
97   Vgl. MMCS, Rauter Box 1, Tagebuch 1947, Eintrag 05.01.1947. Hier wirkten vor allem Laienpriester. Eine eigene Christian Community existierte in Aberdeen mit Heidenreich als Priester. Rauter besuchte mitunter die Weihehandlungen dort.
98   Trude Amann geb. Blau stammte aus Wien und lebte bis zu ihrem Tod 1987 in Camphill. Vgl. www.Vision einer heilenden Gemeinschaft/Leseproben/Content – Zeitschrift für gemeinsames Leben, Lernen und Arbeiten (zeitschriftmenschen.at) [Zugang: 02.06.2021].
99   Vgl. MMCS Rauter Box 1, Tagebuch 1946, Eintrag 06.05. und 13.05.
100 Vgl. MMCS, Rauter Box 1, Tagebücher 1945, 1946 und 1947.
101 Vgl. MMCS, Rauter Box 1, Tagebücher 1945, 1946 (Karl König 11.12.) und 1947 (Karl König am 09.01.)
102 Vgl. MMCS Rauter Box 1, Tagebuch 1946, Eintrag 25.09.: ‚Dann beginnen wir die Geheimwissenschaft.'
103 Vgl. MMCS Rauter Box 1, Tagebuch 1947, Eintrag 25.02.1947.

zogen sich oft und zum großen Verdruss Rauters bis nach Mitternacht hin. Freie Tage gab es selten, da die bedürftigen Kinder rund um die Uhr betreut werden mussten. Andrea Rauter ergänzt dazu: ‚Die Mitarbeiter schliefen bei den Kindern, denn sie mussten die kleineren auch nachts, wenn sie krank waren, versorgen.'[104] Ein gemeinsames Appartement war dem jungen Ehepaar Rauter erst nach der Geburt des Babys zugestanden worden. Das extreme Arbeitspensum und das hohe Arbeitsethos der Camphill-Pioniere erinnert an das Vorbild Steiners,[105] dem auch Dr Karl König mit seiner Lebensleistung als Arzt, Autor, Vortragender und Gründer von Camphill nacheiferte.[106] Ein Arbeitsvertrag Rauters ist nicht überliefert.

8   Die Arbeit mit Kindern

Bereits vor seiner Abreise nach Camphill hatte Rauter 1945 mit Kindern im Rahmen der Christengemeinschaft gearbeitet. In Camphill spielte er an Sonntagen kontinuierlich bei den ‚Kinderhandlungen' bzw. ‚Kinderservice' Klavier oder möglicherweise Harmonium. Singstunden mit den Kindern gehören auch zu seinen feststehenden Aufgaben. Dazu wurde er auch bei Tagungen der ‚Christian Community' in Kidbrook und Sunfield Children's Home in Clent bei Birmingham herangezogen.[107]

Der Idee der Gemeinschaft entsprechend, waren die Betreuer und Heilpädagogen immer präsent, und der Botaniker Rauter erklärte den Kindern auf den gemeinsamen Wegen zwischen den Häusern die Natur und einzelne Pflanzen. Rauter als Klavierpädagoge ist Fachmann darin, unterschiedlich begabten bzw. lernfähigen Kindern Lehrstoffe zu vermitteln. Ergänzend dazu hält Dr. König für die Mitarbeiter auch Vorträge über Kinderpsychologie wie etwa ‚über 12 Sinne und Nidanas'.[108] In seinen Musikstunden improvisiert Rauter und begleitet Lieder am Klavier. Als Klavierlehrer, erfahrener Begleiter Engel Lunds und als Kammermusiker ist er es gewohnt, auf das Spiel des anderen zu achten, im gegenseitigen Geben und Nehmen sich einzufühlen.

---

104   JRH, Interview Andrea Rauter, London, Februar 2020.
105   Vgl. http://steinerdatenbank.de/Titelseite/Titelseite_Frameset [Zugang: 05.09.2021].
106   König, A Biographic Synopsis, www.karlkoeniginstitute.org/images/downloads/Koenig_Biographic_Synopsis.pdf. [Zugang: 22.09.2022].
107   Anthroposophische Jugendarbeit stand im Mittelpunkt. Vom deutschen Heilpädagogen Fried Geuter (1892–1960) und dem englischen Musiker, Dirigenten und Chemiker Michael Wilson (1901–1985), der eine Farbtherapie für die Kinder entwickelte. Vgl. http://www.kulturimpuls.org [Zugang: 17.04.2021].
108   Vgl. MMCS Rauter Box 1, Tagebuch 1946, Einträge vom 22.05.1946 und 04.07.1946.

All das trägt zu seinem intuitiven Erfassen der seelischen Situation der Kinder bei, wie ein Eintrag Rauters bei einer Rückkehr nach zehntägiger Abwesenheit zeigt:

> im Taxi nach Murtle – der Empfang ist so unglaublich, dass ich beinahe weine – die Kinder freuen sich so ehrlich und stark, wie es nur Kinder können, aber Klärles Freude und auch die der meisten Erwachsenen ist ganz groß – ich koche gleich das Abendessen, bleibe dafür aber mit Klärle, die erkältet ist, zu Hause.[109]

Diese spontanen Reaktionen zählen für Rauter als besonders glückliche Momente in Camphill. Ein Tagebucheintrag deutet auf eine Erweiterung seines Angebots in Richtung Improvisation mit Instrumenten hin: Im März 1947 fährt Rauter nach Aberdeen, ‚um Schlaginstrumente für die Kinder zu bekommen'.[110] In der gegenwärtigen Musiktherapie nimmt die Instrumentalimprovisation einen wichtigen Platz bei verschiedenen Indikationen ein. Nach Aussagen seiner Tochter Andrea war Rauter eine Zeitlang auch im Committee von Nordoff/Robbins,[111] die 1954 in Sunfield Children's Home ihre anthroposophische Musiktherapie für Kinder mit Lern- und Verhaltensschwierigkeiten begründeten. Kinder mit Autismus, ADHD, Down-Syndrom, Epilepsie und PDA wurden dabei zum gemeinsamen Improvisieren mit Therapeuten angeregt. Leider hinterließ uns Rauter nicht, was er mit den Kindern in Camphill weiter vorhatte und woher er die Anregung dazu nahm. Dazu kam es nicht mehr. Ein wichtiger Teil der Arbeit von Rauter in Camphill waren die den Jahreszeiten oder dem christlichen Kalenderjahr zugeordneten Aufführungen, an denen die Kinder unter Mitarbeit von Ferdinand und Claire Rauter mitwirkten.

Rauter war nicht nur Musiker, sondern ein großer Naturliebhaber, Botaniker und Mykologe, kannte sich in der Bibel und Literatur aus. Darüber hinaus durchbrach er die damaligen Klischees von Männer- und Frauenrollen. Handwerklich geschickt, repariert er das Auto oder defekte Stromleitungen, reinigt Öfen, baut Lampen, weiß mit wenigen Mitteln für eine große Runde zu kochen und macht danach den Abwasch.

---

109 Vgl. MMCS Rauter Box 1, Tagebuch 1946, Eintrag vom 19.10.1946 bis 01.11.1946.
110 Vgl. MMCS Rauter Box 1, Tagebuch 1947, Einträge 21. Und 25.03.1947.
111 Paul Nordoff (1909–1977), US-amerikanischer Komponist, Musiktherapeut und Anthroposoph; Clive Robbins (1927–2011) britischer Musiktherapeut, Pädagoge, Anthroposoph, vgl. www.nordff-robbins.org.uk [Zugang: 19.04.2021]. Interview JRH mit Andrea Rauter, Februar 2020 in London.

9   Rauters Repertoire als Pianist

Aus den vorliegenden transkribierten Tagebüchern, in denen Rauter seine Beschäftigung mit einzelnen Musikstücken und Aufführungen im privaten und öffentlichen Rahmen erwähnt, ergibt sich etwa folgendes Bild: Die bevorzugten Komponisten, die er als Solist oder Kammermusiker aufführte, waren Schubert (20) und Beethoven (23), Mozart (18), Schumann (4), Chopin (3) und Johann Sebastian Bach (32).

Eine Zeitlang favorisierte Rauter die Diabelli-Variationen, die er seit September 1945 im Steiner House in London, in der Christengemeinschaft in Chalk Farm und im privaten Kreis vortrug, und die er im Februar 1946 noch einmal in Heathcot zu Gehör brachte. Es fällt auf, dass Rauter sich seit Januar 1947 und seiner schwierigen Selbstfindung bis zu seinem Weggang im Juni 1947 zunehmend dem Studium und Vortrag von Bach-Kompositionen für sich selbst und auch die Kinder widmete.

10   Vorspielen zum Zuhören

Zu Rauters regelmäßigen Verpflichtungen gehört das Klavierspiel sowohl für die Kinder als auch die Erwachsenen. Denn die einzige Möglichkeit, Instrumentalmusik in Camphill hören zu können, waren Aufführungen von Musikern bzw. das gemeinsame Proben und Singen im Chor. Radiomusik oder Plattenspieler gehörten nicht zum Konzept Königs. Nach König hatte insbesondere das Zuhören und Lauschen eine wichtige Bedeutung.[112] Mit Rauter, dem erfahrenen Musiker, Lehrer und Improvisator, waren qualitativ anspruchsvolle Aufführungen ‚zur Seelenpflege' aller gewährleistet.

11   Lebenskrise in Camphill

Rauter hatte bereits zehn Jahre in London gelebt, als er Ende 1945 nach Camphill aufbrach. Die von ihm mit Kriegsbeginn angeregten Committee und Gesellschaften waren auf den Weg gebracht. Seine Aufgabe dort erfüllt. Es

---

112   Später in den 50er Jahren wurden in Camphill dazu neue Erkenntnisse gemacht. Vgl. Katarina Seeherr, ‚Karl Königs Beitrag zur Musiktherapie in der Heilpädagogik', in *Musiktherapeutische Umschau*, 41:3 (2020) (Göttingen: Vadenhoeck & Ruprecht), 242–51 (248).

scheint, als ob er auch mit Camphill Abstand zu dem Leben in der vom Krieg gezeichneten Stadt suchte.

Damit entschied er sich nach einem Jahr der Trennung deutlich für das Zusammensein mit Claire. Außerdem eröffnete ihm Camphill die Möglichkeit, mit sich selbst als Mensch und anthroposophischer Christ weiterzukommen. Die Lebensumstände in Camphill waren jedoch viel schwieriger, als er es sich bei seiner Zusage vorstellen konnte. Zudem wurde Claire schwanger und nach seiner Geburt benötigte das Baby besondere Aufmerksamkeit. Obwohl Rauter alles tat, um sämtlichen Aufgaben innerhalb der Gemeinschaft gerecht zu werden, war er hin- und hergerissen zwischen den Anforderungen der Community, glücklichen Stunden mit den Kindern, ihn erfüllenden anthroposophischen Einsichten und dem Verlust seines produktiven Lebens als Musiker. Er zweifelte oft an sich selbst und Depressionen[113] quälten ihn nicht nur in Camphill, sondern insbesondere bei seinem letzten Londoner Aufenthalt im Frühjahr 1947.

12 Abschiedskonzert

> Am Abend beinahe die ganze Community kommt – nur Carlo [Pietzner] ist nicht da, weil er das Haus hütet – ich glaube aber, dass er auf mich böse ist – ich spiele mit Jürgen die 1. und 3. Schubert-Sonatine und die 1. Beethoven-Sonate nach der Pause, dann allein die große c-Moll Schubertsonate – es macht großen Eindruck und K[önig] ist sehr lieb – halb tot ins Bett.[114]

Der Österreicher verabschiedete sich aus Camphill von seinen Kollegen, überwiegend Flüchtlingen aus Österreich, mit Kompositionen von Schubert und Beethoven.

---

113 Seine Tagebucheintragungen vom 10. bis 12.03.1946 sind mit einem schwarzen Kreis am Rand gekennzeichnet, womit Rauter seine Stimmung ausdrückt. Am 27.04.1946: ‚Ich fühle mich ganz unerholt und bin unglücklich, versuche aber stark zu bleiben, schon um 10 Uhr im Bett, Klärle ist schrecklich müde.' Am 30.05.1946: ‚Ich bin kaum auf der Welt und wie im Chaos.' Vgl. MMCS Rauter Box 1, Tagebuch 1946.

114 Vgl. MMCS Rauter Box 1, Tagebuch 1947, Eintrag vom 22.06.1947.

13   Zusammenfassung

Die Berufsbezeichnung des Musiktherapeuten, die Rauter in dem zitierten Bericht von 1973[115] verwendet, setzt sich erst seit Ende der 1950er Jahre als Spezialisierung in Zusammenarbeit mit anderen professionellen Therapien durch.[116] Für die Zeit von 1946 bis 1947 in Camphill kann man von einer musiktherapeutischen Arbeit im eigentlichen Sinne noch nicht sprechen. In dem einmaligen Kontext einer heilpädagogischen Dorfgemeinschaft, die sich selbst trägt und differenziert mit Handwerkern, Landwirten, Therapeuten und Heilpädagogen den Bedürfnissen und Fähigkeiten der Behinderten entgegenkommt und sie fördert, war davon noch keine Rede. Rauters Arbeit war jedoch ein wichtiger Meilenstein im Neuland der Musiktherapie, die Karl König dann in seinem erwähnten Aufsatz von 1959 weiter ausführte.

Für Rauter gab es Ende 1945 noch keinerlei Lehr-Modelle auf musiktherapeutischem Gebiet, die er im Umgang mit unterschiedlich behinderten Kindern hätte anwenden können. In seinen Tagebüchern finden sich keine Spuren einschlägiger Literatur dazu. Es scheint gemeinsam mit den Mitarbeitern keine Auswertung der Reaktionen bei den Kindern in den Musikstunden oder beim Vorspielen für Kinder gegeben zu haben. Vergeblich sucht man in seinen Tagebüchern nach Besprechungen mit Dr. König, in denen die heilpädagogische Situation einzelner Kinder erörtert und die Indikation bestimmter Therapien festgelegt werden. Dennoch kann Rauter bei seiner Arbeit mit den Kindern auf seine Erfahrungen im Umgang mit Blinden zurückgreifen. Diese bestanden im Zuhören und Raumlassen, ferner in sensibler Zuwendung zum individuellen Gegenüber, um Spannungen zu lösen oder innere Sicherheit und Selbstbewusstsein zu fördern.[117]

1938 bereits hatte Rauter in London Anna Freud[118] kennengelernt. Nach Andrea Rauter schätzte sie über Jahre hin seine Arbeit und vertraute ihm mitunter Kinder an, mit denen nur er arbeiten konnte. Andrea Rauter schilderte dazu ein Beispiel:

---

115   80. Aus: Bericht von Ferdinand Rauter über dessen Internierung sowie die Entwicklung der Austrian Musicians' Group und Anglo-Austrian Music Society 1940–1973, o.D. (1973), 451.
116   König, ,Zur Musiktherapie in der Heilpädagogik', 77–88.
117   Seeherr, 248.
118   London, 28.11.1938; neben Anna Freud (1895–1982) lernte Rauter dabei die Kinderpsychoanalytikerin Dorothy Tiffany Burlingham (1891–1979) kennen, die sich blinden Kindern widmete und Rauters Urteil und Erfahrung wertschätzte. Vgl. MMCS, Rauter Box 1, Tagebuch 1938.

> Anna Freud Centre brought him a blind child who was autistic, and nobody knew what to do with her. It was miracles he worked with her, and she was eventually able to go to a normal school for the blind, which was quite extraordinary. But he had this relationship with her. She used to come to the door downstairs, two floors down, 72 steps down. And one of us would go and open the door downstairs, and Jill would come in. And my father would start playing upstairs, the march he had written for her. And, so, this child who could hardly stand, learnt to walk, and walking up the stairs, and then without the banister, and then into the music room. ... He had a total understanding, and the music therapy he did was wonderful.[119]

Nach seiner Rückkehr aus Camphill arbeitete Rauter eine Zeitlang mit Pionieren der Musiktherapie wie Juliette Louise Alvin (1897–1982), Paul Nordorff und Clive Robbins zusammen. Der Ansatz von Nordorff/Robbins kam dabei eher Rauters therapeutischem Umgang mit autistischen und entwicklungsverzögerten Kindern entgegen.[120] Es schließt sich der Kreis: Das natürliche Verhältnis, das der junge Ferdinand den blinden Kindern gegenüber an der Schule seines Vaters erlernte, bewahrte er sein gesamtes Leben zum Dienst an anderen.

Seit seiner Rückkehr nach London im Juni 1947 lebte und arbeitete Rauter weiter als Pianist, Kammermusiker und Liedbegleiter von Engel Lund. Doch als vielseitiger ‚Renaissance-Mann' war er zugleich als Pädagoge, Mykologe, Botaniker, Referent und später Fotograf tätig. Sein offenes Haus in 74 Carlton Hill war über dreißig Jahre lang Begegnungsstätte für Menschen, denen Rauter zuhörte, die er inspirierte und mit denen er musizierte. Claire Rauter entwickelte sich zu einer erfolgreichen Pädagogin und angesehenen Schulleiterin, weit über die Grenzen Londons hinaus bekannt.[121]

---

119 Transcript Andrea Rauter Interview by Norbert Meyn, Royal College of Music, Project Music, Migration, Mobility.
120 E-Mail von Andrea Rauter vom 22.10.2021 an JRH.
121 Stahrenberg, ‚Claire Rauter', in online *Lexikon verfolgter Musiker*, 2017.

FIGURE 13.2   Rehearsal in Rauter's home, 74 Carlton Hill, London NW8: Norbert Brainin, violin; Ferdinand Rauter, piano; photomontage on the back wall portrait by Hans (Peter) Schidlof, violist
PHOTO COURTESY OF ANDREA RAUTER, YEAR UNKNOWN

14

Mischa Spoliansky's Music for the Movie *Mr. Emmanuel* (1944)

Jörg Thunecke

Abstract

Russian-born *Mischa Spoliansky* (1898–1985) was a well-known composer of cabaret music during the Weimar years. In 1933 he emigrated to England and wrote music for numerous British films, among others in 1944 for the movie *Mr. Emmanuel*, based on an eponymous novel by the Jewish writer Louis Golding (1895–1958), published in 1939. In both novel and movie Isaac Emmanuel, a retired secretary of the Jewish Board of Guardians in Doomington, goes on a quest in Nazi Germany to establish the whereabouts of the mother of a Jewish refugee boy, Bruno Rosenheim (the time frame of the plot is moved from 1936 to 1938). In Berlin he is wrongly accused of conspiracy, is tortured in a Gestapo jail, only to be released following the intervention of Elsie Silver – a famous cabaret singer. Emmanuel ultimately establishes the fate of Bruno's mother, who has become the wife of Karl Heinkes, a NS official. Spoliansky's background music for the movie is primarily based on the melody of the Zionist anthem 'Hatikvah' ('The Hope'), which in the form of a *leitmotif* accompanies the plot's development. The film represents a turning point in Spoliansky's career and reflected his identity as a Jewish refugee in Britain.

Mischa Spoliansky (1898–1985)[1] was born into a musical Jewish family in Białystok, then part of the Russian Empire. His father Pawlov was an opera

---

1 Cf. Micha Spoliansky, *Ich schreibe ein Buch* (London: 1980). A typescript is kept at the Akademie der Künste (Berlin): pages 1–151 deal with Spoliansky's career prior to his emigration to England, the remainder (appr. another 100 pages) cover his life in England until his death in the 1980s, however, there is no mention of *Mr. Emmanuel* in this document; see also 'Zeittafel' 'Mischa Spoliansky', in Alan Lareau et al. (eds.), *Mischa Spoliansky: Musikalische Stationen zwischen 'Morphium' und Widerstand. Eine Hommage zum 100. Beilageheft zur CD* (1998), 25f; and Carolin Stahrenberg, *Hot Spots von Café bis Kabarett. Musikalische Handlungsräume im Berlin Mischa Spolianskys 1918–1933* (Münster: Waxmann, 2012), 99–120: '"im Halbdunkel des Dazwischen" Mischa Spolianskys Wege und Stationen', 99–120 u. 244–66: 'Das Kabarett der Komiker'.

singer, his sister Lisa a pianist, and his brother Alexander a cellist. After the birth of Mischa, the family moved to Warsaw and later to Kalisz, now in Poland. After the early death of his mother in 1904, the family split up: Mischa's siblings relocated to Warsaw, while he stayed with his father and eventually moved to Vienna and then to Dresden, where Spoliansky's early musical education continued. He made his public debut at the age of ten, but shortly thereafter, in 1907, his father died, and Spoliansky moved to Königsberg in East Prussia, where he had relatives. In 1914, following the outbreak of the First World War, he fled to Berlin, where his brother worked as a cellist.

There, Spoliansky worked in coffeehouses as a pianist to finance his musical education at the Stern'sche Konservatorium. His first compositions were played by the UFA-Filmtheater Orchester on Friedrichstraße and also by Giuseppe Becce's (1877–1973) Kino-Orchester. In addition to that he also worked as composer and pianist at a Russian émigré cabaret in Berlin, where Friedrich Hollaender (1896–1976) and Werner Richard Heymann (1896–1961) spotted him. They invited him in December 1920 to compose and play for the literary cabaret 'Schall und Rauch' in the basement of the Große Schauspielhaus, founded by Max Reinhardt (1873–1943).[2] Spoliansky set texts to music by well-known writers like Walter Mehring (1896–1981), Kurt Tucholsky (1890–1935), Klabund (1890–1928), and Joachim Ringelnatz (1883–1934). Additionally, he also accompanied stars such as Gussy Holl (1888–1966), Paul O'Montis (1894–1940), and Rosa Valetti (1876–1937), as well as Trude Hesterberg (1892–1967) on the piano. In 1920, under the pseudonym 'Arno Billing', he composed the melody for the first homosexual anthem called 'Das lila Lied', with lyrics by Kurt Schwabach (1898–1966), which he dedicated to the sexologist Magnus Hirschfeld (1868–1935), while at the same time churning out amusing dance tunes like the *valse boston* 'Morphium', performed by the scandalous dancer Anita Berber (1899–1928). In 1922 he became acquainted with the poet Marcellus Schiffer (1892–1932), as well as the French chanteuse Margo Lion (1899–1989);[3] and in the same year he married the dancer Elsbeth Reinwald (1900–88).

---

2 Cf, Kevin Gough-Yates, 'The British Feature Film as a European Concern. Britain and the Emigré Film-Maker, 1933–45', in Günter Berghaus (ed.), *Theatre and Film in Exile. German Artists in Britain, 1933–1945* (Oxford/New York: Oswald Wolff Books/Berg Publishers, 1989), 135–66 (137): 'The composers Allan Gray, the Polish-born émigré, and the ubiquitous Mischa Spoliansky had composed for Max Reinhardt as well as for cabaret in Berlin; they incorporated classical and popular themes into their arrangements for the cinema.'
3 Marguerite Hélène Barbe Elisabeth Constantine Lion (1899–1989), known as Margo Lion, was a French chanteuse, parodist, cabaret singer and actress, best known for her role as Pirate Jenny in director G.W. Pabst's 1931 French language adaptation of Bertolt Brecht and Kurt Weill's *Threepenny Opera* (*Die Dreigroschenoper*).

In early 1923 Spoliansky became the house composer of the cabaret 'Wilde Bühne' in Berlin.[4] Here, in cooperation with Schiffer, he caused a sensation in October of that year, when Margo Lion performed 'Die Linie der Mode'. According to Alan Lareau 'Spoliansky's subtle and elegant musical setting complement[ed] the text to grand humorous effect.'[5] When the 'Wilde Bühne' closed, the veteran entertainment entrepreneur Wilhelm Bendow (1884–1950) opened the cabaret 'TüTü'. Spoliansky, who also worked at the Munich Kleinkunstbühne 'Bonbonniere', was one of the main contributors. In 1926 Spoliansky, after composing the music for the movie *Victoria* (screenplay by Somerset Maugham), accompanied the famous Austrian tenor Richard Tauber (1891–1946) in a recording of songs from Schubert's 'Winterreise', having recorded an album of twelve German folk songs with the singer during the previous year.[6]

The artistic pinnacle of Spoliansky's career during the Weimar Republic was the revue *Es liegt in der Luft* (text by Marcellus Schiffer) in 1928, staged at Reinhardt's 'Komödie', which made him famous throughout Germany.[7] In 1928 Marlene Dietrich (1901–1992) performed in this revue, being discovered one year later in Spoliansky's *Zwei Krawatten* (text by Georg Kaiser [1878–1945]) by Austrian-American film maker Josef von Sternberg (1894–1969), who was searching for a leading actress in the movie *The Blue Angel*. There followed in 1930 the revue *Wie werde ich reich und glücklich?*, with a libretto by Felix Joachimson (1902–1992), and in 1931 the burlesque *Alles Schwindel*. In March 1932 the Berlin 'Kabarett der Komiker' offered a 'cabaret opera', an artistic novelty, for which Spoliansky and Schiffer (who committed suicide later that year), under the direction of Kurt Robitschek (1890–1950), contributed *Rufen Sie Herrn Plim!*. The plot was set in a department store, starring Harald Paulsen (1895–1954) and Irene Eisinger (1903–94).[8] Spoliansky's last contribution to the 'Kabarett der Komiker', prior to his emigration, was *100 Meter Glück* in 1933. In the early 1930s Spoliansky also started writing music for movies (e.g. *Nie wieder Liebe* [1931]), and the song 'Heute Nacht oder nie' for the film *Das Lied einer Nacht* (1932) made him world-famous.

---

4   At that time, Spoliansky was also working at the cabaret 'Rakete' (1922–24) in Berlin.
5   Cf. Alan Lareau, 'Mischa Spoliansky: Berlin's Cosmopolitan Maestro', in Lareau et al. (eds.), *Mischa Spoliansky: Musikalische Stationen*, 27–30 (28).
6   Cf. Habakuk, 'Spoliansky at the Piano', in Lareau et al. (eds.), *Mischa Spoliansky: Musikalische Stationen*, 34f.
7   Cf. Lareau, 'Mischa Spoliansky: Berlin's Cosmopolitan Maestro', in Lareau et al. (eds.), *Mischa Spoliansky: Musikalische Stationen*, 29.
8   Cf. Alan Lareau/Gerhard Zeyen: "'Rufen Sie Herrn Plim!'", in Lareau et al. (eds.), *Mischa Spoliansky: Musikalische Stationen*, 30–32 (31f.).

When Hitler came to power in 1933, Spoliansky, like most Jewish artists in Germany, was no longer allowed to work in the 'Aryanised' entertainment industry. Consequently, he emigrated via Austria to England, where he started a second career as composer of film music, being taken under the wing of the local expatriate cinematographic community, as well as British producers and directors.

Spoliansky was thirty-four when he arrived in London and quite a mature composer whose work changed little during the remaining fifty-one years. His first film music in England was for the movie *The Lucky Number* (1933). Lilly Darvas (1902–1974), the wife of Ferenc Molnar (1878–1952), had recommended him to Alexander Korda (1893–1956), and he thereafter became Korda's most important prewar musical collaborator, composing tunes for *The Private Life of Don Juan* (1934), and the animated short *The Fox Hunt* (1936), among others. His music was widely recorded, and his songs, especially those for the Afro-American singer Paul Robeson (1898–1976), starring in *Sanders of the River*, and the Gaumont-British films *The Ghost Goes West* (1935), *The Man Who Could Work Miracles* (1938), *King Salomon's Mines* (1937) and *Paradise for Two* (1937) became instant successes. However, at the end of October 1939, with Britain now at war with Germany, filming came abruptly to an end for a while.

Despite this, the Second World War – according to Kevin Gough-Yates – became the most fruitful period of Spoliansky's career.

> He wrote characteristically imaginative and varied scores for over a dozen films, including *The Man from Morocco* (1945), the remarkable Co-operative Movement short, *Song of the People* (1945), and *Wanted for Murder* (1946). *Mr. Emmanuel* (1944), set in the England and Germany of 1938, produced one of his finest examples of the incidental music of which he was an advocate. The war brought him into regular contact with the BBC, especially with the Foreign Section which broadcast propaganda to Germany.[9]

Spoliansky's music, along with that of numerous other exiled composers, was banned by the BBC; however, its Foreign Section valued his flexibility to write under pressure and continued to employ him. Thus, he not only composed the signature tune for the Austrian Cabaret *Alle Achtung* (February 1941), and a number of German and Italian programme signature tunes, but he also wrote

---

9 Kevin Gough-Yates, 'Mischa Spoliansky in Exile', in Lareau et al. (eds.), *Mischa Spoliansky: Musikalische Stationen*, 35–37 (36). In his Ph.D thesis (cf. fnt. 10) Gough-Yates mentions Spoliansky only in passing (250).

various propaganda songs, sung by artists such as Martin Miller (1899–1969), Albert Lieven (1906–71), Walter Rilla (1894–1980) and Peter Illing (1899–1966), at times even singing himself under the name of Tony Galante. His version of Brecht's poem 'The Soldier's Bride' was so successful that it was broadcast in translation on the domestic service and sung by Irene Eisinger (1903–1994) at a recital at the Wigmore Hall in London in January 1942. His expertise and professionalism was greatly admired, not least by the department's wartime producer Marius Goring (1912–1998),[10] and he was contracted for a number of broadcasts throughout 1943/44 at Bush House. According to Gough-Yates 'Spoliansky composed best for small orchestras and bands that sounded as though they were playing with a spontaneous and unrehearsed naturalness, with seemingly stray solo instruments, a harmonica or violin, suddenly appeared from nowhere.' However, '[h]e eschewed new recording techniques and multi-track sound recordings, selecting to compose scores that did not stand alone as "great symphonic" or impressive works, but were an integral part of the films'.[11]

During the war years Spoliansky wrote film music for movies like *Secret Mission* (1942) and *Take This to Heart* (1944), not to mention *Mr. Emmanuel* in 1944[12] – often subtle, modest, and sometimes brilliantly detailed scores. And during his later career in the postwar era, he composed scores for some fifty films, such as *Wanted for Murder* (1946), *A Voice in the Night* (1946), *The Happiest Days of Your Life* (1950), *Trouble in Store* (1953), *Saint Joan* (1957), *The Whole Truth* (1958), *North West Frontier* (1959), *The Battle of the Villa Fiorita* (1965), *The Best House in London* (1969), and *Hitler: The Last Ten Days* (1973), containing some of his finest compositions, based on the conviction 'that film music, at its best, is incidental, and should support the drama without drawing attention to itself.'[13]

Louis Golding (1895–1958) was an English writer, famous in his time for novels, though nowadays largely forgotten. He also wrote short stories, essays, fantasies, travel books and poetry.[14] Born in Manchester into a Ukrainian-Jewish

---

10   Cf. Kevin Gough-Yates, *The European Filmmaker in Exile in Britain 1933–1945*, Ph.D. Dissertation (Open University, 1990), 212–14; Goring became Head of the BBC's 'German Dramatic Production' on 23 March 1943.

11   Gough-Yates, 'Mischa Spoliansky in Exile', 37.

12   There is no mention of *Mr. Emmanuel* in Gough-Yates' Ph.D. thesis (cf. *ibid.* pt. 1: 'Empire and Diversions: Europe, Aliens, Exile and British Film 1930–1945', 11–69); neither is there any mention of Spoliansky's film music (cf. 'The International Appeal of German Music', 268–90).

13   Gough-Yates, 'Mischa Spoliansky in Exile', 37.

14   J.B. Simons, *Louis Golding: A Memoir* (London: The Mitre Press, 1958), especially Chpt. 17: 'The Summing Up', 112–39.

family, Golding was educated at Manchester Grammar School and Queen's College, Oxford, using his Manchester background (as the fictive Doomington)[15] and Jewish themes in his fiction. *Magnolia Street*,[16] based on the Hightown area of Manchester, became a bestseller in 1932. In the two decades between 1934 and 1954 Golding wrote the so-called 'Doomington Saga', a pentalogy consisting of *The Five Silver Daughters* (1934), *Mr. Emmanuel* (1939), *The Glory of Elsie Silver* (1945), *The Dangerous Places* (1951), and *To the Quayside* (1954). Of this series of five books, *Mr. Emmanuel* became by far the best known due to the fact it was turned into a successful movie in 1944.[17]

Mr Emmanuel resides in Magnolia Street, in the Jewish quarter of Doomington (Lancashire), next door to Sam Silver on Oleander Street. Recently retired as secretary of the Jewish Board of Guardians he receives, in July 1935, a letter from Rose Cooper in Hampshire, the daughter of another Jewish neighbour of his. Mrs Cooper is temporarily putting up five German-Jewish refugee boys and is asking for Mr Emmanuel's help; for one of these boys, Bruno Rosenheim, whose father was a resistance fighter murdered by the Gestapo, suffers from severe depression since he has not heard from his mother in Berlin for several months. Isaac Emmanuel accepts the invitation, despite the fact that he was supposed to join his son in Palestine, and travels to Ringwood near the New Forest. There he promises Bruno he will travel to Germany in an attempt to uncover what happened to the boy's mother, following unsuccessful attempts by the Head Office of the Jewish Board in London to ascertain details via the jüdische Gemeinde in Berlin. At the end of January 1936, Mr Emmanuel departs by train for Berlin, where he stays at the Pension Kahn, Bambergerstraße 13, subsequently making inquiries with the Jewish Committee regarding Bruno's mother's last known residence at Motzstraße 65, and finally also at the *Einwohnermeldeamt* at the Police HQ on Alexanderplatz. In the course of these inquiries, he becomes – wrongly – implicated in the assassination of Wilhelm Gustloff (1895–1936), since 1932 National Leader of the Swiss

---

15 Cf. Louis Golding, *The World I Knew* (London: Hutchinson, 1940), 7–27 (23): 'I incorporated the word "doom" in the name [Doomington], because for me doom presides over that city [Manchester]. I mean not only doom of the factory-hands in the factories and the clerks in its warehouses, but the doom of the Jews who live in its Ghetto, the doom that has presided over their dispersal and is frustrating, perhaps not forever, their reuniting on the hill-tops of Zion and the fields of Sharon.'
16 Louis Golding, *Magnolia Street* (London: Victor Gollancz, 1932); the novel was also translated into German under the title *Die Magnoliastrasse* (Paris: Europaeischer Merkur, 1934).
17 Louis Golding, *Mr. Emmanuel* (London: Rich & Cowan, 1939). There was also an American edition, published by Viking Press in New York in the same year. All page references follow the English edition.

Group of the NSDAP 'Auslandsorganisation', by David Frankfurter (1909–1982). Frankfurter was a Croatian Jew, who, while studying in Germany, witnessed the Nazis' rise to power and the introduction of antisemitic laws. The banning of Jews from German universities forced him to move to Switzerland in 1934. There, among Germans and German-speaking Swiss, he witnessed the Nazi movement, led by Gustloff (*Landesgruppenleiter*), gain ground. Convinced of the danger posed by the Nazis, Frankfurter shot Gustloff at his Davos residence on 4 February 1936, and although the assassination was well received by the largely anti-Nazi population of the country, the Swiss government prosecuted him owing to concerns about the country's neutrality. Frankfurter was duly convicted and sentenced to eighteen years' imprisonment. At the end of the Second World War, he applied for a pardon, which was granted; nonetheless, he was expelled from Switzerland, moved to the British Mandate of Palestine, and settled in Tel Aviv. He later became an employee of the Israeli Ministry of Defence and an officer in the Israeli Army.

On 8 February 1936, Mr Emmanuel is arrested by the Gestapo on a trumped-up conspiracy charge. The headline in the local newspaper *Beobachter am Abend* read: 'ACCOMPLICE IN GUSTLOFF MURDER ARRESTED. INTERNATIONAL ANGLO-RUSSIAN JEW SPY UNMASKED' (249). Attempts by His Majesty's Consul-General and even the British Ambassador in Berlin to secure the release of Isaac Emmanuel (*1871[18]), who is detained in Schloß Kastanienburg, an SS prison outside Berlin for months on end and tortured to obtain a confession, fail. However, in the latter part of 1936 he is suddenly moved to Moabit Prison in Berlin and eventually released due to an intervention by Elsie Silver, one of the daughters of Sam Silver, Emmanuel's neighbour in Doomington. Ms Silver, officially still Lady Malswetting, but for the past year lover of SS Gruppenführer Wilhelm Brockenburg,[19] is a celebrated cabaret artist at various Kurfürstendamm theatres, singing songs composed by Mischa Spoliansky, to lyrics by Marcellus Schiffer (339).[20] Elsie spotted the news of Isaac Emmanuel's

---

18   According to the movie, Isaac Emmanuel was born in Russia in May 1875 (in the novel 1871).

19   Golding's claim in the novel that Brockenburg found himself attracted to Elsie Silver two and half years after the Nuremberg Ordinances (334) is incompatible with the historical facts since the so-called *Nürnberger Gesetze* were decreed on 15 September 1935, i.e. the novel's plot would be based in spring 1938 rather than in summer of 1936.

20   Cf. Golding, *Mr. Emmanuel*, 339: 'She went back to the stage, and in a year or two was one of the most successful artists at the Kurfürstendamm theatre. [...] Fritzi Massary was getting on a bit, Marlene Dietrich was just a novice, Margo Lion and Elsie Silver were the reigning queens.' Cf. also Louis Golding, *The Glory of Elsie Silver* (London: Hutchinson, 1945), 81: 'Then it came back to her. Music by Spoliansky, Book by Schiffer. One of the glorious revues the Jew-boys had turned out during the twenties for the Kurfürstendamm

arrest in a local newspaper and persuaded her Nazi lover, a close friend of Hermann Göring's, to intervene on Emmanuel's behalf. She also succeeded in obtaining the current address of Hertha Rosenheim, Bruno's mother, who had remarried, become the wife of Karl Heinkes, a prominent SA official, and had since moved to Hamburg-Altona. Isaac Emmanuel visits her there and informs her that her son is still alive, despite her husband's claim that Bruno was dead after having burned all letters from England. When challenged by her husband: "'So you want your little Jew-bastard back? You can have him. Take him off to Palestine, pig-Jewess, where you belong. You and your stinking brat!'" (422),[21] she disowns Bruno. The Nazi bully for his part threatens Isaac Emmanuel with violence but is rebuffed:

> You can beat me up. You can beat up a thousand other Jews. You can kill all the Jews in your country. [...] Where will you be then, I ask you? I will tell you. You will be, sooner or later, where all the enemies of Israel are now. You will be where Egypt is, where Moab is, where Rome is. And it will not be so long like you think, either. And we, where will we be? We will be where we always have been. (426–27)

Subsequently, in late summer of 1936, Mr Emmanuel finally returns to England and tells Bruno a white lie to the effect that his mother, working for the underground in Germany and being hunted by the Gestapo, though never caught, eventually died from natural causes (447–48). Bruno in turn swears:

> I can forgive them, in a way, for killing my father. I can even forgive them for killing my mother. My father and mother were their enemies. They were working against them. But you? An old man like you? An old man who has done nothing? I cannot forgive them for that! I will never forgive them for that! I will not forget! I will not forgive! Some day I will have my revenge. (450)

Louis Golding co-authored the script for *Mr. Emmanuel* with veteran screenwriter Gordon Wellesley (1894–1980), who had already penned several British anti-Nazi movies, most notably *Night Train to Munich* (1940). Apart from many

---

theatre and the delectation of all Europe. [...] The words suddenly came to her lips, it was hard work not to start humming them ... "Nur ein Tropfen von L'Heurs Bleu / Vermischt mit Juchtenduft". The haunting tango out of "Es liegt in der der Luft". The snaky metal-sheathed hips of Margo Lion. It had been a toss-up between Margo Lion and Elsie Silver.'

21 In the movie, Hertha Heinkes, alias Rosenheim, is not Jewish but an 'Aryan'.

minor alterations and omissions, some of them referred to below, the main change in the movie, compared to the plot of the novel, is its time frame: the former takes place two years later in 1938, as can be gleaned from the fact that Mr Emmanuel's passport is signed by Anthony Eden (1897–1977), Foreign Secretary in Neville Chamberlain's Government until 20 February 1938, whereas in the novel, his brand new passport is signed by John Simon (1873–1954), Home Secretary in Baldwin's Government until June 1935 (147). Another important change is a key scene, approximately halfway through the movie, when Mr Emmanuel goes to a show where Elsie Silver, one of the foremost Berlin cabaret stars, sings a song in the style of Spoliansky's hits of the 1920s, a scene which has no counterpart in the novel. Neither have the repeated tête-à-têtes of Elsie Silver's with Willi Brockenburg, a Nazi bigwig, during which she pressurises her lover to use his influence to get Mr Emmanuel released. Ample coverage, however, is given to Isaac Emmanuel's encounter with a street vendor, who turns out to be a former professor at Berlin University. The secret meeting of the two men at a telephone box near Zoo station, where 'ROT FRONT LEBT' has been scrawled in red crayon onto the cover of the directory (205), was changed in the movie to a rather explicit drawing of Hitler hanging from the gallows.[22] Mr Emmanuel's incarceration in Schloß Kastanienburg and Moabit Prison was merged into a single confinement, though the scene of a lawyer's visit, trying to persuade Emmanuel to sign a confession, was kept. Completely omitted, on the other hand, was Emmanuel's religious turn in jail, repeatedly chanting psalms. Another omission was Emmanuel's excursion to Lubbenau in the Spreewald, the place where Bruno used to spend his summer vacations, which quite obviously was extraneous to the plot of the movie. And altered in the movie was also the eventual meeting between Mr Emmanuel and Hertha Rosenheim, alias Frau Heinkes, which for no apparent reason takes place in Berlin and not in Hamburg as it does in the novel. Left intact, however, were the opening scene of the novel, which take place in Doomington, the various events at the Coopers' residence in Hampshire, and Bruno's stay at Greystones, a public school near Haslemere in Surrey.

∙ ∙ ∙

Louis Golding's book *Mr. Emmanuel* sold well and was recommended to Warner Brothers in 1939. In Britain, the Italian producer Felippo Del Giudice

---

22   He later meets the scholar again in the exercise yard of Moabit Prison (327).

(1892–1962)²³ acquired the film rights, and he – under the directorship of Harold French (1897–1997) – turned the novel into a black and white movie (*Eagle-Lion. A Two Cities Film*, released in Britain at the beginning of October 1944²⁴). Del Giudice probably accepted the story on account of its attractive plotline, which enabled him to praise the virtues of British democracy, while denouncing European Fascism in general and Nazi antisemitism in particular.²⁵ In fact – as pointed out by Lawrence Baron – Harold French's *Mr. Emmanuel* (1944) holds the distinction of being the first and only wartime British commercial feature film to focus on Nazi antisemitism.²⁶ The cast consisted – among others²⁷ – of Felix Aylmer (1889–1979) = Mr Emmanuel, Greta Gynt (1916–2000) = Elsie Silver, Meier Tzelnicker = Mr Silver (1898–1980), Walter Rilla (1894–1980) = Wilhelm Brockenburg, Peter Mullins (1931–2006) = Bruno Rosenheim, Elspeth March (1911–1999) = Rose Cooper, Norman Pierce (1900–1968) = John Cooper, Maria Berger (?) = Frau Kahn, Arnold Marlé (1887–1970) = Herr Kahn, Irene Handl (1901–1987) = Trude, Oscar Ebelsbacher (1882–1952) = Professor, Frederick Schiller (1901–94) = Gestapo Examiner. As previously mentioned, Golding co-authored the script for *Mr. Emmanuel* with veteran screenwriter Gordon Wellesley, and '[w]hile the film version of *Mr. Emmanuel* toned down the Jewish content of Golding's 1939 novel, it remained faithful to his conviction that Jews had achieved acceptance as fellow citizens in Great Britain, and faced an implacable foe in Germany'.²⁸ As Laurence Baron notes, the author considered:

> Jews a separate race bound together by a common ancestry, history, and religion. He firmly believed that most Jews possessed a vestigial memory of their collective past that compelled them to protect their vulnerable Jewish brethren in the present.²⁹

---

23 Filippo Del Giudice fled Fascist Italy in 1933 for England where, four years later, he founded with Mario Zampi (1903–1963) 'Two Cities Films' and became responsible for creating some of the most quintessentially British films of the 1940s.
24 In the USA, United Artists released the movie in 1945.
25 *None Shall Escape* (1944) was the only wartime Anglo-Saxon film to recognise that the Third Reich planned to eradicate the Jews of Europe.
26 Lawrence Baron, '*Mr. Emmanuel* (1944). A Belated British Film about Nazi Antisemitism', in Nathan Abrams (ed.), *Hidden in Plain Sight. Jews and Jewishness in British Film, Television, and Popular Culture* (Evanston, IL: Northwestern UP, 2016), 69–90 (69).
27 Unfortunately, not all members of the cast could be identified.
28 Baron, 72.
29 *Ibid.*, 74. Golding visited Palestine 1927 and wrote *Those Ancient Lands* (1928); he later also published *The Jewish Problem* (1936) and *Hitler through the Ages* (1937).

What is striking about the opening scene of the movie, located in Magnolia Street, Doomington, in July 1938, is the mention of Palestine, accompanied by the background melody of the 'Hatikvah' ('The Hope'), the anthem for the first Zionist Congress in 1897, later becoming the Israeli national anthem.[30] The harmony of 'Hatikvah' follows a minor scale, often perceived as mournful in tone and uncommon in national anthems. Yet, as the title 'The Hope' and the words suggest, the song is optimistic and the overall spirit uplifting. It continues as 'Hintergrundmusik' in Isaac Emmanuel's house, who – in the presence of Sam Silver, his next-door neighbour of Oleander Street and father of Elsie Silver – decides to postpone his planned emigration to Palestine and instead assist the Cooper family in Hampshire in looking after three – not five, as in the novel – German-Jewish refugee boys, and Bruno Rosenheim in particular. By choosing this tune, Mischa Spoliansky undoubtedly meant to imply that Jews should be given shelter from oppression in Palestine, and 'Hatikvah' thus 'served as a subtextual message',[31] which would easily have been deciphered by contemporary Jewish audiences, though not necessarily by gentile ones. It recurs as a *leitmotif* in subsequent scenes, when Isaac Emmanuel, for instance, takes residence at a Jewish-run boarding-house in Berlin, and when he finally returns to England from Nazi Germany.

The next scene in the movie is located at the Coopers' cottage 'Shipscar' near Ringwood, a market town in south-west Hampshire on the River Avon, close to the New Forest. The pastoral setting of the English countryside, the dwelling's spacious and sunlit rooms, and the joyfulness of the Cooper children identifies the abode as a happy, safe place, underpinned by Spoliansky's cheerful, light-hearted, carefree background music, a cinematic strategy which, according to Baron, was further highlighted in the pressbook promoting the film:

> The background of the film is a vivid contrast of light and shadow, the peaceful, lovely English countryside stands out against the more subdued

---

30   'Hatikvah' (Hebrew: הַתִּקְוָה, lit. 'The Hope') is a 19th-century Jewish poem. The theme of the Romantic composition reflects the Jews' 2,000-year-old hope of returning to the Land of Israel, restoring it, and reclaiming it as a free and sovereign nation. Its lyrics were adapted from a poem by Naftali Herz Imber, a Jewish poet from Złoczów (todays Zolochiv, Ukraine), which was then in Galicia under Austrian rule. Imber wrote the first version of the poem in 1877. 'Hatikvah' was chosen as the organisational anthem of the First Zionist Congress in 1897. When the State of Israel was established in 1948, 'Hatikvah' was unofficially proclaimed the national anthem. It did not officially become the national anthem until November 2004.

31   Baron, 79.

atmosphere of Doomington's Magnolia Street, the brittle luxury of Berlin's night resorts and drama of its sinister prison.[32]

The initial cheerful mood soon changes, however, when Bruno Rosenheim, one of the refugee boys whom the Coopers are temporarily hosting, repeatedly fails to receive mail from his mother in Germany, accompanied by a rather mournful tune. And in connection with a road trip to fetch Captain Cooper from nearby Southampton, Bruno, in the company of Isaac Emmanuel, is seen walking along the nearby coast singing 'Drei Lilien', an old, and rather sad, German folksong,[33] the first and final stanza being indicative of the Jewish youth's gloomy disposition:

> Drei Lilien, drei Lilien,
> die pflanzt ich auf mein *Grab*,
> da kam ein stolzer Reiter
> und brach sie ab.
> Juvivallerallerallerallera,
> juvivallerallerallerallera,
> da kam ein stolzer Reiter
> und brach sie ab.
>
> [...]
>
> Und *sterbe* ich noch heute,
> so bin ich morgen *tot*;
> dann *begraben* mich die Leute
> ums Morgenrot.
> Juvivallerallerallerallera,
> juvivallerallerallerallera,
> dann *begraben* mich die Leute
> ums Morgenrot [emphasis added].

This depressing atmosphere finds further musical expression in the American folk ballad 'Oh My Darling, Clementine', intoned during Bruno's birthday party at the Coopers and at a subsequent camp party on the Channel coast, a popular song in trochaic metre, triggering Bruno's suicide attempt:

---

32   *Mr. Emmanuel* Press Book, LGP, BRBML-YUL (Yale University Library), cited in *ibid.*, 79, 89.
33   'Drei Lilien, drei Lilien' ('Three Lilies') is a German folksong ('Volks- und Trauerlied') the text having first been recorded around 1830. The composer is unknown.

> Oh my darling, oh my darling,
> Oh my darling, Clementine!
> *Thou art lost and gone forever*
> Dreadful sorry, Clementine [emphasis added].[34]

Bruno is rescued from drowning by Klaus, another refugee boy, but subsequently falls ill with rheumatic fever. When he threatens to repeat his suicide attempt, Isaac Emmanuel promises the lad to travel to Germany and make on-the-spot inquiries as to the whereabouts of the boy's mother. Once again, the *leitmotif* melody of 'Hatikvah' is intoned, accompanying this rather optimistic scene. On his arrival by train at Berlin-Friedrichstraße, however, Isaac Emmanuel is confronted near the station exit with a huge and brutal portrait of Adolf Hitler, accompanied by a brief, but rather dramatic, musical flourish signalling imminent danger, a tune repeated each time the protagonist is in mortal danger.

The doleful melody of the German 'Heimatlied' 'Im schönsten Wiesengrunde', initially intoned in D minor, makes up the background music during Isaac Emmanuel's arrival at the Pension Kahn at Motzstraße 3a. It is symptomatic of the sufferings of the Jewish owners, reduced to letting rooms in their own home to eke out a living, while at the same time indicative of the anxiety of the few remaining Jewish guests, as well as that of the landlady and her maid Trude, who are both constantly looking over their shoulder to ensure that the only 'Aryan' female employee does not spy on them. The song is based on a *Volksliedweise*, composed by Wilhelm Ganzhorn (1818–80) in the middle of the 19th century, and the *Heimwehton* of its three stanzas made it very popular among German emigrants and *Auslandsdeutschen*.

> Im schönsten Wiesengrunde ist meiner Heimat Haus;
> da zog ich manche Stunde ins Tal hinaus.
> Dich, mein stilles Tal, grüß ich tausendmal
> Da zog ich manche Stunde ins Tal hinaus.

---

34 The lyrics were written by Percy Montrose in 1884, based on an earlier song called 'Down by the River Liv'd a Maiden', but the origin of the tune is unknown. In his book *South from Granada* (1957), Gerald Brenan claimed that the melody was from an old Spanish ballad that was made popular by Mexican miners during the California Gold Rush. It is unclear when, where and by whom the song was first recorded in English, but the first version to reach the charts was that by Bing Crosby, recorded in 1941.

Müsst aus dem Tal ich scheiden, wo alles Lust und Klang;
das wär mein herbstes Leiden, mein letzter Gang.
Dich, mein stilles Tal, grüß ich tausendmal!
Das wär mein herbstes Leiden, mein letzter Gang.

Sterb ich – in Tales Grunde will ich begraben sein;
singt mir zur letzten Stunde beim Abendschein:
Dir, o stilles Tal, Gruß zum letzten Mal!
Singt mir zur letzten Stunde beim Abendschein.

In his pursuit to uncover Hertha Rosenheim's fate, once a resident of Motzstraße 3a,[35] Isaac Emmanuel pumps a street vendor – once an academic at Berlin University, now selling cigarettes – for information. The professor agrees to meet him clandestinely at a telephone booth near Zoo Station. However, the two men must abruptly abort their secret rendezvous when they come across an egregious Hitler-sketch on the cover of the telephone directory. Mischa Spoliansky gave expression to the two men's *angst* in a jarring and extremely scary musical accompaniment, which was to become a standard feature (*Begleitmusik*) of quite a few of the protagonist's perilous encounters with the NS authorities. And from this point onwards, Ray Redman's assertion in the *Saturday Review* that Golding's novel 'gathers pace and increases its claims upon our interest as it proceeds' and that 'the curve of excitement mounts to a climax and a denouement',[36] also applied to the movie. To the haunting melody of 'Hatikvah', Isaac Emmanuel receives Mr Kahn's warning that it is dangerous to ask questions in Nazi Germany and decides to write a letter to England, dated 3 February 1938, to this effect, the day before Felix Frankfurter (called Pawłowicz in the movie) assassinated Wilhelm Gustloff (called Kempner in the movie). He then notices on the opposite side of the street the name 'Elsie Silver' emblazoned in front of a nightclub called 'Kit Kat', advertising a show starring one of the five daughters of Mr Emmanuel's Doomington neighbour, Sam Silver. Though Louis Golding mentions in his novel that Ms Silver returned to the stage after her father's bankruptcy, eventually becoming one of the most acclaimed artists of Berlin's cabarets, reminiscent of Margo Lion (the reigning queen in the 1920s), and even though there is also a reference to Ms Silver singing to lyrics by Marcellus Schiffer and music by Mischa Spoliansky (339), there is no mention in the book of the following scene, which takes place exactly

---

35 The street numbers differ in novel & movie!
36 Ray Redman, 'Voice of a People', in: *The Saturday Review* (22 July 1939), 6–7 (7).

halfway through the movie and plays a pivotal part in it. Elsie Silver in fact – as in the novel – had become an irresistible feature of the light entertainment industry in Berlin and sings a song especially composed by Spoliansky for the movie in the style of his 1920s cabaret tunes. The initial stanza is in German:

> Wir sind uns fern und doch so nah,
> die einen hier, die andern da.
> Wann […] und sehnen sich,[37]
> laß uns vereinen, du und ich.

but then it switches to English:

> Oh, the world is full of wonders still,
> and it lies right at your feet at will.
> I have seen and learned and met, such as never I'll forget,
> only one thing I have not discovered yet.
>
> I don't know you, you don't know me,
> what wasted all that unity?
> We lived together under one same sky,
> but every day we passed one another by.
>
> Please tell me why I don't know you, you don't know me,
> what everybody's fate will be.
> When we are strangers walking down the street,
> it's time that you and I should meet.[38]

The actual singer in the movie was the Norwegian-born actress Margrethe Woxholt, who in England adopted the stage name Greta Gynt, a glamourous blonde who added sparkle to British movies from the late 1930s through to the 1940s. Both parts of her song consist of quatrains remotely reminiscent of the rhyme pattern used by Alfred Lord Tennyson (1809–1892) in his famous poem 'In Memoriam A.H.H' (1849). Until Mr Emmanuel's return to England, this cabaret song is the last genuinely pleasing music in the movie; from that point

---

37 The following two lines are unfortunately inaudible since Mr Emmanuel addresses a member of the audience at the cabaret 'Kit Kat'.
38 This song is reminiscent of another one that Mischa Spoliansky wrote only a few years later during the immediate postwar era. See 'Ausklang' in Spoliansky, *Ich schreibe ein Buch*, 190.

onwards, shrill dissonances dominate the subsequent key scenes of the film, interrupted only occasionally by odd interludes, when the background music slightly mitigates such jarring parts.

One such example is the official farewell party for Anton Kempner (the fictional counterpart of Wilhelm Gustloff), which was spoiled by the Nazi leader's assassination. Other instances include sequences during which Elsie Silver persuades her lover, the Nazi grandee Wilhelm Brockenburg, to use his influence to obtain Isaac Emmanuel's release.[39] The scenes at the Coopers' place and another scene at Bruno's boarding school are further examples. However, the most striking scenes during the second half of the movie consist of the repeated interrogations and floggings of Isaac Emmanuel, and a number of executions in jail, one being that of his professorial informant. Gruesome background music accompanies each of these scenes, highlighting the humiliation and degradation of human beings in Gestapo custody.

The concluding scene in Mr Emmanuel's quest for the whereabouts of Bruno's mother occurs in Berlin (and not in Hamburg-Altona, as in the novel), Elsie Silver supplying the address. As discussed earlier, Hertha Rosenheim ultimately turns out to be a certain Frau Heinkes, wife of a high-ranking Nazi official, who insists having been informed by her husband – who intercepted and destroyed Bruno's letters – that her son is dead. In view of the evidence to the contrary, she initially acknowledges that Bruno is still alive, but subsequently, under pressure from her husband to choose between him and her Jewish offspring,[40] disowns her son, to the consternation of Mr Emmanuel. The scene following Isaac Emmanuel's departure, warped by the image of a huge swastika at the Heinkes' residence, switches abruptly to the tranquil pastoral surroundings of the boarding school in East Sussex, following Isaac Emmanuel's eventual return to England. There he is reunited with Bruno, informing the

---

39   Of particular interest in the context is the question why Elsie Silver exerted herself to obtain the release of Mr Emmanuel. Lawrence Baron's claim that she was Golding's favourite creation 'because she began to redeem herself by rescuing Isaac' (Baron, 82) – though true in *Mr. Emmanuel* and certainly in later novels like *The Glory of Elsie Silver* (1945), *The Dangerous Places* (1951), and *To the Quayside* (1954) – is unfounded in the movie, in which she rescues her father's friend for sheer sentimental reasons (cf. J.B. Simons, *Louis Golding: A Memoir* [London: The Mitre Press, 1958], 112–39 (132): 'The outstanding personality is one daughter, Elsie Silver, a girl of remarkable beauty, and gifts who marries an English lord and subsequently weds a Nazi general and lives the life of the rich and the perverted. She reaches the Warsaw ghetto during the war [= 1943], escapes and flees to Hungary and becomes conscious of her Jewishness and endeavours to repent for her former life and the betrayal of her people.')

40   In the movie, Frau Heinkes is an 'Aryan', who had been married to Norbert Rosenheim, a Jew.

boy that his mother died of natural causes, taking refuge to even more blatant white lies than in the novel, thus forestalling future suicide attempts by the youngster. The *Begleitmusik* of the movie's final scene is once more the melody of 'Hatikvah', the musical accompaniment thus returning full circle to the opening scene. In the end, the message of this *leitmotif* tune is therefore quite an optimistic one, and its overall spirit uplifting, suggesting, as the song's title ('The Hope') does, that Spoliansky, in conclusion, meant to give vent to his belief that the Jewish people had a future after all, despite the fact that, by that time (in late 1944), details of the Holocaust were already widely known.

By and large then, as exemplified in his music for the movie *Mr. Emmanuel*, Mischa Spoliansky's emigration to England in 1933 was a turning point in his life; henceforth, 'der leidenschaftliche Bühnenkomponist schr[ieb] fast ausschließlich Filmmusiken.'[41] Carolin Stahrenberg fittingly summarised this turnaround of Mischa Spoliansky's checkered musical career as follows:

> Seine eigentliche Erfüllung fand Spoliansky jedoch im Theater. Hier zeigte sich sein besonderes Talent, musikalisch auf Texte zu reagieren, Stimmungen zu erfassen und seine Musik den Figuren anzupassen. Durch das Kabarett mit seinen Kurzsketchen und Chansons war er in diesen Formen bereits versiert. Noch Spolianskys spätere Filmkompositionen erschienen als Weiterentwicklung des zuerst im Kabarett, dann im Theater Erprobten, der Weg zur Leinwand die folgerichtige Fortsetzung des dort Erlernten. Gerade zu Beginn des Tonfilms war die Situation der Musiker den Gebräuchen im Theater ja noch relativ ähnlich, spielten diese doch am Filmset hinter den Kulissen – eine Situation, die der im Graben oder auf der Seitenbühne glich. Auch die Musik bestand neben 'Hintergrundmusik' aus Tonfilmschlagern, so dass die Arbeitsweise der Operetten- und Musicalkomposition verwandt war.[42]

The cinema production of *Mr. Emmanuel* – according to Kevin Gough-Yates's evaluation of the film – 'deserves to be remembered as a touching British movie that was unique in its focus on Nazi anti-Semitism and a Jewish protagonist.'[43] The question, though, remains, as to why British cinema should have produced

---

41   Habakuk Traber and Elmar Weingarten (eds.), *Verdrängte Musik. Berliner Komponisten im Exil* (Berlin: Argon, 1987), 205–359: 'Biographische Dokumentation', *ibid.* 'Mischa Spoliansky', 332f (332).
42   Stahrenberg, 107.
43   Baron, 85.

so few films with Jewish themes? According to the same critic, 'the answer lies in the complex interplay of ideologies which existed in England in which Jews are not identified as a single cohesive social group and in which, at some level, at least partial or complete assimilation occurs.'[44] Mischa Spoliansky's *Filmmusik* for *Mr. Emmanuel* undoubtedly helped, at least, to partially overcome this obstacle, and his repeated use of a musical *leitmotif*, gleaned from the Jewish 'Hatikvah', typically instilled optimism against a backdrop of Nazi horrors.

---

44 Kevin Gough-Yates, 'Jews and Exiles in British Cinema', in: *Year Book of the LBI* 37 (1992), 517–41 (540).

Index

Abraham, Paul 209
Adama Zijlstra, Anthony 44
Adenauer, Konrad 189
Akademie der Künste Berlin 221
Allied Nations 83
Altmann, Elsie 199
Alvin, Juliette Louise 282
Alwyn, William 174
Amadeus Quartet 3, 8, 115, 121, 125, 225
Anderson, Martin 219
Anna Freud Centre 282
annexation (see also *Anschluss*) 10–12, 16, 22
Anschluss (see also annexation) 4, 8, 15, 18, 25, 29, 39, 51, 57, 121–22, 126, 204, 243–44, 259, 267
Apprahamian, Felix 180, 186
Arlen, Walter 4, 23–26
Aschendorff, Jacob 89
Ascher, Leo 203
Asriel, André 98–99
Asscher, Abraham 34, 44
Association of Jewish Precentors (Gemeinschaft Jüdischer Kantoren) 75, 78–79, 88–93
Association of Jewish Refugees (AJR) 113, 118, 121
Auschwitz 12, 32, 37, 45–49, 140, 143, 154
Austrian Centre 2, 8, 264, 271
Austrian Musicians Group 115
Aylmer, Felix 293

Baar, Josef 48
Bach, Johann Sebastian 66
Back, Oskar 31, 46, 50
Baer, Hans 80
Baer, Werner 72
Baldwin, Lord Stanley 292, 54
Barber, Samuel 23
Bartók, Béla 97–98, 100, 172, 222
Bax, Arnold 100
BBC 7, 11, 63, 65, 123, 127, 157, 162–63, 168–81, 187–90, 217, 248, 257, 274
  European Service 2, 172–73
  Foreign Service 264, 287
  Home Service 2, 172–73
  Proms 231
  Singers (Chorus) 231, 236
Beal, Hilde 126
Becce, Giuseppe 285
Beethoven, Ludwig van 28, 70, 99, 104, 119–20, 123–24, 220, 271, 279–80
Belsize Square Synagogue 130
Ben Uri Art and Literary Society (Ben Uri Art Gallery) 5, 113–33
Benatzky, Ralph 194, 203, 206, 209
Beneš Decrees 13
Bendow, Wilhelm 286
Ben-Haim, Paul 130
Benjamin, Arthur 158, 162
Benjamin, George 231
Berber, Anita 285
Berg, Alban 17, 28, 34, 148, 183, 187
Bergen-Belsen 48, 154
Bergmann, Stefan 32, 49
Berlin Philharmonic Orchestra 32, 220
Berlin State Academy 170
Berlin State Opera Orchestra 120
Berson, Lazar 114
Bettelheim, Antonia/Toni 49
Bettelheim, Dolf 50
Bettelheim, Heini 49
Bismarck, Otto v. 10
Bittner, Julius 18
Blau, Trude 267–68, 276
Bliss, Arthur 172–73, 175
Bloomsbury House 265
Blum, Klaus 177–78
Borchert, Wolfgang 134, 149–50
Boschwitz, Ulrich A. 72
Boult, Sir Adrian 173
Brahms, Johannes 28, 103, 124, 135
Brainin, Norbert 3, 113, 115, 121–22, 125–26, 225, 264–65, 283
Brav, Ludwig 98–99, 103
Brecht, Bertolt 20, 27, 288
Britten, Benjamin 100, 157, 171, 178, 180, 186
Brooke, Rupert 174
Bruno Kittel Choir 120
Buchenwald 7, 23, 200, 247

Bunge, Hans   26
Bunzel, Julius   47
Bunzel, Laura (Lotte)   41, 47
Bureau of Stateless Refugees Affairs   86
Burian, Emil František   143
Busch, Fritz   230
Bush, Alan   158, 162, 173
Bush, Nancy   158
Butting, Max   21

Calmeyer, Hans   46
Camden Theatre   176
Canetti, Elias   264
Carl Rosa Opera   229, 236
Carner, Mosco   180, 189
Cecil (Abraham), Alfred   36, 50
Central British Fund for Germany Jewry   53
Central Chinese Musicians' Union   87
Cesoli, Kuno (see also Holzstein, Konrad)   39
Chajes, Julius   129
Chamber Orchestra of 1939 (Kammerorchester 1939)   81
Chamberlain, Sir Neville   53, 67, 292
Chopin, Frédéric   172, 271, 279
Cleverdon, Douglas   170, 174–82, 189
Cohen, David   34, 44
Cohen, Harriet   131
Cohn, Siegfried Salomon   53, 55–56, 64, 66, 68, 70–73
Colijn, Hendrik   35, 43
Comité van Waakzaamheid   40
Comité voor Joodsche Vluchtelingen   34
Concertgebouw Orkest   31, 36, 38, 50
Concertgebouw Trio   49
Connely, Tilly   226
Conservatorium of the Vereeniging Muzieklyceum Amsterdam   31, 34, 49
Constant, Marius   177
Contreras, José   85
Cooper, Ernest N.   265
Cooper, Martin   180
Copland, Aaron   23, 123
Courtauld, Samuel   117
Cross, Joan   229

Dachau   38, 56–57, 59, 61, 154, 200, 247
Dante   27

Daumer, Georg Friedrich   245
de la Mare, Walter   226
de la Martinez, Odaline   163
de Sarasate, Pablo   70
del Mar, Norman   176
Dessau, Paul   100, 143
Deutekom, Christine   50
Deutsches Symphonie-Orchester Berlin (RSO)   163
Dickens, Charles   158
Dietrich, Marlene   286
Doderer, Heimito von   15
Dollfuss, Engelbert   12, 15, 17, 35
Doniach, Shula   121
Dreifuß, Alfred   79–82, 92
Dresden, Sem   41
Dumas d. Ä, Alexandre   156
Dunera   4, 53, 68, 70
Dvořák, Antonín   70

Ebert, Carl   230
Eccles   124
Egk, Werner   178
Ehrenberg, Max   89
Eichendorff, Joseph v.   26
Eichmann, Adolf   44, 58
Eisinger, Irene   286, 288
Eisler, Hanns   4, 11, 20, 26–28, 97–98, 100, 103–4, 110, 143
Eisner (nee Loeser), Brigitte   124
Elman, Ralph   119
Erdmann, Eduard   21
Esslin, Martin   157, 160–61
European Jewish Artist Society   75–83, 92–93
European Piano Teachers' Association   128
Eysler, Edmund   203, 212

Farkas, Karl   192, 196, 201–2, 214
Fauré, Edgar   124
Federatie van Nederlandse Toonkunstenaars   36
Federation of Shanghai Musicians   86–87
Felber, Erwin   83
Feuchtwanger, Lion   97
Fimmen, Edo   31
Fischer, Betty   198, 204
Flesch, Carl   31, 44–46, 121

Flesch, Hans   102, 107
Flothuis, Marius   52
Foreign Pao Chia   83
Forsdyke, Sir John   264
Fortner, Wolfgang   21
Frank, Ernest   123
Frank, Paul   196
Frankel, Benjamin   123, 176, 179
Free Academy of Arts   145
Free Austrian Movement   115, 264
Free German League of Culture   2, 5, 94, 98–99, 102, 107, 111–12, 130
French, Harold   293
Freud, Anna   281–82
Frid, Géza   45
Fried, Oskar   120
Friedmann, Walter   80
Fromm-Michaels, Ilse   143
Fruchter, Josef   91
Fürstenthal, Robert   4, 21–28
Furtwängler, Wilhelm   46, 220

Gál, Erna   126
Gál, Hans   11, 13, 19, 126, 168, 171–72, 196, 219, 227, 264, 273
Galimir, Felix   28
Ganther, Heinz   80
Geiger, Hans   122
Geiger, Isy   122
Gellhorn, Peter   176, 217–36
George, Stefan   41, 254
Gestapo   7, 25, 56, 63, 289–91, 299
Geyer, Siegfried   196, 201
Ginastera, Alberto   156
Glahs, Rudolf   89
Goehr, Alexander   128
Goehr, Laelia   127
Goehr, Walter   127, 173, 178
Golding, Louis   8, 284, 288–89, 291–93, 297
Goldscheider, Ludwig   124
Goldschmidt, Adolph   116
Goldschmidt, Berthold   2, 6, 8–9, 98–99, 134–69, 171, 219
Gombrich, Dea   264
Gombrich, Sir Ernst Hans Josef   8, 125
Gorge, Marianne   272, 275
Goseling, Carel   39
Goslich, Siegfried   178

Gottfurcht, Fritz   102
Goudstikker, Jacques   38
Gough-Yates, Kevin   287–88, 300
Graener, Paul   242
Graff, Friedrich   61
Granados   124
Grand Opera Shanghai   77
Granichstaedten, Bruno   192–215
Grant, Rosalie   208–11
Grillparzer, Franz   14
Grindea, Carola   113, 128
Grindea, Miron   128
Grossberg, Mimi   39
Guildhall School of Music   121, 127–28, 219, 236
Gustloff, Wilhelm   289, 290, 297, 299

Haas, Joseph   21
Haas, Karl   63, 66
Haas, Pavel   20
Hadda, Gerhard   98
Haes, Margaret   126
Haggard, Stephen   174
Haitink, Bernhard   50
Halban-Kurz, Dési   38, 42, 49
Hamburg Chamber Theatre   151
Hamburger, Paul   113, 118, 121–25, 227, 264
Harris, Roy   23
Hartmann, Karl Amadeus   21
Hassall, Christopher   169–70, 174–77, 182–91
Hatikvah   294
Hausdorff, Martin   83
Haydn, Joseph   28, 60, 122, 225
Heidenreich, Alfred   270–71, 274
Heim, Emmy   264
Heim, Melitta   119, 130
Heimeran, Marta   270
Heine, Heinrich   164, 240
Heinemann, Alexander   238
Heiß, Hermann   21
Hermann, Hugo   21
Herzceg, Géza   196
Hess, Myra   115, 265
Hesterberg, Trude   285
Heymann, Werner Richard   285
Heyse, Paul   26
Hijman, Julius   32

Hindemith, Paul   101, 104, 170–71, 220–22, 225, 239
Hinrichsen, Klaus   117
Hinze, Gerhard   102
Hirsch, Fritz   37, 45
Hirschberg, Rudolf Walther   131
Hirschfeld, Magnus   285
Hitler, Adolf   13, 16, 21, 25, 33, 67, 95, 98, 100, 105, 242, 287, 292, 296–97
Hochberger, Simon   64, 68, 72–73
Hoffnung, Gerard   171
Hölderlin, Friedrich   27, 254
Holl, Gussy   285
Hollaender, Friedrich   285
Holroyd-Reece, John   265
Holst, Imogen   265
Holzmair, Wolfgang   240, 251, 254
Holzstein, Konrad (see also Cesoli, Kuno)   39
Hopkins, Anthony   174
Horenstein, Jascha   10
Horovitz, Béla   124
Horovitz, Joseph   8, 124–25
Hotter, Hans   249
Huberman, Bronislaw   38
Hugh-Jones, Elaine   125
Humboldt, Carolina von   14
Hupka, Felix   37, 50–51
Husmann, Mathias   164
Hutchinson camp (see also internment)   117

Illing, Peter   288
Imperial Philharmonic Society   126
International Artists' Lodge   85
International Musicians Association   84
International Transport Workers Union   31
internment   2, 40, 53, 99, 115, 117, 172, 217–18, 220, 226–29, 233, 235
Isaacs, Leonard   172
Isepp, Helene   264
Isepp, Sebastian   264
Isle of Man (see also internment)   2, 115, 117, 121, 126, 130, 172, 217–20, 226–28, 235–36, 265–66, 268
Isserlis, George   125–26
Isserlis, Julius   125

Jacob, Bernard   122
Jacob, Gordon   176, 179

Jacob, Heinrich Eduard   18
Jacobi, Martin   80
Jadassohn, Salomon   194
Jaeckel, Willy   117
Jansen, Simon C.   50
Jewish Community of Central European Jews   83, 88
Jewish Cultural League (Jüdischer Kulturbund)   80, 92–93, 130, 239, 241, 244
Jewish Institute   118
Jewish Music Council   132
Jewish Music Institute   218
Joachimson, Felix   286
Joint Distribution Committee   38, 129
Jolson, Al   201
Joodsch Symphonie Orkest   49
Joodsche Raad   43
Joodsche Schouwburg   45
Josephus Jitta, Bertha   31
Joyce, James   26
Juda, Jo   46
Juon, Paul   56

Kaiser, Georg   286
Kálmán, Emmerich   196, 209, 212
Kamm, Walter   87
Karpeles, Maud   265
Kästner, Erich   164
Katscher, Robert   7, 192–215
Katz, Erich   98
Katz, Hans Werner   53, 56, 59, 61, 66, 68, 70–74
Kauder, Hugo   38, 41–42
Keller, Hans   227–28
Kerker, Joachim   40
Kienzl, Wilhelm   18
Kindertransport   32, 42, 53–54, 269
Kitchener Camp   53–74
Klabund   244, 250, 285
Kleiber, Erich   249
Klemperer, Otto   28, 230, 249
Knepler, Georg   264
Kodály, Zoltán   231
Kokoschka, Oskar   102
Kolisch Quartet   28
Kolisch, Rudolf   28, 126
Komor, Paul   81

König, Karl   8, 259, 267–81
Koninklijk Conservatorium Den Haag   41
Korda, Alexander   287
Korngold, Erich Wolfgang   18–20, 143
Kossoff, Leon   131
Kösten, Claire (Clarisse)   266–67, 271–72, 274
Kösten, Josef   266
Kösten, Manfred   266
Kowal, Michael   237–242, 246–47, 250–54, 257–58
Kowalski, Max   237–58
Kozenn, Marguerite   129
Krása, Hans   20
Krasselt, Rudolf   56
Kreisler, Fritz   28
Kreiter, Franziska (Fanny)   36, 49–50
Krenek, Ernst   4, 12, 16–17, 19, 38, 97
Kreutzer, Leonid   170
Kristallnacht (see also pogroms)   7, 53, 129, 247
KRO-Radio orchestra   50
Kuttner, Fritz A.   82

Lambert, Constant   100, 171
Landau, Anka   126
Landauer, Alfred   70
Lareau, Alan   286
Lechthaler, Joseph   17
Lehár, Franz   18, 194, 196, 203
Leichter, Käthe   31
Leinsdorf, Erich   28
Leisten, Oskar   84
Lessing, Gotthold Ephraim   80
Lessing, Kolja   145, 164
Levarie, Sigmund   44
Lewandowski, Louis   91
Lewin, Ossi   80–81
Lewkowitz, Mendel   89
Licht, Rainer   52
Lichtenstern, Paul   107, 113, 129
Lidka, Maria   225, 233
Lieven, Albert   288
Lilien, Ignace   32
Lindt, Charlotte   38
Lion, Margo   285–86, 297
Lipton, Marcus   115
Lloyd Hotel (Amsterdam)   49

Loesser, Brigitte   113
Loewe, Carl   70
London Chamber Symphony   163
London Contemporary Music Club   171
Lovett, Martin   121, 125, 225
Lowen, Hanna (also Johanna Löwenstein)   125
Löwenherz, Josef   44
Löwy, Herbert   85
Lund, Engel   7, 113–15, 231, 259, 261–64, 271, 274, 277, 282
Lüps, Mili   46

MacNiece, Louis   178
Magid, Tatjana (See also Riester, Tatjana)   119–20
Mahler, Gustav   18–21, 31, 33, 144, 148, 163
Maly Trostenets   39
Mann, Heinrich   97
Marcus, Paul   196
Margolinski, Henry   81–83
Marischka, Hubert   195, 198
Marsh, Edward   174
Martinů, Bohuslav   19–20, 178, 180
Marx, Joseph   17–18
Maugham, Somerset   286
May, Gisela   27
May, Phineas   57
Mehring, Walter   285
Meller, Wilfried H.   158
Mendelssohn, Felix   119, 123, 172
Mengelberg, Willem   31, 38
Metternich, Klemens von   14–15
Meth, Hildegard/Mady   37, 50
Metropolitan Opera New York   41
Meyer, Conrad Ferdinand   254
Meyer, Ernst Hermann   5, 94, 98, 102–7, 110, 112
Miller, Martin   9, 288
Miłosz, Czesław   23
Mislap-Kapper, Marianne   113, 121
Molnar, Ferenc   80, 287
Monteux, Pierre   36
Moravia, Alberto   156
Morgenstern, Paul (see also Pella, Paul)   34
Morgenstern, Soma   11, 15
Mörike, Eduard   27
Moser, Hans   196, 199

Mozart, Wolfgang Amadeus 28, 64, 99, 104, 119, 122, 128, 144, 225, 230–32, 235, 272, 279
Müller-Hartmann, Robert 143, 264
Murray, Gilbert 115
Myers, Howard 24

National Gallery 115, 231
Naumbourg, Samuel 91
Nederlandse Operastichting 40
Neufeld, Max 200
Nissel, Siegmund 121, 125, 225, 264
Novello, Ivor 174

O'Montis, Paul 285
Okladek, Eleonore 45
Olof, Theo 46, 50
Opera Forum Enschede 50
'Oranjehotel' 46
Overijssels Philharmonisch Orkest 50

Pannwitz, Rudolf 41–42
Paulsen, Harald 286
Pearl Harbor 5, 82
Pears, Peter 229
Pella, Paul (see also Morgenstern, Paul) 33–34, 40, 47, 50
Pepping, Ernst 21
Petersen, Jan 97
Petyrek, Felix 21
Pietruschka, Majer 53–55, 59, 66, 68, 70–73
Pietzner, Carlo 267
Pisk, Arthur 48
Pisk, Paul Amadeus 17, 33
Pleeth, William 173
pogroms (see also *Kristallnacht*) 40–41, 53–55, 57, 63
Prees Heath transit camp 121
Pro Arte Artist-Agency 82
Pro Arte Quartet 28
Pro Musica Chorus of London 163
Prüwer, Julius 56, 220
Puccini, Giacomo 18, 207
Purcell, Henry 60, 128

Raabe, Peter 34
Radio Hilversum 33, 37, 43, 45
Rankl, Karl 4, 20, 158, 162, 219, 229, 230, 236

Rathaus, Karol *4, 10–11, 13, 15, 19*
Rattle, Sir Simon 143, 145, 164
Rauter, Andrea 261, 277, 281
Rauter, Ferdinand 2, 7–8, 115, 227, 231, 259–83
Ravel, Joseph Maurice 28, 124, 126, 261
Raybould, Clarence 176
Refugee Musicians Committee 115, 259, 265
Reich Chamber of Music (Reichsmusikkammer) 34, 45, 55, 92, 262
Reichert, Heinz 212
Reinhardt, Max 285–86
Reiniger, Lotte 218, 222–24, 231–32, 234–35
Reinwald, Elsbeth 285
Reisch, Walter 198, 201
Reizenstein, Franz 6–7, 9, 98, 100, 113, 118–19, 168–91, 219
Reizenstein, Lotte 119, 187
Residentie Orkest 37, 41
Respighi, Ottorino 17
Reznicek, Emil Nikolaus von 18
Riester, Tatjana (see also Magid, Tatjana) 119
Rilke, Rainer Maria 25, 237, 240, 254–57
Rilla, Walter 288, 293
Rimbaud, Arthur 27
Ringelnatz, Joachim 285
Ristow, Nicole 229
Robbins, Clive 282
Robeson, Paul 287
Robitschek, Alfred 82
Robitschek, Kurt 212, 286
Rosé, Alma 37, 44–46
Rosé, Arnold 37, 264, 272
Rosé, Robert 80
Ross, Cyril 116
Rostal, Max 3, 121, 225, 265
Rosza, Suzanne 125
Rota, Nino 180
Roth, Alix 267–68
Roth, Joseph 12, 15
Roth, Peter 267–68, 274
Rothschild Family 58
Royal Albert Hall 173
Royal College of Music 7–8, 113, 120, 123, 133, 171, 217, 219, 225, 231, 234, 236

Royal Opera House   7, 11, 127, 217, 229, 236, 249
Różycki, Ludomir   156
Rückert, Friedrich   245
Rudolf, Max   250

Sackville-West, Edward   178, 180
Safir, Margarete   32
Sagon Collick, Betty   219
Salaman, Esther   118, 123
Salaman, Redcliffe   118
Salzburg Festival   35–36, 38, 50
Saint-Germain-en-Laye, (treaty of)   16
Sassoon, Victor   81
Schellenberger, Hans   102
Schenker, Heinrich   37
Schidlof, Peter (Hans)   115, 121, 125–26, 225, 264–65, 283
Schiffer, Marcellus   285–86, 290, 297
Schlesinger, Kurt   48
Schmidt, Franz   17–19, 22
Schmidt, Joseph   37
Schnabel, Artur   28, 100, 249
Schnitzer, Fritz   80
Schoenberg, Arnold   17–18, 20–21, 28, 31, 33–34, 95, 97–98, 104, 122, 127, 242,
Schonthal, Ruth   143
Schrattenholz, Leo   220
Schreker, Franz   12–13, 16, 18–19, 165
Schubert, Franz   2, 28, 66, 99, 120, 128, 271, 279–80, 286
Schulhoff, Erwin   20
Schumann, Robert   103, 119, 271, 279
Schuschnigg, Kurt   17, 35, 38
Schwabach, Kurt   285
Schwieger, Hans   73
Seiber, Mátyás   98–100, 122, 219, 231
Sekles, Bernhard   239, 244
Serkin, Rudolf   28
Seyss-Inquart, Arthur   38, 42–43
Shanghai Art Club   82
Shanghai Municipal Orchestra   77, 79, 83
Shanghai Musicians Association   75, 78–79, 84–85, 93
   of Central European Musicians   86–87
   of Stateless Refugees   85
Shanghai Opera Company   77
Shanghai Philharmonic Orchestra   82

Shelley, Percy Bysshe   156–57, 159–61
Shostakovich, Dmitri   185, 222
Silberstein, Markus   57
Silberstein, Otmar (also Otto Silverstein)   53, 57, 59, 68, 72
Silberstein, Robert   57
Sladen, Victoria   176
Sluzker, Eduard   47
Smetana, Bedřich   128
Sobibor   48, 200
Solomon (Solominski), Rabbi Frederick   116–17
Sonnenberg, Jenny   113, 120–21
Sowerby, Leo   23
Spanjaard, Ed   45–46
Spanjaard, Martin   45
Spanjaard, Millie   45
Speelman, Michel   81
Spinner, Leopold   219
Spira, Camilla   48
Spiro, Eugen   116
Spoliansky, Mischa   284–301
Stadlen, Peter   98, 264
Städtische Oper, Berlin   130, 230
Stalin, Joseph   11, 64, 102, 105, 111
Stein, Erwin   264
Stein, Marion   264
Steinberg, Wilhelm   28
Steiner, Rudolf   259, 267, 270, 272, 276–77
Sternberg, Josef von   286
Stiedry, Fritz   28
St. John of the Cross   24
Straus, Oscar   203, 212
Strauss, Johann   59, 60
Strauss, Ludwig   244
Strauss, Richard   34, 104
Stravinsky, Igor   95, 97, 221, 225
Sulzer, Salomon   91
Swaap, Sam   46–47
Sweelinck Conservatory Amsterdam   50
Székely, Zoltán   32
Szell, George   32, 37

Tauber, Richard   2, 37–38, 286
Tauský, Vilém   219
Telemann, Georg Philip   27
Tellegen, Marie Anne   45
Theresienstadt   12, 47–49, 139, 151, 249

Tiessen, Heinz   21
Tobin, John   226
Toch, Ernst   11, 19–20, 130
Toynbee Hall   215, 218, 224–26, 233, 235–36
Trapp, Baron (Georg Ludwig Ritter von)   15
Tromp, Samuel   46–47
Tucholsky, Kurt   285
Turina, Joaquín   128

Ulbricht, Walter   27
Ullmann, Viktor   12, 15, 100
Ullrich, Hermann   264
Urbach, Eva   121
Ury, Peter   98

Valetti, Rosa   285
van Leeuwen Boomkamp, Constant   45
Vaughan Williams, Ralph   101, 171–72, 174, 265
Verdi, Giuseppe   103, 186
Vereeniging voor Hedendaagsche Muziek   32
Verwey, Albert   41
Vienna Music Academy   32, 34, 36, 40, 45, 49
Vienna Philharmonic Orchestra   37
Vienna State Opera   33, 36–38, 41
Viertel, Berthold   27, 102

Wagner Vereeniging   41
Wall, Ingeborg   98
Wallerstein, Lothar   33, 40, 41, 50
Walter, Bruno   33–36, 38, 41, 52, 249
Walter-Buchebner-Gesellschaft   164
Walton, William   100, 174–75
Webern, Anton von   17, 100
Webster, David   229

Weigl, Karl   19, 32
Weigl, Vally   31–32
Weihs, Anke   268
Weihs, Thomas   267, 275
Weill, Kurt   97, 104
Weimar Republic   97, 239, 286
Weingarten, Paul   32
Weinheber, Josef   22, 25
Weiss, Max   139, 153
Weisz, Franz   32
Wellesley, Gordon   291, 293
Wellesz, Egon   4, 16, 17, 19, 20, 38, 98, 171, 219, 264
Wertheim, Rosy   32
Westerbork, Central Refugee Camp   40, 45, 48–49
Whiteman, Paul   196–97, 215
Wigmore Hall   119, 218, 270, 288
Wijsmuller-Meijer, Gertruida (Truus)   42
Wilson, Stewart   162
Winterberg, Hans   12–13, 15, 20
Winternitz, Carl Maximilian   83
Wittenberg, Alfred   80
Wolf, Hugo   21
Wolf, Ilse   264
Wolpe, Stefan   97, 143
Wood, Sir Henry   173
Woxholt, Margrethe   298
Wright, Kenneth   173

Yad Vashem   46, 48

Zagrosek, Lothar   163
Zentralstelle für Jüdische Auswanderung   43–45, 47
Zimmering, Max   97
Zweig, Stefan   97